URBAN LIFE AN

Suburban Alchemy

1960s New Towns and the
Transformation of the American Dream

♦

NICHOLAS DAGEN BLOOM

Ohio State University Press
Columbus

12\01

Library of Congress Cataloging-in-Publication Data

Bloom, Nicholas Dagen, 1969–
    Suburban alchemy : 1960s new towns and the transformation of the
American dream / Nicholas Dagen Bloom.
        p. cm. — (Urban life and urban landscape series)
    Includes bibliographical references and index.
        ISBN 0-8142-0874-6 (cloth : alk. paper) — ISBN 0-8142-5075-0
(paper : alk. paper)
        1. Suburban life—United States. 2. Civic improvement—United
States. 3. New towns—Virginia—Reston. 4. New towns—Maryland—
Columbia. 5. New Towns—California—Irvine. I. Title. II. Series.
    HT352.U6 B56 2001
    307.76′0973—dc21

                                                            00-012786

Text design by Sans Serif, Inc.
Cover design by Leanne Whitford.
Type set in Minion 10.5/13 by Sans Serif, Inc.
Printed by Thomson-Shore, Inc.

9 8 7 6 5 4 3 2 1

For my parents

Contents

Acknowledgments

In the 1970s, my parents very nearly exchanged our old house in Baltimore City for a shiny town house in the new town of Columbia, Maryland. Like many liberals at that time, they were attracted to Columbia's combination of social experimentation and high-quality schools. We did not move after all, but even in Baltimore I grew up surrounded by planning experimentation. Just down the street was Coldspring New Town, an incomplete and unconventional new-town-in-town project designed by architect Moshe Safdie. We also lived near the Village of Cross Keys, James Rouse's first planned residential community. I spent many an afternoon waiting for my mother in the courtyards of Cross Keys' shopping plazas, listening to the Muzak and playing in the whimsical ceramic sculptures. No Baltimorean could escape Rouse's presence: he played a leading role in Baltimore's urban renewal plans, built malls both inside and outside of the city, and brought fame to Baltimore with the creation of Harborplace, a lovely waterfront marketplace. Planning was in the air.

In graduate school at Brandeis University, on a hunch that there might be a good story and excellent documents at Columbia, I was elated to find an archive with superb materials. Barbara Kellner, the head of the archive, has been very helpful, as have archivists at George Mason's Planned Community Archive (where much of Reston's material is now stored). I have drawn on resources at Brandeis University, the University of California-Irvine, the library of the Graduate School of Design at Harvard, the New York Public Library, the Enoch Pratt Free Library in Baltimore, and the Fairfax Regional Library in Reston. In trips to new towns I have been well treated by all of the Larsons, Joseph Stowers, Ray Watson, Jack Peltason, Mark Petracca, and Robert Tennenbaum. Stephen Johanson, Pamela Weller, and Samantha have provided a home in Baltimore on numerous research trips.

As the dissertation developed I received invaluable guidance from James Kloppenberg of Harvard University. Morton Keller and Casey Blake also shared insights that have helped shape the text. Richard Fox, David Hackett Fischer, Jacqueline Jones, and Jane Kamensky provided a satisfying graduate career at Brandeis. Scholarships from the Brandeis University History Department and the Graduate School of Arts and Science allowed plenty of time for writing and research. Those seeking more details and further documentation to support arguments made here should consult my dissertation of the same title. Jeffrey Kahana, Jennifer Ratner, Clark Hantzmon, Mark Taylor, Dara Mulderry, and Mark Rennella, fellow students at Brandeis, provided good company. Talkative friends like Chad Cover and Brian Brost have kept life very interesting.

Zane Miller has been a patient supporter of the book, and it is better for his comments. I would also like to thank Malcolm Litchfield, Darrin Pratt, and Emily Rodgers at Ohio State University Press for their guidance. The anonymous reviewers' comments helped tighten my arguments, as did Tonia Payne's sharp eye. A year in the Tulane University Department of History provided timely support for which I am very grateful.

As I have spent pleasurable hours in pottery studios during the making of this book, I would like to thank the friends I have made across wedging tables. Thanks to John Addison, Triesch Voelker, Gayle Lakin, Amy Nolan, Ellen Leopold, Diana Blade, Christine Gratto, Judy Brown, Donna Lorenzo, Nick Corroneos, Daniel Anderson, and many others. Hats off to Jane Sinauer, Avra Leodas, and Nancy Selvage, great leaders and institution builders who have made space for me within their organizations.

Thanks to my parents for their comments, discussions, and support over the years. Visits to my sister, Rachel, and her husband, Scott, have opened my eyes to the delights of Portland, Oregon. Brenda and Chuck Whitford have been very kind to me, as has their daughter Leanne, an unconventional soul with whom I have wandered through many towns both ancient and new.

Introduction

The American city is moving to suburbia. For decades suburbs have been accumulating growing numbers of corporations, stores, and residents, while city centers and urban neighborhoods have crumbled. The story of how urban boosters, civic activists, and intellectuals have tried to save cities and stall suburban expansion is well known. Less familiar are the efforts that have been devoted to helping suburbia adapt to its leading role. This book tells the story of an innovative reform effort that began in the 1960s and remains alive today.

The 1960s new-town movement—most strongly reflected at Reston, Virginia; Columbia, Maryland; and Irvine, California[1]—sought to reshape how Americans built and nurtured new suburban communities. Like most reform movements in American society, it demanded the collaboration of social critics and citizen activists with enlightened business interests. Working together most of the time, they successfully expanded the boundaries of suburban culture.

Intellectuals distilled the sense of frustration many people experienced when confronting the mass-produced suburbs of the post-World War II era. Critics in the national media of the 1950s and 1960s enumerated, and sometimes overstated, suburban flaws. The housing tracts and strip malls of the new suburbs, according to the critics, threatened individuality, suppressed regional differences, and inhibited the growth of strong civic institutions. To make matters worse, developers, with the help of the new suburbanites, successfully excluded the poor and racial minorities. The suburban blight, warned the critics, threatened to infect and destroy American society.

The popular books and essays of these intellectuals emboldened some wealthy businessmen, who had already come to their own conclusions about the dangers of suburban sprawl, to attempt experiments in community development. Robert Simon, a dashing New York real-estate mogul, founded Reston in 1961, the first of America's postwar new towns to respond to suburban criticism. Striking modern architecture nestled around a man-made lake generated admiration and attracted residents. Riding on this wave of excitement, James Rouse, a mall developer and mortgage banker, established Columbia in 1963. Rouse invested more money in social planning than modern design; visitors flooded the new town, and many thousands stayed as residents. Across the country, the Irvine Company, an old ranching operation just south of Los Angeles, commissioned innovative plans for its new town in the late 1950s. By 1970, the company announced that it intended to build the largest planned community in America on central ranch lands. The new-town developers of Reston, Columbia, and Irvine not only constructed housing and roads but sought advice from social scientists, created informative public-relations materials, established local governments, commissioned public art, and donated money and land to cultural and social institutions.

Developers also hired idealistic urban planners who shared a desire to create new kinds of American communities. These planners, under direction from the developers, fused their own unique ideas with traditional suburban designs and modernist new-town innovations. Rouse recruited Morton Hoppenfeld, a young visionary who hoped to promote diversity and community through design; Reston's developer hired Julian Whittlesey, a veteran of international new-town planning efforts who integrated striking architecture into the Virginia countryside; and the Irvine Company rapidly promoted Raymond Watson, an architect who created an innovative system of village design based on the ideas of innovative theorist Kevin Lynch. These planners mixed land uses and housing types; refined architectural, graphic, and landscape design; offered well-defined village and town centers; and pioneered institutional planning. Their efforts did not uniformly succeed, and efforts to reshape community life through design notably faltered, but the goal of rendering these communities distinct from more conventional suburbs reached fruition.

Working with public-relations experts, planners provided a community-wide education in new-town philosophy. They sought to demonstrate to prospective residents and visiting journalists how the new town would improve upon standard subdivisions. Multimedia welcome centers with photographs and scale models greeted visitors; talks by well-known planners and architects edified new residents; and publications that promoted the new-town spirit appeared in visitor centers and resident mailboxes. Many planners even became public figures in the new communities. Development professionals wrote columns in newspapers, often lived in the communities they planned, and were the frequent subjects of features in local newspapers and national magazines. Through this educational process, developers hoped to attract residents, assure long-term support for their master plans, and make connections between their planning and the suburban critique.

Once the initial planning had been completed, these communities began to grow not just of brick and sheetrock but people. Many of the middle-class citizens who came to the new towns saw that opportunity for participation abounded. These residents took seriously the ambitious reform goals featured in company-produced public relations. Reston inspired Embry Rucker, a renegade Episcopal minister, to create a mass-transit system; Columbians read articles by Jean Moon, a local muckraking journalist who fought to preserve the new-town vision; and Irvine elected Larry Agran, a liberal mayor who expanded the city's commitment to social justice. These residents and many others developed a wide range of institutions. They created civic and social-service organizations, maintained and improved recreational and community facilities, supported mass transit, and even founded historical societies and archives for records and public history projects. This wide range of civic activism helped distinguish the new-town scene from more conventional suburbs.

Idealistic residents initiated traditions and a language that reflected their civic spirit. The experience of building a community created a self-identified group of resident "pioneers." These "pioneers" saw themselves as different from later arrivals in the community, united as they were in the early days by being part of an innovative communal experiment. Developers and residents sponsored festivals and parades to build public spirit. Paternalistic developers encouraged these activities and helped personalize communities. Rouse, Simon, and Watson along with Donald Bren have provided steady, personable leadership. This unique civic culture bolstered the sense of new-town identity.

The progressive reputation of the new towns in the 1960s and 1970s attracted liberals interested in building a socially just suburb. The developers and residents promoted the creation of subsidized and more-affordable housing and prohibited racial steering by real estate agents. Local newspapers featured black residents, and black-oriented events proved popular. Feminism and female politicians thrived in this liberal atmosphere. Adolescents, considered by many critics to be lost in suburbia, benefited from teen centers and special programs. Many of these reforms met with mixed results, but the effort built excitement for the new-town experiment and proved satisfying to many residents.

Cultural patronage accompanied the ambitious civic and social activism. The developers initially provided concerts, public art installations, and nature preserves to attract residents and set a sophisticated tone for their communities. They also worked to attract colleges and universities. As the towns grew, some of the developers retreated from cultural sponsorship. Residents had to create their own venues for artistic expression and environmental education.

The new-town residents and developers hoped that their example might inspire national reform. These few communities, however, remain singular models of an alternative future. Reston, for instance, is an island in the midst of northern Virginia's endless suburban sprawl. Within its borders are tree-lined boulevards, shaded bike paths, extensive forests, a thriving town center, and clusters of apartments and homes. Residents of a variety of races and classes work in booming industrial parks, shop at convenient and attractive village centers, and swim at community pools. Local social-service agencies, civic associations, and cultural institutions thrive. Outside its borders has grown unattractive suburban sprawl, including growing numbers of gated communities, strip malls, and office parks.

The idealism that inspired places such as Reston may have diminished, but it is time to revisit the new-town experiment. Forty years have passed since the movement's beginnings, and these towns are now much more than just plans and buildings; they have grown into large, dynamic communities. A number of scholars over the past four decades have examined the towns in this study from relatively narrow disciplinary perspectives. This book combines the earlier works, many of great value, with original research to offer the first integrated look at new-town design, politics, society, and culture. By blending different aspects of community life in one text, the wider significance of the new town emerges.

The self-conscious creation of difference in so many aspects of community life has made these places powerful models of reform. Although it is true that those who built and inhabited new towns aimed to create comfortable suburban communities and a majority of the residents came for the quality of life rather than ideals alone, the developers, their staffs, and a sizable group of activist residents pursued more ambitious goals. The reformers believed that their new towns served a critical function for society by remaining recognizably suburban while supporting a wide range of reforms. By being grounded in suburban realities and avoiding utopianism, new towns gained cultural force. Visitors and those who read about the new towns did, in fact, compare these places to more conventional suburbs. The new-town landscapes themselves proved even more important than the original written criticism that had inspired them.

Those designers associated with the contemporary New Urbanist movement will find the new-town story, as presented here, unsettling. New Urbanists believe that in order to have healthy communities there must be observable gatherings on streets and in public places, not merely historicist architecture. They have, in general, not found these elements in visits to 1960s new towns. Recent visitors found that many of the quaint village greens and piazzas of the new towns were either relatively empty or being transformed into what looked like strip malls. These visitors recognized the attention to architecture, planning, and landscaping in new towns, but they also found what they considered to be an overabundance of conventional suburban housing, cul-de-sacs, and highways. On the surface, community life did not seem very successful.

New towns, however, have developed a much more complicated kind of community life that is only partially visible to the casual visitor. Planners of the 1960s shared with New Urbanists a hope that they could create viable public spaces and discreet neighborhoods in suburbia. After forty years it is clear that although the planning and architecture of Reston, Columbia, and Irvine have contributed to community life by offering new amenities, creating a more diverse population, and physically distinguishing new towns from conventional suburbs, most of the attempts to use physical design to bolster community interaction on an informal, daily basis failed to change the automobile-oriented culture of even these special communities.

Planning has, however, yielded long-term results. At these towns, the comprehensive vision of a reformed suburbia, paired to the new-town design concepts, proved important by inspiring decades of local activism in politics, society, and culture. The new-town idea attracted activists who pushed the boundaries of suburban life in ways that would make New Urbanists blush. Substantial and pathbreaking social and racial integration, powerful citizen organizations and local governments, strong-minded and idealistic local journalism, the women's movement, and ambitious cultural projects all found their way into new towns of the 1960s and have not become part of the more conservative New Urbanist vision.

Residents of the new towns might not have utilized the public spaces created for them, but they have been busily recasting suburban stereotypes. Political and social reform flourished in local papers and magazines, in lectures, on cable television, and at meetings of civic and social organizations; creativity found support at nature and cultural centers and at museums, galleries, and archives; alternative values developed at interracial gatherings and women's and teen centers; and community spirit found expression at parades, festivals, and newly created historic districts. Through the cultivation of this active public life, even with its frequent disappointments and compromises, residents have kept new-town ideals alive for more than four decades. These residents have produced a vital form of suburban community that is far more complicated and interesting than the early vision promoted in the glossy publications and visitor centers of the new-town planners.

PART I

Prelude to the New Town Movement

◆

1

The Suburban Critique

While the suburb served only a favored minority, it neither spoiled the countryside nor threatened the city. But now that the drift to the outer ring has become a mass movement, it tends to destroy the value of both environments without producing anything but a dreary substitute, devoid of form and even more devoid of the original suburban values.

LEWIS MUMFORD, *The City in History*

The application of mass-production techniques to housing construction in the 1940s and 1950s, in combination with federal subsidy of highways and home mortgages, opened the suburban fringe to millions of working- and middle-class Americans. Suburbia, previously considered to be the geographic and cultural periphery of American urban civilization, took center stage.[1] This dramatic social and geographical shift attracted considerable attention in the national media. Intellectuals and journalists began to visit the new suburbs, interviewed residents, and observed daily life. In the numerous books and articles that flowed from their research, a pattern of analysis emerged. Intellectuals believed that the growth of mass-produced suburbia threatened not only the beauty of the American landscape but was undermining traditions of civic activism, social cooperation, and cultural creativity.

Many critics expressed sympathy for suburbanites, but most intellectuals detested the new suburban order. Many could not help but look down upon what they considered to be the provincialism of suburban residents. For all their many errors and oversights, however, the critics correctly understood that the mass-produced suburbs of the 1940s and 1950s represented an important shift from earlier traditions of American community development.[2]

For these critics, standardization in the new suburbs had reached crisis proportions. It appeared to them that endless housing tracts filled with identical-looking homes threatened to eliminate every trace of the American rural landscape. John Keats's popular critique of suburbia, *The Crack in the Picture Window,* described the process with economy and humor: "The typical postwar development operator was a man who figured how many houses he could possibly cram onto a piece of land and have the local zoning board hold still for it. Then he whistled up the bulldozers to knock down all the trees, bat the lumps off the terrain, and level the ensuing desolation. Then up went the houses, one after another, all alike."[3]

Residential subdivisions may have been standardized, but this emphasis on control, observed the critics, did not extend to the new suburban commercial strips. The automobile, the main form of suburban locomotion, stimulated the creation of large and unregulated signs, cheaply constructed and garish buildings, and acres of asphalt parking lots. Compounding problems both in residential neighborhoods and suburban strips was the failure to create public spaces that would unify disparate elements. The store, the car, the school, the highway, and the home on the cul-de-sac became the primary spaces of the new suburbia. Suburbanites, said the critics, were living in a privatized, decentralized landscape.

These journalists and intellectuals extended the critique into other aspects of social and cultural life. Critics believed that suburban residence was changing how Americans lived in community. According to them, suburbanization was encouraging the growth of a new and potentially destructive American society. While critics admired older cities for incorporating a mix of social and racial groups in a rich cultural ferment, a bit of a romantic notion itself, they believed that the suburban environment encouraged political isolation, social elitism, and mass culture.

The lack of clear civic boundaries, public spaces, and large-scale municipal governance seemed to the critics to discourage civic activism. Peter Blake, one of suburbia's most vocal critics, argued, "We find ourselves with 50 million suburbanites most of whom are totally disinterested in local government, refuse to participate in it, and frequently don't even know what community . . . they belong to. The only local issue that arouses any degree of passion is taxes."[4] Disinterest in civic affairs led to a lack of interest in larger metropolitan needs as well. Keats noted that cities faced financial crises when they were "deserted by a middle class that flocks to the suburbs."[5] With the aid of the federal government, suburbs encouraged black isolation in inner cities. William Whyte, in *The Organization Man*, reported an "acrid controversy over the possible admission of blacks" in Park Forest, Illinois. A few residents favored integration, but most did not. According to Whyte, "the sheer fact that one had to talk about it [racial integration] made it impossible to maintain unblemished the idea of egalitarianism so cherished."[6]

The critics also believed that isolation within suburbia led to unhappiness; the uniformity of the physical landscape mirrored and magnified social conformity. Residents were encouraged to have similar ideas on consumption, child rearing, and even politics. To many observers, like Whyte, the conformist pressure on suburban residents reflected the wider bureaucratic culture developing during this period. Feminist critics like Betty Friedan also believed that a suburban culture of domesticity had supplanted the idea of the active, public woman. Friedan believed that many women suffered in the isolated suburban fringe. Other critics reported that adolescents chafed under suburban restrictions. Lacking street corners for casual socializing and possessing little domestic privacy, they seemed to be turning in large numbers to aggressive and socially destructive behavior.

Many observers believed that this landscape of uniformity, privatization, decentralization, and conformity stifled cultural achievement. Intellectuals criticized the lack of cultural nourishment in the suburbs as compared to urban centers. According to historian Richard Pells, "as the quintessential inhabitants of the city ... [intellectuals] could barely fathom the appeal of suburbia. . . . Were PTA meetings and the Little League adequate substitutes for evening concerts and spontaneous excursions to the art gallery?"[7] Other critics worried that "passivity, mechanization, and commercialization of leisure would prove to be just one more link in the chain of suburban tyranny."[8]

The suburban critique, which questioned everything from design to social life, unintentionally provided the groundwork for reform.[9] The frightening, if stereotypical, portrait of suburbia they created lent legitimacy to idealistic plans that promised real changes in suburban community development. The positioning of new towns as the suburban antidote quickly became a task for the new-town developers, planners, and residents. They minted a local version of the suburban critique in publicity materials and in interviews in local and national publications. Prominent intellectuals and journalists quickly reinforced the claims of the new-town supporters in important books and periodicals for a national audience.

Rouse, Columbia's personable developer who had benefited from the growth of suburbia as a mall developer and home mortgage broker, found much to dislike in the suburban landscape he had helped to create. He borrowed liberally from the suburban critique in defense of his ideal suburb: "Sprawl is inefficient. It stretches out the distance people must travel to work, to shop, to worship, to play. It fails to relate these activities in ways that strengthen each. . . . The vast formless spread of housing pierced by the unrelated spotting of schools, churches, stores, creates areas so huge and irrational that they are out of scale with people."[10] Columbia residents shared Rouse's opinion that suburbia had numerous problems. Their language also reflects the suburban critique. For instance, Tom Lorsung, an early resident, delighted that Columbia was different from the "stereotype suburban community—sterile, dropped out in the middle of nowhere."[11]

Simon, Reston's first developer, found even the most exclusive suburb frustrating. A *Fortune* article of 1964 described Simon's experience living in Syosset, Long Island: "Expecting the best in family living, he found instead a series of frustrations; long drives and waits to play tennis, difficult arrangements for playmates for his children, a dearth of interesting things to do evenings. After his first wife's death, he tore up his commuter's card and drove back to Manhattan."[12] Simon expressed his belief that most suburbs had failed to develop in a rational manner. "Urban development in the last generation in the United States," he wrote, "has consisted mostly of sprawl because we have been gobbling up the land and developing it in little pieces—here a sub-division, there a gas station."[13] Early Reston residents shared Simon's distaste for standard suburbia. A letter to the editor in the 1967 *Reston Times* reflects the frustration many felt about suburban sprawl: "For once [at Reston], aesthetic value was considered foremost and we felt people who came to live here had an appreciation for something more than a plot of grass and a very ordinary house."[14] An editorial in the *Reston Times* of 1970 described "Reston [as] a prototype . . . for what is a much more attractive alternative to traditional development of lands in the suburbs."[15]

The Irvine Company envisioned Irvine as a community "where urban sprawl is stopped before it starts." It explained in a 1977 publication that "the people of the Irvine Company faced a decision" in the 1950s. "They could sell off the company's acreage piecemeal to speculators and developers . . . and let suburbia sprawl across the land," or they could "plan for its orderly development themselves." They decided on the latter course because "in Southern California, people are scattered across shapeless suburbs. With few shared interests, little sense of community, nothing to bring them together. Now, more than ever, people want a place they can belong to. That they can identify with."[16] William Pereira, Irvine's first planner, also complained about "the tragedies of helter-skelter planning, of the impossible traffic, the sprawling disorganization."[17] Irvine residents shared this view and felt happy, as one resident explained, to be living with a master plan that "assures us that there won't be urban sprawl here."[18]

Many journalists and intellectuals, some of whom had attacked suburbia in earlier years, were heartened by the movement and believed that the new towns would remedy suburban failings. Intellectuals and reporters offered their support in books and articles during the early years of development and helped spread the new-town gospel. Ada Louise Huxtable, the architecture critic at the *New York Times,* explained in 1964 that "what the new town is supposed to provide is what the standard suburb leaves out: good transportation, good public utilities, good open space, and good over-all design. Above all, it is concerned with the better use of land."[19] And Whyte welcomed the new towns as antidotes to suburban sprawl in his 1968 book, *The Last Landscape:* "[the new towns] provide excellent prototypes for future community development. . . . What they promise to be are first rate communities in the suburbs."[20]

The planned new town had emerged from the clamor of critical voices as a potential solution to the suburban crisis. Criticism, while not actually offering a solution to suburban development, had created an opening in which alternatives might prosper. Without the years of negative commentary on suburban growth, in combination with eventual intellectual support of these innovative planned communities, the new-town movement would have received scant notice and probably would have faltered. Instead, the concept gained rapid momentum.

PART 2

Planning and Designing the New Suburb

◆

2

Reston, Virginia

Lake Anne was . . . the catalyst that attracted people to live in
Reston. . . . There were ducks, there were paddle boats. It was
totally un-suburban, it looked like nothing we had ever seen in
the suburbs. No neon signs, everything was designed architecturally to fit with the surroundings. There was an area you could
walk . . . around the town houses, where you could walk up to a
swing and just swing looking out on the lake.

PAULINE DONATUTI, Reston resident, Reston Oral History Project

Most middle-class Americans of the 1960s faced a difficult choice. They
could remain in city centers as urban violence increased, schools declined,
and urban renewal replaced old neighborhoods with crude middle-class
high-rises, or they could move to an anonymous suburban subdivision
surrounded by ugly strip malls and highways. Pauline Donatuti's admiration for Reston reflected the designers' success in creating an alternative to
both cities and conventional subdivisions.[1] Here was a new community
well integrated with its pastoral surroundings and free of the ugliness that
many middle-class Americans thought they had to accept as essential in
both suburban and urban living.

The master plan for Reston of 1962 envisioned a bold new concept
for American suburbia. High-density corridors of apartments and town
houses rather than single-family homes were to give definition to the landscape. Residents of these high-density complexes and those living in a limited number of single-family homes would be able to walk along wooded
pathways or drive on landscaped parkways to convenient and attractive
"village" centers. There they would find not only shopping but public

space, theaters, galleries, recreational facilities, and meeting halls. Residents would also find a striking high-density town center with more cultural and commercial resources. Finally, bisecting Reston along a new highway, planners envisioned a series of office parks that would ease residents' commuting woes. The developer and planners pictured Reston as a sophisticated, adult-oriented suburban city housing nearly 75,000 residents when complete.

The land for the new development was originally purchased by Robert Simon. In 1961, with money he made from the sale of Carnegie Hall to New York City, Simon purchased 6,800 acres of land in rural Fairfax County, Virginia, on the outer edge of Washington, D.C.'s suburbs. There, he planned to build a new type of American community.

When Simon sat down to craft this new community, with the help of the well-known New York architectural and planning firm of Whittlesey and Conklin, he had many options before him. New-town design in America remained largely unexplored, and the suburban critique had not specified what, if anything, might replace sprawl. The first phase of the planning concerned human needs. Simon explained to prospective buyers in early publicity materials that he and his planners "started with a program rather than a plan. We asked what people could be offered when they move here, rather than what we were going to do with the land. It was like Christmas. Whatever we could dream up, we would write down. And, in the end, we actually used many of the ideas we wrote down."[2] He then gathered a group of consultants, including psychologists, sociologists, and recreation and religious specialists, who helped him to select what they considered the proper mix of educational, cultural, residential, and industrial facilities.[3]

In the next phase of planning, these community functions were organized into a physical plan. Simon, after much consideration, supported a hybrid of conventional and radical traditions that he thought might prove successful in America. Simon's team at Reston borrowed and adapted innovations from both the "community builder" suburban tradition—which began in America with Llewellyn Park, New Jersey, constructed in the 1850s—and the more radical "garden city" or new-town ideals. The planning team then merged these elements with concepts created particularly for Reston. Because the developers of Columbia and Irvine pursued a similar strategy, it is worth considering this early mixture in some detail.

As in the finest suburbs in America, visitors to Reston (and Columbia and Irvine) would find a master plan guiding development, mandating cul-de-sacs, nature preserves, and shopping centers, and formulating covenants to enforce maintenance and architectural styles. Notable examples include Riverside, Illinois (1868), and Country Club District, Kansas (1906). Unlike many suburban builders, the developers at these towns commissioned an attractive community environment for what was usually an affluent audience. During the 1950s and 1960s, this tradition of suburban building was expanded and democratized at large-scale new towns like Park Forest, Illinois; Levittown, New York; Clear Lake City, Texas; and Mission Viejo, California.

The mixture of the suburban tradition with innovative planning styles distinguished Reston, Columbia, and Irvine from the more conventionally planned towns such as Park Forest. Many of the ingenious elements borrowed by the new towns in this study originated in the work of Ebenezer Howard, a visionary British stenographer. In the late nineteenth century, Howard first conceived of the new town, or garden city, as a solution to the problems of urban society. His garden city was a complete community, not just a bedroom community like American suburbs, and included residential, agricultural, commercial, and industrial areas. Howard hoped that the garden city would decentralize large urban centers, create a more just society through communal ownership of land, and bring people into closer contact with nature. The towns of Letchworth and Welwyn, both in Britain, were created by Howard and his followers in the early twentieth century and included municipal land ownership, greenbelts for agriculture and nature, commercial and civic town centers, and a range of picturesque housing types.

This concept traversed the Atlantic and found fertile ground in the New York region. Lewis Mumford, Clarence Stein, and others joined together in the 1920s to create an innovative garden city known as Radburn, New Jersey. Stein, an architect and planner, designed Radburn and adapted Howard's plan for American suburbia. His most important innovation was the "superblock," which replaced individual yards and alleys with landscaped common spaces behind houses. The designers made schools the focus of neighborhoods, developed a mixture of housing types, offered grade-separated walkways, pioneered cul-de-sacs, and organized a community association with extensive recreational responsibilities. This partially constructed project failed during the Great Depression and exerted little influence on other suburban developers until Simon (and developers at Columbia and Irvine) adapted Radburn innovations in their communities. Stein continued to develop his style at the unpopular Greenbelt towns built by the Resettlement Administration during the 1930s, but these also failed to find a wider audience, and government support evaporated.[4]

The garden city's next breakthrough came during the modern European new-town movement after World War II. Governments seized on the new-town concept as a way to erase the bitter memories of war, rebuild and decentralize older urban centers, and improve life for the average person in a time of optimistic social democracy. The modernist movement in architecture and planning, in vogue at the time, naturally played a significant role in these new-town projects. Planners at European new towns, following modernist design concepts, distilled the messiness of the industrial city into mutually exclusive planned zones of housing, work, recreation, civic functions, and traffic. Modernist architectural styles, reflecting the streamlined machine aesthetic, also characterized European new-town environments. These communities, in both plan and form, made a clean break with older urban centers.

Such new towns appeared in profusion across Europe. A large British planning program brought forth new towns like Runcorn and Harlow that featured daring residential design and innovative, modernist town centers. In Finland, the town of Tapiola integrated cutting-edge residential designs with natural surroundings and also grouped an elegant collection of contemporary buildings around an artificial lake in the town center.[5] Many designers from Reston, Columbia, and Irvine visited new towns in Europe before or during work on their own plans. Like European designers, they aimed to create a mixture of residential, commercial, cultural, and industrial activities in freestanding new communities. American designers, although often impressed by what they saw, drew selectively from the modernist planning and architectural styles. Village and town centers at Reston, Columbia, and Irvine, for instance, conformed most closely to European models, with modernist buildings surrounding natural features or plazas. Developers felt that it was here they had to make a splash in order to impress visiting journalists, visitors, and intellectuals.

Simon's choice of planners reflected his personal commitment to the more radical new-town vision. Not only had his father participated in the development of Radburn, but the firm he hired, Whittlesey and Conklin, had played a central role in American new-town planning. Julian Whittlesey had worked with Stein on the creation of Kitimat, a mining community developed in British Columbia during the 1950s. Albert Mayer, a partner in the firm, participated directly in the creation of Radburn. These planners and members of the firm such as William Conklin and James Rossant were eager to reintroduce the new town to American suburbia.

The planners at Reston adapted Radburn innovations for their project. As at Radburn, they replaced individual yards and alleys with landscaped common spaces behind houses. This arrangement, which also protected children from cars, was designed to facilitate community and neighborhood cohesion. Reston's designers offered physical elements similar to Radburn's and organized a community association (not an incorporated city or town government) that would be controlled by the development company. Unlike the case in Radburn, Reston planners preserved the picturesque landscape in the areas surrounding the residences, and they favored modernist architecture for village centers, the town center, and some of the new housing, reflecting the influence of Tapiola and other modernist new towns. The goal of establishing a balance of industry, residence, and commerce also reflected the influence of European new towns.

As influential as these antecedents were, they did not determine every aspect of Reston's design. Not only did its planners integrate conventional suburban styles, but also they decided not to make the schools the focus of residential neighborhoods or villages, as had been done in Radburn and most other new towns. Conklin, one of the leading planners, noted that they had placed schools "relatively independent of the village clusters rather than as a central focus of neighborhood life."[6] Schools were to be convenient but cultural, recreational, and commercial facilities were to anchor the community.

This difference in planning philosophy came from Simon's beliefs about the nature of the good society. He believed that the leisure society had already arrived for most Americans. "The main idea," he wrote, "is that in this age of leisure people should have a wide choice of things to do which are stimulating, pleasurable, exciting, fun." Reston's planners, under Simon's direction, associated "each village with a particular type of recreation, such as a lake for sailing, facilities for riding or even a golf course. The appearance of the architecture would even be influenced by the activity toward which it was oriented." This was an innovative concept. Lake Anne, the first village, was to be a "sailing and fishing town," and the village center was modeled after Portofino, an Italian fishing village. Hunters Woods village center, to follow Lake Anne, was planned to be "in the woods and would have a horseback riding character with hitching posts and all." Neighborhoods would have their own pools and recreational facilities, and village centers and their connecting "urban sinews" would offer abundant public space for interaction, relaxing, and people watching. Simon believed that these abundant diversions would help give form to the new leisure society.[7]

Planners accentuated the sense of repose by making a conscious effort to maximize the natural beauty of the site. They envisioned higher-density housing following the ridgelines and sought to preserve valleys for open space and lakes. An article in *Industrial Design* praised Reston's planning team for taking an ecological approach to suburban development: "In March, 1961, the firm's planners went there [to Virginia], and walking over the land, picked the sights best suited physically to contain village center clusters. . . . Such planned use of topography may seem obvious, but it contrasts refreshingly with the practice of builders who move through an area leveling land and trees and putting up rows of look-alike housing."[8]

The master plan, approved by the Fairfax County Board of Supervisors in 1962, gave the planners almost everything they desired. Incorporating what became known as Residential Planned Community (RPC) zoning, the plan permitted a mix of high- and medium-density housing clusters, single-family homes, open space, and commercial zones. Planners promised a total of seven villages (with 10,000–12,000 people each) featuring village centers with shopping, cultural, and recreational facilities; a series of connected, grade-separated pedestrian walkways; districts of light industrial parks; a hierarchical transport plan with low- and high-volume routes; a high-density town center; a series of man-made and natural lakes, golf courses, and recreation areas; and numerous neighborhood pools, tennis courts, and play areas. This comprehensive and innovative planning, while building on a number of traditions and influences, was unheard of in contemporary American suburbia. The physical plan, in its conscious revision of suburban development patterns, should be seen as an early manifesto of the new-town movement (map 1).[9]

As the master plan indicates, Simon and his team sought to create an urbanized suburb. The developer sought to build 70 percent town houses, 15 percent single-family homes, and 15 percent apartments. The mix of dwelling types in higher density corridors would give Reston many qualities of a healthy city: rich architectural variety, park space, and a more cosmopolitan range of income and age groups. Conklin explained the general framework in 1966: "High density housing, with apartment houses and cluster houses, instead of being tightly packed in concentric rings around a single center, is placed throughout the body of the town." Conklin thought this dispersion of density, what the planners called an "urban sinew," gave "structure and comprehensibility to the town."[10] Even the walking paths were designed as community sidewalks. Simon admitted in 1990 that he "didn't put lights on the roads"; instead, he put "them on the walking paths" so people would walk from village to village—to create pedestrian, active street life supported by this high-density concentration.[11]

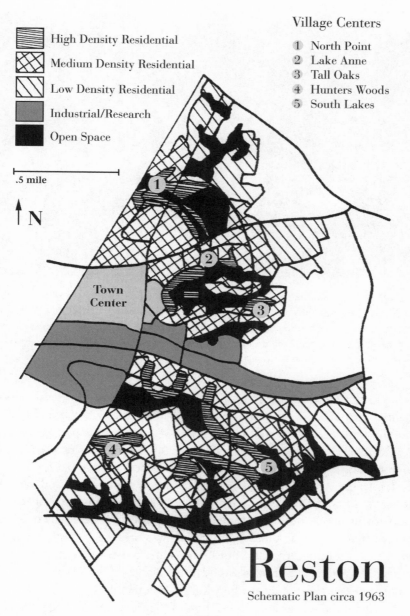

High Density Residential

Medium Density Residential

Low Density Residential

Industrial/Research

Open Space

.5 mile

N

Village Centers

1 North Point
2 Lake Anne
3 Tall Oaks
4 Hunters Woods
5 South Lakes

Town Center

Reston

Schematic Plan circa 1963

MAP 1

FIGURE 1 The American new town at its most picturesque. Lake Anne village center boldly combined apartments, town houses, shops, a lively piazza, and a canal. Although the center languished for decades, it has of late become home to cafés and restaurants that benefit from its romantic design. Later village centers mixed civic and commercial uses but did so in a more conservative style. (1999)

Simon and his staff completed the high- and medium-density residential area around Lake Anne Village, including a high-rise apartment building and tight clusters of modernist town houses and apartments surrounded by woods. At Lake Anne village center, Simon's desire to create an architectural expression of a leisure society reached its culmination. This is certainly the American new town at its most picturesque and lyrical. Rossant, the center's architect, reinterpreted the picturesque style of Italian port towns like Portofino in a modernist, concrete idiom.[12] His plan included a semicircular plaza surrounded by stores, second-story apartments, and community institutions. The center opened dramatically onto a canal, with a dock running alongside, and a large artificial lake (figure 1). Lake Anne remains the most whimsical of Reston's village centers.

Surrounding clusters of town homes (figure 2) received equal attention. For instance, Louis Sauer, a prominent mid-Atlantic architect responsible for the design of the Golf Course Island homes in Reston, planned his complex so that "the grouping of individual units, with their bold exterior features, looks very much like an entire village." Cloethiel Smith, a

FIGURE 2 Reston town houses, designed by architect Cloethiel Smith, accented the contemporary design of the nearby village center. Clusters of housing throughout Reston conserved land, offered architects the opportunity for innovative design, and gave a sense of community to new-town residents. (1999)

prominent Washington architect, created a colorful complex of town houses at water's edge that imitated row houses in Portofino. Architects at Reston understood that they were being asked to promote community development through design and site planning.[13] Reston was one of the first suburban communities in America to include large quantities of architect-designed housing, and its innovative design helped assure its legitimacy among critics of conventional suburbia.

Simon invested in an impressive variety of design innovations. He commissioned sophisticated signs and lighting to distinguish Reston from other suburban communities. The signs at Reston grew out of semiotic research pioneered in the 1930s and made popular in the 1950s and 1960s by corporations and the government. Semiotic signs replaced words with symbols believed to be part of a universal, visual language.[14] The signs at Reston included graphic representations of parks, schools, swimming pools, and even a yacht club. Designers created even more original signs. In Lake Anne village center, oversized pills, a thermometer, and razor blades advertised the pharmacy.[15]

Reston designers even manipulated lighting to its best effect. Lighting consultant Seymour Evans made an effort to make the community glow at night: "Where there is clear glass next to a solid wall, the wall will be lit, bouncing light onto the surrounding walks, lawns, or trees. In the parking lots . . . the walkways leading to them will be lighted and behind the lots a wall of light may be bounced off surrounding trees, silhouetting cars." Evans also created streetlights for village centers with "six lamps covered by clear butyrate globe. Each lamp has a diode that cuts power reaching lamps so that they give a soft yellow-orange glow much like candlelight." Although later developers substituted fluorescent lights, the parts of Lake Anne still lit by the special lamps have a romantic feeling, and their effect emphasizes the architecture and the lake.[16]

Critics in general praised Reston, even though it included many conventional elements, and the town received positive reviews in a variety of professional and popular magazines and newspapers. Visitors flooded in to see this bold place, but they did not readily buy homes. Reston was still far from downtown Washington, and the contemporary designs attracted a select audience. Although one of the original consultants to Simon, the accounting firm Arthur D. Little, had promised that the site "could be developed as a sound investment in the form of a new town for 75,000 people"[17] (and they would be proved correct in the future), these optimistic predictions did little to calm investors impatient with Simon's artistic vision. Gulf Oil, Simon's main backer, assumed management of the town in 1967 because of fears that the whole project was nearing bankruptcy.[18]

Gulf's subsidiary created to manage the project, Gulf Reston, abandoned the innovative architecture of Lake Anne and filled the high- and medium-density corridors with more typical suburban garden-apartment complexes and town-house clusters. Gulf Reston also increased the rate of construction and sales. The combination of these new approaches helped the company achieve financial stability for Reston after only a few years.[19] The county, however, created a temporary setback by implementing an antigrowth sewer moratorium in the early 1970s. After a favorable resolution in court, construction resumed and then quickly slowed again due to the national recession of 1974. Construction, even after these setbacks, continued throughout the 1970s.

Gulf sold the project in 1978 to Reston Land Corporation (RLC, a subsidiary of Mobil Oil), and the new company slowly began to turn a profit in the 1980s. RLC, like Gulf, abandoned the idea of village centers built around thematic leisure activities and switched from the sophisticated architectural styles pioneered at Lake Anne to more conventional designs for garden apartments and town houses. But RLC, like Gulf, followed the master plan in most other respects. The company created clusters of town houses, apartments, and single-family areas, a hierarchy of roads and pedestrian paths, mixed-use village centers, industrial and commercial developments, recreational facilities, and plentiful open spaces.[20]

However, the experimental Lake Anne village center struggled. Shops failed in the center in the 1970s because of resident unwillingness to walk there from the more distant parking lot, competition from surrounding shopping areas, and lackluster management. One early resident, an economist, described the 1960s at the Lake Anne village center as being "like a European city. Sundays you could stroll down to the plaza and see your friends. Families would walk by with the baby. You'd buy a paper, get a sandwich and sit around and watch the scene." In 1971 he lamented, "Now I never see anyone I know there. There's less pride in the place: there's littering. . . . Also, the teenagers congregate there with their alien folkways and sometimes make things unpleasant for others." Drug dealing became notorious on the plaza in the early 1970s, and the outlook seemed grim.[21] Most nonprofit organizations could not afford the commercial rents at the village centers and were forced out of Reston or into office space in the community.

Yet, these problems did not dissuade RLC and Gulf from building mixed-use village centers including Tall Oaks, Hunters Woods, and South Lakes. Hunters Woods village center, for instance, developed by Gulf Reston in 1972, included extensive public plazas, shopping, professional offices, a community center, a library, adjoining town houses, and senior housing. The designers abandoned the picturesque designs of Lake Anne and the planned thematic recreational elements for the second village that had included hitching posts and bridle paths. It was not clear, after all, that Simon had succeeded at Lake Anne in creating a "sailing and fishing" town. Hunters Woods however, did include a series of enclosed plazas, pedestrian underpasses, and a reflecting pond and fountain. Hunters Woods was less ambitious than Lake Anne but still evinced new-town idealism.

Under the leadership of the later development companies, Reston continued to gain population in the 1970s and 1980s. Approximately 50,000 residents had chosen to live in the new town by 1987, and buoyed by northern Virginia's high-technology economy, new industries located there (over 28,000 people employed by 1987). In the 1980s, commuters also found Reston more convenient to Washington, D.C., with the creation of access ramps connecting Reston to the Dulles Access Highway. At the

FIGURE 3 Reston town center features a popular mixture of stores, entertainment, and offices. A crafts fair, holiday parades, and concerts attract both local and regional audiences. Although not opened until the 1990s, the center adopted the urbanistic spirit conceived by the developer in the 1960s. (1999)

same time, RLC added historically inspired homes in both South Lakes and North Point villages as part of a plan to attract a broader audience to Reston and continued to build apartment complexes and condominiums, bike paths, and recreational amenities.

RLC's creation of the Reston town center during the late 1980s began an exciting phase in Reston's development by renewing the recreational and cultural ideals of Lake Anne (figure 3). RLC patterned the town center along lines laid down by Simon. He had predicted in the 1960s that the future town center would "be more like an urban center without cars, because the cars will be underneath it or in several parking fields removed from it." Simon hoped that, as for other areas of the new-town plan, this kind of center would help counter the suburban malaise by replacing the auto-oriented shopping mall. However, he was unable to begin work on the town center, which in schematic renderings incorporated bold modernist design, and instead a few shopping areas and other community resources developed haphazardly during the 1970s and 1980s.[22]

The initial RLC plans from the 1980s called for what was essentially a "suburban town center," according to J. Hunter Richardson Jr., development manager for the project. He noted that the developers took their first plan to the Urban Land Institute (a think tank focused on planning and development issues) for criticism, and the reaction was negative. The experts told them that their plan failed to reflect the vision of Reston and that the design should be "more urban and less suburban, and also more cultural." Richardson's staff began to integrate taller office buildings, brought in a mixed-use development team, and expanded the retail plans.[23]

Kenneth Wong, RLC's lead developer for the Reston town center, grafted urbanistic ideas onto what Richardson called a "suburban town center." Wong's team, using architectural design by the international firm RTKL and landscaping by Sasaki Associates of Watertown, Massachusetts, expressed "a very strong commitment to the values of familiarity and comfort that a perfect stranger gets from a new environment he's visiting, the feeling that he's in a place."[24] Wong believed that the town center would serve as a public space: "We wanted to create a main street with a town square the way people used to do it." Wong successfully brought "new urbanist" design to Reston.[25]

The center, clothed in an updated nineteenth-century commercial style, combines a hotel, offices, restaurants, stores, a large neoclassical plaza, a seasonal ice-skating rink, and a thriving movie complex. These elements are picturesquely sited in a grid that is surrounded by parking lots hidden from the interior of the complex. The developer has consciously promoted events including holiday parades, art fairs, and concerts.[26] Nearly 100,000 people per year came for these special events and an estimated 5 million people use the center each year. Due to its popularity, the complex is being expanded to include more shops, restaurants, and offices. Even Simon liked the design. At the dedication, he said, "this is not a mall, this is an urban phenomenon—a place for shopping and socializing."[27]

But at the town center, the illusion of urbanity does not extend far. At its border are large parking lots and the Spectrum shopping area, a more traditional, although attractive, strip mall. The Spectrum's architecture mimics that of the town center, but its siting amid a sea of parking lots and its scale, at most two stories, fails to relate to the town center with its high rises and public spaces. The same is true for the other elements of the town center. For example, the Fairfax Regional Library is an attractive modern suburban structure, but it is concealed from the main commercial development. Some residents also feared, correctly, that the high-density center would add thousands of cars to local streets. Congestion on surrounding parkways has indeed grown even after road expansions. Reston town center is both a center for Reston and an attractive destination for people throughout the region.

The office parks near the town center have taken on a role that Simon could scarcely have imagined. Reston has become a leading "edge city" in northern Virginia. By 1988, over 1,400 companies operated in Reston, employing 31,000 people, "more than an average of one and one-half jobs per household."[28] By 1999, nearly 40,000 people worked in Reston, far exceeding the immediate employment needs of the approximately 60,000 residents, many of whom commute to other areas to work. The consequent traffic has become a sore point for many residents, and it is clear that Reston's success has encouraged sprawl in the region. Planners overestimated the amount of commercial development necessary to create a balanced town, and they underestimated the degree to which conventional sprawl would surround and disturb the residents if the parks succeeded.

The 1990s brought not only a new town center and booming office parks but also significant changes to the village centers. Lake Anne village center experienced a renaissance as residents and visitors found new appreciation for its unusual design. One of the first urban-style gourmet restaurants to open in Lake Anne (in 1983) had been Il Cigno, and by the 1990s other urbanistic restaurants had crowded into Lake Anne, and a variety of small stores and cafés completed the scene. A renovation, paid for by the shop and restaurant owners and aided by a HUD grant, spruced up the concrete and restored the plaza fountain, making the center seem brighter and more animated. Lake Anne village center commercial tenants in the 1980s also took on a condominium form of ownership that has allowed successful diversification of shops. The plaza attracted small crowds on weekend nights in the summer and provided a charming environment unlike anything else in Fairfax County. After thirty years, the Lake Anne center had become successful as the investment in good design finally yielded dividends. It was not a truly nautical place, nor a particularly successful community public space, but it was becoming a destination for residents of Fairfax County in search of an elegant evening in an ersatz European environment.[29]

Older Reston village centers of less architectural distinction, Hunters Woods and Tall Oaks, underwent more drastic renovation in the 1990s. The Hunters Woods village center, for instance, had been plagued by safety problems and had difficulty maintaining retail businesses in the 1970s and 1980s. While crime rates were relatively low, the perception of crime, a few prominent incidents, and the isolated and enclosed feeling of the center made residents feel unsafe. Except for loitering teenagers, residents did not linger as they were supposed to in the enclosed plazas. They either completed their business and left, or they gravitated to more conventional areas with shops facing directly on parking lots.[30]

A major renovation of Hunters Woods village center by its current owner, a commercial property-management firm, is now complete (1999). Larger parking areas have replaced retail development that enclosed a plaza, and a new, smaller plaza has been created to link new residential and retail development with existing institutions (like the Reston Community Center). The new center is much more popular but aside from its mixture of uses has become nearly indistinguishable from conventional shopping areas. The center is now a collection of buildings that lacks unity or style, and the new public spaces are small and unimpressive.[31]

For North Point, the last village center to be developed, the RLC created an attractive strip mall. One resident architect in 1994 explained that North Point had become popular because "it's just common wisdom that you would put something splashy on the road with a big parking lot to attract customers."[32] Later development companies have also created strip malls in various parts of Reston, including Fox Mill Center and the Hechinger Center (neither of which were part of the original plan for Reston).[33] These changes from the early plans resulted from the developers' acknowledgement that not enough people walked, biked, or lounged to justify the expensive and sophisticated planning of early village centers.

Simon was the first developer to create a landscape that offered a comprehensive solution to perceived suburban failings, and later companies largely followed through on the initial concept. The development of Reston has been complicated by the changes in its management, planning, and architecture over the last forty years. Modernist design has been replaced with more conventional suburban styles; the ambitious recreational ideals have been lost; booming office parks have created traffic nightmares and contributed to sprawl in the region; and most of the pedestrian-oriented village centers have been turned into mixed-use strip malls. The idea that alternative physical design could automatically change people's behavior, particularly at the village centers, proved optimistic. The long-term success of Lake Anne and the instant success of the town center, however, illustrate that excellent design—in certain places, at certain times, and if well managed—can play an important role in changing people's habits. Reston, now a mixture of different architectural and planning styles, has served as an important laboratory for suburban experimentation.

3

Columbia, Maryland

Urban planning deals with highways, land uses, densities—even with crime, delinquency and disease—but it almost never begins with the simple question: "How can we best provide for the happiness of a man, his wife and family?"

JAMES ROUSE, in *Life*

The faith that James Rouse stated in his California speech was that a better environment could create better people. The faith could be questioned philosophically—indeed, theologically, but that faith was nevertheless the assumption on which the planning took place.

WALLACE HAMILTON, Columbia Archive Collection

The excitement generated by Reston in the early 1960s was complemented by the founding of another new town within one hour's drive only two years later (1963). Columbia, Maryland, established in rural Howard County, halfway between Baltimore, Maryland, and Washington, D.C., made an even bigger publicity splash than Reston. Limiting the modernist architectural design that had proved problematic at Reston, Columbia gained fame as a carefully planned, socially innovative suburban community.

Rouse envisioned his new community as a series of intimate small towns; the target population of 100,000 residents was to be divided into a number of "villages" of approximately 12,000 residents. Each village was to have its own center that would combine in one location public space, stores, a high school or middle school, community center, churches, and recreational facilities. Each village was subdivided into a series of residential neighborhoods that included a range of housing types from single-family homes to apartment buildings. The neighborhoods themselves focused on elementary schools, smaller neighborhood stores, and neighborhood-center buildings. Columbia, like Radburn and unlike Reston, was family oriented and emphasized schools and community facilities as the center of life in villages and neighborhoods (map 2).

Columbia's planners oriented the community to family needs, but they also hoped to attract a sophisticated audience that usually avoided suburbia. In the center of town they planned what they hoped would become an urbanistic town center with public spaces, a stylish shopping mall, a community college, an entertainment district, and offices. In addition, planners hoped to integrate modernist housing design with conventional suburban styles in apartment, town-house, and single-family developments. Surrounding the housing and other community facilities, future residents would find a green canopy created by thousands of acres of open spaces. Pathways and landscaped parkways were to wind through these lands. Adding to the sophistication of the plan was the developer's openness to blacks and low-income residents. Columbia quickly developed a reputation for cutting-edge experimentation in social mixture. Finally, the developer created an activist community association and foundation that he hoped would facilitate participation in local cultural and social activities.

In the 1950s, Rouse created some of the earliest covered shopping malls and during the 1970s pioneered the creation of downtown "festival marketplaces" such as Boston's Fanueil Hall and Baltimore's Harborplace. The Rouse Company that he created remains one of the leading managers of malls and communities in the country. During the 1950s Rouse served on Eisenhower's Advisory Committee on Housing and was chairman of the subcommittee that recommended the creation of an urban renewal program, an effort that led eventually to the Housing Act of 1954.[1] He lamented often that so much talent was devoted to business and the space program but not to a truly comprehensive program of urban renewal. He asked, "Why not take on the whole city—and all its pieces—in exactly the spirit in which we would take on a war—if we had it to wage—or in which we send a man to the moon."[2] Columbia, although located in suburbia and reflecting suburban styles, became his attempt to create large-scale urban rethinking.

Like many American reformers, Rouse wholly believed in the ability of the physical environment to improve community and individual

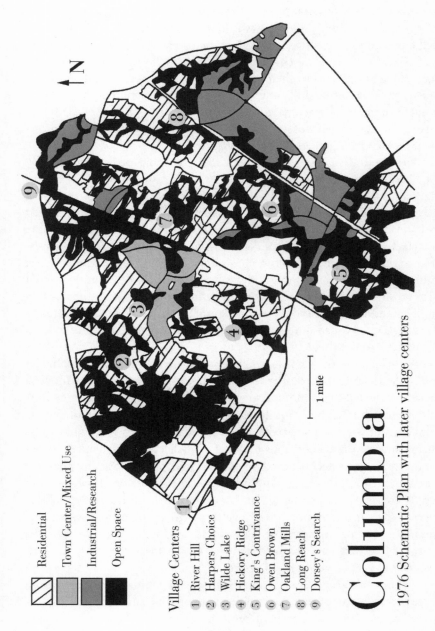

Columbia

1976 Schematic Plan with later village centers

MAP 2

Residential

Town Center/Mixed Use

Industrial/Research

Open Space

Village Centers

1 River Hill
2 Harpers Choice
3 Wilde Lake
4 Hickory Ridge
5 King's Contrivance
6 Owen Brown
7 Oakland Mills
8 Long Reach
9 Dorsey's Search

N

1 mile

character. In a 1969 speech, when discussing Columbia's budding civic life, he explained that "physical plan matters—in allowing community to naturally come into being."[3] In other words, an improved environment would facilitate community cohesion. Further, the speech reflects this philosophy as it related to individual character: "We must believe, because it is true, that people are affected by their environment—by space and scale, by color and texture, by nature and beauty; that they can be uplifted, made comfortable, important; become more productive workers, more agreeable clients, more expansive customers."[4] This belief in the effect of environment on character guided his new town's design.

Rouse and his associates began the Columbia project quietly. By 1963, Rouse had secretly assembled a tenth of rural Howard County in Maryland—nearly 14,000 acres—for his new community. He created a separate subsidiary of his Rouse Company, known as Howard Research and Development Corporation (HRD), to develop Columbia. The name reflects Rouse's belief that his undertaking was both a profit-making enterprise and a "research" project in community building. This company has until the present taken responsibility for planning the community, worked with governmental agencies, set construction requirements, sold land to builders and industry, and developed special facilities needed in the early years. HRD had broad powers in establishing the life of Columbia and did not hesitate to use them.[5]

Although he knew how to make a profit, Rouse acknowledged that he and his staff, and most planners in general, knew little about how modern society worked at the community level. Simon had hired a number of consultants on a limited basis, but Rouse spent $250,000 on a group of experts from a variety of fields to participate in the planning process. Unlike most businessmen, he had enormous respect for intellectuals, particularly social scientists. He genuinely believed that intellectuals would offer city planners a new way of approaching planning: "There is no dialogue between the people engaged in urban design and development and the behavioral sciences. Why not? Why not bring together a group of people who knew about people from a variety of backgrounds and experiences to view the prospect of a new city and shed light on how it might be made to work best for the people who would live there?"[6]

The work group served another purpose: public relations. Rouse possessed extensive experience in pleasing the public and knew the intricacies of marketing a development project, but he lacked legitimacy in the eyes of the intellectual elite he needed to impress in order to receive positive national publicity. Simon primarily used architecture and design to gain notice; Rouse chose intellectuals to attract attention. From a public-relations and marketing standpoint, Rouse's work group filled an important need and succeeded better than imagined. The idea of living in a community designed by intellectuals and wise planners impressed journalists and attracted many residents. In the long run, the work group's participation in early planning helped preserve the legitimacy of the plan as Columbia filled with many academics and educated professionals.

The work group in 1963 included mostly noncelebrity experts in the areas of government, family life, recreation, sociology, economics, education, health, psychology, housing, transportation, and communication. Hoppenfeld explained that they avoided big-name intellectuals because "we were anxious for the planning of this town to come from unfrozen minds. So we assembled a rather distinguished group of relatively unknown names in a wide variety of fields."[7] The group nonetheless included Herbert Gans, who at the time was writing *The Levittowners,* a balanced assessment of contemporary suburban society. Less well known but equally respected figures included Henry Bain, a government consultant, Nelson Foote, a sociologist, and Chester Rapkin, a professor of city planning, as well as nine other experts and intellectuals. Rouse and select members of his staff participated in the meetings.

The academics, while well paid for their services, needed to be convinced during the initial meeting of the practicality of a new town. A Christmas message to Columbians in 1970 from Rouse recounted how at the work group's first meeting they had been making little progress because "each invited expert proceeded to set forth the roadblock, the perils, the futility of undertaking the idea of a rational and humane city." That Saturday, however, a change took place:

> After an hour or so of heavy going, Chester Rapkin, Professor of Sociology at Penn, now at Columbia, a gentle, earnest man, and a deeply religious Jew, leaned across the table and said to the group: "We have been missing the point of this whole effort. . . . We are diagnosing the ills of the city, but what we are being asked to do is help bring forth the community structure that will nurture the growth of love." The moment was right. The impact was immediate. The spirit of the group transformed. There was a new light that guided the discussion—and it never faded. . . . The new morale of hope and high expectancy was sustained. Conviction grew that the new city (then unnamed) could, in fact, bring forth new structures, new

relationships, new attitudes—a new community in which understanding, trust, respect—yes, love—might flourish.[8]

Rouse, a very spiritual man, recounted this experience many times, and it
provided an excellent secular mythology for the new town. As with the
telling of any good religious tale, skeptics are converted and become part of
a crusade. These intellectuals did not become devotees of a religious creed,
however, but joined a humanistic project of community design.

After overcoming this initial hurdle, the work group, under the full-
time direction of Donald Michael, a psychologist, met twice monthly for
about six months. A series of papers on each expert's particular specialty as
it might operate in the community "served as grist for the interdisciplinary
mill, and traditional boundaries crumbled." Many Columbia institutions
received initial impetus from the group: the Johns Hopkins Hospital medical plan (one of the first health maintenance organizations in the country), the cooperative ministry, a minibus system, the Columbia Association
(CA), the Columbia Council and village boards (resident governance), a
community magazine, and a community amphitheater. The intellectuals'
guidance distinguished Columbia from conventional suburbs in numerous
ways, in both social and physical planning. Social scientists advocating innovations in social, cultural, and educational life could be found nowhere
else in suburbia.[9]

Most importantly, the work-group meetings yielded guiding principles for the plan. The intellectuals established the scale of the nine villages
(10,000 to 15,000 residents) and neighborhoods (2,000 to 5,000 residents).
They believed that this smaller scale would help community cohesion and
reduce residents' sense of anomie. This group of intellectuals, perhaps reflecting the importance of education in their own lives, also agreed that
"learning . . . is the basic foundation for the human community." Just as
recreational themes had been designated to give character to Reston villages, education was to give structure to the different community levels in
Columbia. Elementary schools nestled in the center of neighborhoods,
middle and upper schools anchored village centers, and institutions of
higher education gave character to the town center. The work group added
neighborhood and village community centers and hoped that all schools
would double as sites for community meetings and activities. Even the
plans for new school structures—changing a six-three-three grade
arrangement to five-three-four—and educational reform, including open
classrooms and self-directed learning, emerged in large part from the

innovative spirit of the work group. Continuing education for all age groups received particular emphasis.[10]

Making the schools the focus of small-scale neighborhoods placed the work group's planning firmly in line with practices as they had developed in new towns like Radburn. The degree to which educational experimentation and continuing education guided the whole plan, however, was peculiar to Columbia. This focus on education as the center of community life would also prove to have its own limitations.

The work group participated fully in the process of creating the new town, but there remained a crucial difference in conception between it and Rouse. Rouse, unlike the group, fondly hoped to create a series of old-fashioned small towns in Columbia. In a speech at the University of California, Berkeley, in 1963, he said, "I hold some very unscientific conclusions to the effect that people grow best in small communities where the institutions . . . are within reach of their responsibility." People could expect benefits not just in organizations but in social life, too, for Rouse explained that "a broader range of friendships and relationships occurs in a village or small town than in a city. . . . There is a greater sense of responsibility for one's neighbor" and "self-reliance is promoted."[11] Rouse had grown up in a small town on Maryland's Eastern Shore and remained nostalgic for small-town life.

Rouse remembered that the members of the work group were all "urban types, urban sophisticates" and that "he didn't dare talk too much about small towns." According to Rouse, however, "as they discussed the 'malaise' of the cities, their conversation often focused on scale—things were too big."[12] Bain, the work group's expert on government, explained many years later that members of the group were "not all that keen on the neighborhood concept," and yet he added, "I don't remember anybody confronting Mr. Rouse and saying, 'Mr. Rouse, the medieval era has passed. We're now in the modern era. It's no longer a viable concept for social organization.'" Gans expressed his opinion during the meetings that "neighborhoods were unlikely to function as cohesive social units."[13] The work group had nonetheless found a way to integrate Rouse's fondness for neighborhoods and villages; they did so by making educational institutions the center of a series of small communities.

The work group's existence helped bring attention and legitimacy to the Columbia new-town reform effort. Newspapers and magazines across the country carried complimentary stories. A 1964 article by J. W. Anderson in *Harper's* provided an insightful analysis. Anderson understood Rouse's social-reform instinct better than most observers, although he had his doubts about the ability of Rouse to create intimate small towns: "[Rouse's] neighborhood planning is an attempt to recreate the old sense of village community in the context of the great Eastern megalopolis. His villages' orientation toward schools—which are for adults as well as children—is an attempt to design a city that will elevate its people morally and intellectually. Although the first customer may think he is merely buying a house, he will in reality become part of a carefully considered campaign to reform the American's view of his neighbor."[14]

A talented young planning team employed by the developer worked concurrently with the work group. Rouse had participated in the affairs of the National Capital Planning Commission, which advocated new towns in the Washington region as a way to reduce suburban sprawl. Rouse naturally hired professionals from that project. William Finley, Hoppenfeld, and Robert Tennenbaum worked on the commission and later joined the team at the new town. Finley assumed the role of general manager, Hoppenfeld became director of planning and design, and Tennenbaum took on the role of chief architect-planner.[15]

The members of the planning staff, unlike most subdividers, first tried to understand their site in order to have the community fit the shape of the land. Hoppenfeld "started with aerial photographs and maps, complemented by field surveys—by helicopter, automobile and on foot—to inspect topographic and land features, to note land forms of particular potential, to plot aesthetic features which would be retained or amplified." They itemized these features "and separated [them] into a series of overlay maps. With deliberate disregard of land ownership, these overlays isolated for inventory such existing features as tree cover, waterways and watershed areas" that would be preserved as part of the final plan. The staff "was determined to preserve the general contour of the rolling farmland and to perpetuate wooded areas where practicable." By 1970, the planners had graduated to even more detailed site planning: "Instead of the 5 foot contour suitable for general planning, 1 foot contours are checked in the field; roads are walked before the final grades are set in order to minimize cuts or fill; trees to be saved are decided upon by size and species, and a road may bend or bifurcate to save a 30 inch oak."[16]

Adaptations to the site changed planning ideals. Wallace Hamilton, who acted as a historian for HRD, notes that the original ideas envisioned a combined greenbelt and park system of 3,900 acres out of the planned 12,300 acre total. The idea of a greenbelt surrounding the community was dispensed with because planners believed that "nature had done a better planning job on the land with three stream valleys." The planners observed that "each of these valleys . . . gave the land a natural definition, and could give the villages their definition." In addition, by the time the planners had made provisions for all of the low-density uses, including golf courses, lakes, parks, bridle paths and other recreational uses, the acreage set aside for the greenbelt had been used.[17]

The village form at Columbia emerged from a combination of work-group discussions and Rouse's admiration for small towns. Hamilton re-counted that "the most significant point about the early plans was that there was no suggestion of the village idea that was to dominate later plan-ning. Residential [and retail] areas were scattered about . . . without any clear sense of coordination." The work-group discussions in 1963, in which the leading planners participated, contributed to the creation of the village concept, and Rouse's speech in California, outlining his admiration for small towns, influenced the planners. He was their boss, after all.[18] The planners adopted the village idea and organized housing and educational and cultural resources around the ideas of compact, nucleated neighbor-hoods and villages.

Neighborhoods and villages connoted hometown friendliness, but small-town intimacy was not the goal of the planners to the same degree it was for Rouse. Hoppenfeld, in particular, had contemporary ideas about modern urban life that guided his and the development team's planning. He believed that "the real community to which individuals belong be-comes a function of personal interest and identification. Sometimes it will correspond to the 'physical community' of their neighborhood or village, but at other times . . . it will cut across service areas resulting in 'commu-nity patterns' as complex and overlapping as in every living city. Freedom of movement and access to community facility centers via transit and car throughout the city should enhance and foster the sense of real commu-nity, based on choice." A community based on "choice" is quite different from a small town where residents have limited choices and a high degree of isolation. Hoppenfeld envisioned Columbia as part of a future Ameri-can society consisting of "alternative cultures and varied life styles, brought together by a social and physical environment and enabled to co-exist, overlap, thrive."[19]

Integrating his interest in creating overlapping communities, Hop-penfeld specified that each village have one special recreational feature "to foster variety and encourage cross village center use." In Wilde Lake, the first village developed in the 1960s, the planners constructed a year-round swimming facility; in Oakland Mills, across town, a skating rink was built. In their own way, planners were breaking down the small-town culture

FIGURE 4 Wilde Lake village center, framed by low-slung commercial and civic buildings, offered residents high-quality public spaces rarely found in suburbia. Although a
mixed commercial success, the center remains a popular destination for many Columbia
residents. (1999)

envisioned by Rouse. They did hope, however, as did Rouse, that they
could create active community public spaces, a feature lacking from the
suburban strip. Rouse and his planners envisioned the centers as village
greens where "teachers, doctors, ministers, parents, merchants, kids come
together . . . in the ordinary course of life." The early centers, with shops
and community facilities grouped around a village "green," were modeled
loosely on the New England town common (figure 4).[20]

Planners added other innovations that they hoped would facilitate
community integration. They placed higher-density housing near the village centers, which were built in the geographic middle of each village.
Through this arrangement, they sought to maximize convenience for the
most people, particularly lower-income residents, who might not have vehicles, as well as to improve the efficiency of the planned minibus system
that would run between villages. Each village also included a mixture of
single-family homes, apartment complexes, and town houses arranged in
smaller-scale neighborhoods. This mixing of styles was revolutionary in
this area at the time. Neighborhoods included their own smaller centers
containing a community facility, a small store, and a pool. Planners pre-

served natural expanses in every village, and the different villages were linked by parkways and grade-separated pathways (pioneered at Radburn). Later villages (a total of ten nearly complete by the 1990s) followed this model in most respects.[21]

Architects played a prominent role in the commercial and community planning of Columbia, but they played a minor role in residential design. Quite a few custom-built contemporary homes and some innovative apartment and condominium complexes were architect designed; these resembled those found at Reston and European new towns (figure 5). But most of the residential design at Columbia was, and remains, the work of builders who repeated the familiar patterns of suburban architecture, fitting them into the framework of the new town. Most single-family homes were split-levels and colonial revivals, and most apartment complexes were little different from any found in suburbia, with cheap materials, conventional designs, and uninspired siting. Over time this has led to a variety of styles, as even conventional modes have changed over the decades, but architectural variety is not as evident in Columbia as it is in Reston. The idea remained, however, to increase the options in a suburban community.

Architects did play a prominent role in the town center, Columbia's urban core. Suburbanites at Columbia would not have to venture into a city, driving long distances to experience urban excitement: they would have a small but dynamic downtown of their own. In the handsome promotional materials for the town created by the Rouse Company in the early 1960s, the planning staff envisioned a remarkable downtown filled with educational, cultural, commercial, retail, and residential areas: "By day, one edge of the lake will be a park—Kittamaqundi—with restaurants, coffee shops, carousels and entertainment for children; by night, it will be transformed into a gay and playful wonderland for people of every age." The plans for the downtown as advertised nationally set a very high standard of urbanity.[22]

Rouse invested most in contemporary, architect-designed structures in the town center, and it is here that the influence of the modernist new towns, particularly Tapiola, is most evident (figure 6). As the high-profile centerpiece of a dynamic new community, it had to look the part. A mall topped with pyramidal glass structures sat in the middle, while modernist buildings lined an artificial lakeshore and plaza. In the early years of his career, Frank Gehry (with his then-partner David O'Malley) designed the Columbia Exhibition building (1967), the Merriweather Post Pavilion (a musical amphitheater built in 1967), and the Rouse Company headquarters (1974) in the town center. Perhaps best reflecting his later work is the

FIGURE 5 Tidesfall town houses in the village of Wilde Lake offered unconventional designs in a natural setting. Although Columbia's developer devoted little attention to contemporary design and most housing followed more conventional suburban lines, offbeat designs were offered to attract as wide an audience as possible. (*Newcomers Guide*, 1983)

pavilion, constructed of "anonymous materials" including rough-finished Douglas fir, exposed steel I-beams, steel joists and concrete to give character and avoid monumentality.[23]

A number of different elements, beyond just architectural design, had to be coordinated to make the downtown a success. An early disappointment came during the initial planning process of the 1960s with the abandonment of Columbia's Tivoli section, adjoining the downtown lake. The work group had pioneered the idea of a downtown recreation/

FIGURE 6 At Columbia's town center lakefront, children frolicked in an inviting fountain or found pleasure in paddleboats rented at the shoreline. Adults found restaurants, public art, walking paths, and convivial outdoor seating areas. Community events often centered on the plaza, and the modern Rouse Company headquarters (at right), designed by Frank Gehry, overlooked the scene. In the background above the lake are town house and apartment complexes of Talbot Springs in Oakland Mills village.

education area modeled on Tivoli Gardens, Copenhagen's famous park and amusement district. Hamilton shared Hoppenfeld's and the work group's enthusiasm for the creation of an entertainment district, but failed to attract an amusement vendor.[24] The lakefront area in the town center, however, did borrow elements from Tivoli. Hoppenfeld explained that the Gardens taught him "the value of trees, of street furniture, of lights, of kiosks, of benches for people to sit and look at something moving." The lakefront therefore included abundant seating, landscaped open spaces, attractive lighting, a dock, and a gazebo with a blue-canvas mansard roof.

An enormous fountain splashed near the shore to add interest to the scene and attract residents.[25]

A galleria shopping mall was also placed in the town center. The Rouse Company believed that the shopping malls it built elsewhere introduced urban-style excitement and helped create community in suburbia. The company promised that Columbia would share in this tradition: "In the center of the downtown will be the Galleria, a multilevel, enclosed pedestrian street of shops, services, and entertainment. Department stores, hundreds of retailers of every description, fine clothing and apparel stores, gift and gourmet shops, street vendors, colorful kiosks and cafes will line the Galleria."[26] At the 1971 opening of the mall, a local reporter raved, "ten thousand people swarmed in. . . . It was all there as promised—the skylights, the famous clock, the fountains, trees and flowers."[27] A perceptive reporter from a trade magazine noticed that the mall, even with a modern pyramidal glass ceiling, had been designed to evoke an historic American main street—it was to be Columbia's main street, as he put it: "The center, attractively landscaped with live trees and shrubbery, was obviously styled in an Early America flavor with brick walkways, simulated gas lamps and an old time sidewalk clock as a focal point."[28]

Planning in the 1960s extended beyond brick and mortar issues. The CA, local village boards, and the Columbia Council constituted a possible solution to suburban civic disorganization. The CA, composed of recreation specialists, was designed to play a wide role in community life. While Howard County was to run the schools, police, libraries, and fire department, the association would manage recreational and cultural resources in the new town. The citizen body, the Columbia Council, which was to oversee the association was dominated in the 1960s and 1970s by Rouse Company officials, who saw to it that the association had a commitment to larger issues like subsidizing a local minibus service and developing cultural resources. By the 1980s, elected council members from the villages of Columbia directed the association, although day-to-day operations remained in the hands of the professionals.

Local village boards were designed by the planners as a means to encourage community participation and incipient democracy, but it was not clear what role they would play beyond covenant enforcement and election of a representative to the citywide Columbia Council. In the 1970s, however, led by activists in Oakland Mills village, most of the boards took on the administration of local services (recreational facilities and social events in community centers) through contracts with the CA.

HRD took responsibility for more than just recreational resources. In addition to helping organize the Johns Hopkins Hospital Medical Plan, the Interfaith plan for shared religious facilities, and the Merriweather Post Pavilion,[29] Columbia's development team also helped transform Howard County's segregated educational system into a leader in integrated education by attracting grants to finance the newest educational concepts, including a new community college. Early schools at Columbia included ungraded classes, team teaching, learning centers, flexible grouping, and multimedia centers.

By creating a mechanism for channeling some of the local corporations' money to local efforts, Rouse helped stimulate a richness in institutional life not duplicated at the other new towns. The Columbia Foundation Inc., a grant-making institution established within the new community, helped citizens create a wide range of social and cultural institutions. In 1970 Rouse committed HRD to giving 10 per cent of its net earnings before taxes to the foundation every year (and the newly formed Columbia Bank and Trust also agreed). The foundation gave grants to local institutions that addressed psychological counseling, women's issues, the arts, and low-income housing. From the 1970s to the 1990s, the foundation continued to support a variety of cultural and social organizations— including dance, low-income housing initiatives, aid for retarded children and adults, and the Columbia Forum (dedicated to preserving new-town ideals). By 1996 the foundation made fifty-six grants valued at $350,000 and had developed an endowment of $3,900,000.[30]

These efforts in institutional planning complemented the innovative physical planning. Under Rouse's guidance, HRD had committed itself to a wide array of reforms. With these many elements in place by the late 1960s and early 1970s, Columbia was poised as an attractive alternative to surrounding suburbs. It began to attract tens of thousands of residents eager for a new life. Columbia grew rapidly in the 1960s and 1970s. The recession of 1973–74 temporarily shook the town's progress. Reduced demand for housing coupled with previous investments in land and infrastructure forced Rouse to cut approximately half of his staff. He also sought and obtained additional financing from his main investor, Connecticut General Life Insurance Corporation. Throughout this period of troubles, Columbia grew rapidly but not as quickly as the Rouse Company's economic models from the 1960s had predicted. Thanks to the deep pockets of the investor and some belt tightening, the community continued to grow. By the 1980s Columbia had become one of Maryland's largest towns. The business parks in the community filled and the many villages gained new apartments, village centers, and community facilities. The population had reached 50,000 by the mid-1980s and has continued rising (to 85,000 in 1999). New roads carried residents, new parks blossomed, and Columbia enjoyed an enviable reputation for superb recreation facilities, booming office parks, excellent schools, and mostly affluent residents (average household income in 1999 was $79,000).[31]

The CA grew in scale with the community. By the 1990s, the association managed 2,900 acres of open space, 144 tot lots (playgrounds), 227 pedestrian bridges, fifteen overpasses and underpasses, three lakes and nineteen ponds, and seventy-eight miles of pathways. Athletic and sporting clubs including pools (indoor and outdoor), golf courses, ice rinks, and more, also run by the association, were available on a membership basis. Temporary downsizing during the recession in the early 1970s was quickly followed by a recommitment to the broader ideals of the new towns under the direction of Padraic (Pat) Kennedy, the leader of the organization. The association also maintained an arts center, a series of community centers (run by village boards) with meeting and performance spaces, a number of camps for children, and child-care programs.

From many perspectives, Columbia was a great success and quite idyllic, but blemishes remained. Persistent problems emerged in the village centers and the town center. The strong focus on education as the core of public life went unquestioned in Columbia's planning, but it has had a negative effect, particularly in village centers. Schools, community centers, and stores became the focus of village centers, not movie theaters, churches, bowling alleys, bars, dance halls, or diners. Although in the late 1960s and early 1970s journalists had found village centers filled with small-town scenes and a variety of alternative venues including coffee-houses and galleries, fewer residents over the decades came to the centers than expected, and those that did chose not to linger as planners had hoped. Village centers did attract teenagers, and occasional crime incidents in the 1970s and 1980s—in a suburban environment with a low tolerance for any violence—gave village centers a reputation, not necessarily deserved, for being dangerous. Centralized management of all the different centers by the Rouse Company also prevented a diversification of ownership, and there were frequent complaints about the company's high rents. Finally, understated signage and the siting of village centers at the geographic middle of each community made them difficult for anyone but residents to find.[32]

Planners at HRD have slowly adjusted the village-center concept. Inward facing village centers (Wilde Lake, 1967; Oakland Mills, 1969; Harper's Choice, 1971; Long Reach, 1974; Owen Brown, 1978) with small

but attractive public spaces enclosed by shopping and community facilities
have been followed by more open—and popular—strip-type village centers with less common space (King's Contrivance, 1986; Dorsey's Search,
1989; Hickory Ridge, 1992; River Hill, 1998). Dorsey's Search and River
Hill most resemble strip malls, whereas King's Contrivance and Hickory
Ridge combine a strip-mall design with narrow plazas as part of their plan.
Renovations of older village centers (Harper's Choice, Oakland Mills, and
Long Reach) to make them more open and to expand the size of grocery
stores have been completed. Internal courtyards are being opened out, signage enlarged, colors brightened, lighting increased, and parking made
more prominent. These changes seem to have made the centers more popular, but it remains to be seen how well these renovations address persistent problems.

These changes in the village centers have led many observers to see
the village-center concept as a failure, but the truth is more complicated.
Many Columbians still use the centers. In a 1997 survey, 17 percent reported using a village center every day, 31 percent used them at least three
times a week, and 42 percent used them once or twice a week. Most residents also believe the quality of the village centers is good. In addition, six
community centers are located in the village centers, and they are well used
for specific events and activities. The village centers, with shopping, community, and educational facilities, remain attractive destinations even
though they have failed to meet the expectations of the planners.[33]

The industrial-office parks on Columbia's edges, designed by the developer, have also attracted many private community facilities that might
have been absorbed in village centers. Although many high-technology
and light-manufacturing businesses have located there (2,900 businesses
called Columbia home in 1999),[34] the parks also have a surprisingly high
number of institutions that would fit better in village centers. Athletic
clubs, discount and specialty stores, churches, nonprofits, and child-care
centers can be found in abundance in these industrial parks. With space
cheap and abundant and parking plentiful, these parks have taken on the
role envisioned for village centers. Planners underestimated the amount of
multipurpose space that would be needed by the residents of the town.
Many of these institutions simply found a more affordable and convenient
space that closely fit suburban expectations.

Columbia's successful office parks, with nearly as many jobs (66,000)
as residents of the town (85,000),[35] also raise questions about the ability
of new towns to tame sprawl. Columbia (rather than older urban cores
like Baltimore) has become a magnet for businesses in the region; new

expensive subdivisions have grown around the community's edges; and traffic has become heavy on local highways and roads. As at Reston, the process of sprawl has certainly received a boost from Columbia's success. If the village centers were too small in some respects, the office parks may have proved to be too large.

The lakefront has experienced its own unique problems over the decades. Teenagers, the residents most interested in lounging in public spaces, began congregating along the lake as early as the 1970s and disturbed the peace of adult residents. According to one police officer in 1971, in the town center "there have been assaults and robberies, an excessive amount of misuse of alcohol by under-age youths, open sexual promiscuity—and we have every reason to believe that there is also drug abuse." A *Columbia Flier* reporter, Chuck Petrowski, described the situation: "A weeknight visit to the plaza revealed perhaps fifty or so young people. . . . Many of them reportedly remain there until after midnight on balmy summer evenings. On weekends, crowds are said to swell to three or four times this." The CA responded to complaints about the teenagers in the early 1970s by transforming the lakefront during the summers into a performance space. The CA focused on adult- and child-oriented offerings "from old time movies to jazz sessions." In response, "hundreds of families have turned out to sit on the lawn and listen" to jazz, bluegrass, country, folk and gospel, African, and West Indian music. The head of the local security force noticed that the festival "edged the rough crowd out" and brought a "more peaceful, more desirable crowd." Some teenagers disliked the new arrangements, although many undoubtedly enjoyed the offerings. This series, with an event planned for every summer night, continues today and now includes a regular "open-mike" night to which many teenagers are drawn.[36] The association turned what had become a trying situation into a valued community resource. Additional festivals and activities, attracting thousands of residents, filled the lakefront on a regular basis. The area developed as the civic heart of Columbia, but it did not became the grand urban center promised.

By the 1980s, in many residents' eyes, the town center as a whole had failed to achieve the level of urbanity envisioned in original publicity materials. The plan, like most modernist plans, had separated the community college, the shopping mall, office buildings, and public spaces into individual zones. Large open areas and sprawling parking lots diluted an urban feeling and made walking difficult. Columbians were skeptical that the downtown offered urban excitement. Lisa Leff, of the *Washington Post*, reported that residents knew that "a city has taxicabs, street-level stores and skyscrapers . . . not parking lots, a giant shopping mall and winding streets that spill into precise town house developments and end in cul-de-sacs. If Columbia were truly a city, they muse, would Columbians get into their cars on weekend nights and head for Baltimore or Washington?"[37]

The primary reason for the failure of urbanity in the town center was the dominance of the Columbia mall. The mall at first developed features usually associated with downtown commercial districts, including small stores, political activity, art shows, and lounging. In 1972, one reporter found the mall "festive with banners and exhibits, way-out specialty shops like Airport as well as standbys like Woody's—and, on a pre-primary Saturday, bustling with McGovern workers."[38] The police also had plenty to do at the mall. One Howard County policeman reported in the 1970s: "Teenagers especially come here from all over. My men call the Mall a giant day care center."[39] The openness to spontaneity and political or other non-consuming behavior did not last long after Rouse left the company in the 1980s.[40]

A 1990s mall expansion and renovation has been accompanied by what many perceive as a hostile attitude toward small, local businesses that have been located in the mall for many years and a greater emphasis on national chain stores. The mall renovation will not address the disconnection of the mall from the rest of town center: it will remain an enclosed shopping center with blank walls and parking lots. Rouse Company executives talk of creating a more dynamic downtown, but the renovation plan does not reflect this. The mall strategy, based on marketing studies of the region, is to bring back wealthy customers by increasing luxury retailing (Lord and Taylor and Nordstroms) and refurbishing the mall, rather than creating the urban-style excitement of the town center at Reston, establishing an exciting connection to the lakeside, or invigorating the mall's civic function.[41]

The mall has problems, but it compares well with later commercial development. The developer permitted the growth of "box" stores on Columbia's edges during the 1980s and 1990s. These shopping centers, such as Dobbin Center on Route 175 along Columbia's edge, are popular for their ample parking and low prices. The shift of commercial activity to these new centers reflects the value consciousness of the American family and the perception of decreasing leisure time. The centers include stores of little architectural interest, and many residents believe they have hurt business at smaller village centers and the mall. One resident noted that "Now we go to BJ's [a wholesale club]. I don't even look at the people's faces when I go to BJ's, because I assume I don't know them." This shift to wholesale shopping and big box stores is not unique to Columbia and reflects an unresolved tension in contemporary American life between the desire for community and the insatiable demand for ever more—and ever less expensive—goods. Rouse Company officials have apparently abandoned elements of the suburban reform movement that opposed strip mall development.[42]

❖

Columbia, like Reston, provides important results from planning experimentation. Certain experiments, such as the town-center lakefront, the later village centers, and extensive institutional planning, improved Columbia's reputation, attracted new residents, and helped build community life. The early pedestrian village centers as community social spaces, the focus on education for the whole community, and the mall as the center of an urbane downtown, on the other hand, proved unsatisfactory in many respects. The phenomenal success of Columbia in attracting businesses has also contributed to sprawl in the Baltimore-Washington area by creating a powerful regional employment and commercial center in a formerly rural area.

Columbia as a whole, even with its blemishes, remains an attractive alternative to the conventional subdivisions it sought to replace. The landscape is dominated by the thousands of trees preserved and planted in the early years, man-made lakes, handsome mixed-use village centers, and a mixture of architectural styles. Cultural and educational institutions have benefited from the Rouse Company's patronage, and an activist community association continues to design new facilities and programs for residents. The 85,000 people who now live in this new town still benefit from the developer's tenacious and unorthodox vision.

4

Irvine, California

In the molasses of suburbia, people did want a sense of place.

RAYMOND WATSON, Irvine Company planner

In the 1950s Los Angeles began to spread into the orange groves and ranches on its southern border. Much of what is now the suburban sprawl of Orange County at one time was part of a productive agricultural region. Glimpses of this former landscape are evident in sections of the Irvine Ranch, which once encompassed 120,000 acres of prime California land (map 3). A few crops still grow on acreage that in a few years will sprout office parks and housing developments.

The Irvine Ranch, unlike much of Orange County, has not been supplanted by conventional suburban sprawl. The original plan for Irvine from the early 1960s envisioned a small college town of 100,000 residents surrounding a new campus of the University of California. A town center adjoining the university was to include a variety of commercial and cultural venues and was to be surrounded by a variety of small neighborhoods and tasteful industrial parks. This concept guided the early years of planning. A more ambitious plan adopted in 1970 superseded this early concept and raised population targets to 400,000. This larger city plan still divided the future population into discrete neighborhoods surrounding the university but now included a linear urban spine featuring commercial and community facilities.

Irvine's developer was building a new kind of city and developed a wide range of housing options, but the company did not commit itself to racial integration. Irvine was created from the beginning as a relatively homogeneous, well-designed suburban city with options for play, work, and

53

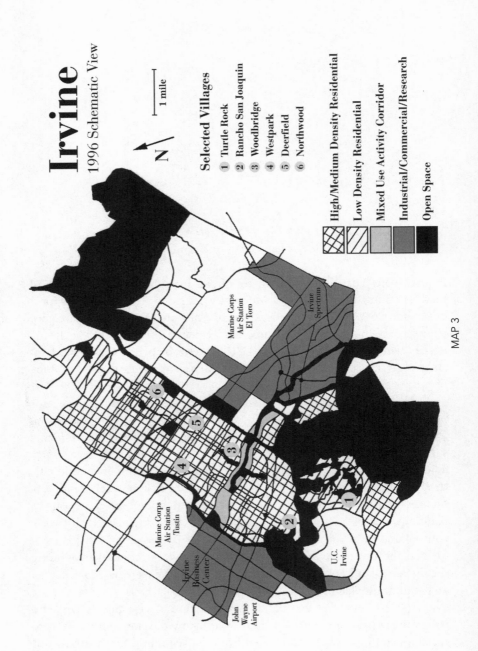

Irvine
1996 Schematic View

N

1 mile

Selected Villages
1 Turtle Rock
2 Rancho San Joaquin
3 Woodbridge
4 Westpark
5 Deerfield
6 Northwood

High/Medium Density Residential

Low Density Residential

Mixed Use Activity Corridor

Industrial/Commercial/Research

Open Space

Marine Corps Air Station Tustin

John Wayne Airport

Irvine Business Center

U.C. Irvine

Marine Corps Air Station El Toro

Irvine Spectrum

MAP 3

study. Although this chapter focuses primarily on the City of Irvine in the center of the ranch, developments planned by the Irvine Company on other parts of the ranch are also discussed in relation to the growth of the city.

The Irvine Company, manager and owner of the ranch, focused on agricultural production until the 1950s and 1960s, when residential, commercial, and industrial development began. The company, established in the nineteenth century by James Irvine Sr. eventually passed to the Irvine Foundation, composed of his descendants and a managing board of directors. As the ranch was located just south of booming Los Angeles, most observers expected it to be carved into subdivisions and office parks. Instead, under the influence of planner/architect William Pereira, the company decided to develop the land as a planned community.[1]

Pereira, designer of the Transamerica building in San Francisco and the community plan for Cape Canaveral, developed the first plans for Irvine in the 1950s. He began his work in 1957 for the University of California system as part of the firm of Pereira and Luckman. After extensive analysis, the university system and the firm selected the Irvine Ranch as a desirable location for a new campus in Southern California. In 1959, the university agreed to build its new branch on the ranch if the Irvine Company would donate 1,000 acres (the company had originally hoped to sell land to the university) and would prepare a plan for the surrounding community. The company agreed to the donation, and the university announced the location of its new campus in 1960. The two institutions jointly hired Pereira (no longer in partnership with Luckman) to "prepare a general plan for the 10,000 acres around the University."[2] The company later commissioned Pereira to create a detailed South Irvine Ranch General Plan (encompassing 35,000 acres), "incorporating basic elements of the original 10,000 acre University Community plan." Orange County approved this plan for a city of approximately 100,000 people in 1964.[3]

These early plans seek to create a small community that the historian Martin Schiesl describes as a "new version of the garden city complete with shopping centers, greenbelts and parks." The plan also called for a town center near the campus with a blend of "professional offices, restaurants, churches, apartments, inns, coffee houses, motor hotels, bowling alleys, theaters, concert halls, dance hall, museums, art galleries, [and] a farmer's market."[4] This list reflects an idealistic notion of a society more reminiscent of university towns Pereira admired, like Oxford and Cambridge, than southern California cities and suburbs as they existed.[5] As one recent observer noted, "his Irvine would be a dense urban core surrounded by carefully designed open space, where cars were unnecessary, the community intertwined with the university, and anyone could afford to live." The Irvine Company's plan would significantly alter this original image.[6]

During the 1960s, a number of important developments by the Irvine Company set the pattern for residential construction to come. At Eastbluff, planner Raymond Watson sought and received approval from the city of Newport Beach (which had annexed the land) to mix housing, commercial facilities, parks, and schools. Watson, an architect by training who later became president of the Irvine Company, also established the signal elements of Irvine in Eastbluff: narrow greenbelts, attached but still expensive housing, extensive recreational facilities, and a village concept. The company initiated a number of similar villages in the 1960s near the university, including University Park and Turtle Rock. These developments proved extremely popular.[7]

These Irvine villages have many similarities to those of Columbia and Reston. Although the population size of Irvine villages varied more than those of the other new towns, the planners also created "neighborhood clusters," fewer streets, open spaces, and convenient schools. Irvine planners, however, hoped to avoid the unending formlessness of suburbia by making villages thematically distinct through planning, architecture, and landscaping. The elements of villages are designed to provide a sense of place, give orientation to outsiders, and make Irvine as a whole comprehensible. Columbia and Reston are distinct from nearby suburban communities, but the coordinated and uniform architecture, planning, and landscaping of the entire community can be disorienting.

Watson, who developed this village-planning model in the 1960s, acknowledges the influence of Kevin Lynch, the pioneering planner and theorist. Lynch's design philosophy, as articulated in his influential *The Image of the City*, encouraged planners to focus on how people actually experienced the city rather than adopting abstract ideals about urban form. He demanded attention to the natural and man-made edges of a city, the elements that distinguished districts or neighborhoods, pathways through the city, and the necessity for landmarks. This sensitivity to the experience of the city from the individual's point of view was evident in Watson's planning at Irvine.[8]

First, the company designed and marketed the villages along three orientations: "a University orientation, proximity to the ocean, and hillside location. This was done to enhance the residents' sense of place within the larger Irvine community."[9] Wider streets defined the borders of villages, and most traffic was diverted around smaller neighborhoods. The com-

FIGURE 7 Multiple-family housing in Irvine's village of Rancho San Joaquin reflects the Mission style. Unlike most garden apartments in suburbia, architects designed these buildings to attractively match their surroundings. Planners at Irvine applied thematic architecture like this to help differentiate the individual villages.

pany hired architects to help distinguish villages and functions. Modernist designs, usually white and geometrically bold, dominated the Newport Center office complex and the University of California campus, affirming the serious purpose and cutting-edge profile of businesses and the new university. Residential areas had warmer, contrasting styles. University Park's architecture was California ranch; Eastbluff featured red-tile roofs and stucco; Rancho San Joaquin employed Mission-inspired buildings (figure 7); and Woodbridge received a Cape Cod-influenced style. One company official explained that "although the great majority of construction throughout the United States is done without the use of an architect, the Irvine Company has always required that any development within its master planned area be designed by a professional architect."[10]

Landscape design added further definition to villages. Rancho San Joaquin was planted with lemon-scented eucalyptus and plane trees, as well as "yellow flowering gazania" as ground cover. At Deerfield, "the flat terrain . . . suggested a city park theme. The many small parks are connected to each other and to the central public park by a mini-trail system."

Planners oriented Woodbridge around its two lakes, which have walking paths, shopping, and recreational facilities adjoining them. Watson explained in an interview that in Irvine, "landscape is more important than buildings" in giving definition and distinction to the new town.[11] Unlike Reston and Columbia, the landscape of Irvine is not rustic. Designers employed manicured nature as a palette to add identity and beauty to villages. In the other new towns, sufficient natural vegetation and water existed to integrate developments with wild areas. In addition, the developers of the eastern new towns set aside larger parcels of open space for the pathways and surrounding landscape.

More than the village design concept separated Irvine planning from that of Columbia and Reston. In Irvine, the developer created two levels of recreational facilities. Neighborhoods, each generally composed of one housing type, focused on a particular recreational facility—usually a pool, tennis courts, or a small recreation center—open only to residents of that neighborhood. This system was different from Columbia or Reston, where planners spread open space and recreational facilities more evenly throughout the town, made facilities available to any resident for a fee, and gave community associations a monopoly on recreational services. Irvine planners added a hierarchical notion to their villages that is not present at the other new towns.

The village-center concept also distinguishes Irvine from either Reston or Columbia. The developers and planners of Columbia and Reston sought to use community facilities and public spaces as a way to bolster village identity and public life. At Irvine, these resources are not found in village centers. Planning, architectural, and landscape elements rather than centralized community facilities, village greens, or urbanistic piazzas affirmed village ideals. Irvine's development team did not place much faith in the ability of design to create an intimate, small-town environment.[12]

Village centers in Irvine became convenient shopping areas with small public spaces, although planners boasted that "we've planned our village centers as self-contained centers of activity, as opposed to the more conventional shopping sites." In Irvine, "self-contained centers of activity" meant a mixture of supermarket, drug store, and specialty stores rather than the more exotic mix of schools, community centers, and religious facilities found at other new towns. Nonetheless, the company made the centers more attractive than those in most of suburbia (figure 8). They hid service areas, landscaped open space and parking lots, created seating areas, and gave each center a thematic element (a covered walkway or clock tower, for instance). Architects always used warm materials, such as stucco,

FIGURE 8 Village center at University Park offered small public spaces and attractive design, but Irvine's planners avoided the more unconventional mixture of uses seen at Columbia and Reston village centers.

adobe brick, and wood, and matched the centers to their surrounding village. Designers also specified more tasteful signage and encouraged the use of semiotic signs.[13]

Pereira's university town center plan languished in the 1960s, in part because of student activism, but Newport Center (located in Newport Beach, but part of the Irvine Company's planning efforts) became the area's new downtown. Designed as a 700-acre complex of high-rise office buildings, hotels, and shopping facilities, it gained popularity quickly. Modern, tall buildings, including Irvine Company headquarters, filled a circular office park that surrounded a central shopping mall. Watson designed the shopping center as a "staggered mall . . . forming a series of individual plazas and changing vistas."[14]

Careful attention to everything from small details to master planning made the Irvine Ranch developments some of the most popular communities in southern California. As the new villages grew in the 1960s and filled with affluent residents and successful businesses, the neighboring towns of Newport Beach and Santa Ana annexed sections of the ranch. The Irvine Company, however, saw that few benefits were to be had from dividing the entire property among a number of surrounding cities. The planners of Irvine, without Pereira at this point, thus turned their attention to unifying the central sector of the ranch. In 1970, the Irvine Company announced, with much fanfare, that it planned to build on the central sector "the largest totally master-planned city on the North American continent: the City of Irvine, to cover 53,000 acres, with a population of 430,000 expected by the year 2000." The city would include twenty-four distinct villages and a variety of "opportunities for life styles, occupation, and recreation." Planners envisioned a hierarchy of roads and paths, a mixture of apartments, attached housing, and single-family homes, a variety of park spaces, commercial and industrial areas, a large commercial center, and an "urban spine" combining park, civic, and commercial uses.[15]

The population targets were high, much higher than Pereira's plan for a city of 100,000, but company planners promoted a decentralized vision of what would be urban space in Irvine: a series of villages with multiple-use urban corridors weaving through them. This plan seems to parallel that of Reston, with its urban sinew concept, but it is quite different. The urban sinew at Reston included high-density housing that wove through the community and connected village centers; by contrast, Irvine's urban sinew is simply a linear planning system for a variety of uses needed by the various communities through which the corridor passed.

Dealing with the problem of drainage paths for the central area of the ranch during planning in the 1970s "led to the imaginative idea that they represented an opportunity for a positive recreational asset, by combining them with open space corridors complete with bridle trails, bicycle paths, pedestrian trails, and recreational activity centers." According to Richard Reese, vice president of planning at the Irvine Company in 1970, the company sought to use, for the first time ever, "environmental corridors to create an 'imageable' urban form." He predicted that "just as Paris is known by its boulevards and Venice by its canals, the City of Irvine will be known by its environmental corridors."[16]

The urbanistic plan helped justify the drive for incorporation of the City of Irvine, an effort led by the Irvine Company and those already residing on ranch lands. Although at that time incorporation was considered undesirable among new-town developers, the idea seemed more appealing to company executives than coordinating planning with a variety of surrounding cities. Incorporation carried its own risk, notably citizen revolt against the plan, but the company chose to risk negotiation with the residents who had chosen to live in a planned environment. In addition, Watson genuinely believed in the value of local democracy.

Company officials like Watson believed in democracy, but they did not hesitate to promote company goals in the public sphere. In 1970, they created two institutions to advance their interests in the new community, the *Irvine World News*, a weekly tabloid with local news and editorials from Irvine Company officials, and the *New Worlds of Irvine* (later re-named *New Worlds*), a colorful magazine distributed bimonthly to all ranch residents. The company also helped organize the upper-income inhabitants of existing developments, and together they succeeded in incorporating the city in 1971. The new city council created its own planning agency and "staffed it with a group of environmentalists" who then commissioned their own plan for the city. This city-sponsored plan lowered population targets but endorsed most aspects of the company's ideas. The Irvine Company had gambled and won.[17]

After incorporation, the rapid pace of growth continued. The village of Woodbridge, founded in 1974, reflects some of the most ambitious planning on the ranch. Woodbridge was shaped out of 1,700 flat, nondescript acres in the center of the new city. The designers first researched market demands and patterns of community use. According to planner Doug Gfeller, "We listened to what [residents] said they wanted . . . and we watched to see how they responded to opportunities offered to them. That's how we ascertained, for example, that the only people who regularly use a park are the people who live quite near it. . . . So in Woodbridge, everyone lives near a park." The company gave character to the site by adding "a magnificent lake, a protective berm, a mixture of nine housing types around a series of parks, [and] bicycle and pedestrian paths." Planners mixed a variety of housing styles—single-family, attached homes, apartments, and condominiums—added smaller parks that featured different recreational elements, and mixed schools into neighborhoods. Woodbridge proved so popular that its early stages were sold through a lottery.[18]

By the 1970s the ranch had become a spectacular success, making it an even more desirable asset. Battles began for control of the company, involving members of the Irvine family, the foundation board of directors, and outside investors. Through a complex series of lawsuits, legislation, and financial deals, in 1983 the company came under the control of Donald Bren. A prominent California builder, Bren was responsible for the creation of the neighboring, and more conventional, new town of Mission Viejo. As owner of the Irvine Company, he initiated a building boom that has not ceased and has brought successful office parks (in 1999 more than 160,000 people were employed in the City of Irvine), commercial developments, and new residential villages (130,000 city residents by 1999). Early architectural styles had focused on California ranch or an improvised Cape Cod style, but later developments completed under Bren's management have been "romantic interpretations of Mediterranean—particularly Italian and Spanish styles." The Westpark development, Newport Coast, and the new Fashion Island are characterized by a style derived from "classic resort towns" of southern France and northern Italy. The application of this style, at first a welcome change from the understated design of the early years, has started to become monotonous. Landscaping has also shifted from a naturalistic to a formal, Mediterranean style. This new approach includes "straight rows of palms that seem to mimic columns, crisply cut hedges, rippleless pools of grass. . . . It is a landscape that is determinedly anti-natural."[19]

New residential and business developments boomed in the 1980s and 1990s under Bren's guidance, but after thirty years it had become clear that some of the original plans had not equaled early ambitions. As at the other new towns, the phenomenal success of the office parks of Irvine has increased rather than controlled sprawl. With employment exceeding the number of residents in Irvine, it is clear the city is a new employment center for the region rather than a balanced community. Booming employment has brought tax revenues but also traffic headaches and more suburbanization of the surrounding area.

The activity corridor as built in Woodbridge and Westpark villages has failed to meet the planners' optimism for their new urban form. A wide variety of uses, including stores, community centers, schools, offices, and churches, has filled in the corridor, but the only unifying factors are a bike path, a drainage canal, and a linear road system. As the corridor lacks coordinated design elements, it is easily overlooked and makes a weak impression.

The town center abutting the campus, originally designed by Pereira to be Irvine's vibrant urban core, remained undeveloped until the 1980s. The Irvine Company concentrated large-scale commercial and retail development in its Fashion Island development in Newport Beach, largely ignoring the original plans. Watson has explained, however, that a mixture of community and company decisions slowed development of the town center. During the 1960s, Watson convinced company officials to move their corporate headquarters to the town center. A bombing of the Bank of America branch in the town center by radical student groups caused these plans to be abandoned. University students later decided to locate their student centers on campus rather than in the town, further isolating the campus. Finally, the city government, against the wishes of Irvine Company planners who wanted city hall in town center, decided to locate it in a more peripheral location.[20]

The Irvine Marketplace, constructed by the company in the town center during the 1980s, filled some of the commercial and entertainment needs of the university community but struggled financially. This open-air pedestrian mall organized around a generous public space includes offices, a cinema, an improvisation club, restaurants, shops, and a weekly farmer's market. The Marketplace, although significantly less ambitious than Pereira's plans, does follow the general pattern he established. One couple recently explained that when attending events at the university (usually by walking to them), "we never forget to consider the Irvine Marketplace for dinner on the way, for cappuccino or frozen yogurt on the way home, or even as goal unto itself for its village-like atmosphere."[21]

During the 1980s, Fashion Island, the shopping area in Newport Center, underwent a complete renovation. It was transformed from a dull modernist mall into a postmodern retail fantasy land on a Mediterranean theme. According to the *Orange County Register*, "Once a ponderous collection of late '60s department stores, the shopping center has been filled with smaller stores aligned along open-air 'streets.'" Bren spent nearly $100 million, applying paint colors and architectural details inspired by his trips to Italy and Spain. Visitors are now invited to "shop outdoors amid sidewalk carts, ocean breezes, tree-lined paseos and sparkling fountains." The complex now includes more than two hundred stores, forty restaurants, and a number of commercial art galleries.[22] A recent article noted, "Fashion Island draws strolling parents and children by morning, hungry workers at noon, and movie-goers at night."[23] Office buildings in Newport Center, on the other hand, failed to grow as rapidly as the shopping area due to resident opposition.

The Irvine Spectrum, started in the 1980s, surpassed Newport Center as one of the most important urban centers in Orange County. The Spectrum, located on Irvine's south side, included numerous white-collar businesses (2,200 in 2000) and open-air entertainment and shopping areas. Located at the meeting point of important highways, the area has assumed a role beyond serving the local community. Commercial tenants at the open-air shopping mall, which has Moorish-style architecture, included movies, restaurants, arcades, stores, a coffeehouse, and a food court around an open plaza. The Spectrum flourished as a regional center (figure 9). A 1990s expansion enlarged the Spectrum to a million square feet. The developer added restaurants, shopping, elaborate architecture, fountains,

FIGURE 9 Residents who visit the Irvine Spectrum find quasi-public spaces, fountains, Moorish designs, and abundant shopping and entertainment. A successful regional center, the Spectrum attracts visitors from throughout Southern California.

courtyards, "glass embedded walkways, tower bell chimes, hanging pendant lamps, colored arcades and seating areas shaded by exotic palms." This expansion borrowed its theme from the Alhambra, Granada's thirteenth-century palace complex. The aim of the developer is to "differentiate Irvine Spectrum in a physical way from any other entertainment center in the United States."[24] The planning of the Spectrum is primitive compared to the model on which it is based, and the center takes only superficial elements from the Alhambra. However, the high quality of materials used (including real tile, stone, and metal), the theatrical lighting, and a series of pleasing fountains and courtyards nevertheless make for an impressive show.

Shopping centers like Fashion Island and the Spectrum are imitating Disneyland, as well as Rouse Company projects such as Fanuiel Hall, in urban fantasy. Disneyland and Fanuiel Hall have demonstrated that Americans will leave their cars and walk if they are promised a safe, consumable, visually stimulating environment. As sociologist Mark Gottdiener explains, it is not merely commerce that is driving the creation of these spaces but the continuing "desire for community and pedestrian communion in public spaces . . . a need created by the destruction of public space in contemporary society through suburbanization and the terror of urban crime."[25] Developments at the Spectrum and Fashion Island, therefore, hold great promise; after all, the developer is building a pedestrian environment in suburbia. For all the fun, however, there remains something disturbing in both centers' flights of fantasy.

The Irvine centers, as well as Reston's, have little aesthetic relationship to their actual locations, thus disorienting the visitor. They are also strictly regulated private spaces, employing their own security guards, who make sure that order is maintained. Yet there remains an important difference between the centers of Irvine and Reston. The Reston town center, after all, functions as a quasi-public space for the town of Reston as well as a regional downtown for many northern Virginians. Irvine's main town centers have self-consciously distanced themselves from the new town and the local population; no public rituals like parades or community festivals occur in either the Spectrum or Fashion Island. These centers focus on entertainment and commercialism to the exclusion of all other activity. Irvine still lacks a civic core.

The Irvine Company, like its counterparts in Reston and Columbia, created a master plan that has led to an attractive and inventive physical environment. A mixture of architectural and landscape styles, a variety of housing types, modern office complexes and a university campus, a linear urban corridor, and attractive shopping areas gave form to an alternative landscape. By adjusting their designs to public behavior, the planners did not have to redesign the commercial areas as has occurred at the other new towns. At the same time, they lost some of the convenience and identity the other new towns gained from innovative village centers. Irvine's village concept as a whole, however, is the most successful of the new towns in orienting residents and establishing identity for residential areas; its new downtown areas may have little connection to the local community, but they are successful pseudo-urban places. The company also played a significant role in establishing Irvine's strong civic and educational institutions. Irvine is not the diverse university town envisioned by Pereira, but it is a decided improvement over the conventional subdivisions it sought to replace.

❖

The new-town development companies created viable alternatives to conventional suburbs. The developers and planners proved to be flexible,

adjusting plans and ideals to suit the tastes of the residents, but they preserved most elements of the master plans, including village concepts, land
preservation, architectural innovation, a variety of housing types, careful
landscape design, and institutional planning. Residents of these communities gave the planning high marks in the 1970s and they still do, as indicated by their attempts to promote and protect the new-town plans in local
civic organizations.[26]

Most planning and architectural historians, who see all American
new towns as overgrown subdivisions, have failed to recognize the inventive planning and design of these three communities. The mediocrity of
most other American new towns has obscured the view of the remarkable
communities in this study. The developers of conventional large-scale
planned new towns of the 1950s and 1960s—such as Mission Viejo, California; Park Forest, Illinois; and Clear Lake City, Texas—did not adopt innovative planning methods, nor did they take a comprehensive approach
to redesigning the physical and institutional landscape of suburbia. Most
of these new towns were, in fact, simply large-scale "community builder"
suburbs. Reston, Columbia, and Irvine remain the experimental stars of
the new-town movement.[27]

There have been notable failures at Reston, Columbia, and Irvine,
and certain attempts to create a new suburban order have fallen flat. The
pedestrian-oriented village centers have generally failed to become community public spaces. The attempt to use design to alter community life
proved unsuccessful in most instances. The popular pseudo-urban "town
centers," although more successful as quasi-public spaces, themselves raise
difficult questions. These privately owned spaces can take on a civic role, as
with Columbia's lakeside or Reston's town center. Developments like the
Irvine Spectrum and the Columbia Mall, however, place unreasonable restrictions on public use that limit the ability of a community to form a
genuine civic core. A controversial change has also occurred because of the
success of innovative new-town commercial and retail planning. By succeeding so well, the new towns have contributed to the very problems of
sprawl that they were supposed to remedy.

The lasting achievement of new-town planning has been the use of
design to distinguish the developments from conventional subdivisions.
Although traditional suburban elements could be found, and more ordinary subdivisions have surrounded them, sufficient changes were made to
indicate a new environment. Modernist buildings and public spaces in
town and village centers, clusters of housing surrounding extensive open
spaces, grade-separated pathways, thematic or unconventional architecture

and landscape design, controlled signs and lighting, extensive institutional planning, and abundant recreational facilities offered an alternative within a familiar context. The layering of different architectural and planning styles added further interest to the landscape over the decades. These new towns were suburbs but they were not ordinary. Strategic changes had been made that commented on what other places lacked, a critique and challenge to convention made not of words but earth, wood, and sheetrock.

PART 3

Civic Renewal in Suburbia

◆

5

The Translation of Ideas

We hope we've created an atmosphere where people *do* care enough about planning and planned development to get involved and help make it happen.

RICHARD REESE, The Irvine Company

The new-town landscape made a compelling argument for the benefits of planning in suburbia, but it did not necessarily follow that visitors or buyers would connect the project with suburban criticism. Many residents came simply because these towns promised to be more attractive than conventional suburbs. Others, perhaps familiar with the suburban critique, might not have readily agreed that new-town planning was the best answer to sprawl. Over time, many residents were likely to forget what made the new towns special and might try to push out the planners and the master plan.

The developers left little to chance. They knew that in order to complete their plans over the many decades of development, they had to connect their communities to the intellectual critique that preceded them. Designers also had to convince residents that their planning offered a potential solution to the perceived failings of conventional suburbia. Professionals like Richard Reese therefore did not hide away in offices but published articles in local papers, helped create innovative and substantive public-relations materials, sometimes lived in the communities they were planning, and regularly appeared at community meetings.

Planners and developers hoped to make money, but they had ideals that transcended the profit motive. Professionals from the development companies, for instance, could be found promoting master plans that included affordable housing, racial integration, and environmental preservation. Through their community involvement they hoped to attract activist residents and assure long-term support for their master plans, and they achieved both goals. Many residents came because of the new-town concept and stood behind those ideals when the concepts seemed threatened by changes in development practices. Some development officials likely wished that they, or earlier planners, had been a little less persuasive in early publicity materials.

One of the neglected aspects of the story is the transformation of new-town ideals into community ideals. Developers found ways on a regular basis to inject ideas into the communities and spent a small fortune doing so. Developers borrowed methods from other traditions—world fairs, television, magazines, model-home tours, academic conferences, and advertising campaigns—to promote new-town concepts. In their welcome centers and publications, the developers' staffs adopted the "seamless flow of imagery overlaid with spoken and typographic messages" popularized by television and a new wave of magazines (imitating television) in the 1960s. This new style was part of a continuing "transition from word thinking to visual thinking" in American culture that has shown no sign of abating. Although this style did not originate in the new towns, the application of these methods to the selling of American communities took on a different meaning. Those who bought homes or moved to new towns bought into a compelling image, a mental map of reform, that raised expectations and eventually inspired civic activism.[1]

Introducing Reston

Reston's development team created a promotion and sales center as unconventional as its planning. Visitors found themselves enveloped in a diverting exhibit that—from its design to the content and mode of presentation—promised a remarkable new environment. The center, a striking circular building designed by Robert Gersin Associates, stood "on a hilltop . . . overlooking the countryside." Inside the center, the exhibit "explains [the] philosophy of planned cluster living and shows photos and plans of recreational facilities." In addition, "using photomurals and occasional slide and sound picture shows, a circular exhibit channels visitors through [the] building where they are never far from the full length glass window wall." Visitors experienced "triangular posts . . . [that] rotate, changing scene and giving [the] exhibit motion." The Reston center further displayed a detailed model of the future community; *Fortune* noted in 1964 that, from the air, the community "looked just the way it had looked in a scale-model from three years earlier."[2]

The developer's team, in fact, made a conscious decision to develop an embryonic, full-scale model of the future community as part of its promotion. The developer constructed Lake Anne, the first village, to be as complete as possible as early as possible—a decision that ultimately taxed Simon's limited resources. One observer noted that Simon "had to demonstrate just how Reston would really be different, and to do that he had to come up with quite a piece of sample goods, not a swatch." Lake Anne rapidly and successfully began to demonstrate these "different" qualities. Visitors in 1965 received tours of the village, in addition to the exhibits: "Since (1963) 270 tours have been recorded. Unscheduled tours, conducted by others than the public relations people at Reston, would bring the total to more than 500. The number of official visitors, not counting week end visitors and home buyers who average about 3,000 each week-end, is now over the 2,000 mark." Philip Goyert, an early architectural historian of Reston, noted, however, that "during the good weather the curious came in throngs to crowd out the residents in the Lake Anne Center."[3] By offering tours and bragging about them, Reston's developer was showing that his community was extraordinary. How many subdivisions needed tour guides for international visitors?

Gulf Reston and RLC also developed visitor centers. RLC's center, overlooking a small lake, included a large model of the community and a sophisticated slide show with narration. In his history of Reston, Tom Grubishich notes that the town had developed a reputation as not being friendly, so the new center built in the early 1980s included a slide show that featured interviews with residents who talked "informally about the town—in their own words and in their own backyards. . . . [The center] presented Reston not so much as a new town but a hometown, and a successful one. The emphasis was not on the future, but on the pleasures and achievements of the here and now."[4] This slide show, utilizing a convincing mixture of words, music, and images, stressed both the sense of community and the natural beauty of the area—and avoided pictures of more avant-garde Lake Anne. The center closed during the 1990s and has been replaced by a trailer in Reston town center. The new Reston Historic Trust for Community Revitalization now displays the old model and offers programs that introduce residents to new-town ideals, but the effect is not the same as the old center with its mixed-media approach to community description.

Simon not only encouraged visitors to become familiar with the innovative community plan but also sought to make the early residents experts in new-town ideas. Planning thus became public property rather than a secret, technical undertaking. The *Reston Letter* in 1963 reported:

> The first lecture series given at Reston was "Planning and Building a New Community: Reston, New Town in Virginia," and featured . . . various experts on the genesis and development of Reston. Primarily for hometown consumption, the series nevertheless attracted students and neighbors from Washington. . . . The opening lecture was given by Robert Simon, Jr., . . . and he was followed by architects, planners, engineers, lawyers, school board, and county and state officials. . . . The distinguished architecture critic . . . Wolf Von Eckardt concluded the series.[5]

For those with even more interest in planning, in 1966, the University of Virginia offered a non-credit course about Reston, entitled "The Community and the Individual." According to the *Reston Letter,* "County, state, metropolitan area, and international planners, specialists, and officials made up the roster of speakers for this interesting and timely eight-week course."[6]

The integration of planning and architects' ideas into the community did not end with the early development years. Irving Wasserman, originally hired by Simon but retained by Gulf Reston as their chief city planner, made a point of being available to the public during his tenure at Reston (1967–72). According to an article praising him on the eve of his departure: "Wasserman's planning techniques have become rather common knowledge to those who have attended the annual Gulf Reston show and tell session in which Wasserman informs residents of development to take place within the next several months and the next year."[7] The developers who followed Simon, in part under pressure from the Reston Community Association (RCA), continued to maintain open lines of communication with residents.

Many of the earliest designers visited Reston to examine the condition of their projects and discuss progress. The architect Cloethiel Smith returned to visit her project, Waterview Cluster, in 1977, after speaking at a Greater Reston Arts Center Gallery show that featured displays on Reston architecture. As she toured, she heard a variety of complaints. "Residents pointed out the smallness of the kitchens, the poor construction of the screen doors, the practical impossibility of changing light bulbs in stairwell chandeliers." Most residents, however, complimented Smith "on the design which provides common areas nearby for recreation, privacy without enclosure fences, and integration with the existing woods." Architects William Conklin and James Rossant returned in 1984 to visit the Lake Anne plaza. They noted its physical decline but "saw more that they liked than disliked, including a number of people taking their pleasure in the sun drenched plaza." They had come to consult with the Lake Anne Revitalization Committee to help with the town's "continued renewal." They offered to help in rebuilding the fountain, which had fallen into disrepair, and endorsed "creating a theme, perhaps restaurants, that would attract shoppers not only from the surrounding village but the entire region."[8]

Simon pioneered a sophisticated public relations machine for Reston. The *Reston Letter* contained information about the new-town staff, development, architecture, planning, and numerous cultural events in the emerging community. The *Letter* focused on design innovations and the cultural activities of the nascent community, with photographs of children and adults enjoying Lake Anne. The *Letter* also summarized the national press reaction to the communities, boasting about regular coverage by publications like the *New York Times, Business Week, McCall's,* and *Life.* Occasionally a bit of sentimentality slipped through, but as the paper was targeted at a highly educated, urbane group, the public-relations experts deliberately tried to avoid sappy presentations. The Simons provided a little poetry, however, for the magazine. In 1966, Anne Simon, Robert's wife, rhapsodized: "Here, a man looks at a tall tower and a tree against the sky and knows that both mark the place of his home. . . . Here, children run free to delight in a bridge, a wooded path. Water glints against brick, music sounds in the village, and men know a sense of joy." In a nearby photograph a child fishes in a pond and the caption reads: "Happiness is a solitary pool." Robert Simon in his dedication speech gushed: "We have all around us, in smiles as well as stone, the fruits of [our] labor. It is a cause for rejoicing." The *Reston Letter* dedicated itself to attracting both the dreamers and the realists among an urban-oriented crowd, but the publication lasted for only a few years.[9]

Gulf Reston published its own public-relations paper, the *Restonian,* reflecting a similar but less-ambitious program for community life. They wagered that "most of us live here because of the fulfillment of a more satisfying life style than that offered in a typical subdivision." Residents were also to realize that planning benefited their lives: "The opportunity to live, work, play and worship in the same community has offered Restonians more free time for family life—for individual freedom and development. The Reston visitor also feels this presence of community and cohesiveness not generally found in American's exurbia. . . . Spread City isn't here."[10]

Mobil Corporation public-relations materials (ca. 1996), accompanied by glossy, full-color photographs of buildings, multiracial groups of residents, and pastoral landscapes, also informed newcomers of the special nature of the community: "Reston. It was among the first of its kind. A community with a plan that offered the best in life by design. . . . The plan for Reston was to build a community with the character of a small town and the convenience of a modern city." They lauded a strong "sense of community" helped by the village centers, the new-town center, and work opportunities. They also explained that "our planners and designers work with the land wherever possible to retain its natural plant life, topography and existing landscape." Recent public-relations materials for the town-center residences, much like the earliest materials, paint Reston as an ideal combination of urban and pastoral living.[11]

The mixture of approaches to public relations—visual, written, personal—built excitement and distinguished Reston from other suburban developments. Visitors and residents, particularly in the early years, could easily see how Reston represented a break with conventional sprawl. Prestigious architects and planners met with the community; tours made the place seem like a monument; new town related courses and lectures were offered; multimedia slide shows welcomed visitors; and special publications stressed the new-town vision. Public relations complemented the physical design by featuring innovations and drawing the intellectual connections between Reston and suburban reform goals.

The Columbia Concept

In rural Howard County, Rouse had to convince conservative county residents that Columbia would be an asset. Whereas Simon had purchased a large estate in a progrowth county and the Irvine Company had owned all of its land for a hundred years, Rouse faced more potential conflict over his secretive purchase of land in a county ambivalent about increased urbanization. The Rouse Company mounted an expensive campaign that included scale models, a multimedia welcome center, tours, public appearances, and printed circulars in order to demonstrate the dynamism and timeliness of their plan. Publicists and planners quickly raised new-town publicity to an art form.

Rouse made a series of announcements in 1963 and 1964 that prepared the county for the coming plan. He took a calculated risk by predicting that it would be ready in one year's time. The team did complete the plan and included everything from financial to recreational projections. Perhaps the most compelling of the public-relations efforts centered on the creation of a scale model of the planned community. The model, "done in four 4-foot sections . . . [including] the town center, almost all of village one, and a segment of the village on the east side of [Route] 29, across from the town center," provoked some doubts on the part of the developer:

> What (Norman) Houk and his staff created was a wondrous thing, a great white vision of Utopia stretching across rolling countryside. . . . The model was almost too magnificent, and James Rouse had some acute last-minute qualms about showing it all as part of the presentation. "Here we are talking about low density, villages, and open space." he said, "And then you look at that big white beautiful thing, and you know it's a *city* we're building."[12]

Like City Beautiful proponents, Columbia's developer sought to substitute clean design and elegant planning for urban/suburban blight. The Rouse Company displayed the model in an existing building on the Columbia site, and visitors poured in to view the plan.

The company followed up in local newspapers with "a sixteen page insert describing the town plan, in word, picture, and diagram." Local print media, county residents, and political figures responded positively, and "television in both Baltimore and Washington made it one of the top local news items of the day." As Scott Ditch, one of the early HRD officials, explained, "No paid advertising of any note was done [during the first two years], but thousands of stories and articles appeared in publications around the world, pointing up the deep dissatisfaction with the course taken by so much suburban development in America and the hope for something better." The intellectuals dutifully aided the new towns they had inspired.[13]

In the Columbia Exhibit Center constructed in the 1960s, visitors experienced a show reminiscent of international expositions. As at Reston, the presentation engulfed visitors in a compelling three-dimensional, multimedia argument in favor of new towns. The exhibit offered "an impressive presentation of the cacophony of unplanned cities then contrast[ed] it with the calmness, orderliness, yet the excitement of a planned community."[14] The exhibition no longer continues; only a short slide show is available at the CA headquarters. Nevertheless, it is possible to reconstruct what visitors might have experienced:

> In the slide theater, the first section of the exhibit, four 35mm projectors present a coordinated show at continuously changing locations on a wide 3-panel screen. . . . From the slide show theater, the visitor walks though a combination of display structures which include floor-to-ceiling photo panels, dimensional maps, and illuminated transparency boxes, some of them with an automatic sound track. . . . The central display of the Next America Exhibit begins with a summary of land use in Columbia, then views downtown Columbia—now and in the future, the villages and their neighborhoods, the extensive use of open space, and employment opportunities. . . . The final portion of the Next America Exhibit is a 3 and a half minute sound color film, summarizing Columbia's early days and discussing the future. . . . In the lobby of the Exhibit Building are 24 panels devoted to the many features of the city including sample homes, apartments, and the recreational aspects of Columbia. Each panel consists of a light box illuminating one or more large color transparencies, and a taped audio message that is heard through an earphone.[15]

By 1971 a million people from around the world had visited the exhibition center. A million more would visit during the next decade. Columbia's goal of offering an antidote to suburban sprawl resounded across the nation. That almost everyone who visited came through the center made it a powerful force for featuring local innovations and connecting suburban criticism with the new-town vision.[16]

The Exhibit Center changed during the course of the 1970s. The Rouse Company added "Columbia scenes captured on film by local residents" and even a cutting-edge computer that contained information about the community. In 1977, Len Lazarick, a reporter for the *Columbia Flier*, gave residents a description of the new and expensive slide show: "A baby is shown being born at the hospital, and the baby's first cries are heard. Children pledge allegiance to the flag, and there's a party at a grade school with kids singing the Beatles' 'With a Little Help from My Friends.'

Baseball and soccer games abound, and the night life of Clyde's [a local restaurant and bar] fades into scenes of a concert at the Merriweather Post Pavilion." Lazarick noted that this "decidedly upbeat propaganda for the new town" contained no mention of the Rouse Company and used "the words of Columbians themselves." Although Lazarick approved of residents in the show describing what they liked about the community, he noted with some irony that "seldom is heard a discouraging word."[17] A few years later, an editorial in the *Howard Sun* commented on the slide show, seeing it as a possible metaphor for a changing community. The article noted a "loss of a sense of 'quest.'" To illustrate the point, the writer described the replacement of "a strong radio-voice narration about the beauty of the Columbia concept" with residents talking about "the convenience of the schools, the variety of sports programs, the niceness of the area."[18]

Complementing the Exhibit Center were publications made available to visitors and journalists. A 1966 brochure, "Columbia: A New City," reflects the talent of Rouse's publicists and provides further clues about the Exhibit Center. The document features color photographic essays (created primarily from stock shots of existing American and European communities) and diagrams in a large-format booklet that reflects "visual thinking." Every conceivable element of life—from villages to industrial parks—is pictured and described in glowing language. The vision of this new community remains enticing, and the vividness of the images has not faded— no wonder so many people became excited about the possibilities of the development.[19]

The magazine *Columbia* developed in the 1960s in a very different manner from the *Reston Letter*. In the early years, it resembled the *Letter*, but it soon addressed more challenging community issues. The work group had promoted the idea of a weekly magazine with an overt social function. According to a final report from the group, "one of the purposes of the magazine would be to show that there are various socially acceptable styles of doing things, that people with differing backgrounds need not act the same in order to enjoy certain activities, that there is fun in the act of learning new activities, and so on."[20]

Columbia took up this challenge. Images and text conveyed a mood of optimism and community happiness, of people in harmony with other people and nature. One finds photographs of wildflowers growing below a new dam intermixed with the photograph of a man riding a bulldozer through the landscape. The caption explained the juxtaposition: "Near the Merriweather Post Pavilion of Music, amid the sounds of building construction, the martins were singing and the spring peepers were the precursors of this summer's first symphony season in Columbia."[21] Despite the jarring juxtaposition of images, the message reinforced the ideal of nature and humans in balance. Other issues of the magazine showed interracial groups that conveyed through visual language the open philosophy of the community; others discussed educational reform and even the concerns of teenagers. The magazine, like other efforts by developers' public-relations teams, helped give the community an identity that other suburbs lacked. However, it ceased publishing in this form in the early 1970s.

The most convincing part of the public-relations effort was the tour of the community itself. As at Reston, the planners designed the town to be instantly understandable to visitors. According to Hoppenfeld, "the community should be staged and developed in a way which would create an early sense of completeness."[22] Wilde Lake was the first to be built, and visitors found two neighborhoods and a village center, a lake, and a variety of housing types. The Rouse Company ran tour buses "scheduled for frequent departures [to] take visitors to The Village of Wilde Lake and through the neighborhoods of The Birches and Bryant Woods. Along the way will be seen the first of the riding trails and pathways, parks and wooded areas, the stream valleys—all preserved as part of the open space system."[23]

Jeanne Lamb O'Neill, a journalist reporting for *American Home* magazine in 1970, noted that "Columbia is set up as a showplace. Out on Route 29, touristy blue and white signs beckon you in with all the graciousness of Colonial Williamsburg. By the lake shore an attractive, holiday-gay exhibit center offers a lively tour of the city in motion pictures, slides, models and graphics." O'Neill noted that "visitors stream through the Exhibit Center every day of the week, including cold, rainy Monday mornings in dreary February. They come from Arizona and Australia, Vancouver and Vietnam."[24] Writing in the Methodist Church family magazine *Together*, Willmon White reported that "Columbia is a booming tourist attraction. Families swarm in on weekends to see the 'Next America' exhibit, visit the model homes, tramp the woods, and skip stones across man-made Kittmaqundi." From the moment they came, visitors understood that they had entered a bold experiment in community reform.[25]

Over the course of development, the Rouse Company attempted not only to make information available but also consciously desired to make the planners community figures. Representatives of the company made presentations and met with community groups on a regular basis throughout the development process. This campaign included Rouse, who popped up at the grocery, at community centers, and all over town.

The executives Rouse hired exuded an iconoclastic, liberal, hip, and caring ethos. Hoppenfeld, a resident of Columbia, remained popular in the town even though he left the Rouse Company in the 1970s to pursue planning projects across the nation. In the 1980s, he rejoined Rouse at the Enterprise Foundation, Rouse's nonprofit foundation for expanding affordable housing, but he succumbed to a heart attack in 1985. The *Columbia Flier* created a poster in his honor and *Columbia* magazine named him Columbian of the Year.

Wallace Hamilton exemplified the Columbia executive. The description of his office in the late 1960s gives the impression of an irreverent character: "[It] is decorated with a pop art poster of an entwined couple with the legend 'light my fire' and a placard asking 'question of the week: does Wallace Hamilton have redeeming social value?'" Robert Tennenbaum, the urban designer, lived in Columbia, and the *Baltimore Sun Magazine* of 1968 featured his fashionable home. Tennenbaum has recently collected articles by himself and others who worked on Columbia and published them as a book entitled *Creating a New City*. Continuing the tradition of public accessibility to planners, Tennenbaum also appeared at Columbia's thirtieth birthday party to sign copies of the book.[26]

Michael Spear, who became the manager of Columbia's development in 1971 at age twenty-nine, was another popular figure. His youth, willingness to communicate, dedication to the new-town plan, and modesty did much to keep the citizens united in support of the plan. Spear also lived in Columbia with his family. He noted in the 1970s that "it's like living over the store. When we go for a walk . . . I'm not just using the paths, but making notes about where they need repair." The long-term involvement of these planners and professionals in community life gave Columbia a very different feeling from most subdivisions.[27]

During Columbia's tenth year celebration, the Columbia Foundation invited members of the original work group to speak. Attendees included Hoppenfeld, Finley, Rouse, Bain, Foote, Paul Lemkau, and Donald Michael. More than six hundred residents attended a talk entitled "Columbia Revisited" in what turned out to be a positive assessment of the city's progress. The size of the crowd indicates the widespread interest within the community in the planning process. Bain praised the growing governmental services of the community. The sense of loyalty in Columbia and the community's willingness to confront racial problems was praised by Lemkau. Foote applauded the growth of city institutions, although he was disappointed by "the dependence on the automobile, trouble with teens, and an inability to provide low cost housing." According to Michael, the city had met the goal of offering "a 'learning context' for 'human growth,'" although he noticed that an unintended side effect of "this success is that residents experience a sense of 'relative deprivation' because everything is not perfect."[28]

In this impressive range of efforts by the development team, new-town planning and community ideals came to permeate the air of Columbia. A multimedia welcome center, stunning scale models, strategic touring of new neighborhoods, unconventional publications, and hip designers, managers, and intellectuals transported visitors and residents into an unconventional landscape. This educational process proved so successful that not only did it set Columbia outside the suburban mainstream, but in the long term it also helped create a language and identity for those residents interested in reforming suburbia.

Irvine's World News

The Irvine Company, unlike the developers of Reston and Columbia, promoted its plans through the control of local media and regular mass mailings. Much of what was produced seems at first glance to be merely self-serving, but the company made a genuine attempt to promote reform ideals. The company, facing many skeptical residents uncomfortable with the growing scale of the city, offered detailed and informative materials on the intricacies of the planning process.

There were some more traditional aspects of the marketing effort. At the Woodbridge opening in 1974, the company made sure that visitors knew that "before opening day 800 people had worked to build nine model home complexes, five parks, streets, a bridge, and a lake as long as ten football fields." Woodbridge needed little advertising: from the beginning, potential homeowners swamped the project. *New Worlds* explained that "Woodbridge is hosting a flood of prospective homebuyers and a stream of builders, city planners, designers. . . . Visitors are welcomed at the Woodbridge Information Center where they find brochures and photo displays, a 'talking' topographic model of the village's northwest quadrant, and where they meet village 'hostesses.'" Visitors could tour any of the Irvine villages, but most came for Woodbridge. On their tour along a "purposely representative boulevard" they viewed "eight housing products, four neighborhood parks, a lake and swimming lagoon, a view of the thematic wood bridge and an adjoining school and park site."[29]

The Irvine Homefinding Center, which originated in the 1980s, now serves as Irvine's visitors' center. Its exterior—a tree-house facade hiding a trailer—reflects the homey aspirations of the Irvine Company. Inside, visitors are registered and treated to large pictures of the town, extensive publications on neighborhoods and facilities, both those under construction and those already existing, and a video presentation on Irvine's development and planning. Important people in the community's development, such as Bren and Watson, appear on the video and discuss how the planning has created a unique community. The presentation pictures Irvine as an ideal mixture of natural areas, leisure opportunities, university culture, and neighborhood life. Newcomers to the ranch can hardly miss the fact that Irvine is a planned community, and if they give some time to the presentations can learn in detail about the planning effort.

Unlike the case in Reston and Columbia, the Irvine Company found it relatively easy to promote their community to outsiders. They faced a much greater challenge, however, in keeping residents of Irvine Ranch lined up behind the plans. Most company printed materials focused on giving residents an understanding of the planning process. A 1977 newcomer's guide accented the expertise devoted to every project. Residents learned that professionals had determined "how much land would be needed for each use. The guide explained how planners carefully balanced these land allocations with vital circulation systems: streets, parkways and highways, plus networks for water, electricity, gas and sanitation." Residents received confirmation that "every element of the Plan had to pass through many phases: design, economics, engineering, financing, approval by the board of directors, public review, and government agency approvals." The planners even explained how the environmental planning affected residents' perceptions: "Stores are built on a scale that makes you feel comfortable. Trees soften the harshness of the necessary parking lots. Signs inform discreetly. Vines and shrubs beautify village walls along the parkways."[30]

The company created publications on a regular basis, at a cost of hundreds of thousands of dollars, to gain resident support. Perhaps the most significant of their public-relations operations has been an eight-page tabloid newspaper, the *Irvine World News*. Since its inception in 1970, it has been for all intents and purposes the City of Irvine's only paper. The newspaper has covered most city events and has provided space for articles by Irvine Company executives and development experts to put forward their opinions in the "Irvine Company Report."[31] Articles often focused on breaking down the wall that separated residents and designers and showing the ways planning directly benefited the community. Experts deconstructed the landscape to demonstrate both the necessity and benefits of planning and the skill of the company planners. Michael Manahan, community-relations manager, showed residents how their reactions to place were being accentuated by designers: "The drive along the proposed activity corridor in Central Irvine, for example, is a planned, visual and cineramic [like the wide, curved movie screen of the 1960s and 1970s] experience in which a eucalyptus tree at this corner or a village center around the bend does not just happen to be there."[32] The director of marketing explained that not only did the company engage in regional demographic and housing-market research, but they also researched "attitudes toward growth, open space, industrial parks, and the convenience of nearby shopping facilities" in Irvine and in the region.[33] Residents learned that "Good Neighbor" ads placed in local publications (at high schools or community events) "have a special purpose. It is to communicate something meaningful to the community and to us." The company also admitted that such postings helped get "our ad, our message, before a reading audience that is very important to us: the people who live here, the young people especially."[34]

The magazine *New Worlds* (originally *New Worlds of Irvine*), published by the Irvine Company and distributed on a bimonthly basis to ranch residents beginning in 1970, contained articles on community history, life and culture, and on the planning effort. The magazine developed a number of innovative styles to promote the interests of the company. One method used impressionistic photographs and texts to establish a sense of community and praise the planning efforts (a clear application of "visual thinking"). Frank McGee, the editor, prepared a number of free-verse poems that strived to create a community feeling. The company might have been destroying every trace of the ranch, but one poem, framed by photographs of old farm tools and cowboys, established a connection between the former agricultural land and the modern new town: "From men who toiled and tilled the soil, who rode the herds, who packed the crops, has grown a love of all this place, a loyalty, and care about its use. That's why people grow here now as well, a new and favored product of a very favored place." One article borrowed from Peter Blake's *God's Own Junkyard* by contrasting photographs of a beautiful field with a junkyard. The accompanying text read: "Once there was a big country, then a lot of it gave way to junk." Text on later pages promised that "it doesn't have to be like that" and featured photographs of a child playing in a fountain, the sun setting through the steel frame of a rising building, teenagers playing ball in a greenbelt, and the budding university.[35]

Many of the articles in *New Worlds* directly addressed planning issues facing the community and the Irvine Company. Staff members, usually in interview or profile format rather than editorials, put forward their best arguments. In one article, readers met Bill Watt, Irvine Company vice president for multifamily housing and a builder with a concern for making a "social contribution through planning and building." Watt played a leading role in the design and construction of "multi-family" units in Irvine in the 1970s. His philosophy about apartments flew in the face of general opinion of many suburbanites, including many Irvine residents: "No one likes apartments except those who live in them. That's the way it's been and it's something we've got to turn around. There are a lot of people out there who can't afford or don't need the single-family residential lifestyle. And over the next 15 years there'll be a big surge of them, young people and old people, divorced people and single people." He encouraged residents to stop thinking of apartments as threats to property values, pointing out that "apartments can be designed attractively, with plenty of amenities."[36] At points in the development process, the Irvine Company's interest in more-affordable and higher-density housing has exceeded that of Irvine residents.[37]

Public-relations methods varied in each new town, depending on audience and timing, but all yielded concrete results. Many of the residents who came to Reston, Irvine, and Columbia became intoxicated by the new-town vision so forcefully projected by developers in welcome centers, scale models, tours, lectures, personal appearances, and publications. Public relations thus served as more than a means to sell homes; publicity became part of an effort to connect the new-town effort to a grander vision of a reformed suburbia. The impact of this vision can be seen not only in its ability to attract idealistic residents but also in the adoption, in later years, of similar imagery and ideas by citizen activists. The activists, however, would often find themselves using the promises embedded in older publicity as a defense against developers as policies, management, and plans changed over time.

6

Civic Activism in the New Towns

The democratic American spirit found a home in the new towns. Citizens of Reston, Columbia, and Irvine have less say over the color of their houses or the length of their lawns than many residents of other less carefully planned communities, but they benefit from a political culture that has been designed, or in some cases forced by citizen pressure, to be accessible. Many residents ignore the opportunities for participation, and some have felt frustrated by what they see as excessive control by community associations and developers, but others have seen that opportunities for meaningful participation abound.

Unlike residents of most subdivisions, those of new towns self-consciously pursued civic ideals that extended beyond property values, local suburban issues, and domestic tranquillity. Like Americans of the previous century described by Alexis de Tocqueville, suburbanites had formed many voluntary associations to regulate their communities. Critics, however, condemned them for "clinging to outmoded forms of government at the expense of the whole metropolitan area, and . . . casting only conservative ballots." The activist residents of new towns, on the other hand, adopted ideals that included ambitious national planning reforms and liberal social goals. Through regulation and reform of their communities, they hoped to create both a high-quality local environment and an alternative model for suburbia as a whole. For reformers, the two goals went hand-in-hand.[1]

The idealism of resident activists set these three towns apart from other large planned developments of the 1950s and 1960s. A majority of residents selected the new towns for the attractive environment and excellent recreational facilities, but an active, idealistic group made its presence felt in all three. Raymond Burby and Shirley Weiss, in *New Communities U.S.A.* (1976), found that a third of the residents interviewed at Columbia, Reston, and Irvine, mentioned "the character of community planning" as one of the three most important reasons for moving to the new town.[2] In other words, at least one third of the residents placed a high value on the new-town concept. New-town idealists thus had more than adequate local support and they also possessed advantages over residents of more typical suburbs when it came time to organize: they shared the language of the new-town concept adopted from the developer's publicity; they had set out for them a series of local and community-wide governing bodies; and finally, the liberal residents who favored the new-town ideals gained power quickly because they did not have to fight an established political hierarchy.

Over four decades, residents have created a wide range of civic institutions. They founded watchdog organizations and nonprofits; many became political leaders at the local, county, or state level; others created local historical societies that offered public history projects and archives. Quite a few became journalists and reported on new-town developments in local newspapers or magazines they started. These citizen efforts have not been equally successful, and compromise became as important as idealism, but residents did score a number of measurable successes.

New-Town Journalism

The journalism practiced in the new towns reflects the belief among local publishers that their audience, a well-educated and often liberal group, had a genuine interest in issues such as planning, social mixture, and cultural development. Most papers were founded by new residents with a journalism background, and although they started small, most became widely read and influential in local affairs. These papers acted as both amplifiers and critics of the original publicity created by the developers. In part through these journalistic efforts, new-town ideals became community ideals.

The interest in planning has never abated in Reston periodicals. The *Reston Times* and the (Reston) *Connection* have consistently provided their readers with extensive information on planning and related issues. The papers, as befitted these sophisticated communities, also featured extensive coverage of cultural events and local black issues and even occasional pieces on "alternative" lifestyles in Reston. In the 1970s, the papers kept residents well informed on the intricacies of real estate and planning as Gulf Reston shifted ownership to Mobil Land.[3]

The *Reston Times* in the 1960s featured "Reston Town Crier" articles directly addressing new town issues. A few of these articles were actually reprints of Simon speeches. Others offered essays by members of the community on a variety of new-town themes—sometimes exhorting, other times describing conditions particular to the new towns.

In 1968, Vernon George, a resident and an urban planner, wrote a two-part "Reston Town Crier" series that encouraged residents to take the new-town effort seriously: "Here in this ideal setting we sense a role in a great American experiment—the 'new town.' An experiment to see what role it can play in meeting the single most important challenge facing our nation—how we can accommodate a doubling of the population in the major urban centers of our nation in the next few decades."[4] During the 1980s the newspaper ran excerpts from a history of Reston by a local resident and reflections on the town's history by local political leader Martha Pennino.[5] A six-part series published by the *Connection* in 1995 as part of a celebration of Reston's thirtieth anniversary reflects the continuing interest in new-town ideals. In the series, "the *Connection* examines whether Reston is succeeding according to its original plan." In the first article, for example, the author offered a combination of community history, development philosophy, interviews with important players, discussion of issues, and quotations from residents. Other articles examined the community from "design to diversity, from shopping to safety."[6]

Only one issue of the *Restonian* (ca. 1967), a magazine by Reston residents, survives. Articles addressed affairs in Reston after the takeover by Gulf Reston, the history of new towns, the possibility for democracy in a planned community, and a critical essay on nearby Columbia. Photographs accompanied the text and accentuated the human scale of development much the way the *Reston Letter* did. A revived *Restonian* ran for a few years in the 1980s and also featured articles on issues facing the new town.

Columbia, like Reston, featured journalism attuned to new-town issues. The *Columbia Flier* carried sophisticated and often critical articles on new towns and planning. The founder and editor of the *Columbia Flier*, Zeke Orlinsky, an early activist, explained on the second anniversary of the paper (1971) that "to reflect the growth of a new city like Columbia is to meet new challenges. It calls on a publisher to throw away the old and tired concepts of journalism. . . . Journalism should excite and guide a community." The *Flier* pioneered an artsy, free paper for suburbia and expanded from a rather modest advertising circular to a full weekly with a large staff of local and arts reporters. As one observer from Baltimore noted, the *Flier* reflected "the 'California East' spirit in its tabloid magazine format" and included "attractive graphics, art and music reviews." The paper ran interesting, forthright, and revealing articles on teenagers, blacks, homosexuals, women's rights, local and state politics, and it even published Jules Fieffer cartoons on a weekly basis. The paper also featured thoughtful articles by local reporters Len Lazarick, Susan Hall, Nancy Baggett, and Jean Moon on planning, community life, and related issues.

The *Flier* staff created remarkable *Newcomers Guides* for the community during the 1970s and 1980s. The guides presented newcomers with histories of the community, the various elements of the planned community, and photographs of lakes, houses, and community areas filled with busy, attractive, happy people. They also presented detailed information on every aspect of the community, including neighborhoods, education, business, health, religion, the arts, and recreation. Negative observations also found their way into many descriptions of community life—a welcome addition to the often unrealistic new-town publicity created by the developer.[7]

During the 1970s, Moon wrote some of the most compelling pieces in the *Columbia Flier* focusing on the town's development. Moon came to Columbia in 1971 with her husband, an architect who worked for the Rouse Company. She cajoled, praised, and pressed for adherence to new-town ideals in a series of spirited articles and editorials during the 1970s. For instance, Moon presented a distillation of Burby and Weiss's *New Communities U.S.A.* The study found much to praise in the towns and also many failings. Although it used a wide definition for new towns and grouped comprehensive communities like Columbia and Irvine with areas like Forest Park, Illinois; North Palm Beach, Florida; and Sun City, Arizona (much more modest endeavors), the authors still found much to recommend in planned communities. They reported that new towns had "better land use planning and access to community facilities . . . reduction in automobile travel . . . superior recreational facilities . . . enhanced community livability . . . and improved living environments for low- and moderate-income households, blacks, and the elderly." The study singled out Columbia as having succeeded best in "population balance, innovation in governance, planning for the provision of better educational, recreation, health care, transportation service systems," and shopping areas.[8] Moon noted for her local readers that while most new towns had not met their original promise, Columbia appeared to be successful: "The notable success of

Columbia—particularly in the area of openness to minority groups— should give pause to those researchers who would discount future new town developments."[9]

A later development, the *Columbia Magazine,* emerged out of the CA. The magazine began as the *Calendar* in 1979, and it included community events and a number of articles on local personalities and trends. Over time, the magazine also included articles on planning, architecture, urban design, community life, and the arts. The association sold the magazine in 1988 to Patuxent Publishing, the owners of the *Flier. Columbia Magazine* continued to feature excellent articles on new-town issues for many years but in recent years has become a lifestyle magazine. In Reston and Columbia, residents could also read comprehensive articles on their communities in newspapers and magazines from surrounding communities (the *Baltimore Sun* and *Washington Post* most notably).

Irvine residents, as discussed earlier, do not have as distinguished a history of journalism as the other new towns. The *Irvine World News* features local stories and has provided abundant coverage on planning issues, but it has never been a genuine forum for discussion. It remains a "good news paper" that tries to steer clear of confrontation while still promoting the Irvine Company's agenda.[10] However, the *Orange County Register* and *Los Angeles Times* have published numerous articles on Irvine, some of high quality. Residents have thus been able to learn about the conflicts within the Irvine Company, outside evaluations of their community, and essays on Irvine social life.

Columbia and Reston cultivated quality publications that went on to become reputable, intelligent sources of local news and problems. Most notable, perhaps, is that these papers (including the *Irvine World News*) did not shy away from covering complicated issues involving planning and community development. The persistence of new-town related coverage in local papers kept the suburban reform ideals alive when developers' efforts flagged.

Civic Activism

Many well-informed, articulate residents became direct participants in the new-town planning culture. Suburbia has from the beginning been characterized as a community of joiners, but the wider civic idealism and the innovative methods and institutions devised by new-town residents distinguished them from conventional suburban communities of the time.

In Reston, the threat of development changes and shifting ownership led to the creation of the Reston Community Association (RCA) and other organizations that fought for the preservation of the new-town plan and developed urban-style community services. In Columbia, although the development company fulfilled most of its promises and power proved accessible at the county level, many residents nevertheless sought a stronger local voice. Incorporation drives and the activities of the Columbia Forum functioned as two very different efforts to raise local awareness and augment resident control. In Irvine, the only incorporated city of these new towns, residents designed a responsive local government that played a significant role in the town's development and transformation.[11]

Residents in all of these new towns refused to be restricted to the governments established by the developers. Such village boards and "cluster" or "neighborhood" associations enforced architectural and community standards. The local village associations communicated to residents through newsletters, which included minutes of important meetings, event calendars, rules and regulations, and general announcements. Many residents found participation in the village governments inadequate. Local boards had responsibility for some recreational and landscape development and enforced architectural covenants, but boards and associations possessed at most an advisory power in higher governmental affairs. Village boards and associations, however, did serve as important training grounds for political leadership of the new towns, particularly for women. In Columbia, some villages took a leading role in developing and maintaining facilities for the community. At Oakland Mills, the village board established a volunteer post office, teen programs, courses for adults, and a performance series. Other villages followed suit.[12]

Reston's Civic Activists

In a speech in 1966, Simon assured the doubtful that liberty, not control, would be the hallmark of the community: "Anticipating what facilities are needed is a matter of social planning. This does not mean telling people how to spend their time, but rather providing a multitude of facilities, social institutions and programs to make possible interesting and worthwhile alternatives for the use of leisure time."[13] Power might have been relatively diffuse when compared to earlier company towns, but the developer made sure that he, and ultimately his successors, would have significant control in the community when it came to local issues. The developer assumed powers usually wielded by representatives of elected governance.

The developer controlled the Reston Association as long as it desired. The development of the association (not to be confused with RCA) began on a sour note. Originally two organizations, one for Lake Anne and one for Hunters Woods, Gulf Reston forced unification of the two for both cost and administrative reasons in the early 1970s. According to Grubishich, this merger "left a residual enmity among Hunters Woods residents that survives to this day and probably has hobbled the combined homeowners association in its attempt to achieve more active resident involvement throughout the community."[14]

The developer continued to exercise great power over the Reston Association and came out against a citizen attempt to create a town government in 1979 (discussed in more detail below). Supporters of local governance hoped that citizens could gain some control over the development of their community, much as other towns in Fairfax County had done. One of the organizers of the referendum, Carol Lindberg, a longtime activist in Reston, explained that "Reston Land Corporation's opposition killed it because the industrial areas would be taxed as in the nearby town of Vienna. RHOA [Reston Association] didn't really oppose it, but they sent out a question-and-answer brochure that sounded negative. Reston Land had influenced them." In 1985, the situation might have changed, because the Reston Association gained a directly elected resident board. Unfortunately, according to Grubishich, the committee charged with rewriting the organization's charter "deliberately avoided language that would encourage a broadening of the association's mandate. RHOA will apparently remain essentially a land-management organization."[15]

The association did play an important role in the creation of the Reston Community Center. Reston was growing rapidly in the 1970s, but no community halls had been created since Lake Anne village. Executives of RHOA in particular developed the early planning process with permission from Gulf Reston and help of volunteers. Residents on committees selected the architect, picked the site (in Hunters Woods village center), and determined the financing method, which turned out to be quite original. Because the developer was not interested in bankrolling such an expensive center (although it did donate the land), it was decided that the most feasible means of financing the center would come through the creation of a special tax district for Reston that would be designed solely to finance the center. In 1975, residents approved the special tax on themselves. The complex includes an indoor pool, art studios, a professional theater, and meeting spaces. The center was and is a resident controlled organization.[16]

As seen in the community-center development, the residents wanted to preserve the new-town plan. The most serious crisis emerged in 1967, when Simon lost control of Reston. In that year the RCA (now known as the Reston Citizens Organization) formed out of fear "that Robert E. Simon's new town dream would be lost." The organization focused on influencing planning but also developed some needed services in the community, including "express bus service between Reston and Washington, D.C." The commuters "chartered the buses, sold the tickets, drew up the schedules, and attended hours of hearings on public transit subsidies."[17]

The RCA's primary emphasis has been planning policy and direction. The association's statement of purpose affirmed new-town goals: "provision of mixed-income housing; better architectural design; open space preservation, balanced development of residences, recreation, culture, industry, and commerce."[18] The very form of the RCA reflected a criticism of the governance of the Reston Association, which was heavily weighted by the developers in favor of property owners. In a 1969 editorial, Donald D. Fusaro observed that "the documents which establish Reston do not support the idea of an open community; they do not serve the idea of a new town in a democracy. They set up a political system which is old, namely, a feudal aristocracy. The effective concept of Reston reenergizes the notion that political power and rights of citizenship adhere to those who own land."[19] RCA leaders instead based suffrage on a one-person-one vote system.

In elections for the RCA board, voters selected from an accomplished group of residents, including planners, architects, political consultants, transportation consultants, attorneys, and housewives. The sentiments expressed by candidates for the RCA board reflect the conscious goal of using the organization as a means for preserving the town's plans and reforming suburbia. Diane Gore, a candidate in 1974, explained to residents that "the 'new town' concept, of which Reston is a star example, is also, many of us believe, a better town concept. In the areas of planning, development, services, programs and life styles, it is a challenge to traditional modes."[20]

Although the hope of many residents that RCA would become a governing body failed to materialize, the organization found numerous ways to influence development. It gained power first by forming alliances: "Powerless in itself, R.C.A. was quick to align itself with Fairfax County and [Centreville Supervisor Martha] Pennino in particular to gain political muscle that could thwart Gulf Reston development plans at the county level." Pennino and RCA ultimately forced Gulf Reston "to disclose significantly more information about its development plans."[21] The other tactics applied by RCA are recorded in a revealing document entitled "Tactical

Considerations for 'New Town' Citizens Groups: An Urban Guerrilla Warfare Manual" (1972), created by Dr. John Dockery, chairman of the RCA Master Plan and Zoning [P and Z] Committee.

Dockery thought that the RCA committee possessed "classic guerrilla" characteristics: "1. a small number of irregulars facing an extensive, and very wealthy, organization; 2. long campaigns over familiar ground; 3. careful husbanding of resources; 4. careful selection of targets and limited objectives; 5. well developed intelligence network; 6. cadre type organization which assists temporary popular front activities." Dockery claimed that the rapid state of development in Reston ("around 2500 dwelling units per year") "creates within Reston an endemic condition of 'future shock' as defined by Alvin Toffler. . . . Since future shock causes people to cope by tuning out, we must develop a hard core organization of persons impervious to future shock, motivated to overcome it, or in some cases thriving in it." Dockery and his compatriots had clearly avoided "future shock."[22]

The planning and zoning committee primarily addressed issues related to the RPC (Residential Planned Community) ordinance and "evolved a feed-back process to the county staff and political hierarchy which compares the promises of design excellence with the reality as built." The committee became involved by directly studying the planning of the community:

> The sheer volume of site plans requires a special strategy. We monitor *all* site plans. This means at least a quick visual examination. This screening produces a very limited number of site plans for serious review. This is generally followed by comment to developer and county staff. Following upon a period of negotiation and compromises, usually directed at principles, as opposed to technical details, an even smaller number are subject to formal appeal and public hearings. Beyond this point are the courts.

Dockery noted that they did not like to go to court because of the cost and the unlikely chance of winning. The organization's credibility, however, increased and was predicated "upon our ability to occasionally turn out 'bodies' for crucial hearings." He explained that "we avoid the politically untenable posture of total obstructionism by addressing a variety of cases" and that "we avoid *ad hominum* attacks." He noted, however, that "to handle conflict of interest cases, we research [Fairfax County] Commission and Board Member involvement in advance. Findings can be 'leaked' as required." The committee was not above using a variety of means to gain their ends.[23]

Some of the issues in which the committee intervened included "entry into cases outside the Reston Master Plan . . . commentary on basic planning documents of the county . . . initiation of a redraft of the R.P.C. ordinance in 1969–70 . . . insistence on a pathway across the Reston Country Club golf course . . . commentary on low/moderate income housing proposals and site plans . . . [and actions] to stop the introduction of strip commercial zoning into Reston; to force eventual commercial development into village centers."[24] The P and Z committee has continued to weigh in on community issues over the last three decades under a variety of leaders including Calvin Larson, Dockery, and Joseph Stowers. According to Stowers, the development companies generally worked with the committee rather than against it, particularly after they realized that the committee was not only forceful but had good ideas and was competent, having a core group of professionals on its side.

RCA has played a signal role in promoting the continuation and connection of the grade-separated walkway system. The pathway system, which began under Simon's tenure, now encompasses eighty miles of trails that wind through park land, private golf courses, open space, and under roads. As early as the 1970s, RCA began criticizing Gulf Reston for its failure to create adequate or well conceived path systems in the community. Dockery, in particular, found difficult and dangerous crossings and too few crossing points. Stowers also placed a high priority on the pathway system during his long tenure as head of the P and Z committee (1977–1993). He "made sure developers integrated pathways in their projects with the existing system" and "pushed developers to encourage walking, bicycling, public transportation, ride-sharing and other alternatives to automobile traffic." In recent years he has noted that although the path system is excellent, residents have trouble at dangerous intersections. With other community leaders, he completed a study that recommended extensive crosswalk improvements and sidewalk upgrades.[25]

During the 1970s and early 1980s the association led an effort to establish a local government for Reston. Supporters saw many reasons to establish such an entity: Reston's governance was split between the Reston Association, a private development corporation, the county, the state highway department, and the FAA managing the Dulles access route. Members of RCA supported the creation of a more modern town government than existed in Virginia at the time, consisting of a six-member town council and a mayor. Activists envisioned a limited town government, with taxing power, recreational management, sanitation, and other responsibilities; the county would retain control over services such as planning and police and fire. Supporters expended significant effort to win the referendum because Virginia law "forbids the incorporation of new towns in counties, like Fairfax, that have the urban county form of government and also that have more than 200 inhabitants per square mile." A special bill was created in the state legislature to allow Reston to hold a referendum on the creation of a town government.[26] Those residents who spoke at a public forum against incorporation expressed their fears that a town government would lead to higher taxes, and RLC came out against the plan as well. Even with RCA support, the move to establish a local government failed to attract even a minimum of the necessary votes for approval, and so Reston remains an unincorporated part of Fairfax County.[27]

The failure of the incorporation issue reflects the fact that from the beginning a small group of residents, elected by a small number of voters who shared their ideas, dominated RCA. These activists were welcome to work within the parameters of the community's governance, but most Restonians evidently did not feel as frustrated by a lack of formal government in Reston. The leadership of RCA, after all, had to deal on a daily basis with the limitations of its power, and as indicated here, did quite well under the circumstances. RCA leadership made guerrilla warfare look easy and professional. Some residents might have even feared giving even more power to local activists. Ironically, had RCA been less powerful and effective, they might have made a better case for incorporation.

The Spectrum development, a 24-acre commercial parcel in the town center initiated in 1994, revealed the fragility of RCA's informal style of governance. The developers, Mobil Land and Lerner Enterprises, created an oversized strip mall that uneasily faced the new urbanistic town center, complete with "category killing" chain stores. The developers received support in their plan from Robert Dix (who had replaced Martha Pennino as the county representative for Reston) and proceeded to take the plan to RCA for approval. In the past, P and Z committee members had received an early look at development plans, and the committee tried to work out agreements before full public or RCA meetings. In this situation, however, RCA and the P and Z found themselves facing a fully formulated public plan. Dix disliked RCA and favored business interests, whereas Pennino had admitted to never having disagreed with the P and Z committee.

When the developer presented the plan to RCA, the trouble began. First, the P and Z committee rejected the plan as unbefitting the new-town center; they felt that the low-rise nature of the center, the overabundance of parking lots, and poor site planning may have fit the letter of the zoning but defied its spirit. After this initial rejection, the developer and architect made changes in the plans. On a second pass, the P and Z committee decided to approve the changes, which included larger sidewalks, more doors and pathways to provide better connections to other areas of the town center, more trees, outdoor seating for restaurants, and better architectural styling. The RCA board, however, led by then-president Ivan Cole, rejected the plan, causing consternation among P and Z members who had come to believe themselves unassailable. The board thought that the design was still poorly integrated with the town center and that pedestrian usage was poorly designed.

The developer's staff threw up their hands in disgust over this rejection. The developer promised space for community use, variation in building height, more trees, bus shelters, miniparks, benches, and street improvements. RCA eventually approved the project that year, not primarily because of the changes made in the plan, which most found superficial, but because the board felt that the community at large supported the Spectrum. Board members also felt that the benefit of having more discount stores would offset the costs from the less-than-desirable development style. The center has now been built and is an attractive strip mall, as its opponents warned and its proponents desired.[28]

RCA helped direct the completion of the new-town plan, but it is not the only innovative civic organization. In 1969, Embry Rucker, a liberal Episcopal minister appointed to Reston, began filling in the gaps in institutional development. According to an article that appeared the year he died (1994), "with scores of volunteers of all ages, [Rucker] helped to create most of Reston's basic social institutions." Rucker and his volunteers established "Reston's first bus service, a day-care center for children, a sitter referral service, an employment service and a traveling nurse service." They also founded a community coffee house (Common Ground) and a counseling service. Bus service started "when residents in 1972 complained of their inability to get around the community without a car. Rucker recalled that two ramshackle buses were for sale. Money was collected, the buses purchased, volunteer drivers recruited, and gasoline donated by the local Gulf station." Eventually the county also helped buy buses. RIBS (Reston Internal Bus System) is still in operation and "provides weekday and Saturday service with routes to most village centers, many centers of employment and social services." Later in the 1980s, Rucker helped establish a homeless shelter in Reston and public housing downtown.[29]

Another institution important to fulfilling the new-town dream is known as Reston Interfaith. It started in 1970 when seven religious organizations joined to form Reston Interfaith Housing Corporation; its goal was to build low-cost housing. The organization succeeded in sponsoring Laurel Glade Apartments, two hundred units of affordable housing. Interfaith has since expanded its mission to include affordable day care (at the Laurel Learning Center), advocacy for affordable housing, emergency food provision, self-help groups for teens, youth employment programs, recreation programs for low-income residents, and support for the Embry Rucker Shelter for the homeless. It faced financial and organizational problems in the early 1980s, but under the leadership of Connie Pettinger, a former assistant dean of students at the University of California, recovered and took on larger projects. By 1987, the organization managed grants totaling over $200,000 and in just six months (between September 1986 and January 1987), "served about 14,000 people, providing food, clothing, job counseling, drug abuse information, transportation, housing and day care." Interfaith continues today to offer this wide range of services. The organization is currently developing an affordable housing project in North Point village, which up to this point has had almost no low-cost housing, and it is taking over management of other affordable housing developments in Reston.[30]

One of the unexpected additions to the master plan is a resident-led preservation movement of sections of the new town itself. In the proposal for creating the Lake Anne Historic District (established in 1983), proponents of historic designation described the Lake Anne center as "the internationally recognizable symbol of Reston, pioneer of the new town movement." At least part of the motivation for attaining historic recognition came from a desire to improve commercial activity in the center. Architect Bruce Kriviskey, a participant in historical preservation efforts in Fairfax County, explained that the village center presented challenges because "these mixed use building were products of the 1960s, and designed to meet current needs with the technologies of the times. As such, they are essentially speculative commercial buildings designed and constructed to last around thirty years." The center underwent major renovation in 1995 and 1996, aided by nearly $1 million borrowed from HUD. The local owners of property worked together to receive the loan, and the newly renovated center is significantly cleaner looking and more attractive.[31]

In 1997, the Reston Historic Trust for Community Revitalization began the creation of a Reston history and new-town culture museum and study center in Lake Anne village center. Sarah Larson, leader of the drive, a historian and Reston native, explained that "the major underlying concept is the problem that with a planned community people think that once it's planned and built that it's done. Well it isn't, a community keeps growing." Larson and other members, including many residents who had been involved as professionals in the early development of Reston, planned to have "exhibition and meeting space, a Reston shop, a collections program of historical artifacts, historic walking tours, school programs, public programs for adults, festivals and public events." The museum is now open, and includes, among other displays, the model of the community that was formerly part of the Reston Visitors Center. The center also has sponsored a series of talks by sales agents and architects involved in the early years of development and offers activities for children on a new-town theme. Residents, then, have come full circle, from consumers of a comprehensive public-relations program to active participants in the planning and public life of the community.[32]

Columbia's Civic Struggles

> When Columbians are sold on Columbia a utopian image is projected. It's strongly implied that the developer has thought of all our needs and provided for these. . . . We awaken to the fact that Howard County is our local government and is solely responsible for government services. . . . therein lies a genuine area of potential disagreement: government services responding to the needs of urbanization. Most Columbians are urban people who are used to urban services.
>
> SYLVIA VOSS, Columbia Task Force Committee

Sylvia Voss, like many Columbia residents, discovered the discontinuity between the developer's publicity and the reality of community governance. The developer stimulated the creation of improved county educational facilities, and the CA provided abundant recreational facilities and opportunities for citizen involvement, but Columbians lacked a local government finely tuned to many residents' urban demands. Over the last three decades a number of unsuccessful attempts have been made to create an urban government, but the process of seeking self-determination has provoked activism and lively community discussion.

Columbia's developers knew that they had to keep enough power to hold the plan together, and part of the desire to keep to the plan arose from social idealism. According to Hamilton, the "ghost" of Phil Klutznick, the developer of Park Forest in Chicago (featured in William Whyte's *The*

Organization Man), hung over Columbia, because Klutznick "having had an honest, integral idea of how a new community could be put together, in the middle of the thing, the residents got control, and they said, 'We don't want anybody here but us.' And Park Forest is now a super upper-income community outside of Chicago, and every vision Klutznick ever had, went down the drain."[33] In a work-group meeting, Hamilton described Rouse's philosophy of development: "James Rouse [mindful of Klutznick's experience] pointed out that political power needs to be held by the developer in considerable measure during the development period." Indeed, the Rouse Company made many decisions that residents disliked, but it also worked to involve their opinion from the beginning and moved rapidly to shift complete control of the CA to residents in the 1980s.[34]

The work group discussed social engineering such as computer monitoring of daily activities, but they primarily advocated against paternalistic control. The members recommended that the development company "not start its own paper, but offer encouragement" to an existing private publisher to "set up a true community press in the new town."[35] In addition, the way to allow citizen participation while preserving developer control was through the combination of village boards, Columbia Council, and above all, the CA, which would become progressively more resident-controlled as development continued.

When first created, the village boards had power to enforce covenants, review architecture, and were supposed to provide a forum for expressing concerns, particularly to higher authorities. The developer and his team of intellectuals believed that the village government could be part of restoring the American democratic system and spirit. The villages were small, like the idealized small town, and the boards had a discrete role to play. When the actual village boards started many residents doubted their legitimacy. Orlinsky noted that at village board meetings, "passing motions . . . doesn't mean a thing. It's just a waste of energy." Orlinsky explained, however, how the residents gained power in the managing and even planning of Columbia: "We are learning to get leverage through counteraction and bad publicity. That's the one thing they don't want, and that's their Achilles heel."[36]

Village boards slowly gained power. Led in the 1970s by Oakland Mills, which took over management of its local community center, the different boards began to operate community-center facilities through contracts with the central association. The CA transferred much of its management authority to villages, although it did not have to do so. This arrangement proved successful: it allowed individual villages more local control and gave their leadership real management issues to address. A typical village board, such as that of Kings Contrivance, on a budget of approximately $180,000 in 1996 ran an active community center, employed a professional staff, monitored architectural changes in the community, and acted as an advocate for village issues with the CA and the county. The village board also rented space in its community center, Amherst House, as a means to raise money, and offered numerous classes and events.[37]

The CA's management presented a more complicated problem. The developer controlled the association in the early years and maintained a strong voice until 1982, when the association came under the control of the elected Columbia Council. Before 1982, many people thought that the association represented the best interests of the developer, not the residents. Moon, for instance, frequently accused Rouse executives of voting to protect their interests on the CA board. Many other residents held the association in high esteem for its success in creating new programs. Although many of these programs had to be scaled back after the recession of the early 1970s, most residents expected the association to return to its emphasis on community needs once it had weathered the downturn in the economy, and the organization did just that.

Even though most residents expressed contentment with the association, it was clear to the leadership of the Columbia Council, and probably to the association itself, that the organization had special problems. The association's bonds, for instance, were not tax exempt, like those of other municipal governments. This higher cost, when viewed in light of the large debt incurred to install amenities in new villages before residents moved in, made the community more expensive to develop and maintain. Columbia also operated under a household vote system, not a one-person-one-vote system, the standard means of voting in most American communities. Voter turn-out at local elections has never been high, in part because of this confusing system of voting rights.

In the late 1970s, as residents tightened their control of the Columbia Council (the association's governing body), a special tax-district proposal originated in an Alternate Finance committee. The members of this committee, with support of the council, hoped that a new public entity, the special tax district, would be more accountable and that it would save money because of tax exemption. The group also sought to limit the tax district to the powers that CA already possessed, primarily "the broad range of amenities that impart to Columbia its unique character or 'quality of life.'" They made clear that the county and the state would still provide essential services like education, transportation, planning, and so on. Not

only did the committee recognize that incorporation would have been unlikely at the state level (the state government generally rejected bids for
new incorporated areas), but they thought "incorporation would give Columbia more powers than it needs or wants." The tax district, on the other
hand, "would be able to issue tax exempt state instruments," assessments
would be tax deductible, citizens would have more control, and a special
district "would not obligate the community to offer services presently
being provided by Howard County." In addition, the new entity would be
more open to public scrutiny. The Columbia Council supported the initiative, but the state government, hostile in general to bids for new levels of
governance, refused to approve the proposal in 1978.[38]

The final transfer of the CA to complete citizen control came in
1982. But that change did not settle the issue of Columbia's unincorpora-
tion. The council and citizens at large, played a role in setting some priori-
ties of the association before the turnover, and they continued to do so
afterwards. Citizens, for instance, forced a complete path around Lake
Elkhorn, created the momentum for the Columbia Arts Center, invented
the pattern of contracts with the association for management of village facilities, supported sister-city programs, and pressured for sliding-scale
membership fees and the earn-a-membership program at association facilities. The council also has the power to hire and fire association staff, although it has rarely done so.

Problems remained, however, with the association in many residents'
eyes. Not only had the question of financing and representation not been
resolved, but the Columbia Association's professional managers still
wielded most of the power even though the Rouse Company officials were
gone. Padraic (Pat) Kennedy, the association's president until 1998, had
been appointed by James Rouse in 1972 and was known to get his way
through a combination of charm and hard work. Most people liked him
for his many years of service and congenial personality, but others saw him
as capricious and aristocratic. Only on rare occasions had the council rejected proposals by the association staff even as an independent body, and
some of those may have been "give-a-ways" to help the council feel useful.
As one observer noted of Kennedy's relationship to the Columbia Council,
its members "like Homer's Ulysses may have to stop up their ears to resist
[his] siren song."[39]

By the 1990s the issues surrounding the idea of incorporation
seemed clear, but the consensus on the shape reform would take was not.
The group pushing for incorporation called itself the Columbia Municipal
League. Many of its members came out of ABC, Alliance for a Better Co-

lumbia, "an ad hoc citizens group established in 1987 to act as the Association's watchdog." ABC pushed for, among other things, rate reductions at CA facilities and careful monitoring of CA's budget.[40] Proponents of incorporation, led by Jim Clark, a business consultant and longtime resident; Chuck Rees, a law professor and Columbia Council member from the village of Kings Contrivance and a participant in the special tax-district formation attempt; and Rabbi Martin Siegel of the Columbia Jewish Congregation made both financial and civic arguments for incorporation.

Proponents began with criticisms of CA's structure and system of governance. They reminded residents that as a private entity Columbia paid more than municipalities on its debt, and residents themselves lacked the ability to deduct lien payments from their taxes. Incorporation proponents also objected to paying a lien on their property to support the association and not receiving free access to recreational facilities such as pools and athletic clubs, which required additional fees. The leaders also criticized what they considered to be a lack of financial oversight on the part of the association and a high-handedness often combined with arrogance.

Although proponents of incorporation thought that the association ran the existing facilities well, they believed that a true civic feeling had not developed because of the association's dominance. Proponents, like many before, objected to the household vote system (which leaves the question of who voted in the household up in the air). Representation on the council was not proportional to population: a small village such as the town center received one representative, the same number as villages ten times as large. The proponents also believed that the Columbia Council lacked the resources to understand or critique all the proposals made by association staff and ended up rubber-stamping proposals. Finally, some incorporation proponents believed that a community-service organization could never be a true government for an American community.[41] Siegel accused the city of having a spiritual crisis that related to its civic form: "What I see now is a kind of pretty playground in which the outer life looks good but the inner life is not real because there is no true entity called Columbia that people can play a role in." The proponents made many compelling arguments, and many Columbians agreed that incorporation would benefit the community.[42] In a 1997 resident opinion poll, approximately 40 percent of Columbians favored incorporation.[43]

The leadership of the incorporation drive had significant community support but made a number of tactical and rhetorical mistakes. First, they never directly or openly specified the form of incorporated government they actually wanted, so it was unclear to residents what shape the future government would take. This vagueness gave opponents of incorporation carte blanche to picture the worst possible outcome. Unlike the proponents of the special tax district, which proposed to limit the role of the new government, the incorporation leaders left open the exact extent of power that the new government would have, powers that might replace not only the association but the county's important role in Columbia. Second, the leadership reacted bitterly to what they considered apathy on the part of residents, particularly after a drive for signatures to place the incorporation issue on the ballot failed to garner anywhere near the required 10,000 names. However, a lack of organization as much as apathy hindered the incorporation movement's efforts to gain signatures. Finally, the leadership, particularly Siegel, mistakenly claimed that Columbia lacked community spirit because it lacked a government. This accusation was provocative and not particularly true. Siegel also made a tragic error by getting into a heated debate with the aged Rouse, who opposed incorporation, on a local talk radio show. They later patched relations up publicly in two letters that appeared in the local newspaper, but the damage was done. In the end, the leadership of the incorporation drive let down the Columbians who favored incorporation.[44]

Opponents, like Rouse and the majority of Columbians, saw no good reason to incorporate. They believed that the association and the county provided excellent services, and that a healthy civic life, although in need of some tweaking, was in place. In terms of community services, the evidence strongly favored nonincorporation. The CA, now under the direction of residents, has continued to uphold the new-town plans, including providing residents with extensive facilities at reasonable or subsidized prices. Most residents are also apparently content with the services provided by the CA. A 1997 survey found that a strong majority of residents thought that the quality of service provided by the association was excellent or good. At the county level, Columbia residents gained the lion's share of power, and the community has largely benefited from its relationship to the county. The county provides excellent schools and adequate fire and police protection. On these arguments alone, the anti-incorporation forces could convince most people.[45]

The question of civic spirit was more complicated, and anti-incorporation advocates took a measured position: they claimed that civic life was healthier than the critics charged and that improvements could best be rendered through reform of the association rather than through incorporation. They noted that the Columbia Council possessed veto power over the CA, even though it had used such power sparingly. Should a crisis in leadership arise in the association, the council could change the management. As one opponent noted as well, "we already have a democratic and immediate government in the village boards and council whom we can freely petition, to whom we can protest or with whom we can participate. In fact, we even have our own separate watchdog organization— ABC, Alliance for a Better Columbia."[46] Hundreds of residents also serve on committees, village boards, and advisory groups. In addition, the meetings of the council are open to the public.

Yet many opponents of incorporation agreed that the association should be reformed. They believed, in particular, that the organization should be made more accountable to the residents. Robert Tennenbaum pointed out in an editorial that "although I agree that the Columbia Association can be unresponsive and arrogant, on balance Columbia's open space and recreation amenities are well-managed. . . . The answer is . . . to entirely re-engineer CA and not to create an even greater problem in the form of municipal government."[47]

Kennedy's retirement in 1999 led to the hiring of Debbie McCarty, a parks administrator from Atlanta, as the new association president. Her selection was seen by many as an attempt to choose someone more willing to work with the elected council rather than through it. Indeed, she began to work closely with the council, much to the chagrin of many pioneers and long-term residents. She proposed further privatizing community centers and cutting back on services (at a time when the association was flush with money). Her bold style set off numerous angry editorials, community meetings featuring early residents such as Moon, and a hotly contested election for council seats that brought her opponents into power and led to her resignation. The tension between old ideals and tighter financial management (supported by many residents) is likely to remain at the center of attention in Columbia. The struggle also showed that residents possess significant power should they choose to exercise it. Lack of participation probably reflected general satisfaction rather than powerlessness.

The Columbia Forum, a citizen-led reform effort of the 1980s and 1990s, produced only a few more practical results than the incorporation drive but played an important intellectual role in the community. The forum, organized by many long-term residents and supported by the Columbia power structure (including the retired Rouse), involved residents in planning issues; sponsored talks, symposia, a video history, and an archive; and generated one of the most insightful reports by residents on the benefits and problems of living in a planned community. The forum has faded from view in Columbia, but it left behind an important intellectual legacy.

A series of large-scale forum meetings held in 1982 and 1983 addressed important issues in the community. Topics for discussion included planning, education, village centers, teenagers, and affordable housing as well as a less-conventional topic, the creation of a nuclear-free zone. These meetings also yielded some practical results. At the first meeting on June 12, 1982, "a discussion group on the last village attracted a large group of interested residents who wanted to take part in this planning effort. As a result, the Trotter Road Village [now known as the Village of River Hill] Planning Committee was established." According to an update on the forum from 1983, "one of the most exciting results is a unique opportunity for residents to participate in the planning of a village, Columbia's last. The Trotter Road Village Planning Committee has been working with the developer to incorporate innovative ideas of energy conservation, housing diversity and affordability, new telecommunications technologies and others into the village plans." The group discussed "village based electrical power systems, using solar and wind power and garbage as fuel, the use of electric and other non-polluting vehicles, video telephones and other futuristic communications systems, water-conserving toilets, shared taxi service and roads free of cars except during peak hours."[48] The Rouse Company failed to integrate these ideas of the committee, most of which did not meet the market standard. The builders at River Hill have constructed typical suburban houses rather than the cutting-edge ideas proposed by the forum. The forum, as well as the community at large, lacked the power or ingenuity to force the company to integrate these suggestions.

The committee did aid in the rezoning of River Hill, a role welcomed by the Rouse Company, which wanted to build higher-density housing. The areas designated for the future village had originally been zoned as single family, low density, detached residential. The committee, which believed rezoning for apartments would make social diversity possible, made concrete suggestions toward changing the zoning. The Rouse Company sought 90 acres of apartments from the county zoning department for the new village, a request that was greeted with much dismay by longtime residents of Trotter Road but supported by the forum. The company eventually agreed to 33 acres of apartments, a significant improvement from the single-family designation of the original planning but far short of the company's and the forum's desired density.[49]

The forum also had limited success in its attempt to improve the town center. During the 1980s, the forum brought to Columbia experts on urban development and design in a series of talks. Wolf Von Eckardt offered a negative analysis of the town center at the first talk by citing banal design, high-speed roads, and lack of pedestrian access.[50] Ronald Lee Fleming, president of the Townscape Institute of Cambridge, Massachusetts, helped residents shape a response to these failings. The resulting wish list included the following exuberant suggestions: "A floating barge for social functions, art on walls and bridges, street vendors, chess and checker tournaments, storytelling, sidewalk inserts, sailboats, drinking fountains." The attendees also "wanted a clear self-image, outdoor eating places, shops, better pedestrian linkages and amenities, places for year-round activities, a cultural center, public transportation, a more urban atmosphere, higher density, and a residential element present." Those attending agreed to begin pressuring the Rouse Company and the CA to begin rethinking the downtown. In part because of pressure from the forum, the downtown underwent minor renovations including new lighting, restoration of the People Tree sculpture, and extension of the lakeside pathway. Unfortunately, these renovations failed to address the problems and opportunities highlighted by the forum, and the residents devised no way of forcing a more comprehensive plan.[51]

The translation of ideas to reality proved difficult for the forum, but the process and ideas themselves proved of value. The forum created an impressive report from a four-year (1988–92) process of discussion called the Columbia Voyage.[52] The report An Agenda for Columbia (the result of four years of effort by "over 1,000 volunteers, commentators, and participants" meeting on numerous committees and task forces), addressed a variety of important issues, including the arts, cultural and religious diversity, downtown, economic development, education, the environment, transportation, housing, health, and "a sense of community." The report affirmed the goals of social justice and sought to expand them; its framers sought to improve mass transit, augment the arts, and recommended some form of incorporated government for Columbia. Again, however, the means to translate these ideas proved elusive. The Rouse Company, the CA, and the Howard County government encouraged the Voyage meetings but did nothing to help turn suggestions into reality, and participating citizens lacked formal means and political savvy to gain acceptance for their ideas.

Although An Agenda for Columbia was generally optimistic, it revealed doubts about the ability of planning alone to reshape community life, a conclusion that was the result of actual experience in a planned community. In a one-page statement of goals, the community criticized Ebenezer Howard, turn-of-the-century pioneer of the contemporary garden-city movement, and the "Rouse company planners" (really Rouse) for believing that "the traditional city . . . was not rational, not 'human scale.' It was inimical to a sense of community. Howard saw the values of the country as more positive and humane, and to the extent they could be imposed upon an area of settlement, 'A Garden City,' a new life, a new civilization would develop." Although an oversimplification of the ideas of both Howard and Rouse, the statement does accurately reflect both individuals' belief in environmental effects on behavior. The report concluded that "the bonding of a community does not result from geography. Communities grow from shared values, purposes, goals, processes, modes and measures of behavior; from the involvement of its people in common endeavors." The report shows that experience had tempered early idealism. Residents added a new vision of community, oriented more around activism than design, rarely seen in new-town planning documents with their emphasis on physical design as a means to better life.[53]

The forum has translated its vision into publicity. It commissioned a documentary entitled "Our Town—Columbia," which, according to the forum brochure, offers "a portrait of Columbia today seen through the prism of its citizens, not through rose-colored glasses." Using quotations from residents and from Rouse and visual images from the community, the video briefly traces Columbia's history and celebrates racial integration, community spirit, and open-space preservation. Unlike Rouse Company documents, however, the video also presents many criticisms, including the perceived sterility of environment, the loss of community spirit, and growing affluence. The video, then, represents an important adaptation of the new-town style by residents to better reflect their own experiences.[54]

The most important intellectual innovation arising from the Columbia Forum has been the Columbia Archive. Columbia is the only new town with a central public archive that has developed history presentations. Established in 1982, the archive has undertaken the task of preserving an enormous volume of materials, most of it related to the new-town concept. The collection includes early plans, photographs, articles, planning papers, and community newsletters. Ruth McCulough, a former information analyst at Westinghouse and archive organizer, "realized the documentation of a planned city would provide a 'marvelous data base for a sociological study of the late '60s and early '70s.'"[55] The archivists sought more than preservation of records; they also viewed the archive as a means of promoting the new town ideals: "The Museum and Archives would . . . develop a sense of place, history and community, and provide a focus for on-going renewal of the concepts underlying Columbia's development."[56]

The archive has taken an active role in educating residents about new-town history and values. The first exhibition appeared in 1983 in the Columbia mall and included early drawings for the community. It also displayed "dozens of aerial photographs taken between 1965 and 1975," including photographs of villages as they grew.[57] In 1987, the archivists created an oral history project focused on people who "participated in the evolution of the various villages—each with its own distinctive personality." At the 1997 Columbia birthday celebration, the archives presented an exhibit, "'Cities are for People' . . . consisting of letters, stories, poems and photographs contributed by Columbia residents." A time line illustrating Columbia's history was added to the CA welcome center in the 1990s. The archive, having demonstrated its importance, became one of the CA's many responsibilities. The donation of Rouse's extensive papers in 1999 has given it a further stamp of legitimacy.[58]

The Columbia Forum should be seen as both a practical political failure and an intellectual and community-building success. Residents have had the opportunity to meet with each other and discuss and criticize their community. The forum helped organize local history, thereby keeping new-town ideals in the public view. It has also indirectly provided important insights into the experience of planned-community living.

Irvine's City Spirit

The incorporated municipality of Irvine has maintained an open style of governance and developed both a responsive school system and a range of community services. This government developed a vision distinct from the Irvine Company, and the citizens gained enough power to challenge the company's plans. Other citizens have organized important voluntary associations and struggled to preserve the history of the Irvine Ranch.

From the beginning, Irvine attracted residents with an interest in self-government. One Irvine Company official remarked: "people who move to Irvine come with high expectations and a desire to become involved. In fact, noninvolvement and a sense of alienation from neighbors and local government helped prompt the move from the old neighborhoods in the first place."[59] As an example, one tireless organizer in the community noted that at Irvine he had been able to take a leadership role in fund-raising, whereas "you could flip pancakes at fund-raisers for years in some of the older communities, and never have a chance for leadership. Here you can get right in on the ground floor and make a real contribution."[60] Marshall Brewer, the author of a study on Irvine governance, noted that from the earliest days "the leaders [of Irvine] were aware of the town's

separate identity and of its being a 'new town.' This can be seen in their
planning documents and their attempt to bring innovation into the community. . . . The new City Fathers have taken the birthright of being a
planned city seriously, and intend to pursue the theme of creating a better
urban environment."[61]

An early form of area-resident participation came in the University
of California, Irvine (UCI), Project 21 from 1971 to 1974, a joint effort of
the university, the local governments of Orange County, and a private leadership group. The project created study teams on downtown deterioration,
transportation, open space, government, and urban planning. Professionals from Orange County filled the team, including planners, university employees, realtors, engineers, architects, and businessmen. The team
advocated federally subsidized low-income housing in all Orange County
communities, and it called for the elimination of racist housing policies.
The university also sponsored other events that, according to Brewer, made
"leaders of the various communities more aware of area-wide problems,
and, in effect, more liberal in their outlook than the community at large."
He also suggested that these efforts by the university might have prompted
the Irvine city council "to move ahead with a low-income housing element
to the city's master plan." Most historians have failed to see that Irvine was
part of a general attempt to reshape suburban life at that time, and that elements of the community's leadership stood behind such ideals.[62]

The Irvine Company developed its plan for the city in 1970, but the
new leadership on the city council in the early 1970s created its own commission and hired professionals to create a general plan. Although the city
plan resembled the company's, with its system of villages, greenbelts, and
transportation hierarchy, the city plan suggested options for the future that
included much lower population levels than those envisioned by the Irvine
Company. In addition, the professional planning firm hired by the city
sought extensive resident input. Martin Schiesl, an expert on Irvine politics, notes that the plan provided for a linked series of paths "to reduce dependence on the automobile," "reserved various sites for schools, churches,
and shopping facilities," and "proposed the establishment of an information network that could closely monitor the housing developments to be
sure they filled the residential needs of all people who worked in the
community."[63]

During the 1970s the residents of Irvine, through their local government, began to shape the city more to their liking and planning ideals. Unlike Columbia and Reston, the city government had the authority to shape
the community. Although the city management staff implemented policy,

the city council clearly set it. In 1977, the then progrowth council approved a land-use plan revision, making 250,000 the maximum population of Irvine (including its northern environs). The plan itself was "a compromise between alternative plans, which had been part of the general plan since 1973." The compromise emerged "after more than 18 months of studies, public hearing and revisions of proposals." The approved plan displeased slow-growth proponents, but it predicted a significantly lower population than that of the Irvine Company, which in 1970 had projected 430,000 residents at completion. The company fully expected the city to adopt lower population goals, but the city has given form to the smaller-scale vision. Instead of favoring single-family homes on large lots, the city has promoted high-density housing in combination with large-scale nature preservation.

This planning vision has been in evidence during the 1970s, 1980s, and 1990s as the council has often rejected or scaled down Irvine Company developments and created open-space preserves. In 1973, the city residents, fighting the fiscal conservatism emerging in California at the time, approved an $18 million bond for park and bike-trail creation. The city also traded high-density development for land to create Heritage Park, site of many facilities and attractive open space. The city has pursued similar land and development exchanges over the years. All told, these exchanges will lead to nearly 30,000 open acres out of the original 90,000 acre ranch. Many of these changes (affordable housing, for example) have been made with the consent and cooperation of the Irvine Company, while others (such as open space exchanges) the company has simply been forced to accept in order to continue to build in the city. A 1989 article summarized the first two decades of city governance: "The council has tinkered with the plan: expanding bicycle trails, cutting back on development, preserving more land for open space, but has held tight to the larger concept of planning since the area became a city in 1971."[64]

Over the decades, the council has created a variety of facilities, including an arts complex and performing-arts center; community centers; extensive parks, bike paths, and walkways; and an aquatic center that have neutralized some of the more hierarchical aspects of the system in which neighborhoods and villages have different levels of amenities. In addition, residents have more freedom of choice: unlike the case in Reston or Columbia, a family can use facilities without having to buy an expensive membership.[65]

Irvine's city government has been involved in social issues, too, a feature difficult to achieve in local governance at other new towns and usually undertaken by a nonprofit organization outside the community association. In 1974, the city mandated 10 percent affordable housing in large-scale new developments, a provision that by the 1990s led to thousands of affordable apartments spread discreetly throughout the community. Irvine's community services department offers a wide range of services. These include community centers and parks, personal-enrichment programs, an extensive child care and camp program, and senior services. The department maintains a program offering counseling, disability services, a referral service for parenting classes, support groups, and emergency shelters. Many of these services exist in other new towns, but they are better promoted and more easily supported through Irvine's system of local government.[66]

Irvine is also the only one of these new towns to run its own school system. The city's school system reflects an emphasis on decentralization and citizen control that has not been achieved elsewhere. Schools in Irvine have individual citizen-advisory boards designed to suit schools to local needs and to develop new programs (the system now operates twenty-eight elementary and middle schools and three high schools with a total of 22,500 students). The system consistently ranks high on college preparation, spends heavily on the arts, and rewards teachers for excellence. There remain alternative schools that offer smaller classes and individualized instruction, an independent-study high school, year-round schools, English-as-a-second-language (ESL) programs, a home-school curriculum, and gifted and talented classes.[67]

The many services and programs of the government are affected by citizen advice. Irvine residents created a municipal government that made citizen action part of the planning and building process: "Instead of adopting the standard structural system used by the vast majority of California's cities, Irvine leaders chose to create a 'charter city' with one-of-a-kind departments and commissions."[68] The city has consistently created citizen "commissions and committees, at all levels of planning and operation. The range of topics is impressive: ' . . . culture and fine arts, day care centers, transportation . . . bike trails, overall planning, alcoholism'" and more. According to councilman Ed Dornan in 1989, "we have hundreds, maybe a thousand people from the community involved in task forces. That kind of citizen participation allows everyone to have a say."[69]

Larry Agran, one of the mayors of the 1980s, with the support of a liberal city council, used the openness of the city government to expand Irvine's commitment to social issues. Issues he addressed included those that expanded attention to the homeless, child care, recycling, chlorofluorocarbons, pay equity, and discrimination. In addition, the council worked to set aside large spaces of the city as open space, initiated a "gray water" recycling program (the use of treated sewer water on greenbelts and open spaces), and adopted international sister cities.[70] Agran lost the election for mayor in 1990 to conservative Sally Anne Sheridan, and the city council became more politically and fiscally conservative, although most programs remained in place.[71] After a quixotic run for president of the United States in 1992, in 1998 Agran returned to the Irvine City Council, and actively opposed plans for conversion of the nearby El Toro marine base into an international airport.

Agran and many other city leaders received support from a small but important citizen's organization known as Irvine Tomorrow. Since the 1970s, the organization has been instrumental in promoting the new-town vision. In an angry rebuttal to an accusation by former mayor Art Anthony and the *Irvine World News,* who claimed that Irvine Tomorrow was "disruptive" and bent on "social planning, tighter and more experimental forms of regulating community goals," the chair of Irvine Tomorrow at the time (1979), Louis Fridhandler, fumed "it was not Irvine Tomorrow that 'disrupted' the original Pereira plan for the community of Irvine." Fridhandler reminded readers that "the Pereira plan aimed at a set of villages centered near the university at Irvine Town Center. . . . The orderly progression toward this gracious, lovely concept was radically changed when the push toward making Irvine a large city was launched about 9 or 10 years ago, before Irvine Tomorrow existed." He accused certain agencies of wanting to profit while "leaving behind a community with citizens facing a possible future plagued by pollution, overcrowding, lowered property values, and frustrating traffic jams." According to Fridhandler, Irvine Tomorrow had organized a "symposium on New Towns with speakers from New Towns all over the country," television shows on local cable channels, "a symposium on proposed and needed commercial and recreational facilities . . . advocacy of bike trails, protection of the San Joaquin marsh, and protection of citizens from noise pollution." The organization also supported politicians who have favored slower growth and social justice. The organization's fortunes have waxed and waned over the decades, but in recent years a renewed Irvine Tomorrow has continued to influence public policy by acting as "watchdog group" of the council. In the early 1990s, members organized a series of referenda designed to slow growth, but they failed to garner the necessary support and faced intense and expensive opposition by the Irvine Company.[72]

Residents, notably those of Irvine Tomorrow, during the last four decades have directed their frustration at the company. Opinion is split on the degree of influence exercised by the company on city government. Thomas Wilk, a company vice president of public affairs, explained that while they might support some Irvine citizens for "boards or agencies . . . whose jurisdiction extends beyond the local community level," they stayed out of local campaigns for the city council and did not endorse candidates. Wilk asserted that "the people of Irvine are in control of their city's destiny. We supported their having that control, and we will not now seek to compromise it with any attempt at Big Brother participation." Irvine's second mayor, Gabrielle Pryor, a frequent critic of the company in the early years, even believed that "good government" free of "favoritism in both the private and public sector" existed in Irvine and that residents had established a city government that ensured "fairness, justice, respect for individual's rights and for the public's right to know what is going on."[73]

Over the last decades, however, the Irvine Company has spent millions of dollars on public-relations efforts to gain approval for projects. Many residents and politicians, moreover, began to see an unhealthy relationship developing in the 1990s between city management staff and the Irvine Company. Christina Shea, a conservative who was elected mayor in 1996, ran on a platform that promised to reduce the control of city managers. Mark Petracca, a UCI professor and a liberal Irvine Tomorrow activist, also believes that the company has exercised undue influence in Irvine. He argues that "structurally, and based on personality, the city manager is controlled by the Irvine Company." This cozy relationship develops, Petracca believes, because "when you sit around and listen to them you end up looking out for their interests." Petracca acknowledged that the Irvine Company is "really smart and really thorough," including being "good at subtly punishing opponents." The domination of local media by the *Irvine World News* helps keep the city behind the company (as do regular company mailings). This being said, the elected council and the mayor have more clearly shaped Irvine than the Columbia Council and the CA have shaped their community.[74]

In Irvine, historical sensitivity has grown over the years, and citizens have added historic preservation to the list of planning goals. The agricultural and architectural heritage of the Irvine Ranch has become the focus of historical preservation efforts even though the Irvine Company originally had no such plans. Many citizens realized that the comprehensive style of development at the ranch would probably obliterate all evidence of its past use.[75] The area known as Old Town Irvine, "the former rural town center" near the Irvine Spectrum, has been the most successful historical renovation completed in any new town.

In the 1980s, the Irvine Company planned to destroy the Old Town area, originally both a service area for workers of the ranch and a shipping center for ranch products. The threat motivated a group of residents associated with the Irvine Historical Society to pressure the city to protect the area. The city council created a special committee, led by a founding member of the historical society, Judy Liebeck, to draw up plans to preserve the center. A development group called Sand Canyon Historical Partners, with help from the city, the historical society, and the Irvine Company undertook a $20 million renovation that preserved and adapted the structures. The renovation features buildings "painted in blue-green, lemon-yellow, engine-red, steamy-peach—bright colors that are taboo in the city's neighborhoods." An architect converted a granary into a La Quinta Motor Inn, a blacksmith's shop into a restaurant, and other bungalows and the old Irvine Company store into commercial space. An old lima-bean warehouse has even been converted into a bakery and a Mexican restaurant.[76]

Founded in 1977, the Irvine Historical Society continues to provide public programs through its displays in an old ranch building adjacent to the Rancho San Joaquin golf course. Exhibits feature material-culture evidence from the days of the ranch, and a collection of old farm implements is on display around the building. Tours are offered on a regular basis, and public presentations feature ranch history. Unlike the Reston Historic Trust for Community Revitalization or the Columbia Archive, the Irvine Historical Society does not focus on or even devote much attention to the history of Irvine as a new town; the agricultural past seems of greater interest. Irvine residents take for granted the high-quality design of the community and seem more ambivalent about the growth of the city around them. They knew when they moved to Irvine that they were moving to a future city, but the reality of Irvine's urban present is undoubtedly disconcerting to people who moved there when it was a series of small communities surrounded by open range and agricultural land. That a new-town plan has guided the development means less than it does in the other communities, which integrate larger, lusher natural areas amidst their many villages.

Irvine's city government is a great success and an asset to the community. Contrary to the fears of those who opposed incorporation in Reston and Columbia, the city government is not a bloated bureaucracy. Instead, it has been well designed to respond to citizen pressure. There is a benefit to having city facilities in an upper-income community like Irvine where some moderate-income people live. Public facilities diminish the feeling of exclusiveness and offer more options for those who would like freedom of choice. Perhaps most important is that the city government gives legitimacy and opportunities for broad action on issues that are of more significance to new-town residents than those of the county at large.

The many citizen institutions of the new towns—community associations, village boards, a city government, historical societies, citizen committees, nonprofits, and newspapers and magazines—have shaped atypical suburban communities. By demanding that their communities be developed as true new towns, rather than subdivisions, residents were upholding their commitment to solving the problems of suburban sprawl.

During four decades, resident institutions have initiated social and planning innovations that have filled in the physical framework established by planners. Their experiences as residents and activists also called into question early faith in environmental determinism. Master plans, cozy village-center plazas, and pathway systems, it turned out, gave residents rallying points but did not build public life. Decades of shared effort on issues like planning, education, recreation, environmental protection, mass transit, and affordable housing not only created tangible benefits for residents but helped establish a strong sense of community for many others.

Participation also yielded occasional frustrations that many residents found difficult to stomach. Unlike the corporations that built the towns, under great pressure to make a profit and sensitive to shifting economic realities, some residents thought nothing less than the ideal was acceptable. As one might expect, there was always sufficient disappointment to excite "end of the dream" jeremiads. Other activists were more pragmatic. They realized that struggles for an ideal inspired public discourse and quite often led to serious bargaining with development companies over plans. Compromise emerged as a singularly important value, one entirely unmentioned in the sunny public relations of the new-town developers.

7

Communal Prodigies:
New Towns and the
Instant Creation of Civic Spirit

> It was a comfortable enough place to live back there, but the
> community, with its thousands of people, seemed so cold and
> faceless. I suppose it was no different from so many other semi-
> suburbs anywhere. There were no organizations, no places to
> meet anyone. People came and went. We began to feel, Larry
> and I, sort of like automatons. We were busy enough, but we did-
> n't like the feeling of aloneness, of alienation, of being involved
> with ourselves and not with the other people all around us.
>
> THE LEGALLOS, an early Reston couple,
> interview in *Family Circle*

Residents of suburban housing tracts initiated numerous clubs and occasional parades but advanced few traditions or leaders that reflected a
grander civic vision. Suburbanites, according to the critics, seemed singularly focused on domestic activities. They might organize around a particular community issue or an interest like gardening, but their emphasis
remained on home ownership and the happiness of the nuclear family.
City residents, on the other hand, supported parades, festivals, and leadership that reflected their civic pride and idealism. In new towns, the attempt
to infuse both civic idealism and rituals into the suburban world set these
fledgling communities apart.

The civic activism described in the preceding chapter extended into other dimensions of community life. The experience of joining together in new towns in the early years created a self-identified group of resident "pioneers." These pioneers saw themselves as different from later arrivals in the community, united as they were in the early days by being part of an innovative communal experiment. Developers and pioneer residents also created a number of events designed to boost community spirit and overcome the anonymity of both suburbia and the city. These included community "birthday" celebrations, July Fourth celebrations and parades, a "Harvest Festival," and holiday pageants. Finally, uniting all these activities has been the paternalism of well-liked developers, the "urban bosses" of the new towns. Figures such as Rouse, Simon, and Watson have provided steady leadership for these rapidly growing communities. Civic life has faced challenges over the years, and certain efforts have simply failed. Overall, however, a unique civic spirit has been created, with a comprehensiveness usually thought to be reserved for more established communities.

Pioneers

The yeasty reform ethos of the early years of these communities had its effect on residents. They understood that their use of the term *pioneer* was primarily rhetorical—they understood the enormous differences that distinguished them from historical pioneers—but they wanted to stress that they were adventurous and daring reformers. These latter-day pioneers gained solidarity through early arrival, mild adversity, and a dedication to new-town ideals. The term *pioneer* also became a way to distinguish the early reform-oriented members of the community from later arrivals and a perceived decline in civic spirit.

The new-town frontier reproduced in miniature the process of town development on America's frontier. In his famous essay *The Frontier in American History,* Frederick Jackson Turner argued that the frontier experience explained much about American life. He believed that contact with the primitive conditions of the frontier reshaped America along more democratic lines by breaking down traditional ideas of social rank and accentuating individualism. Turner theorized that while the pioneer phase had ended, "the democratic aspirations" and strong individualism kindled by the pioneering process remained a central aspect of Midwestern life— and had become part of American society in general.[1]

New-town residents also believed that democracy and idealism flourished on their edge of society, and they hoped that their pioneering efforts would inspire national reform. As residents piled in, many with little interest in new-town ideals, and suburbs outside the new towns continued to sprawl, some pioneers became discouraged. Most, along with many who came after them, continued to shape their communities along more democratic and tolerant lines. The growing pluralism, which included residents with no interest in new-town ideology, made the towns more compelling models of social reform.

Reston's Communal Frontier

Jane Wilhem, a member of Simon's original staff and still a resident of Reston, explained in 1984 that "part of the reason for Reston's success is the traditions of community involvement established by the original settlers and continued institutions which encourage community participation."[2] Pioneering took on powerful metaphorical significance in Reston. In the *Restonian*, a 1967 editorial made a connection between earlier pioneers who settled the western frontier, suburban growth, and the new-town movement:

> Even as America pressed up against the ocean the migrations continued. This time the movement was internal—from the cities to the neighboring countryside. . . . In the story of urban America, it can be found under the heading "Urban Sprawl." There are Americans today who are trying to write a new hopeful chapter to this story. They are the pioneers of the New Towns. Like pioneers before them, they too are pushing outward. But their towns are not just new places to live. The New Towns, looking toward the future but remembering the past, offer an alternative to the sprawl of the suburbs and blight of the cities.[3]

A surprisingly strong communalist spirit underwrote much of the pioneer spirit. A dedication article by a settler named James F. Grady in 1968 set the tone for the newly inaugurated "Town Crier" column by establishing a connection between Reston and earlier American communal efforts:

> As our early 17th century new towns moved though the processes (and the developing pains) of building a sense of community, the Town Crier performed an essential function and became a respected, vital part of town life. If each settler in

the early new towns had gone his own way without regard for the interest, needs and rights of his fellow-settlers and neighbors, however close or distant, there would have been no need for a Town Crier to announce important news and to summon the settlers to discuss major issues.[4]

The pioneers of Reston focused on communal values, rather than individualism or the nuclear family. Many residents commented on the communalism of town life. Thomas Huth, an early resident, pointed out that "if Reston is a pioneer, a model of a more perfect life style, it will truly show the way because its residents, given a suitable atmosphere, learn to live in harmony and happiness with each other."[5] Jacqueline Vergin, who moved to Reston in 1967, remembered "the 'sense of adventure . . . commitment and financial risk' that united those living and investing in Simon's then-unproven design."[6]

Many early pioneers found much to appreciate in this new environment. Successful, ambitious members of the government and corporate worlds, they were pleased to be pioneering a communal life without the taint of communism or hippie-style communes—an alternative for those who wanted to preserve capitalism and the nuclear family. There were many in the middle class at this time who were attracted to less individualistic modes of living yet not ready to shed all conventions. Reston, then, was a middle ground between the extremes represented by family life in standard suburbs at one end and the formlessness of communes sprouting up around America in the 1960s and 1970s.

The Reston story would be less interesting if every resident shared the pioneering, communal spirit, but the fact is that residents came for a variety of reasons. Huth also revealed that "as nearly every Restonian knows, there is a great social distance between Hunters Woods and Lake Anne, more than the five miles shown on the map. There is a rivalry, often resentful, built around differing life styles (the urban oriented Lake Anne vs. the more cloistered Hunters Woods) and around snobbishness (the pioneer, socially involved, longhair vs. the respectable, property oriented)." A particularly interesting description of this divide appeared in a "Town Crier" article of 1970:

> Reston's Rededication Festival on May 23 was an exciting attempt to recreate the mood and spirit of the early pioneering days of the New Town. One highlight was a truly impressive group of speakers on the New Town theme. . . . Yet with this

marvelous array only a meager band of perhaps 200 townsfolk grouped near the podium to listen—and, as an early settler, I must admit that most of the faces in that group were ones I saw in a similar gathering back in '66. Milling around the Center, not listening and apparently not caring, were one thousand more Restonians. It occurred to me that many newcomers to Reston during its past few years of great population growth may not know of the magnet that attracted its early settlers; of the New Town concepts put forth so beguiling by Bob Simon.[7]

For those upper middle-class residents milling on the fringes of these speeches, the new town offered a good place for family life, amenities for different generations, protective covenants, shopping and cultural opportunities, and contact with nature, not new-town idealism.

Pioneers of Reston not only socialized but formed the core group of leadership in organizations like the RCA, the Reston Association, and the Reston Community Center. These organizations did much to preserve plans during the changes in ownership. In recent years, a group of younger, newer arrivals have asserted themselves. Most of the pioneers have adjusted to this change, which has brought a more conservative, more "realistic" attitude to community politics. Most newcomers do not realize how hard residents worked to preserve the new-town plan after Simon's departure. Now that the first wave of development is largely complete, and most Restonians accept that the new-town ideals have created an exceptional community, the decline of the pioneer spirit is less threatening. Because one aspect of the pioneering spirit was greater tolerance, this change to a more pluralistic community is not necessarily the decline that many residents believe.

Columbia's Liberal Frontier

> The fact that a band of residents in voluntary association with a visionary mortgage banker just might "get it together" without doing violence to all the middle-class values or dropping out of the mainstream of life, may prove a surprise.
>
> CHARLES SIMPKINSON, *Columbia Flier*

After Rouse's death in 1996, the *Columbia Flier* described him as a kind of prophet, followed by his flock: "Thousands of idealistic settlers followed Rouse, like Moses, colonizing 'The Next America,' as it was dubbed—an open community founded to nurture its citizens. Columbia, Rouse said, was never meant to be Utopia; what was remarkable was that it was unusual."[8] These idealistic followers were not hippies: they were ordinary middle-class liberals like Charles Simpkinson, who wanted to improve the world without resorting to violence or communalism. The flock of liberal pioneers flourished for many years and continues to flourish, although the attitudes of most have been tempered by age and experience.

The pioneers of Columbia, even more than those of Reston, defined themselves as liberals: "The capitalist visionary and his utopian community was to attract a whole slew of hairy liberals, concerned about the decline of the city, racial inequality, religious intolerance, the plight of the poor, the desolation of the environment and the war in Vietnam."[9] As at Reston, these residents also saw pioneering in communal rather than individualistic or familial terms. Ruth Seidel, an important Columbia leader, explained that "we felt like pioneers . . . and we felt like everyday there was change. There was an opportunity to meet people from all over, all kinds of backgrounds, and we became friends very quickly."[10] Mimi Mathews and her husband Bob looked at Columbia before they moved there and decided that "'this is the sort of thing pioneers going west did,' settling new territory, establishing new towns. 'Columbia was small, it had new concepts, it had new people from all over the country and all over the world.'"[11]

Living in distant exurbia, residents came to depend upon one another. In a 1970 article, Harriet Scarupa explained that pioneers had "a willingness to cope with inconveniences, a spirit of adventure and an all-encompassing sense of community [that] seemed to give those earliest residents a lot in common with the Westward Ho set." She interviewed many people who affirmed this identity. Jeri Akers, an early resident of Bryant Gardens apartments, remembered that "the people who were here had to want to be here—to not be tempted to throw up their hands and say, 'Let's go back to civilization.' . . . There was a real sense of adventure—a willingness of people to commit themselves to things that weren't certain. . . . There was a lot of visiting back and forth—not just to borrow a cup of sugar—but to really talk. In some ways you had no life of your own. It was closer than any other experience I've had, even college." Barbara Russell, another early resident, explained that "since we were the only people here, we were all very close. It was like a family."[12]

According to Scarupa, the occasion of George Wallace's speaking at the local Merriweather Post Pavilion acted as a further stimulus to community feeling. Residents put an ad in local papers affirming Wallace's right to speak, but they reprimanded him: "We hope that while you and your followers are in Columbia you will be able to sense the spirit of true freedom, of unity of purpose and of belief in brotherhood that character-izes our city." Scarupa's description of the counter-rally gives a sense of the tenor of those days: "On the night of June 27 [1968] while the Wallace rally was taking place, almost all of Columbia's residents packed Slayton House for an 'I believe in Columbia' rally and heard spokesmen reaffirm their belief—and the new city's—in human values. Residents joined in prayer and singing of the 'Battle Hymn of the Republic' at the meeting's close." Heady words and doings for a suburban community![13]

Pat Carto, an early Columbia resident, described the excitement resi-dents could feel for something as simple as minibus service. Once she and others were on the bus, community began: "'Let's see,' says the driver, 'the library,' and he whips out a map. Fantastic, absolutely fantastic. . . . At the sight of the map, people crowd around the driver like explorers choosing the best route to the summit of Mt. Everest. They all know there is only one route the bus takes to the other side of Rt. 29, but to go that route without a little participation sayso would be unthinkable and spoil the whole point of riding the minibus or moving to Columbia."[14] She also described a "long twisting ride home, accomplished with a fine, European sense of his-tory and time. . . . Passengers got on and off, but we were the hard core, the sightseers watching the dream glide by, hardly believing it wouldn't melt in the sun. Pleasantries, lively conversation, a kid's happiness, forehead and nose pressed to the windowpane, hot sun trapped inside—was I in Colum-bia or on a rollicking ride to Naples, passing a wayside shrine, or ready to get off at a dusty, Greek village?" This resident's sense of being out of nor-mal time and location (while only twenty minutes from Baltimore) marks her as a pioneer, as does her enthusiasm for community-building exercises.

True pioneer status seemed to have been conferred only on those who arrived within the first year or two, but the pioneering spirit never re-ally died. The 1977 commemorative issue of the *Columbia Flier* reflected some of that spirit. Moon still felt as though the community was engaged in a bold experiment: "Columbia is particularly fascinating because we are breaking new ground, trying to live in a way different from the way we were brought up. The people here are special, if for no other reason than that they are involved in a collective experience rare in our lifetime. We have an identity, an identity so distinct that a teen living here observes it is almost as if there is an invisible 'fence' around the city." Moon acknowl-edged, however, that "all of this community-building, ground-breaking and experimenting, of course, may be invisible to many of the people who

choose to live here for other reasons." Lurking in the background, as at
Reston, were the thousands who came without any interest in a full complement of liberal ideals: residents who saw Columbia as a community of
pretty streets, good schools, recreational activities, and shopping centers.
At the same time, Columbia pioneers were well known for profiting from
their early purchase in the community. They benefited from rapid appreciation in housing prices, and many either bought larger homes or moved to
fancier areas within Columbia.[15]

Regional and national publications celebrated the new towns' pioneering spirit. In the *Washington Post*, Mary Strasburg noted in 1968 that
"no matter that Columbia's pioneers are not hewers of wood and drawers
of water, but drivers of station wagon and captives of outdoor Muzak.
These hardy 'natives' consider themselves on the threshold of a new era in
planned community living which they are helping to build."[16] An article by
Jeanne O'Neill in *American Home* described the pioneers she encountered
in Columbia in 1971: "Before you've spent one hour in Columbia, you
bump into the Concept. It's the idea of Columbia that sets everybody's face
aglow. This is a city of 'believers.' A young mother shopping for baby food
tells you, 'We came because we like what it stands for.' A graying insurance
executive explains that he took a drastic cut in salary to work in Columbia
because he 'believes' in it. A black junior high school vice-principal says,
'It's the answer to my problems and dreams.'" The optimism of Columbia's
early pioneers is striking indeed.[17]

It took longer, it appears, in Columbia than in Reston for the pioneering spirit to fade, but by the 1980s and 1990s, many people noted that
conditions had changed with the growing population and success of the
town. In a 1992 article on Columbia, one woman raised in a Columbia
neighborhood reflected that "the original residents' simultaneous arrival
inspired the interdependence of souls that Rouse envisioned for all. . . . As
pioneers move on though, many Columbia neighborhoods foster the cool,
nodding acquaintances that [Herbert] Gans and others foretold. . . . New
arrivals choose Columbia for its location, its safety, its trees, and give little
weight, or none, to the myths of the city's beginnings. Old-timers bemoan
this, calling for a return to the fire-in-the-belly pioneer days, when idealists
flocked here, despite the valid threat of the new town's failure, of being
stranded in a cluster of town houses, out among the moo-cows."[18] George
Martin, who arrived in 1967, remembered that in the early days "people
were accepted for who they were instead of what kind of car they drove or
where they lived or how they dressed, their family or background. It was a
place to grow, instead of just a place to live." The egalitarianism of the early

years is probably overstated in these remembrances; after all, Columbia residents were from the beginning divided into different levels of housing. Still, that many residents have felt a movement to greater stratification cannot be easily dismissed. The new-town rhetoric and pioneering spirit provided a common language in the early years that appears to have faded over time. Without this common language and feeling of shared adventure, many people of different classes probably did have less in common.[19]

Not all early arrivals to Columbia believed there was decline. Adele Levine, a leader in local politics and of the Columbia Forum, described one factor that may have played a role in the transformation of the town's spirit. She described not only a society more motivated by "consumerism and individualism" but a more complicated demographic shift in family life and work:

> It was easier for me to know what it meant to be a good neighbor when I moved to Columbia in 1971 than it is for me now. *Then* we were a street of young traditional families. Most women did not work outside the home. We welcomed each other with plates of cookies and included newcomers in our daily lives. In 1987, on this same street, the children are growing up, the neighborhood is almost deserted on weekdays, there are more non-traditional households than there are traditional two parent families, residents have less free time to participate in the life of the neighborhood, and somehow the plates of cookies no longer get delivered.[20]

People like Levine were not frustrated by this situation and used the Columbia Forum as an opportunity to re-invigorate that early sense of community. The liberal pioneers also played a central role, as at Reston, in establishing local institutions—including the Columbia birthday party, the *Columbia Flier,* and the Columbia Forum—that have played an important role in community development. Pioneers have helped attract many other liberals to the community and have been the ones defending the most liberal aspects of the town's mission. As at Reston, there is a new, younger group of residents moving into positions of power in Columbia, and only time will tell the degree to which they adopt or reject the vision so clearly put forth by the pioneers.

Columbians may have pioneered a liberal frontier, but the community's success can be read as much in its accommodation of more conservative residents. The democratic openness extended to those with whom the pioneers had little in common and thus offered the new-town experience to a more representative sample of America. This openness led to both a decline in some of the earlier ideals and to the fulfillment of the new town as a viable alternative to mainstream communities.

Irvine's Western Frontier

Most early residents of Irvine saw themselves as pioneers because they moved so far from the city and conveniences, lived in attached housing, and had settled in the middle of an active ranch operation. Of all the new-town residents, these pioneers came closest to experiencing actual frontier conditions, but only for a few years before shopping centers, schools, highways, and the university brought new residents and conveniences. One early resident remembered that "the fragrance of the orange groves was stronger than carbon monoxide. . . . A deer would come out of the groves occasionally and be frozen in the car lights." Another resident remembered that "crops separated north from south, and Turtle Rock was just a rock. These were the days when Farmer's Market was on real farmland, and Woodbridge didn't even have a lake to cross."[21] These early years produced a more open political society as well. Judy Liebeck remembered that in the 1970s, "there were no cliques. Anybody could run for office and, with a couple hundred votes, get in. You could start any club. It was theirs to mold."[22]

Some residents had a broader idea of the pioneer spirit. Gabrielle Pryor expressed views similar to those of her peers in other new towns. She explained that she had heard "there would be low-cost housing in the residential mix and that in the undeveloped area next to the campus, a craft village of artisans would be coming any day." Pryor remembered, "We were idealistic, but we didn't want to live poor. . . . We were pioneers."[23] She wanted "to help create a place where people will wish to stay for more than a year or two." She detailed the costs that came from too much social and geographic mobility: "That's so destructive to family life, it's damaging to children, and it really hurts the people who do it." She believed, however, that, "we're getting people in Irvine now who won't move for any reason and that pleases me. I think what people are trying to say is, hey—let's forget our possessions for a minute and think what it means to be alive, to be part of a family, to stay in one place, to help a neighbor." Pryor saw it as her goal "to make Irvine so attractive as a community and as a society—not just physical attractiveness, but as a decent place to live for all kinds of people—that they won't want to go anywhere else." She even noted, "I get very upset when someone leaves. I really think it's almost kind of traitorous."[24]

In 1980, Pryor looked back on the community's growth and admitted that "she's not altogether pleased with the way Irvine has been unfolding. When her family moved in, the community held the promise of being a true university community with an intellectual climate and liberal coloration to match." The article noted that "changing social patterns, however, have lent the city a more conservative hue built on the kind of affluence won by individuals." And so she even admitted that "she's thinking about moving. 'I'd be happier in a more heterogeneous community. I'm more liberal than the average Irvine resident. . . . If we move [however], there won't be as many people like us.'" Another pioneer raised in Irvine who returned to raise her family with her husband (also an Irvine native), observed that "I keep seeing more and more Mercedes. I wonder how long our Volkswagen will fit in." This couple had, unlike most Irvine residents, "made a conscious decision to limit our material expectations. But not our expectations for quality of life." They took advantage of the many low-cost or free resources in Irvine, including concerts, recreation programs and the bike trails even as the community became more affluent around them. Irvine has a more conservative reputation than Reston or Columbia, but the success (up to the present) of a number of liberal politicians like Gabrielle Pryor and Larry Agran indicates that Irvine is a more complicated place politically and socially than most observers realize.[25]

The pioneering spirit in all these communities faded fast, but it left a legacy of idealism. Pioneers have often been in the front line of battles to preserve new-town ideals and have created community institutions that preserved the democratic spirit. Still, the pioneer era rapidly passed as modern conveniences and more-traditional residents arrived. Like the communities of the frontier, the idealism or democratic spirit seemed muted as the communities became larger and richer. One can mourn this loss of community idealism, but many of these residents continued to lead their communities, and the new residents brought important ideas with them.

The growing pluralism can be seen as a healthy contribution to the creation of a viable suburban alternative. Had the pioneers made life uncomfortable for those with different ideals, the new towns would likely have failed to attract the hundreds of thousands of residents they now possess. Because the towns proved open to a more diverse population, including those with little interest in reform ideals, they have had greater influence both locally and nationally. Many Americans who might not have supported issues like affordable housing and racial integration often found themselves living near subsidized developments or black residents. Journalists and academics paid more attention to these communities because they continued to grow in popularity. That the new towns fell from perfection made them more compelling models for suburban reform.

Community Rituals in New Towns

American towns and cities have been blessed with a wide variety of community celebrations. Rituals, some brought by immigrants and adapted to American life, others developed within the nation's borders, have included a wide variety of parades and festivals that commemorate national, religious, and ethnic holidays.[26] Suburban subdivisions, however, faced a number of obstacles to the development of civic traditions. Not only was ethnic assimilation dominant during the period of suburban ascendance, but these new communities lacked an organizational structure that could mount community rituals. Most suburbs also lacked a corresponding civic vision that could inspire public events.

The new towns sought to bring back community rituals such as parades and festivals, and residents devoted significant energy to adapting traditions to suit new-town ideals. The most common form of festivity celebrated the community's achievements rather than those of any particular group. Other rituals focused on nonreligious national holidays like July Fourth. Many of these traditions persist, some have been replaced, and others have disappeared. In all, however, the new towns proved that suburbia could host community rituals of some originality and longevity.

Celebrating Reston

Reston developed a yearly public birthday party that gathered residents together and affirmed communal goals and ideals. It has been complemented by a series of popular holiday festivals in the town center. Reston also features neighborhood pool parties sponsored on a regular basis by the Reston Association, and individual clusters of townhomes often organize their own events. The community still values the civic celebrations that originally distinguished Reston from conventional subdivisions.

The RCA organized the first Reston Festival in 1968 to raise money and to illustrate its growing influence. The schedule for the festival included a children's parade to the plaza, designed to rouse "late sleepers Saturday Morning." RCA even arranged for the parade, "complete with drums, trumpets, noise, banners, to march through the paths of Reston converging on the Plaza for the opening ceremony at noon." At noon, many residents, some probably awakened by the parade, gathered in Lake Anne village center for a "Reston Town Portrait, (or can 1500 people fit on the Plaza?)." The festival featured a film, *The Four Seasons of Reston*, modern dance, arts exhibitions, folk songs, square dancing, and jazz. The day closed with a flourish when trumpeters from the shores of Lake Anne announced the arrival of "a decorated flotilla . . . gaily decorated and illuminated."[27]

Dick Hays, then RCA president, explained that the festival commemorated the original dedication of Reston by Simon. Simon, according to Hays, had hoped that "someday the community . . . the people of Reston . . . would choose to congregate annually in celebration of this dedication." Hays boasted that "this Festival is a product of the people of Reston. . . . We planned it and we will oversee its operation. Our goal is to commemorate the original dedication by assisting in developing and nurturing a community spirit and pride, a rededication, if you will, 'to provide a sense of place, not the anonymity prevalent in so much residential development today.'" This community leader understood the festival as a means both to entertain and to build community spirit.[28]

By 1970, RCA materials explained that "every Spring, to commemorate the founding of Reston, R.C.A. sponsors a two day festival featuring local and national dignitaries, entertainment, arts and crafts exhibits, amusement and other highlights."[29] On the eve of the festival, the editor of the *Reston Times* wanted "residents to encourage visitors to disregard signs for just one weekend and tour the place by shank's mare. The fact of exclusivisim is encouraged by barring visitors from our common lands."[30] The parade continued to be popular and included a growing number of Reston institutions and businesses. Simon attended the festival in 1972, and he attended later festivals, too. The festival in 1977 still included music, speeches, dancing, and plenty of drinking. In 1978, "people literally packed Lake Anne Plaza," where they found "games, music, clowns, food, and, most of all, other people." RCA used the event to introduce its officers and present a Restonian of the Year award.[31]

By 1982, the festival had nearly 5,000 attendees and included an enormous crab feast as well as other food and entertainment. By 1987, 8,000–10,000 people attended.[32] The festival had become too commercial for some residents: "We had rug merchants from Alexandria, people selling art, people selling stained glass and it turned into more sales than celebration."[33] RCA president Jack Gwynn explained in 1990 that not only did the festival lack local commercial participation, but "the Festival is not family-oriented and it's not representative of the community." In 1990, the emphasis turned to creating a more "tasteful celebration" that would be community oriented. Local school groups were invited to play music; craft booths were to be screened by a jury; and a beer garden was established to limit alcohol consumption to one area. The last festival, in 1995, was a small community celebration at a local park. By giving up its commercial aspects, the festival ultimately gave up its popularity. In a surprising renaissance, a renewed summer festival, organized by older residents and a new generation raised in Reston, attracted thousands back to Lake Anne in 1999 for live music, performers, children's activities, and food. A resident organizer from RCA explained that she remembered fondly the old days and "wanted to bring back the original feel that Reston had during the festival."[34]

The festival has been complemented with larger, urban-scale events. A holiday parade in the town center, beginning in 1990, has helped establish a new civic ritual. The parade, like the festival that preceded it, combined elements of big city and small town life. By 1993, thousands of people turned out for "a parade that featured Santa Claus, as well as more than fifty sections, including marching bands, cheerleaders, unicyclists, antique cars, a RIBS bus, Cub Scouts, Girl Scouts, [and] former Washington Redskin Tony McGee." In addition, local politicians appeared, Santa Claus arrived in a horse-drawn carriage, and in Fountain Square "at 6 p.m., after darkness fell, Santa appeared in front of Fountain Square's giant Christmas tree and asked everyone to hold hands and wish for happy holidays for all children. Lo and behold, the lights turned on."[35] The town center is also the site of Easter festivities, a Thanksgiving parade, an Octoberfest celebration, and a regional arts-and-crafts show.[36] The shift of most community rituals to town center reflects an aggressive effort on the part of the management to make it the heart of community celebrations. The town center is, in fact, well designed for these big events and parades, and residents seem to enjoy festivities that combine both community feeling with more traditional holiday symbolism.

Reston, then, does not lack for community rituals. Community residents demonstrated to the skeptical that suburbs could develop innovative civic events. The community birthday party may have temporarily faltered, but it has been complemented by a new set of celebrations better suited to the town's growing scale and diversity.

Columbia's Celebratory Spirit

Public-spirited celebrations began early in Columbia. Before Columbia existed, during construction of the Cross Keys development in Baltimore, Rouse had promised to build a community that would give "a spirit and feeling of neighborliness and a rich sense of belonging to a community."[37] As discussed earlier, planners at Columbia went to great trouble to design a communal environment. Planners also constructed residences around cul-de-sacs and grouped mailboxes together to encourage social interaction and neighborliness. Residents have, to a certain degree, picked up this neighborly spirit, particularly as reflected in community celebrations. Many community rituals also have developed out of Columbia's unique civic spirit.

Especially in the early years, there seem to have been numerous gatherings. An impromptu party, for instance, celebrated the completion of a pedestrian underpass. O'Neill described the party for the readers of *American Home* in 1970: "Last fall they gave an Underpass Party, to celebrate the newest link in a network of underpasses and pathways designed to keep the children off the streets. There were psychedelic lights, a bonfire, a rock band, hot dogs and beer. *IN* the underpass? Of course."[38] In Harper's Choice in 1975, the community sponsored a community-building event with a country fair theme.[39] During the summer of the tenth anniversary of Columbia, 1977, villages held a variety of festivals, and thousands of residents turned out for food, ceremonies, games, and music.[40]

Columbians seemed particularly adept at inventing their own community traditions. The *Newcomers Guide* of 1983–84 gave a good overview of the numerous events:

> As the city matures, the neighborhoods develop their own identities and their own traditions. For instance, residents of Longfellow organize their own Fourth of July parade each year. And then, there are the traditional summer block parties that take place all over town. . . . On one cul-de-sac there is an annual birthday party for all the neighborhood kids, and on another there is a Halloween party for the children. Neighbors mobilize neighbors around political issues, And often, entire cul-de-sacs get together to sponsor one huge garage or "carport sale."[41]

A 1986 article also praised the "village fairs, festivals and parties: From the Long Reach Village Fair to Hickory Ridge's Volunteer Appreciation

Night, to block parties (or 'circle' parties to be more accurate) all over town."[42] These events in the numerous villages changed from year to year, but it is fair to say that Columbia has not lacked for community celebrations, and residents use holidays and community anniversaries as excuses for festivities. A resident gave a description of what one Wilde Lake celebration felt like in the mid-1970s: "It was a very Columbia event. People sipping wine instead of lemonade. Babies abounding in the backpacks and snugglies." She noted that she and other residents "needed this face-to-face contact with the architects of our city [Rouse attended]. . . . As we stretched our necks to see the birthday children release their balloons . . . tears came to my eyes. Tears of gratitude and appreciation, because somehow I had known life could be better than it was B.C. [Before Columbia] and because I found Columbia in time to make it so."[43] Community rituals like these helped bridge the gap between the planners and the residents and helped remind residents of the special quality of their community.

Not only have there been numerous village and neighborhood events, but Columbia developed an annual Columbia birthday party. This party directly celebrated civic ideals and offered entertainment for the community. The 1970 event boasted movies, puppet shows, a community-wide picnic, dances, and a fair along the edges of the lake that included not only a Ferris wheel, but a German beer garden, folk dancing, and pony rides.[44] In photographs from the 1973 event, the sixth birthday, young people and teens of mixed races watch a jazz concert, and residents lounge under trees. Rouse usually attended these festivities, and there are many pictures of him cutting cake for residents—a symbolic action that reflected his humble nature and recapitulated the idea of the developer serving the residents.[45] The birthday parties have continued to the present, although they are now merged with the arts festival during June. Activities in 1997 included the cake cutting, a mural project with Gail Holliday, one of the early graphic designers for the community, and an exhibit on Columbia history. Tennenbaum appeared to sign his book *Creating a New City*, and local dancers and musicians performed by the lake.[46]

Columbia has also featured a popular July Fourth festival each year along the lakeshore, and thousands of residents usually attend. In a community with so much non-traditional activity, a July Fourth affair added a nice touch of small town intimacy and American traditionalism. One resident of Columbia, who had left to live for two years in Englewood, New

Jersey (where there was no July Fourth community celebration), reflected in 1985 on the meaning of the Columbia festival at the lakefront: "This fourth of July, we were right down there at the Lakefront watching the fireworks. It's easy to think that sort of thing doesn't mean much or is silly, but it's not. All these things give a sense of community." Although silly to some, the opportunity for socializing and community solidarity has meant a great deal to many residents.[47]

The July Fourth weekend is the time for the Longfellow neighborhood parade, a popular and irreverent celebration. The parade illustrates the good humor of the community, the high degree of civic awareness, and its conscious attempts to be simultaneously countercultural and traditional. Claire Lea, a resident who keeps an archive on the parade, described the parade's values: "Our underlying thing was to provide that small-town type of thing for our kids, but it grew to become an art of its own kind." Jon M. Files, one of the founders also explained that "we don't have any marching bands. If we're lucky, we may have a few instruments. . . . One year, we had so many people in the parade that there was nobody along the sides to watch it."[48]

The parade's unconventional appeal has been described many times in local publications: "The Longfellow Fourth of July is always good for a laugh—either their drill team buzzing Sears drills or their float with half-naked couples standing in bathtubs—'Save Water, Shower with a Friend,' their signs proclaimed."[49] Local politicians often came under fire. One year, a woman dressed as stick of dynamite destined for a controversial water tower in the community, and another anti–water tower costume mocked a county executive, Omar Jones: "the Friends of the 4th secured a weather balloon shaped like the controversial tower, painted it pink, and paraded it as 'Omar's Last Erection.'"[50] A 1990 parade included a front-end loader with a sign saying it was a "pooper-scooper" for cleaning up after the village meetings.[51] Some Columbians seem to take genuine pleasure in this offbeat community celebration with a serious civic purpose.

Columbia, then, has been particularly successful in nurturing rituals well adapted to community values. The birthday party celebrates the community itself, its achievements, and its leadership. The events in different villages have attempted to celebrate the individual spirit of each village and some of the alternative values that seemed to have blossomed in many of them. Like Reston, Columbia has developed civic events that appear to have genuine meaning for a number of residents.

Irvine's Harvest of Spirit

Festivals and parades have been features of Irvine life, too. Like Columbia and Reston residents, residents of Irvine have borrowed from older traditions and created their own to suit the local community. Irvine began to sponsor an elaborate July Fourth celebration in the early 1970s. In 1972, a celebration incorporated a giant American flag, a hot-air balloon, games and food, a steam engine that ran around the park, fireworks displays, and a community parade that lasted for more than an hour. The city still sponsors a July Fourth picnic and fireworks in Heritage Park.[52] One early resident explained that growing up in Irvine had helped make him patriotic: "Our Independence Days always felt a step purer amid a national climate of declining patriotism (I didn't word it that way as a child, but I got the idea). Maybe it was the proximity of the Marine Base, or perhaps the general sentiment that did it, but the Fourth of July was always grand. When Sousa blared and fireworks boomed in the skies above Heritage Park, the unanimous reverence of the crowds etched in me a love of God and country. Irvine helped make it real."[53]

Some villages had their own festivities, too. During the 1970s, community "associations are literally turning them away at mid-summer luaus, Memorial Day celebrations and other events." According to *New Worlds* in 1973, these rituals had a purpose: "Such activities are a throwback to pre-mobile-society America. And they're a partial answer to the notion that a neighbor is someone you wish you'd gotten to know before he moved away."[54] One article announced that children on "big wheels lead the parade at Woodbridge's July 4th celebration."[55] The parade in 1979 included a parade of five hundred decorated trikes and bikes as well as a treasure hunt, games, picnic, Dixieland band, disco dance, free flags, lemonade and popcorn, and a gigantic fireworks display.[56]

Irvine developed its own unique community festival. In the early years Irvine became the site of a festival entitled "Irvine Is . . ." that incorporated arts, crafts, games, music, and theatrical performances. According to *New Worlds*, "the Irvine festival was an affirmation of the community-participation life-style that flourishes under these sunny skies." Journalists working for the Irvine Company thus celebrated the participatory orientation of the residents of Irvine.[57] The Harvest Festival replaced "Irvine Is . . ." in the 1970s.

The Harvest Festival, as its name implied, took place in harvested fields on the Irvine Ranch. The festival featured in 1975 a Harvest Moon Ball on Friday night, and booths during the weekend with food, activities ("dunking . . . throwing pies . . . pitching pennies, hayriding" and so forth), and goods for sale.[58] Another year, 1976, brought symphony music, a western barbecue, and a Sunday breakfast and interfaith church service, as well as a full-scale junior rodeo.[59] In 1981, the *Irvine World News* noted that "it's Harvest Festival Time again . . . our once-a-year community bash; the biggest civic party for miles and miles around." They predicted that thousands would attend as usual.[60]

The Irvine Harvest Festival continues to be popular and features pumpkin carving, craft displays, home baked goods, and live entertainment, and it serves as a fund-raiser for local nonprofits. One longtime resident explained that the Harvest Festival "was a kind of annual affirmation that Irvine was 'Our Town' and not 'Our Metropolis.' You'd see people you knew and booths from groups you knew. And you'd eat food that wasn't imported or microwaved."[61] The festival is announced with five hundred blue-and-white signs posted on parkway crossings and empty lots.[62] A pair of scholars who studied other Orange County festivities noted that the festival "is billed as a 'home-grown fair' and attempts to re-create older festive occasions by bringing together the local population for informal socializing." In recent years, the Harvest Festival has reflected the growing multiculturalism of Irvine. The 1995 festival not only provided carnival rides and game booths, but international foods and musical troupes representing China, Scandinavia, Ukraine, Poland, India, Latin America, and Mexico. The 1997 festival featured offerings like country music and rock-and-roll alongside the Tyagga Folk Dance Philippino-American troupe.[63]

The new towns pioneered a wide variety of events that adapted older traditions (such as July Fourth) and transcended older categories with entirely new kinds of events: the Reston Festival and holiday parade, the Columbia birthday party, the Longfellow parade and the Harvest Festival. That these events, for the most part, have continued reflects the need many residents have for community rituals and the possibility of creating new ones in communities where there are high degrees of social diversity and geographic mobility. Not everyone in these towns attends or even likes these events. That they exist for those residents of suburbia who want them is perhaps most significant.

Benevolent Paternalism

New towns inadvertently became test communities for corporate penetration of local, middle-class, civic culture in modern America. Corporations had played an important role in national economic, political, and cultural life but had played a less-direct role in local communal life. High-ranking officers from the corporate world dominated local social and political affairs, but (except in the case of paternalist developments) they usually did not directly represent their corporation or its goals. In the new towns, however, a single corporation set the standard for planning, designing, and maintaining the community over time; contributed social and political leadership; determined initial governmental forms; and established many cultural, educational, commercial, and recreational institutions, maintaining a strong role in the community after development was well established. These communities looked much more like nineteenth-century paternalist communities for a largely blue-collar population than like traditional middle-class planned suburbs.[64]

Long-term developer interaction in the local community arose partly by accident and partly through necessity. Suburban developers of the past, working on smaller parcels of land, maintained only a brief period of construction and sales. The scale of new towns, however—ranging from 7,000 acres (at Reston) to nearly 100,000 acres (at Irvine)—lengthened the construction phase. Even after thirty years, construction is still under way. Many middle-class residents inadvertently found themselves living in more paternalistic communities than they wanted simply because companies had a long-term stake in local construction and land sales.

As discussed earlier, quite a few residents complained in local newspapers about excessive corporate control and created their own institutions to counter the developer or provide for community needs. The story of paternalism in new towns, however, is not a story of conflict but a balancing of institutions and goals among competing interests. Most remarkable, perhaps, is that developers such as Simon, Rouse, and Watson became community leaders as well as businessmen, and their influence lasted long after their actual control of the community had ended. Many residents and many developers, in fact, saw the paternalistic role of developers in a more positive light. It turned out that corporate developers could participate extensively in civic life, as long as they did not appear to be seeking to dominate the community. Many residents, in fact, were attracted to the higher level of community control exercised by what they perceived as a responsible, honest, cultured authority.

New towns have been enormous construction projects, incorporating billions of dollars of investment and radically altering the landscape. To have a human face directing such an enormous undertaking made a difference to many residents. Developers worked hard to cultivate a paternal image on the model of a likable urban mayor and made appearances at events where they invoked new-town ideals. Developers also avoided public heavy-handedness by never trying to stop the development of any community organization, even those established to criticize or monitor the developer. Because of their adroit management, optimism, and genial manners, many developers took on the role of civic leaders, a role that elected leaders had generally assumed in urban communities and a figure absent in most suburban communities.

RESton=R.obert E. S.imon+ton

Few people in Reston realize that their community's name derives from the founder's three initials. Many more know Simon as a local community activist, dedicated to preserving the new town vision. Even during the three decades when he did not live in Reston, he remained an admired and influential figure. Simon's position in Reston's civic life has transcended his role as initial developer.

The degree to which Simon had become a welcome and important part of the community became evident when Gulf Reston fired him in 1967 as the project neared bankruptcy. Mrs. Karl Ingebritsen, an early resident, explained that "there is a sense of loss and a feeling of anxiety in Reston this fall. Mr. Simon is greatly missed, with his fine taste, charm, and perhaps above all an imaginative, innovative plan for the town. To a considerable extent his commitment fired and was the measure of our own. For the sake of all of us I hope he will continue to exert an influence on Reston's development."[65] Not only did some residents burn their Gulf credit cards,[66] but the community gathered in the fall of 1967 at the Reston Festival to honor him:

> Mr. Simon, accompanied by Mrs. Simon, stood silent as the Plaza resounded with applause for him. . . . Admiral Lyle [an early resident] summed up the crowd's feeling when he said, "the festival is a demonstration of our affection for and faith in Reston and the Reston way of life . . . and in some way [we] want to thank Bob for it. . . . So all the Reston types, with all their enthusiasms for all the things that Reston represents are

gathered here today to say to Bob Simon: for your vision, for your courage, for your perseverance, for your uncompromising integrity and for Reston as it stands today, the products of all these qualities, we thank you and bless you."

It is hard to imagine many developers being so honored by their communities.[67]

The leaders of the later development companies established cordial relations but did not see themselves as community leaders. Simon, however, never completely lost touch with Reston, was a regular visitor to town, and attended the Reston festivals. Occasional letters by Simon appeared in the local newspapers, too. In 1978, for instance, he wrote a letter responding to an article in a local paper that accused him of having wanting to establish a "monopoly" on services in Reston. He countered that he had in fact set up a number of cluster associations that could determine for themselves how they wanted to structure maintenance. In the article, he claimed that he wanted to "shed the monopolist robe" in which he had been cast by the writer.[68] In 1979, he appeared at the dedication of the Reston Community Center and gave an interview on local cable television in which he gave his ideas on Reston's future.[69] In 1987, he sent a letter, published in the local paper, to the family that pushed Reston over the 50,000 population mark. In the letter he addressed himself primarily to the daughter of the new residents. He fantasized that "she will be the connecting link between me and her great grandchildren and their friends who will be living in Reston in 2064, 100 years from the time when the first residents and first office workers moved into Reston." He hoped that Reston of 2064 would "be a place where all sorts of people can grow up, mature and age gracefully" as well as "find opportunities for stretching their minds and bodies to the full."[70] In 1990, on one of the visits he made a "couple times a year," Simon was described in terms that reflected his role: "He is the very persona of a community patriarch, in looks and actions. . . . It is the eyes that strike you at first glance. They are dark, humbling eyes, full of ingenious youth. These are the eyes that envisioned the buildings Restonians work in, the playgrounds your children play in, the homes you live in, and the paths you walk on."[71]

In 1993, at the age of seventy-nine, Simon returned to live in Reston and took an apartment at the top of Heron House in Lake Anne village. Local papers made much of the return of the "father" of the community and reviewed his accomplishments. A reporter from the *Reston Times* followed him as he ambled about the community and admired some older sculptures and details.[72] Another article described Simon as saying he looked forward to being "within walking distance of many of his friends. He'll also be steps away from Lake Anne Plaza's stores, restaurants and services—permitting him to enjoy the pedestrian oriented conveniences he built into the master plan for Reston." He was also described joining "a table of late morning kibitzers" at a local grill. Jane Wilhelm, the first community-relations director and a Reston resident since 1987, noted, "I find it very fitting that the founder of Reston will live at the highest point in Reston." She added his apartment had a "270 degree view of Reston."[73]

Since 1993, Simon has been "a public relations machine." He was the host of a half-hour cable television show, wrote a column for the *Reston Times,* and frequently had letters published in local papers. Simon became a community activist in Reston, and his activities included "opposing development of the Spectrum retail center in the Town Center District, supporting the creation of a public-supported community arts center at Lake Anne," fighting funding cuts by Reston Association for Lake Anne maintenance, and serving on the association's board of directors.[74] He constantly exhorted the community to improve education, open space, and planning.[75]

Simon, a whirlwind of energy, also became an annoyance to some community leaders, many of whom did not hesitate to criticize him. Ivan Cole explained in an interview that he considered Simon an impediment to the full development of Reston, because Simon did not understand the ways the community has changed over time.[76] Other residents respect Simon as a genius but feel that they benefited from having had to organize themselves. They are convinced that this organizing not only helped preserve the new-town plan but brought them friendships and a sense of community. Still, Reston would be a very different and less interesting place if Simon had decided to abdicate the role of community patriarch.

None of the succeeding developers attained Simon's level of influence, but one figure did earn Reston's affection: Embry Rucker. Jane Wilhelm was concerned about Reston's future after the loss of the original development team. She recalled, however, that in 1969, "I saw this new person standing at the head of Lake Anne just kind of gazing into space." That person turned out to be Rucker. She remembered, "I talked to (Rucker) for about 10 minutes and I knew right away that I didn't need to worry anymore. The community of Reston was in good hands." Simon also recalled that Rucker "stepped into a vacuum and filled it. Gulf was there for the money and so was Mobil—Rucker was there for the people."[77] Rucker, like Simon, had spent much of his life in business and even successfully mass produced furniture at one point. In the 1950s, however, he decided to become an Episcopal priest. "For Rucker, bearing witness to Christ meant getting totally involved in the community."[78]

Rucker, with many others, helped found the Common Ground Coffee House (which served as a social meeting place), FISH (Friendly Instant Sympathetic Help), local bus service, a child care center, a nursing service, an employment service, teen and counseling programs, a homeless shelter in Reston town center, and public housing initiatives. In 1970, he was voted Man of the Year by the *Reston Times,* which cited his "do, don't talk" philosophy. According to the article, "because of his willingness to try (almost anything) Rucker appears to be a universal source of advice and an inexhaustible fountain of encouragement for anything that will fill a need."[79] The *Times* also praised his combination of a pragmatic attitude and idealism. This attitude did not fade. In 1981, for instance, when Lake Anne village's supermarket closed, "he and his companion, Priscilla Ames, quickly marshaled a group of volunteers and opened a small food store that provided milk, bread and other basics and stayed in business until a new supermarket was started." Reston mourned Rucker's passing in 1994.[80]

Restonians have been lucky, then, in having honorable public figures who have helped give direction to their community. Simon began as a businessman and enlightened developer, became something of a legend and exiled hero, and now has become a sometimes controversial community leader. Rucker, who fostered many of the social innovations of Reston, also acted as a unifying force for the community, particularly after Simon's banishment. These individuals helped establish a vibrant civic life and added some personality to Reston.

Columbia's People Man

> I find I don't feel all the things people attribute to me or want me to feel. I always feel concern about the credits people attribute to me—I chalk it up to the human desire to personalize things.
>
> JAMES ROUSE, in *Columbia Times*

Columbia residents could have done worse than give credit to Rouse, because adulation and wealth never seems to have gone to his head. Padraic Kennedy recounted an amusing and revealing story of Rouse's modesty:

> Kennedy once tagged along on a driving tour Rouse gave David Rockefeller, head of Chase Manhattan Bank. Rouse, an

erratic driver, was enthusing over Longfellow Elementary School when he ran a stop sign, Kennedy said. "Rockefeller slid down in his seat and mumbled something about the police."

The officer handed Rouse a fifty dollar ticket, causing Rockefeller to quip that Rouse obviously lacked influence in Columbia.

"Rouse loved it," said Kennedy. "It showed that Columbia worked."[81]

Indeed, Rouse combined a remarkable financial touch with a humility, public-spiritedness, and gentleness that have been extremely rare in American public life. For all these qualities he became a much loved and respected person in Columbia, and he seemed genuinely to enjoy playing the loving father figure to the community. At the same time, because he was such a dominant personality and because so much more was done for inhabitants of Columbia than was done at Reston, Columbia does not seem to have felt a comparable sense of resident leadership. By providing everything—high-quality development, rapid growth, and community leadership—Rouse may have succeeded too well. Still, most communities never have a figure like Rouse to look back on, and he provides a wonderful founding mythology that is alive and well. He also sustained the legitimacy of the new-town project in the first decades when, out of necessity, developer control had to be stronger and residents reacted bitterly against their powerlessness.

Some journalists picked up the scent of this benevolent paternalism quite early in Columbia's history. As early as 1964, J. W. Anderson in *Harpers* saw the necessity of paternalistic control in developing a place such as Columbia and the problems it might bring. Anderson realized, as did the developer, that many residents might reject the ideas for apartments and commerce in the midst of Columbia. He predicted that "no one can doubt that thousands of families will come to live in the new houses. But whether they will come to sustain its values and carry out its high moral purpose is quite another matter. Rouse is now in the position of a painter who knows that his dealers can sell whatever he produces, but who is personally concerned about the history of art and his place in it." Anderson ended on an optimistic note, pointing out that "perhaps the only man who can lead [this new departure in community building] is this new aristocrat with his massive holdings, his institutional backers, his staffs of planners and scholars, and his consuming interest in the art of creating the good city."[82] In *American Home* of 1970, O'Neill explained that Columbia should be called "Rousetown or Jamestown II" after Rouse. She gave a particularly good description of how paternalism functioned in Columbia: "'You know,' confided a vivacious 'Villager'-garbed guide in the Exhibit Center, 'Mr. Rouse doesn't have employees—he has disciples.' The others are just on his bandwagon. Surely Columbia has problems. It's new-house owners gripe as much as any other new-house owners. But if the plaster peels or the doors stick, people blame the builder. Nobody blames Jim Rouse. That would be like blaming Columbia—and *nobody* is mad at Columbia."[83] Rouse appeared at Columbia birthday parties, at the local supermarket and village center, and seems to have been a genuinely affable man. A 1972 address to a small audience featured his understated approach, and according to an article that described the speech, "the homespun orator managed to create an atmosphere and enthusiasm far exceeding his self-effacing description." Rouse affirmed, as he always did, that Columbia would be a place for all ages and professions and that "the city affords the opportunities for the 'deep relationships' denied in large metropolitan areas and isolated suburbs." According to Rouse, "we are living out a new way of relating to one another. This offers us the opportunity and responsibility to fashion what American society can really be. We deserve more for ourselves than the old habits and patterns." The article described how Rouse took questions from the audience after reviewing the state of Columbia: "His patience and equanimity in the face of complaints was rewarded by one resident's observation, widely applauded by all present, that Columbia was a success because the developer had the 'guts, brass, love and hard-headedness to make it work.'"[84]

Rouse did not shy from airing his personal opinions in the community either. He printed a Christmas greeting in the *Columbia Flier* of 1970 that reflected his willingness to advertise his own strong religious convictions: "The call was sounded thousands of years ago by the prophets of the Old Testament. It was reinforced at the first Christmas. It rings in our ears today: 'Love the Lord Our God with all your heart, with all your soul, with all your mind—and love your neighbor as yourself.' Merry Christmas!" This message reflected both his spirituality and his communal idealism, qualities that attracted many residents to Columbia.[85]

A meeting of the CA executive council during the early 1970s also reflects Rouse's tolerance, particularly as it related to teenagers. Rouse generally seemed more tolerant than many of Columbia's residents. After complaints about rock concerts at Merriweather Post Pavilion, the developer was asked to take action:

On the question of future regulation of programs at the Merriweather Post Pavilion, such as the recent performance of "The Doors," which caused much resentment among residents because of the allegedly unsavory character and quality of the entertainers, no one present at the meeting had actually attended the performance. Mr. Rouse said he felt the publicity in the local newspapers, criticizing the performance, was exaggerated. He said his son attended the Doors' show and did not find it objectionable. Mr. Rouse stated that he and the developer's staff are very much aware of the feelings of Wilde Lake residents about future bookings at the Pavilion, and that action will be taken to insure that these performances are in good taste and not of an immoral or objectionable nature.[86]

A similar incident—a community meeting on young people, drugs, and disorderly behavior—was described by Wolf Von Eckardt in the *Saturday Review* of 1971. During the meeting "a woman spoke up and told Rouse rather emotionally that he must consider the reputation of his town and throw the freaks out. Applause." Eckardt noted that Rouse sympathized with the woman, but "said he hoped the lady did not mean to suggest that the problem be swept under the rug. There must be a more creative answer. The hippies, he added, 'may be saying something that we should hear.' He got far more applause than the woman."[87]

Rouse began his adult life as a Republican, but he had a good dose of the counterculturalist in him that grew with time. Dan Beyers, a reporter for the *Washington Post*, described how people in Columbia did not worry about the innovations in Columbia because "the plan was the brainstorm of James W. Rouse, a mortgage banker-turned-visionary who drove around town in a tiny yellow electric car and wrote open letters to President Nixon calling for an end to the Vietnam War."[88] Not only did he print protests against the Vietnam War, but one reporter found him "participating in a 'communications workshop'" in Columbia in 1972. The reporter wondered whether "this earnest, slightly rumpled, balding 58-year old man could be the big, big money boss who testifies before congressional committees." She gives this vivid description of his willingness to engage in some fairly unconventional community activities: "He and his wife are with a group of 200 persons, mostly Columbians in jeans and bells, divided into groups of three, going through exercises in which they assume different roles (the placater, the blamer, the super reasonable, the distracted person) as they pretend to go to the beach or perform common activities."[89]

In 1982, Rouse stated his commitment to open-ended debate: "'you can even damn the developer in Columbia as many others have . . . and the developer will like you, too.'"[90] He was not overstating the case.

Residents came into contact with Rouse not only at public events but through local newspapers and national magazines. Rouse did not avoid publicity and during the thirty years of Columbia's development was interviewed in publications as diverse as the *New York Times,* the *Columbia Flier,* and *Look.* Most reporters wrote favorable reports on Rouse, seeing him as both a dynamic businessman and an earnest urban visionary. Local papers and magazines contributed to the development of Rouse's image. In 1974, Moon reflected on Rouse's tight connection to the community:

> Sitting in James Rouse's office, one cannot help but reflect on how much the new city bears the personal imprint of one man. . . . He is Columbia, its commitments, expectations and disappointments. Rouse, who just celebrated his sixtieth birthday, is that rarity in contemporary culture—an individual who has lived to see his visions become reality. A businessman with a social awareness, dedicated to improving the quality of American life and circumventing technocratic inroads on human dignity, Rouse had the money and power to initiate change. And, he used it. It is not surprising that Rouse is sensitive to criticism of his brain child. One does not expect parents to be objective about their offspring.

Moon had her own reservations about Columbia's commitment to social justice, but she explained that Rouse pointed with pride to the community's racial openness and community vitality as reflected in "community conflicts, volunteer efforts, city governance and plethora of organizations."[91]

Community magazines also promoted Rouse's paternal image. A boy featured in *Columbia Today* of 1970 drew his impression of the new city. It included two hands, with cufflinks and jacket sleeves, holding a small globe on which were houses, people, and parks. He described his work in a revealing sentence: "The hands are Mr. Rouse's." From a child's perspective at least, Rouse had the whole world in his hands.[92] *Columbia Magazine* also helped cultivate Rouse's paternal image. The editors one year selected Rouse as one of Columbia's "favorite things."[93]

To outsiders, the extent of Rouse's popularity has sometimes seemed a little bewildering, even unbelievable. But Rouse successfully completed a multi-billion-dollar project with no visible corruption or compromise, and throughout his life he gave away enormous sums to good causes. After retiring in 1980, for example, he established the Enterprise Foundation, an organization that has been a leader in the national fight to improve and construct affordable housing (with billions of dollars now invested). Most residents understood that James Rouse made an excellent community leader.

When Rouse died in 1996, the full extent of his paternal influence in Columbia became apparent. In Columbia, a funeral service was "held in the open-air Merriweather Post Pavilion" and was "attended by about 2,500 people."[94] Rouse, always a stickler for detail, had scripted his own funeral service: "Leaving little to chance, Rouse had left specific handwritten instructions to his family about how to organize his last good-bye. . . . He was a planner, after all." A positive thinker even in death, he explained to his dearly departed, "I've just left on a trip to my next life. . . . Make this an opportunity for happy memory-sharing." Martin Siegel, who at times argued with Rouse, felt that "one of Rouse's 'great legacies' . . . was his belief 'that we do not have to agree but we can all respect one another.'" The *Columbia Flier*, a week later, embroidered on these descriptions, beginning with a vision that Rouse himself would have appreciated: "On Friday afternoon, as the famous people on stage at Merriweather Post Pavilion spoke eloquently about James Rouse, his ideals were embodied in two boys. One white, one black, the youths had wandered off to the side of the hall to play together in a shaft of sunlight." The article noted in particular the popular affection for the man: "Rouse's dreams were made manifest in the thousands of ordinary people who turned out to honor him at a celebration of his life last week. Neighbors came in groups, senior citizens car-pooled to the service because they loved the man."[95]

It is unlikely that Columbia will ever produce another figure like Rouse, but he has left behind a rich legacy of ideas, images, and institutions. He demonstrated that the real estate developer need not remain a cold businessman concerned only with the bottom line. The vision he cultivated and the image he created of a new kind of leader give Columbia a unique heritage after only thirty years.

Family Men on the Irvine Ranch

Reston and Columbia activists identified strongly with Simon and Rouse, who provided community myths and a human side to development, but the Irvine situation is more complex. Most Irvine Company presidents, although respected by many in the community, have been private individuals who showed less interest in being paternal figures. Residents in Irvine have also disagreed more with the developers than those in Reston or Columbia: In Irvine, there never has been one plan, as in Reston and Columbia, on which both developer and residents agree.

Organizations such as Irvine Tomorrow have complained about the Irvine Company and its leaders, but it would be a mistake to believe that most residents do not at least respect the company and its officials for the care they have shown in developing the community. As one resident grudgingly admitted, "We complained when houses took the place of orange groves. We grumbled when streets were widened and more shopping centers were built. But now, we will cherish the memories of exploring new parks that sprang up with the development of each new tract of homes."[96] Another longtime resident admitted that "we like the neighborhoods, the schools, [and] the Irvine Company's good planning."[97] Even Louis Fridhandler, long an opponent of the Irvine Company, acknowledges that although he does not think much of recent company planning, he liked the combination of schools and parks in his neighborhood, University Park (constructed in the 1960s).[98] Many residents, after all, paid more for the reputed high quality of development. Ray Watson expressed his opinion that to be successful in Irvine electoral politics, a candidate has to "run" against the company, yet a survey of residents by the company found that they trusted the planning abilities of the Irvine Company more than the city and county government.[99]

The company made some early attempts to humanize leadership through public-relations materials they distributed. Through a *New Worlds* interview, residents met William Mason, the president of the company who began large-scale residential development during the 1960s and 1970s. Mason had made himself unpopular in Irvine by fighting a battle over the preservation of open space in Upper Newport Bay. One article in *New Worlds* made it clear that Mason was not an irresponsible man. On the contrary, the article argued that he was worthy of respect. They learned that Mason "neither smokes, nor drinks, limits his swearing to a soft 'damn' . . . and spends most of his free time working on youth programs." Mason explained his development philosophy, which also appeared rather moderate: "People look at our hills, our shoreline properties, our orange groves, our bayfront and island properties, with a special proprietary interest. Long ago I faced up to this public concern and our corporate goal of creating a better place for man, the size and scope of our operations, would continue to put us in the middle of issues that stir emotions on every side."[100]

Mason died suddenly in 1973.[101] Watson, who replaced Mason, proved more popular and cultivated a more flexible style of leadership. A younger man than Mason and a graduate of the University of California at Berkeley, he better understood the zeitgeist, and he used it to his and the company's advantage. *New Worlds* described his attempt to humanize Irvine Company leadership during the 1970s: "Raymond Watson stood in the crowded multi-purpose room at University High School and applauded along with the citizens of Irvine. A spokesman named Art Anthony had just completed an attack on the company's plan for a new project. 'You're not supposed to applaud,' chided a company staff member. 'Sure I am, this is real democracy in action, with each of us respecting the other's role.'"[102] Watson made every effort to appear as flexible as possible while pursuing the goals of the corporation. In public relations materials he explained, "I see our place in society and in this community as that of a responsible corporation with a strong sense of mission, but never to the point of not listening or yielding to better ideas. That's the public image I hope we have." He believed in working "with regulating agencies, not against them" and accommodating the "public's concern about unregulated growth." In fact, much of his tenure as president did reflect his willingness to work with residents rather than against them. He expected his opponents to meet him halfway, however: "Rigidity won't work. Flexibility within the framework of what's reasonable will. That goes for the conservationists too."[103]

One of Watson's opponents, an environmentalist named Judy Rosener, acknowledged his integrity in 1996, reflecting on her past disagreements with him: "We disagreed greatly on development of the [Newport] Back Bay, but we've disagreed agreeably. He's a really socially conscious guy who cares about the area and the community." Another friend noted, "I've talked to some people who are wild-eyed liberal environmentalists, and they'll stop complaining about the Irvine Company in midsentence to say something nice about Ray Watson." Gabrielle Pryor also believes that Watson helped fulfill the dream of a more diverse community. She recalled that after residents objected to the creation of affordable housing in the early years of development, Watson still found a way to integrate lower-cost dwellings with the help of the city government: "Watson really did believe in democracy. He also believed in Pereira's original conception of the city. Watson's solution to the city's dilemma over low-income housing was to put it in first when developing future villages. That way, no villager could object."[104]

Residents learned through company public relations that Watson is a "family man," although he shied away from taking on the role of a community paternal figure. Residents saw photographs of him with his family and in the community, and learned that he loved camping. In most major interviews, Watson, like Rouse and Simon, was seen to maintain a modest home life, in tune with his modest background. He has "lived in the same Newport Beach tract house for 32 years—in the Irvine Co. development of East Bluff."[105] Corporate papers rendered him as a kind of Irvine everyman that residents could respect and trust.[106] Watson served as president until 1977, when the company was sold to an outside group of investors, including Bren. Watson went on to develop his own company, but he rejoined the Irvine Company board of directors in the 1980s as part of Bren's team, in large measure to restore the company's reputation for responsible development.

Since 1983, the ranch has been under the near complete control of Bren, who is a very different kind of developer from Watson, Mason, Simon, and Rouse. These other developers made an effort to be accessible leaders of the community, figures who might possess money and power in abundance but for whom money and power were secondary to building a better community. Bren did not have the same approach and was reticent about taking on a prominent public role.

Bren is the son of Milton Bren, the producer of the "Topper" films, and the actress Claire Trevor. He grew up in an elite and cosmopolitan atmosphere that has played a significant role in shaping his sense of community. For him, community is high society, in a way that it is not for the other developers. One of the highlights of Bren's teenage years was his participation with his father in the Newport to Ensanada International Yacht Race. He was charmed by Mexico's "rustic beauty, its charm and its warm, lively people." Bren also reflected on how sailing shaped his view of community: "As I reflect on that experience, it occurs to me just how much sailing has been a glue that helped mold our community and that has helped keep it together for so many years. It is deep in the spirit and soul of Newport Beach—a major part of our history and character."[107] Bren's Newport Beach world is quite distant from the rest of the City of Irvine, which lacks access to the boating world.

Bren had some embarrassing moments in the 1980s and 1990s, as communities and residents protested his massive building program for the ranch. Times have changed, however, and Bren is showing he can gain the upper hand in public relations. A society reporter for the *Orange County Register* chided Bren for his aristocratic distance at a fund-raiser for the University of California at Irvine in 1998: "So Sir, why is it so rare you come out to play among your adoring philanthropic subjects? 'I get out more than you think,' Bren quipped."[108] Indeed, in recent years Bren has raised his profile. He decided, for instance, as early as 1983, that he "wanted a project that he could build, not litigate" along the Newport Coast areas of the ranch. Over the course of twenty years the scale of development had shrunk from 50,000 single-family homes, to 2,600, with two office towers. Environmentalists challenged even this small number, and Bren agreed in 1988 to eliminate the office towers, add "two golf courses . . . and place homes in tighter clusters to allow more room for habitat. Executives agreed to set aside three sensitive canyons and impose new policies to protect native plants and animals. In all, 75 percent of the Newport Coast would remain open." This plan was approved and Newport Coast is being developed at a rapid pace.[109]

The Newport Coast development was part of a larger agreement from the 1980s that Bren made with governments and environmentalists in the area. As discussed earlier, nearly 30,000 acres will be preserved on the ranch in exchange for rights to build more densely in other areas—this is the Open Space Reserve system. Bren has used the creation of the Open Space Reserve as a means to diffuse the criticism that extended across the political spectrum in many communities both within and adjoining the ranch. In a 1992 article, Bren explained that "there's been an increasing focus on (preservation) in the last four, five years. . . . My thrust has been to bring about a balance between man and nature."[110] He has also endowed an environmental science and management graduate program at several University of California campuses, including UCI, and ten chairs at UCI, particularly in the biomedical sciences, part of his hope to nurture Irvine as Silicon Valley South.[111]

Bren, like Watson and the other new-town leaders, now provides civic leadership to the community. Although not as liberal as other developers in new towns, he is involved with the community and is demonstrating to the residents the importance of social prominence, compromise, and business acumen. Bren is, in short, an excellent leader of an upper-class California community.

❖

Civic life has developed in a complicated fashion in these new towns. Early residents developed a sense of solidarity, only to feel it dissolve in later years. Residents created community rituals, many of which became popular and enduring events while others faltered. Paternal figures mostly from the development corporations have provided civic leadership for mammoth building programs but have also sometimes been controversial community members. The addition of civic character to new towns has not been without its challenges.

Many residents of these communities have known little about the activities or personalities discussed in this chapter, but many others appreciated the lively civic activities. The suburban individuals who wanted a strong sense of adventure, community, civic spirit, and even community guidance—like that they imagined in small towns or urban neighborhoods—found these qualities in Reston, Columbia, and Irvine. The new towns, then, served as one of the most important experiments in shaping a new American civic spirit in suburbia. Even in the face of rapid growth, social and geographic mobility, and increasing ethnic diversity, the new towns created institutions and efforts that brought the residents together and gave a sense of place and community. This unique political culture widened the gap between these new towns and conventional subdivisions.

PART 4

Suburban Social and Cultural Innovation

◆

8

The Shame of the Suburbs: Reforming Suburban Social Homogeneity

> A city is physically created, more or less, expensive and cheap housing intermixed with shops and community activity centers, and people from different backgrounds—not necessarily urban at all—are encouraged to move in. The idea is that a city lifestyle can be imposed on anyone not hopelessly addicted to the economic and racial segregation of suburbia.
>
> MICHAEL KERNAN, *The Washington Post*

New-town reformers, as Michael Kernan observed, hoped that new suburbs could be designed from the start to be socially inclusive. Most conventional suburbs restricted the variety of housing types and residents in the hopes of guaranteeing social stability. Growing on the edge of many American cities were endless housing tracts of single-family homes filled with white middle-class families. Mired in older urban neighborhoods were racially and socially heterogeneous populations, cut off from the resources lavished on the new suburbs.

Most of the American middle class during the last two centuries has pursued social exclusivity, but a renegade portion of that same class has valued social justice and ethnic diversity. Settlement workers and Progressives, participants in New Deal efforts, civil-rights activists, and 1960s student activists have shared a commitment to questioning the status quo and aiding the disadvantaged. Many middle-class liberals from this

153

tradition gathered in the new towns and helped to build a more socially equitable suburb.

Spurring on the liberal search for more diverse suburban communities was the urban violence of the 1960s, including race riots, that frightened many middle-class liberals. Precipitous urban decline, in no way mitigated by urban renewal policies, highlighted the need for genuine suburban reform. The new-town reformers believed that they could mitigate or relieve the urban crisis and slow the pattern of middle-class "flight" in American cities by helping to create more diverse suburban communities.

The Suburban Social Critique in the New Towns

The suburban social critique assumed a unique form in the new towns. According to their residents, communities worked best when people of different classes, races, ages, and religions (reflecting the diversity of American life in general) lived in close proximity. The interaction brought on by residential propinquity served an educational and cultural function. People's horizons broadened and they could feel satisfied that their community was not contributing to social injustice in the nation as a whole. Although many new-town residents came to question this belief in the course of community development, it nevertheless constituted the overarching social philosophy of the new-town movement.

Simon sought to create a suburb with urban characteristics. A 1972 article on Reston revealed that "the original residents attracted by the Simon concept were not typical suburbanites. They were, if anything, anti-suburb, traveling further from Washington and paying more to live in a unique community." Simon remembered "that 20 of the original town houses in Reston were bought by single people at a time when suburbia was almost exclusively made up of married couples." Indeed, the early residents seemed committed to a more urban vision. A 1966 *Reston Times* editorial hoped that Reston would "become the diversified city that it should be. Economic, ethnic, and racial pressures will shape Reston as an embryo is shaped by physical pressures."[1] Vernon George wrote an editorial that appeared in the *Reston Times* in 1968:

> Many of us came to Reston believing, at least hoping, that
> the town was the answer to the urban dilemma our nation
> faces—that the vast economic gap between the haves and the

have-nots could somehow be bridged. Not only would our town have all races and all economic groups, but in substantial number and share of our total population, so that our town and tens and hundreds of others like it could provide the "release valve." And by providing for the escape of large numbers of low income ghetto dwellers the new town movement would give a dimension of realism to efforts to revitalize the economic social and physical life of the inner city.[2]

This "release valve" idea of urban development now seems outdated because it oversimplified complex urban problems, but George, and many others at the time, believed it could work. He even modestly argued that new towns provided "the environment which brings together the kind of people with the philosophy, the dedication and the abilities to lead suburban America out of the dark ages." Walter Knorr, editor of the *Restonian,* remembered that "Reston was this way out new experiment put up by a bunch of ambitious New York architects, a haven for certain types: utopian HUD govies, activist civil rights and anti-war types, [Central Intelligence] Agency people, Foreign Service officers (who were also often Agency people) . . . [and] it seemed like a magnet for progressives from Big Ten universities." Reston attracted residents who were looking for an alternative social environment in the suburbs.[3]

Rouse remained a constant critic of the social order of suburbia throughout his life. In a 1967 interview he discussed suburban and urban limitations as they related to the life of his first wife, Libby. At that time he and his family still lived in an old suburb, Roland Park, that lay within the city limits of Baltimore. He explained that "as a woman and a mother with the responsibility for children and a family, she has felt the inadequacy of the city and its fracturing impact, the absence of rich community. I have come to see through her eyes the requirements of family and community."[4] Perhaps Rouse projected his own marital problems on the environment (he and Libby divorced in the 1970s), but he seemed to believe genuinely that both city and suburb failed to meet human needs. Rouse idealized the communal intimacy of small towns, but he envisioned Columbia as sociologically urban: "Like any real city of 100,000 Columbia will be economically diverse, polycultural, multi-faith and interracial."[5] Rouse set in motion the institutional framework for the development of this yeasty social ferment and succeeded in attracting people with similar goals. He observed in 1979 that Columbia had attracted urban oriented residents: "The kind of people who live in the center city also live in Columbia, whereas they don't like suburban development."[6]

Indeed, many Columbia residents saw themselves as engaged in the creation of a reformed American suburb. Ray Bird, in an article celebrating the (low-income) Interfaith Housing effort, argued that "if Columbia is to work, we must leave behind the suburban snobbery of homogeneous communities and status symbol price tags."[7] Paul Imre, a Columbia resident and high-ranking official in the Baltimore County Department of Health, explained that "the New America was designed so that each neighborhood was not to be another builder's subdivision. The social and emotional meaning of neighborhood in Columbia was to prevent social breakdown, encourage health, individual growth and a feeling of community responsibility."[8] Reverend John Walsh of St. John's Catholic parish at Wilde Lake village and president of Interfaith Housing Corporation reminded Columbians in an interview of 1969 that "it has always been a stated goal that we will be a complete city and not a suburban enclave. . . . I see Columbia as being the most significant effort being made to establish a community with the wide range of individuals that you would need in order to have a real city . . ." Although residents may seem to us overly optimistic, even a bit naive in retrospect, the evidence indicates that many residents made a genuine commitment to creating a socially diverse community.[9]

Even Irvine's developers, although not initially committed to building a truly diverse city, sought to create a more variegated suburb. The company condemned "the monotony of typical suburban development, where everyone's the same age, at the same point in their career, with the same number of children, living more or less the same lifestyle."[10] Bill Watt defended apartments in Irvine in a 1973 article: "There is a definite need . . . for apartments in a community. . . . Cities should provide a variety of housing types which correspond to the economic cycles which most people go through." Critics have been quick to jump on the Irvine Company's lack of social responsibility, but there is significant evidence that the company did not remain static in its approach to affordable housing and religious and ethnic (if not racial) diversity. Many residents have been attracted by the idea that Irvine offers an alternative to traditional suburban society. One early resident, Helen Hurd, remembered that "part of our dream was the knowledge that anyone who wanted to could be a part of the development of the new town; there was no entrenched political structure to overcome. There were only a lot of people with a common desire to find better answers to the urban and suburban problems which were so common elsewhere." As in most new towns, the achievement of this openness has been difficult, but not without some success.[11]

The new towns attracted a number of idealistic reformers, yet many others came simply because the community offered better schools, more open space, and aesthetic controls. Even these residents, however, had to be at peace with the social experimentation in the community. As Albert Mayer of the *Village Voice* noted in 1971, in an article on Columbia, "the people who have been settling here have been attracted mainly by the good values and conveniences and facilities. Attracted by these, they were ready to accept these [socially innovative] frameworks and resulting ground rules or help to modify them." It mattered very little that all residents, or even a majority of residents, agreed on the founding liberal principles. Because the developer and a strong minority openly and vocally supported progressive social goals, the rest of the residents generally followed.[12]

Affordable Suburbs

Exclusive, homogenous suburbs, disliked by most liberal reformers, emerged around American cities for complicated reasons. American cities, more than their European counterparts, suffered from a successional pattern of neighborhood and city development. The United States, a society with rapid industrial growth, high social and geographic mobility, and often violent racial and ethnic conflict, has had difficulty establishing stable neighborhood or community life; even wealthy neighborhoods have declined into slums or industrial areas at a rapid rate. Such transformations occurred in most American cities and varied only in speed and intensity. A pattern of outmigration spurred by neighborhood change and urban growth had established itself as early as the late nineteenth century and showed no sign of slowing in the twentieth. Inner ring, streetcar suburbs, and older urban neighborhoods changed hands from white Protestants to Jews, Germans, Irish, and Italians, and eventually to blacks and Hispanics. Examples of such transformations abound in American cities, including Harlem, New York; Roxbury, Massachusetts; and Chicago's West Side.

Some communities, however, stalled this successional process through regulation. These were the famous planned suburban communities including Llewellyn Park, New Jersey; Riverside, Illinois; Roland Park, Maryland; and Shaker Heights, Ohio. These suburbs preserved their cachet by the use of restrictive covenants and limitations on housing types (primarily single-family homes). Through such deliberate measures, these communities remained the preserve of white, wealthy families.

When the expansion of the automobile suburbs began in the 1920s, the growing middle class, more ethnically diverse than ever before, moved to stripped-down versions of these elite suburbs. They collected in new suburbs that contained only one class and purposely kept apartments and lower-cost housing outside the community. Their goal, like that of the upper-classes who preceded them, was to create stability and stall the pattern of successional decline. Many new suburban residents, after all, had watched their former neighborhoods decline and their homes lose value. Still, as the suburbs expanded and, in the 1940s, 1950s, and 1960s, seemed destined to become the dominant urban form of America, many liberal observers worried that this stability had its own price: an even sharper division between the haves (in suburbia) and the have-nots (trapped in dying city centers). The elitism of these middle-class suburbs became intolerable to many liberal Americans.[13]

The new-town movement initiated a search for a different kind of communal stability. New town residents and developers believed that long-term stability would not result from a society or city cleaved into different sections. Instead, they believed that the only way to build more stable neighborhoods was to make racial and economic integration as essential a part of every neighborhood as architectural covenants. This socio-economic integration would remove the incentive to abandon neighborhoods, because no one area would be more exclusive than the other. Fear of social change, rather than social change itself, would be shown to be the driving force of neighborhood decline.

The new-town developers and planners initiated this mixture through the addition of more affordable and low-income housing. These communities became more affluent than originally planned, but the desire to preserve a mixed population remained. Developers in all these communities provided a wide range of housing styles—including apartments, town homes, and single family houses—some of which were simply more affordable, while others used government subsidies. The creators of the *New Communities, U.S.A.* study found that people who moved to subsidized housing in new towns (including those less innovative than the ones in this study) found better facilities than where they had come from and were happier with their living environments than those in more conventional developments. Residents of nonsubsidized apartment complexes in new towns rated their environment much higher than those in conventional suburban apartment communities "in terms of appearance, privacy, quiet, safety, maintenance, and places for children's outdoor play."[14]

It now seems remarkable, however, that developers and many early residents believed they could accrue all the benefits of social innovation and avoid any problems or complications. Inevitably difficulties did arise, and the social attitudes and values of residents changed. Some of the market-rate apartment and town-house complexes have become lower-cost housing and may be contributing to a negative perception of certain areas of new towns. Many of the subsidized complexes developed problems with crime and maintenance. Tensions sometimes mounted between poor and affluent residents. Friction between black and white teenagers was not uncommon. Some residents felt that their communities were carrying an inordinate share of public housing in their respective regions. Nor did the construction of low-income complexes keep pace as federal support for subsidized housing withered in the 1970s.

A core group of individuals dedicated to the social mission of the new towns did not give up hope. Rather than responding to fear of social change, many community leaders have chastised developers, the federal government, and their fellow citizens for failing to achieve the high standards of social mixture on which the community was founded. Other residents created institutions and events to augment and support the growing social diversity. Many residents simply went about their lives in a socially integrated milieu and refused to dignify complaints or tension with their attention. Diversity has thus become a matrix of different ideals and organizations that transcend the idealistic, but also simplistic, notions of the initial developers. Social diversity also became the most vivid reflection of a new suburban landscape for many visitors and residents. Low-income residents in apartments mixed in with an affluent population occupying single-family homes provided a strong contrast to conventional suburban towns.[15]

Opening the Gate in Reston

Reston began as a high-income community and has remained one of America's most affluent suburbs. From the beginning, however, the community has included market-rate apartments and lower-income housing. Including lower-income housing in primarily middle-class communities like Reston has worked relatively well and has stimulated greater social responsibility among many middle-class residents. As will become clear, even problems with low-income housing in a community like Reston need not lead to the pattern of successional neighborhood abandonment experienced in so many American cities.[16]

The inclusion of this mixture of housing types in Reston was not accidental. Simon and succeeding developers created apartments and town houses from market-rate to more expensive units (apartments and town houses constituted approximately two thirds of all construction). Even in the early days of development, Simon believed that different classes would coexist at Reston: "The acceptance of the wide variety of housing prices within a given neighborhood has proven the validity of the idea that people do not insist on living in rigid economic stratifications. This range will be increased as time goes on to provide housing in Reston for all who are employed here and want to live here."[17]

This mix of apartment styles touted by Simon offered both promise and problems. Some local residents reported greater social egalitarianism. The Le Gallos, a struggling young couple, enjoyed life in a Reston apartment: "Joan and Larry have learned something else about a new town—that status, so-called 'social standing' based on income matters little, if at all. . . . The Le Gallos are finding that money and possessions are not the keys to social acceptance. 'It's you yourself,' Joan says simply."[18] "Diversity is what I have sought, and I do believe that Reston has it," explained another early resident, bragging that "we have poor kids from public housing, and we have affluent kids."[19]

At the same time, differences in economic status caused occasional tension. In 1970, one resident reported that "within the community, the renter is considered to belong to a lower economic class, to be prone to hang wash on his balcony and allow his children to run free." He observed that "when Hickory Cluster posts signs on its common land saying 'Private Property,' the renters in Vantage Hill believe (with justification) that they are the ones who should 'keep off.'" This resident also noticed a further divide between upper-income Restonians and the rural residents around them: "The Herndon and Chantilly people work as Reston's soda jerks and grease monkeys and janitors and return home at sunset. The Reston people wonder, without charity, why all the help have Southern accents." Over the last decades, a growing divide has developed between the upper-income areas near the North Point village center and the Lake Anne and South Reston villages, which are more economically and ethnically diverse.[20]

Although developers incorporated a variety of apartment styles and price levels, much of the focus of local media and the community has been on low-income housing developments. The commitment to low-income housing grew out of new-town idealism and competition for industries in its office parks: the community would need to have living space for lower-income workers in local industries. Reston's developers chose to create a series of low-income apartment complexes rather than spreading low-income housing around the community. In Columbia, designers believed that this isolation of units would reduce social conflict, and the same idea probably motivated the developer of Reston. Still, construction of low-income housing started slowly.

In 1966, Simon explained that construction of low-income units up until that point had been slow, but "we have been working with the seven industries that have moved or are moving to Reston and we've told them if any of their employees want to live in Reston and don't find something here that they can afford or that they like, that we will build a government subsidized low-rental project."[21] In fact, a number of subsidized housing units were constructed in Reston, but mostly after Simon had been replaced in 1967. By the late 1970s, approximately 1,000 units of subsidized housing had been built, concentrated in a series of complexes (then representing about 10 percent of the available units in Reston).[22] Gulf Reston had constructed many, but not all, of these units as a result of a "suit by a Washington D.C. organization which made construction of a number of units mandatory in connection with the relocation of the U.S. Geological Survey from Washington, D.C. to Reston."[23] Low-income units were grouped in apartment clusters at Cedar Ridge, Island Walk, Fox Mill, the Green, Stonegate, and Laurel Glade.

Some of the low-income housing proved successful and allowed a number of low-income residents access to the jobs, schools, and natural setting of Reston. Island Walk, a cooperative housing project designed by the well-known firm of Gwathmey Siegal in 1974–75, was the "first newly constructed cooperative in the country to be approved by (HUD) under the Section 8 rent subsidy program."[24] The architects believed that the complex was "tailored to Reston with the architectural aspects reflective of Reston." These special touches included "a sequence of pedestrian mews and walkways to plaza spaces. The mews are enclosed by individual court-yards, and each courtyard serves as the entrance to the private dwelling of the resident."[25] The Island Walk apartments have continued to offer affordable housing to those who might not be able to afford to buy homes or even rent in Reston.

Long-standing maintenance and safety problems plagued many of the other low-income housing projects because private developers constructed housing for low-income tenants but failed to provide the additional services and maintenance demanded by this population.[26] The

Stonegate Village apartment complex, for instance, received help from the county in the 1980s because of maintenance, crime, and drug problems. The complex was surrounded by a number of other lower-income complexes that shared many of the same problems. Many residents, in fact, feared that Reston was developing a low-income "ghetto." The county took over the project in the 1980s, introduced community policing, expanded social services (relating to education, employment, and drug and alcohol services), and began renovating the complex. These changes brought a substantial decrease in crime.[27] Stonegate today appears externally attractive, but Ivan Cole, who, in addition to his role with RCA was coordinator of job counseling and development for Reston Interfaith, explained that appearances are deceiving. The project continues to have a large number of social problems, including drug dealing. Even so, conditions have improved enough so that a number of units have been successfully converted to market-rate rentals by the county.

There has been no significant increase in the number of low-income complexes since the 1970s due to problems with such developments as well as the loss of federal financing. Complicating the situation was a concentration of Section 8 recipients in apartment complexes close to existing subsidized housing. Section 8 tenants were known to be living in the Shadowood, Southgate, and Glenwood complexes near subsidized Stonegate, Fox Mill, and Laurel Glade. This concentration led to Martha Pennino's opposition to more subsidized housing in Reston until problems with existing units were resolved and the concentration relieved.[28]

The county government and local residents have taken a comprehensive approach to redeveloping the low-income projects of Reston during the last two decades. During the last decade, the county took over Stonegate, Cedar Ridge, and the Green from private managers and also controlled the public housing in the town center. In 1998, there still existed 1,134 project-based public and assisted units in Reston, but some of these will be lost in redevelopment. The county, in general, has improved the management of the complexes and has started to convert some of these apartments into market-rate rentals. The idea of these conversions is to reduce problems brought on by the concentration of low-income tenants. Reston Interfaith and the county have also found 774 other apartment units (and 187 town houses) in public and privately owned developments spread throughout Reston, most under the Section 8 program. In 1990, Simon and other community leaders successfully advocated the construction of thirty units of affordable housing as part of the town center. This housing, known as Bowman Terrace, is notable for its attractive design and is indistinguishable from more expensive housing—a conscious attempt by the developer to avoid the problems in other low-income developments.[29]

Jerry Geary, an official with Reston Interfaith, explained in an interview that low-income employees are needed in the new businesses of Reston, but even with the existence of some subsidized apartments, many are unable to find housing. Reston Interfaith, however, is currently building a new low-income complex in North Point village and recently assumed management of Cedar Ridge apartments, thus preserving it as low-income housing. The community leadership is trying to expand lower-income opportunities but faces resistance from many residents who feel Reston has enough low-income housing, especially compared with similar communities in Fairfax County.[30]

Cole explained a more subtle problem for low-income residents in Reston. He has observed that many low-income residents try to move too quickly from the low-income complexes into higher-cost housing in Reston. Residents want to shed the stigma of living in these complexes and to avoid the problems associated with them. According to Cole, however, Reston is particularly weak in intermediate-price rentals, and the cost of living in general there proves challenging even for working families. Still, Cole observed that many children from low-income projects, although often identified in schools as disruptive and academically limited, eventually attend some of America's best colleges.[31]

Much of the discussion in Reston has focused on making low-income projects acceptable for their residents and the community as a whole, but low-income residents face their own challenges. Poor residents, for instance, have often been unable to pay for participation in the recreational facilities in the new town.[32] Donald Grant, a HUD attorney who lived in Reston, noted in 1975 that "a poor person in a new town is at a unique disadvantage because he can't afford the amenities, and without those things there's no meaning to the idea of new town. If you transplant poor people who don't have the wherewithal to enjoy these things, you're creating a whole new problem for them." Fox Mill, a federally subsidized housing project, had trouble with its neighbors because "Reston's planners placed Fox Mill and Laurel Glade . . . directly alongside the community swimming pool [and] children from the low-income families can stand at the gate and watch while families from the nearby middle- and upper-income areas splash and swim."[33] Poor children had access to nature, and poor families had access to low-cost activities and events, but they lived quite differently from high-income residents. Over the last thirty years, the income gap has increased in Reston, as it has in the United States as a whole. Participation in recreational facilities became more affordable over the years, now only a few dollars for a year's access to pools, but problems remained. One resident explained why: "Because of the rising property values in general, Reston has some very low-income families but not very many middle-income people, and then many high-income families . . . and that creates tension in the schools, in the community between the haves and the have-nots."[34]

South Lakes High School, in particular, is known to be split between the "gifted and talented" group of middle-income students and regular-education lower-income students. In addition, some of the low-income, minority, and immigrant residents are visible waiting at bus stops in Reston, while the more affluent members of the community drive by in their cars. These lifestyle gaps have not led to open conflict, but they have made life difficult for those at the bottom of the social ladder who are so visibly cut off from the good life that surrounds them.

Low-income complexes have also been stigmatized as the source of crime in Reston. Although they have been a source and location of criminal activity, crime also originated from outside the community and from higher-income residents within the community (many of whom buy drugs from lower-income dealers). Still, many Reston residents instinctively blamed low-income residents for crime that occurred throughout Reston. Early tension centered, for example, around one of Reston's earliest projects, Cedar Ridge. According to a *Washington Post* article of 1971, "social division showed up when some residents blamed . . . window-breaking on children from the town's one limited income apartment complex, Cedar Ridge." The article noted, however, that discussion went on for months in Reston, and this had to do "with the fact that it is a town full of activists." The reporter chronicled a "mass meeting" where the police and the district attorney's office "exonerated Cedar Ridge youngsters."[35]

When crime grew at Hunters Woods village center in the late 1970s, retailers blamed "Reston's problems on low-income renters. They singled out Stonegate, a racially and economically mixed, subsidized housing project . . . as the main source of trouble." Unlike a conventional community, however, where nobody would be expected to defend the honor of poor people, some leaders in the Reston community defended other residents. Pennino "accused Reston merchants of looking for a scapegoat for chronic business ills." She and leaders from the county police maintained that the crimes had been "done by well-educated, well-off kids." Although many Reston residents probably believe that they have a higher crime rate than nearby communities because of the existence of low-income housing, Reston has generally been one of the safest communities on the East Coast, according to a variety of police reports. There are high-profile crimes—rapes on bike paths, occasional crime at village stores, property crimes, and drug traffic concentrated in low-income areas—but overall Reston remains a very safe community, even with its subsidized housing.[36]

Although some residents have opposed low-income complexes, an important and vocal segment of Reston's population has stood firmly behind low-income housing and its residents. Editorials in the local paper reflect this attitude. As early as 1967, one reminded residents of the new town vision:

> While some people may have bought or rented at Reston on the assumption that they were moving into a "nice," or "acceptable," or "untainted" suburban development, we feel sure that the vast majority moved here with the knowledge that Reston was to be a genuine New Town in the fullest sense of the word—a town rich in diversity of incomes, race, occupations, and social and political outlook. . . . If we treat the residents of low-cost housing as lepers, if we isolate them from the rest of the community . . . then we will probably become the victim of a self-fulfilling prophecy. On the other hand, if we welcome them into the community as we have welcomed one another, if we show even a modicum of human decency and kindness, we may find ourselves living in a much richer and healthier community.[37]

George Hickey, director of a 1977 community study for the Reston Homeowners Association, explained that even though the spirit of "social experimentation and community spirit" was fading, "the 'urban character' of the town . . . has been strengthened . . . as a result of an increase in apartments and rental units and the greater number of blacks, poor, singles and the elderly that now live here." He explained that these residents came for services and amenities in the new town and a more open acceptance of nontraditional suburban residents.[38] During a review of proposals to renovate one complex during the 1980s, "residents of the area around [the subsidized project] say the looks of the apartment complex are adversely affecting property values—but they're not packing their bags." One of the nearby residents, in fact, explained that "we want to improve what's going on in the neighborhood. We'd like to develop a more cohesive neighborhood."[39]

The local organizations of Reston acted on behalf of low-income residents. Although Reston's developer and planners thought little about what services would be needed by low-income residents, community members have developed an impressive range of social services. These institutions—such as Reston Interfaith, RIBS mass transit, FISH (mentioned previously), and the Embry Rucker Shelter for the homeless—provide services for needy residents. Many of Reston's residents need the affordable child-care, ESL instruction, elderly and youth services, job counseling and training, temporary and long-term affordable housing, mass transit, and emergency financial assistance that these institutions provide. These nonprofit organizations have attracted both private donations and government grants and often operate in tandem with county, state, and federal programs.

As stated before, Reston Interfaith has advocated low-income housing and services in the Reston area. In 1985, Connie Pettinger asked the RCA board a difficult question: "Is Reston willing and ready to make a new commitment to the goals of an inclusive community offering housing and population diversity? . . . Reston Interfaith maintains that diversity and pluralism should be promoted in Reston and that providing affordable housing for a full range of income levels is critical to encouraging diversity." Pettinger noted that Interfaith services to low-income families included child care, job counseling, emergency shelter and transitional housing, subsidized housing management and construction, education and career aid, as well as support to Section 8 recipients searching for apartments in the area.[40]

The RCA has also been an advocate for affordable housing. A 1970 brochure described its efforts to improve conditions for low-income people in Reston: "RCA is currently working with various county, state, and federal groups to insure that adequate low and moderate income housing will be provided by the time the new U.S. Geological Survey headquarters opens in Reston. RCA and the Cedar Ridge Tenants Association worked together with Gulf Reston in order to improve the general conditions and landlord-tenant relationships at Cedar Ridge Apartments."[41] RCA has consistently fought for low-income housing.[42] In 1979, the association even found itself promoting low-income housing when many residents, along with Pennino, felt Reston had its share. Under Janet Howell's leadership, the RCA lobbied in the 1980s to bring a homeless shelter to the town center and to create thirty units of low-income housing in town center.[43] In the 1980s as well, a proposal to curb drug trafficking that included a six-foot metal fence around the Stonegate complex was defeated by RCA.

Vicky Wingert, director of open space for RCA, explained that "the proposed fence is counter to the Reston concept."[44]

Outsiders have been particularly interested in social mixture in the new towns. During the early years of construction, Wolf Von Eckardt gave a very revealing view of one possible outcome of class mixture in new towns:

> Mixing rich and poor holds new and largely unthought of advantages for the American middle class. Wouldn't it be nice to have women in the neighborhood who'll be glad to iron your shirts and men who won't be above sweeping out the garage? If growing numbers of unskilled people are unemployable because of automation, why don't we offer them work sprucing up and maintaining our streets and public spaces[?] . . . Sure, we run the risk that a few of them might throw empty whisky bottles into our front yards. On the other hand, they'll learn about garbage disposal and deportment much faster from their neighbors than from Sargent Shriver's domestic peace corps. . . . And if all this sounds condescending toward the poor, it is far less so than present programs of "human renewal."[45]

Eckardt's comments are prescient in certain respects. The current workfare programs, for instance, integrate aspects of this program. Workfare programs, however, generally perpetuate the residential income segregation of cities and the distance between the haves and have-nots. But residential propinquity in a community like Reston encourages, even demands, middle-class attention to low-income housing issues. There has been conflict and negative attention, but residents have developed some creative solutions for improving the lives of low-income people. In part owing to these efforts, Reston has so far been successful in halting a successional pattern of neighborhood disintegration by reducing the fear associated with a more diverse socioeconomic profile.

Columbia's Open Society

It has never been difficult to build handsome communities for the rich. So the developer's vow [to build a more complete community] presumably rests upon the conviction that all people,

not just the affluent, deserve a community conducive to the development of the best in life.

RAY N. BIRD, Columbia resident, *Columbia Today*

Rouse became famous for saying that the company janitor and president
might be neighbors in Columbia. Residents such as Ray Bird came to Columbia believing that the community would achieve a level of social mixture lacking in typical suburbs. More than thirty years later the goal of
social mixture has been preserved. Columbia still boasts residents with a
wide range of incomes living in a variety of housing types. In addition to a
wide range of styles, it has added subsidized housing to its stock. Although
problems with low-income developments stalled their expansion in the
late 1970s, they still exist in Columbia and have been augmented by new
subsidized units spread evenly and discreetly throughout the community.
Columbia remains the primary location of low-income housing in
Howard County. Furthermore, the community leadership is still committed to preserving a more mixed population.

Planning for the mixture of classes in Columbia began early. A humorous but revealing work-group discussion can be found in notes by
Wallace Hamilton:

> [Herbert] Gans felt that the upper-middle-class would be
> predominant at the new town and pointed out—to the dismay
> of some other members of the work group—that the lower and
> lower-middle-classes were unlikely to take much interest in . . .
> civic affairs. . . . This point led to a discussion of "upward mo-
> bility" and the possibility of drawing other class groups into the
> upper-middle-class way of doing things. Since all members of
> the work group were upper-middle-class, the meeting became
> fairly evangelistic about upper-middle-class virtues until finally
> [one member] suggested that everybody in the new town
> should be given a free subscription to the *New Yorker* magazine.
> At that juncture the work group rather sheepishly decided that
> value judgments on class characteristics was a tenuous business
> at best.[46]

The work group did not accept Gans's view of upper-middle-class leadership, but this quotation does reveal the group's class consciousness. And
they actually took most of Gans's recommendations seriously.

Gans explained that "there were going to be class differences in the new town, that the differences tended to be related more to education than to income, and that the differences would show up in a variety of ways, including child-rearing, relations with relatives, social habits, and degree of civic activity." He suggested that the planners stay away from "putting diverse people side by side in a community" because it "did not necessarily lead to an enriched community; it may instead lead to a lot of unresolvable conflicts." The planners only partially implemented Gans's ideas, according to Hamilton, because "neighborhoods were not as homogeneous as perhaps Gans had in mind, and included a variety of housing at a variety of prices. But the houses were in homogenous segments—single families, garden apartments, town houses." There has been tension among classes in Columbia, even with the separation of groups, but it may have been far less severe because of the attempts at some residential isolation.[47]

This failure to create complete homogeneity affected the educational planning of the schools. The work group recommended that small, "homogeneous" neighborhood schools be built "to provide a better opportunity to bring the lower-income children and their parents into the orbit of aspirations and behavior which would prepare the children to take full advantage of the middle-class, competitive environment of the upper schools." The report noted that "if the neighborhoods are relatively homogeneous, there is a fair chance that, with the right kind of teachers . . . lower class parents and youngsters could be drawn into the school orbit more easily than if they are expected to be inadequate."[48] The neighborhood schools created by planners, however, did not develop as homogeneous schools in large part because there has never been sufficient concentration of low-income families in neighborhoods. The potential benefits, then, of class homogeneity in schools has been lost, but so too has the threat of rigid class segregation that might have resulted.

The work group believed that social interaction between classes would best take place in village centers. According to a later summary of the work group's efforts, "contact [among classes] in the village center would be over matters of joint interest or under circumstances that are relatively low in emotional content, such as shopping in the supermarket." The document explained that "those emotionally loaded circumstances, such as keeping up with the Joneses and coping with the neighbors' child training standards, would be minimized at the village level of interaction. Thus the opportunities for felicitous integration would be high in the village center."[49] Even the village centers proved "emotionally loaded" in many circumstances, as low-income teenagers and other adolescents loitered there. However, a great majority of Columbia's diverse population used the village centers with almost no conflict. The discussion and planning during the work-group and planning phase, while not implemented as envisioned, and perhaps not as prescient as could be desired, did establish the community's interest and concern for social mixture.

The developer has over the decades followed through on the creation of a broad range of housing options. By 1986, "35 percent of the housing units in the new town district were single-family, detached houses. Another 27 percent were attached units (e.g., town houses, multiplexes), and 38 percent were apartments and condominiums."[50] However, these statistics do not reflect the fluidity of housing patterns. A survey of households in the early 1980s found that many "apartment dwellers moved to town houses, and later to single-family dwellings. Renters, in general, moved toward ownership."[51] In the late 1980s, nearly 7,000 apartment units existed in Columbia, with models for a full range of incomes.

Many of the residents of Columbia have shared interest in providing more affordable housing and social egalitarianism. Mrs. Barry, an early resident of Columbia who moved to the New Jersey suburbs with her family in 1982, moved back to Columbia only a few years later: "It became obvious to us when we moved up there that different types of people live in different communities. There wasn't a liberal attitude." Her husband explained that in New Jersey "there is prejudice built in. People were judged by what they owned, what they had." The belief that Columbia is more egalitarian than many communities, as reflected in this couple's observations, has been expressed quite often by residents.[52]

Not all the residents of Columbia, however, have believed that the community has escaped suburban social homogeneity and snobbery. Zeke Orlinsky wrote in 1977 that "many of us came to Columbia because we were attracted by its openness, by its promise to be an integrated community. One of the biggest disappointments has been the lack of housing available for low- and moderate-income families. We are fast becoming an upper-middle-class ghetto, rather than the diversified community we originally sought to find here."[53] One high-school student confided to a *Washington Post* reporter in 1987 that "everyone in Columbia knows which [neighborhood and development] is which, and a classmate was distraught when a sudden drop in his parent's economic status forced them to move to one of the 'less desirable' town house developments."[54]

Ernest Erber, a retired professor of planning and Harper's Choice resident, described in 1995 how the residents over the years had self-segregated "by income, lifestyle interests, education and possibly even race as development continues." According to Erber, "initially there's a more egalitarian distribution of people in the new town. They come with no prior concepts. Once there, they find that one thing is more desirable than another and associate in different ways. There's a tendency for self-segregation."[55] Columbia's residents remain overwhelmingly professional and well-educated. In 1997, "the average household income [was] $72,000 a year—about three times higher than Baltimore's, and one of the highest in the country."[56]

Within this community, as at Reston, there are demarcations between the older villages (considered more ethnically and socially diverse), such as Wilde Lake and Long Reach, and new villages, such as River Hill and King's Contrivance, that attract a more uniform upper-income group. The newer areas such as River Hill have fewer apartment and town-house developments, and lavish new homes command higher prices. Yet even Columbia's older villages are only thirty years old and remain as a whole affluent and attractive. Furthermore, the decline of certain complexes and areas offers opportunities for first-time buyers or lower-income renters who otherwise would be locked out of Columbia's high-priced real estate. Columbia has served, and still serves, as both a prestigious community and a stepping stone to home ownership for many members of the lower and middle classes.

Working-class residents of Columbia who can afford to live in some of the older areas gain access to the high quality educational system of Howard County. All of the high schools in Columbia either meet or exceed national SAT average scores, and college attendance rates are very high.[57] Even with this impressive record of achievement, not everyone is happy. Conflict, for instance, has occurred over schools in the 1990s: "largely white, affluent parents [fight] student transfers from high-achieving Centennial High to more ethnic, less affluent Wilde Lake High." Wilde Lake, however, was only "less affluent" in the Columbia context. Wilde Lake High School in 1998 received a $20 million renovation and students in 1999 had average SAT scores of 1098 (Centennial had 1166 and the national average was 1016). The high standards of social mixture sought at the new town have exaggerated any differences.[58]

The primary means to gaining a more heterogeneous community came from Columbia's commitment to building significant numbers of apartments and town houses, but subsidized housing also became part of the formula for community diversity. This housing, as at Reston, has been the focus of a great deal of community discussion, even though it has not been built in the original proportions. The original plans called for 10 percent subsidized housing, but according to Len Lazarick, this goal "was easier to achieve before the Nixon administration scuttled many housing programs and before inflation made the costs prohibitive." Lazarick noted in 1977 that "low income dwellings are now only 5 per cent of Columbia's housing mix, not 10 per cent as planned."[59] The residents of subsidized housing, moreover, tended to be working poor people, not members of the "underclass." Of the 1000 residents of Interfaith projects, "46 per cent of the residents are in single-parent families; 12 per cent are students; 15 per cent come from local government and industry; 14 per cent are clerical workers; 6 per cent are military personnel; 5 percent are nurses; 2 percent are teachers . . . less than 5 per cent depend entirely on welfare. By race, 40 per cent of the residents are white; 60 per cent black." In addition, residents of Interfaith projects used the low-income housing as a transition to buying homes: "the average length of residence is 24 months and over 30 percent of the turnover results in home ownership here in Howard County."[60]

Subsidized units have been created through a variety of means. As stated previously, the Interfaith Housing Corporation, initiated by the Columbia Cooperative Ministry (an ecumenical organization of Protestants, Catholics, and Jews), was organized to build low-income housing. A 1967 statement reflects the organization's understanding of what was at stake in Columbia and how it related to national and international planning efforts: "We believe that the housing needs of those with low income in this country confront us with a . . . human crisis of chronic and emergency proportions. The new capital of Brasilia in South America suggests to us a 'parable' on housing needs. In that well planned and architecturally sophisticated city, no provision was made for the poor to live there; as a result, satellite slums cluster about this ambitious new urban design."[61] This statement repeated common misconceptions about Brasilia (there were some provisions for the poor), but it reflects well the idealism that motivated Columbians.

In 1971 the Interfaith Housing Corporation created a program of church-sponsored housing for Columbia. Projects included three hundred apartment and town-house dwellings on scattered sites at affordable rents.[62] By 1988, the corporation, now known as the Columbia Housing Corporation, managed 484 rental units in Howard County, most of them in Columbia. The majority of these units are complexes relatively isolated from surrounding developments.[63]

Many other subsidized complexes have been developed and managed by Columbia Management, a subsidiary of the Rouse Company created to develop and manage low-income housing. These complexes include Abbott House, Copperstone Circle, Tilbury Woods, and Locust Park (about seven hundred units in all).[64] Since the 1970s, hundreds of other units of subsidized housing have been spread more evenly throughout new developments in the community by the Howard County government, primarily through the Section 8 program. Of the 2,631 units of subsidized housing in Howard County, 1,793 were in Columbia in 1998 (and Columbia constitutes only 10 percent of Howard County's land area). Through this variety of efforts, then, Columbia now possesses an impressive number of subsidized housing options and almost all of Howard County's subsidized housing.

As attitudes to class diversity varied, so also have attitudes to low-income housing. There are some signs that the units were positively integrated into the community. Columbia residents favored a mix of housing when interviewed in a survey created by the University of North Carolina Center for Urban and Regional Studies. According to Jean Moon, in a 1974 *Columbia Flier* review of the survey, researchers found that "Columbians are not only more open to racial and income mix in their neighborhood, they favor further expansion of housing to meet the needs of these groups." She noted that while other residents of new towns had placed transportation as their first choice where more money should be spent, in Columbia, "50 percent of the respondents placed 'housing for low income families,' as their choice."[65] Dan Beyers, in a 1992 article looking back on Columbia's early years remembered that "we welcomed subsidized housing, town houses and apartments next to single-family subdivisions because economic integration was the Columbia Concept."[66] In 1978, the community even "raised $100,00 in seed money for a 50-unit subsidized housing complex."[67] An upper-income Hobbit's Glen resident, Roselle Cummins, still believed in 1995 that "affordable housing being in close proximity to where I live is just a fact of life being in Columbia." She explained that low-income housing and a troubled shopping area did not affect her decision to live in her village.[68]

Not everyone has had such a positive view of the low-income housing developments. June Caldwell, a psychologist residing in Columbia, argued in 1971, "I don't consider $99 a month really low-income housing. The Interfaith apartments . . . were stigmatized as low-income places before they were even built. They're dispersed around, but you can tell 'em, all right. All the American prejudices about low-rent housing are being preserved intact here. If something is stolen, everyone looks at the Interfaith kids."[69] Indeed, subsidized housing became the focus of much criticism by residents both inside and outside of complexes. Efraim Ben-Zadok, a doctoral student at New York University, completed a dissertation in 1980 that examined racial and social integration in Columbia during the late 1970s. One of his most notable findings was that residents had a much higher enthusiasm for racial integration than economic integration and there existed widespread concern about the effect of low-income developments on property values and safety in Columbia.[70]

In 1977, complaints about low-income residents found their way into the local papers. A series of letters that appeared in the *Columbia Flier* reflect persistent tensions. Stephen Ater, a neighbor of Fall River Terrace, an Interfaith development, wrote that he believed residents of Fall River littered and intimidated children. He complained, "I am tired of The Rouse Memorial Ghetto being thrown in my face and then having to pick up after it . . . only to be laughed at. . . . I am tired of seeing my neighbor's little girls being stripped of their clothing by 7–10 year old boys of the Rouse Memorial Ghetto."[71] J. Michael Marshall, chief executive officer of Interfaith, wrote a heartfelt response in which he speculated that "there is nothing more caustically violent than this type of attempt to strip a community of its dignity." Michael Riemer also wrote on behalf of the directors of the Harper's Choice Village Association. He affirmed, "We stand committed to the principle of race and income integration. . . . We feel that the struggle to learn to live together will strengthen us individually and collectively." These kinds of responses to attacks on low-income housing residents are part of the community leadership's commitment to low-income housing.[72]

There is a significant amount of evidence that indicates how low-income residents felt about their treatment in Columbia. Many of them, but not all, criticized housing projects and Columbia in general. One resident of subsidized housing, Gene Collins, explained in 1987 that he had lived for two decades in subsidized housing and considered "Columbia home." He "chose to be here because of the green grass and open space. Here I don't have to deal with the druggers. I don't have to deal with the high crime rate, the insecurity." He noted, however, that the town seemed to be becoming more class conscious, he considered his apartment poorly constructed, and he felt that recreational amenities in the community were too expensive.[73]

Many other residents identified problems in their projects. One resident of low-cost housing described her complex as an "urban ghetto complete with racial tension, street gangs armed with knives, and an obvious disinterest by the 'landlords' in the rights and problems of their tenants."[74] In a 1975 letter to the editor, Margaret Taite, a resident of subsidized Copperstone Terrace, complained about new signs installed by the property management company in response to disorderly activity in the area. The signs read: "Notice: No Drinking of Alcoholic Beverages. No Loud or Abu-sive Language. No Unlawful Conduct . . . Property Supervised." Taite pointed out that in no other Columbia complexes did one find similar signs and criticized the attitudes of the managers of the complex: "Con-trary to some beliefs, Columbia is no 'Utopia' and although problems do exist in Copperstone, there are misconceptions inherent in a changing structure forced by the growth of the Columbia community, and I feel very strongly that a reaffirmation is in order to rectify the signs that suggest that I, Margaret Taite, a resident in the City of Columbia and residing in a gov-ernment subsidized apartment, namely Copperstone Circle, is some sort of intolerable being and must be 'kept in line' or else."[75] Although there are few records of low-income residents' own feelings about living in Colum-bia, many undoubtedly did feel uncomfortable.

A sociologist, Neil Sandberg, conducted a comprehensive study of one low-income housing project in Columbia in the late 1970s. His study, *Stairwell 7: Family Life in the Welfare State,* focused on the residents who lived around one entry in a low-income project. Sandberg found that low-income residents had difficulty adjusting to Columbia because they were cut off from traditional family and community support and lacked the economic means to mimic middle-class life. He found that residents did not share a "culture of poverty" but desired to be participants in the middle-class life around them; unfortunately, they lacked the skills and re-sources to be full participants. Most residents failed to establish a strong local community for a variety of reasons: they had little control over their neighborhood; many suffered from physical and psychological problems; many moved through the project, and few people wanted to identify or be identified with living there; many objected to the racial and ethnic hetero-geneity, one of the supposed new-town improvements; and many others objected to the high cost of amenities. Sandberg's book coincided with a general turn against the project-style development in Columbia and in America at large.

In recent years, residents of villages in Columbia have fought the in-troduction of additional low-income housing, pointing out that almost all the low-income housing in Howard County is in Columbia (for instance, Long Reach alone has 12 percent of Howard County's subsidized homes and Harper's Choice has 17 percent). The disproportion of Columbia's share of such housing is magnified because Howard County has one of the lowest levels of affordable housing in Maryland, and few communities in the county outside of Columbia have built low-income developments. Subsidized housing also attracts attention because some of Columbia's

market-rate rental and town-house developments in older villages have become more affordable over the years, thus alleviating some of the elitism
subsidized housing is supposed to address. The resident objections, then,
when viewed in conjunction with the internal failure of the projects,
brought an end to big projects in Columbia but did not spell the end of
low-income housing there.

The Rouse Company, Howard County, local builders, and local nonprofits have shifted strategy since the 1970s. The newer subsidized units in
Columbia, mostly designated Section-8 units within higher-income developments, are spread more evenly throughout the community. It might
come as a surprise to most Columbians that Hickory Ridge, a newer village, has 20 percent of Columbia's subsidized housing. King's Contrivance,
another new village, has nearly 13 percent of the subsidized housing. Other
older villages, however, such as Owen Brown (18 percent of the total),
Wilde Lake (11 percent), Harper's Choice (10 percent), and Long Reach
(17 percent), are more closely associated with low-income projects. And
Oakland Mills, which has had numerous problems with its village center
and low-income residents, has only 6 percent of Columbia's subsidized
housing.

The reason for the difference in perception is clear and correlates
only slightly with actual percentages. In older villages, low-income residents found themselves isolated in poorly maintained projects adjacent to
village centers. The planners hoped to increase shopping and transit convenience for low-income residents, many of whom would lack cars, by
placing low-income complexes near the community's shopping and cultural resources. The planning actually succeeded in making the problems
of these complexes evident to all residents, increasing the stigma of living
in subsidized housing and turning the village centers into living rooms for
low-income teenagers.

In later villages, low-income residents are mixed discreetly into
market-rate apartment complexes. In Wilde Lake, for instance, the 197
subsidized units are concentrated in three completely subsidized projects
(Fall River, Roslyn Rise, and Rideout Heath); in Hickory Ridge, by contrast, the 366 units are spread among eight different developments and
generally do not exceed forty subsidized units per project. The Rouse
Company, local builders, and Howard County then, deserve credit for
abandoning the flawed reasoning of the early planning sessions but maintaining the commitment to low-income housing.[76]

The *Columbia Flier* also has been a consistent booster of low-income
housing. In a 1974 article that accompanied an interview with Rouse in

which he defended the community's commitment to low-income housing (especially compared to other suburbs), Moon goaded her fellow citizens:

> All the good things about Columbia—its community identity, its religious and racial tolerance, its lovely physical environment and social services—poignantly point to the fact that they continue to be offered only to the predominantly upper-middle-class. . . . If Columbians do, indeed, have an 'unorganized concern' for the poor, they can do one of two things. They can, like Rouse, settle for what is already good about Columbia and abandon their notion of extending these crucial amenities to those less fortunate. Or they can rally behind this concern and demand that our community recourse—the Columbia Association—immediately seek ways to remedy the worsening situation. We do have the money in Columbia.[77]

Moon exaggerated in saying that the resources of Columbia were offered "only" to upper-income residents, but her goal, to shame residents and the CA into more decisive action, demanded hyperbole.

The *Flier* played an indirect role in promoting Columbia as a destination for low-income residents. In the *Newcomers Guides* of the 1980s and 1990s, created by the *Flier* staff, the low-income housing in Columbia filled a prominent part of the section on "Housing in Columbia." The *Guides* included detailed descriptions of apartment units and phone numbers for further information. Those who came to visit or had purchased in Columbia would know that low-income residents were welcome.[78]

The political leadership of Columbia complemented the *Flier*'s efforts. The Columbia Council, for instance, in 1979 created a resolution, largely for symbolic effect, that affirmed "Columbia's original goal of becoming an economically integrated community." The council lent "its support [to] efforts both to provide more subsidized housing for low and moderate income families throughout the city and to improve the appearance and quality of Columbia's existing subsidized housing units."[79] The Columbia Forum also discussed affordable housing during the 1980s. The committee with responsibility for reviewing low-income housing "decided there is a definite need to support low and moderate income housing. Some of the major issues discussed were what groups should be served and what criteria should be established for ability to pay."[80]

It is easy to dismiss these ceremonial actions on the part of residents,

178 ◆   CHAPTER EIGHT

but they contributed to an atmosphere that supported low-income housing. A resident and an executive involved in low-income housing in Columbia, John Brandenburg, explained in 1987 the problems and strengths
of a community like Columbia: "I don't get the feeling that there is any
kind of consensus in the community as a whole that there need to be more
poor people here. There is a commitment on the part of Columbia's leadership, but I think most people would just as soon seal up the borders."[81]
The fact that community leadership stood behind increasing low-income
housing opportunities is significant in itself.

The CA did take some action to improve life for low-income residents. Beginning in the 1970s, it made discount memberships to facilities
such as pools and fitness clubs available to low-income residents. These
discounts are significant, up to 50 percent off on a package plan that covers
a wide variety of facilities and 75 percent on pool memberships. By the
1990s about 1,000 residents per year took advantage of these discounts.
Teenagers also have the option of earning a membership to facilities.

These discounts illustrate the community's commitment to improving the lives of low-income residents. After all, poor residents frequently
complained that they were cut off from the facilities of the community. In
recent years, the association has also lowered the cost of attending one of
the many camps run each summer and provides slots for low-income
children. The maintenance of the internal Columbia bus system, despite
poor ridership and fiscal insolvency, also reflected the CA's and Columbia
Council's commitment to providing services to those less fortunate.
Many low-income residents would have suffered if the service had been
discontinued.[82]

The community successfully integrated apartments, houses, and
single-family homes. Problems have surrounded low-income complexes,
but they continue to operate in Columbia. The community has continued
to add low-income residents through the creation of scattered subsidized
dwellings, and the so-called decline of older villages will open homeown-
ership and rentals in Columbia to a wider group. The leadership of the
community, particularly at the CA, has also made a genuine effort to improve life in Columbia for low-income residents. There is some talk of a
successional pattern developing between old and new villages, and it may
well transpire, but for the moment most Columbians seem to focus more
on moving into different types of dwellings than into different types of
neighborhoods. Although it has not achieved its idealistic plan, the community has achieved more social diversity than the suburbs it sought to
replace.

Irvine's Slow Progress

. . . as much diversity as a capitalistic society can provide.

RAYMOND WATSON, in *Orange County Register*

Irvine's experience with affordable income housing has been completely overlooked by most observers because no low-income subsidized housing has been constructed there. On the other hand, there has been a consistent effort to build more affordable housing and apartment complexes. The city and its residents have also created social services for the less fortunate. Residents and the developer have been engaged in a process of compromise over the last three decades that has both achieved substantive results and avoided more radical social experimentation.

The Irvine Company began its development without a significant commitment to low-income or affordable housing. Nevertheless, the company faced enormous resistance from residents even to the prospect of market-rate apartment complexes. Watson and his staff, including Bill Watt, supported apartment complexes in Irvine when there was talk of banning them from the ranch area in the 1970s: "It's wrong, morally and legally, if the reason behind it is a bias against people who live in apartments." Watson noted, finally, that "without diversity, you can't have a real village. You just wind up with another subdivision. That's what we believe in and we'll do everything we can to pursue that belief even if it's politically unpopular." Watson genuinely believed that the community would benefit from mixing apartments and affordable housing with high-income developments and often fought residents to achieve this progressive goal.[83]

The magazine, *New Worlds,* made a number of attempts to promote apartment living in Irvine by featuring the wholesome residents and community life in apartment complexes, as well as emphasizing their contribution to the tax base of the new city. The company also made much of its investment in better design, exceptional recreation facilities, and high standards of maintenance that would make their apartment communities an asset to Irvine. Looking at those complexes today, it is clear that the company did indeed build high-quality complexes. Through a subsidiary, the company now manages approximately 8,000 apartment units.[84]

Irvine has a reputation of unrelenting elitism, but many upper-income residents overcame their aversion to more affordable housing. One of the residents of a luxury development on the ranch, the Colony, asked rhetorically, in reference to a proposed affordable housing project nearby: "Who am I to deprive a man as good as I am who earns $10,000 or less a year, from this city? And who wants to exclude a young man with a baby and a young wife, the promise of tomorrow's life, from living in this nice place?"[85] One homeowner, during a controversy over affordable housing, explained, "I am concerned with the way the city is growing without any mechanism for a young adult to live in the city where he is raised." Another resident noted "I do not feel that simply because a person has a low income he is not as good as those with higher incomes, nor does the fact that a person earns more money make him better, smarter or nicer than those who earn less." Many more people, however, turned out to fight subsidized projects and units in their community.[86]

The inclusion of apartments and attached housing diversified Irvine and, according to some residents, gave the community a more egalitarian ethos. Carol Littschwager, society editor of the *Irvine World News,* boasted that "private clubs such as country clubs just aren't a big thing in Irvine, as they are in cities like Newport Beach. We're more interested in quiet get-togethers and recreational activities with neighbors and friends." She also claimed that there existed (in 1983) "very little stratification among neighborhoods. There's very little keeping up with the Joneses, either. Instead, people would rather help create what the community needs, like the new Boys and Girls Club."[87] The political and social system of Irvine does appear to be more open than that of many communities, yet it is largely an equality among equals, those who have already succeeded in the world. Irvine is a democratic city for upper-income residents. Average household income in 1999, for instance, was an impressive $57,000, and median home value was $245,000. The very fact of buying a home in Irvine reflects social success, so the need for social stratification within the community is probably not strongly felt.[88]

During the 1970s, the Irvine Company began to agitate for more affordable housing in the community, in large measure because of its hope of developing Irvine as an industrial center. But during the early to mid-1970s, when the Irvine Company finally sought to create high-density, more-affordable housing, the city government began to oppose such developments. The City of Irvine has struggled to provide more affordable housing because of alliances between conservative progrowth officials opposed to social welfare schemes and slow-growth environmental groups opposed to the higher densities that lower-cost housing demands.

In the early 1970s, elements of the city government had seemed solidly opposed to not only subsidized housing but also moderate-cost housing. John Burton, then mayor of Irvine, explained that he had opposed Valley View—a high-density project aimed at moderate-income groups—because it threatened property values. When asked by a reporter from *New Worlds* if Irvine would be a "city for everyone," he countered with a convincing but decidedly elitist retort: "Is Newport Beach a city for everyone? Is San Clemente?"[89] Burton was not alone in his resistance to the program. He had joined other councillors, under considerable public pressure, to defeat Valley View. After all, Gabrielle Pryor and her like-minded councillors elected under the Irvine Tomorrow banner, "pledged support for fair housing" yet also "vowed to oppose certain large-scale projects." Still, the Irvine Company had enough projects in the works that a certain number of high-density complexes succeeded in gaining approval, thus leading to the thousands of apartments now in Irvine.

The city failed to support not only many high-density projects with more affordable components but subsidized housing programs entirely. Unfortunately, the master plan of 1970 that guided the company, even though it was never officially adopted by the city or county, "said nothing about income diversity and subsidized housing." This omission proved a mistake on the company's part, as they would face even fiercer opposition from residents, who could rightly state that this type of housing was not part of the plan. Dr. Thomas Ashley, an economic planner for the Irvine Company, argued in 1972, however, that "the promise of improved housing in better environments for low- and moderate-income families is a goal that cannot be ignored."[90] Residents and the city council have successfully fought off the construction of any subsidized housing in the community from the beginning of the city's history until the present. Pryor expressed her disappointment in 1976, saying "there are those who just can't stand anyone who is in the low-income category and especially can't stomach those who must be subsidized."[91]

Subsidized housing failed to gain approval, but affordable housing projects have become part of the community's fabric. In 1998, Irvine had a total of 2,200 affordable units spread throughout the city in market-rate apartment complexes. The development of this affordable housing began in the early 1970s. In 1973, the city council hired the planning company Wilsey and Ham to create the plan for the city. Their plan, unveiled in 1973 "outlined specific procedures for builders to follow so that they provided housing in different price ranges and for different income groups in specific areas of the city." The city council followed up on this recommendation. In 1974 the council adopted a measure that forced inclusion of "a certain number of lower-priced rental and sale units" in large developments. This first inclusion occurred in 1974 when "the council required that 10 percent of the units be moderate-income housing" at Woodbridge

Village. The city began to apply this 10-percent rule generally after that time with developer cooperation. The Irvine Company, which had an interest in keeping its research and industrial parks growing, supported and lobbied for this provision of affordable housing, and it continues to cooperate. As discussed in the previous chapter, Watson recommended that, as a means to reduce resident resistance, affordable housing be incorporated into developments during construction rather than after. According to historian Martin Schiesl, under Pryor's leadership, in 1974 "Irvine . . . became the first city in the county to require that some inexpensive housing be permanently available in residential developments."[92]

Irvine Company officials sought to avoid the "boxy drabness of 'Project' units in older urban areas" by spreading the affordable units throughout the city.[93] Company officials boasted that, in 1992, the company had "7,800 apartments in Irvine. Of those, nearly 25 percent offer below-market rents for qualified families with more modest incomes. These affordable units are spread throughout the city. Thus, individuals and families with limited incomes are able to live and enjoy these high quality apartment communities and amenities without being singled out or identified."[94] Even the more conservative city government in power since 1990 has stood behind the 10 percent inclusion, although they now require that the company provide 10 percent affordable units anywhere on the ranch each time a major project is approved, rather than in the particular project approved. At the same time, it is not clear how lower-income people find out about these units. The city prints a guide to them, but prospective renters must put themselves on a waiting list at individual apartment complexes.

Related efforts by residents, often in tandem with the city government and the Irvine Company, have attempted to increase Irvine's social diversity. Since the mid-1980's, Irvine Temporary Housing has provided short-term shelter to homeless families, along with food, clothing and financial and job counseling. This emergency housing organization received support from the city, and the Irvine Company provided "the organization with 10 apartments at reduced rental rates and two renovated ranch houses."[95] The city also created special services, transportation, and housing for the disabled in the 1990s. The city's program of affordable child care provides a service much in demand by low-income families. Finally, UCI has created more affordable home-ownership opportunities on 530 owner-occupied residences for faculty and staff and has set price appreciation limits. A compromise in Irvine has thus been established. While the city consistently fought high-density development, it did meet its commitment to a more economically diverse community by working with the Irvine Company and the university to expand options for affordable and transitional housing.

❖

In each of these new towns, middle-class developers, planners, and residents have sought to reform the homogeneity of suburbia by creating a wider range of housing and income styles than found in most suburbs. The leadership of developers and residents encouraged the creation of a variety of housing as part of a better community life, even as certain aspects of the planned economic integration failed to meet expectations.

In Reston and Columbia, the disintegration of certain low-income complexes became a community issue—as it would not in many other communities where rich and poor are separated by more than a slice of woods or open space. Irvine demonstrated from the beginning the wiseness of integrating affordable housing units in market-rate complexes. As in other areas of reform, physical planning set off a complex social result. Although redesign of low-income housing programs along more decentralized lines played an important role in reducing social conflict, long-term citizen action has played just as important a part in preserving the idealistic vision.

At all these towns there are threats to maintaining social equality. Increasing affluence, the disappearance of federal subsidies, the conversion of low-income to market-rate rentals, and continuing problems in low-income complexes coupled with middle-class intolerance may erode the social mixture. The next forty years will be just as important in determining the degree to which the early vision can be maintained.

These communities together demonstrated that social diversity, even when accompanied by conflict, need not lead to middle-class flight, especially if the community is committed to creatively solving its problems. Some conventional suburbs have made progress in social mixture since the founding of the new towns, but most have not achieved anywhere near the success of these three communities. As an alternative to suburban social exclusivity, the new town experiments in social mixture made a clean break with conventions of community building.[96]

9

Colorblind: Race Relations in the New Towns

It's not fashionable to be a bigot in Columbia. If you don't want to live next door to a black or a Jew, you're probably not going to move here.

BEBE PRICE, Columbia resident, in *Baltimore Magazine*

The belief in racial integration as a social benefit thrived in two of the new towns. Reston and Columbia attracted numerous affluent black individuals and families who directly participated in the formation and growth of the community. Numerous liberals, both black and white, many of whom had been involved in civil-rights efforts, also piled in. Although racial integration at Columbia and Reston has not been without its challenges, and there has been plenty of hand-wringing over the decades, it has stood the test of time. Irvine might well have been able to duplicate the experience of Columbia and Reston, both of which were built in segregated counties, but it did not.

Since the inception of the new towns, the black population of suburbia has grown rapidly. The fair-housing legislation of the 1960s, which legally challenged discriminatory practices, helped open suburban communities. Cities like Washington, Atlanta, St. Louis, Los Angeles, and Baltimore experienced meteoric growth of their black suburban populations. But the increasing overall diversity of suburbia belies a more troubling picture. The black population of suburbia may be growing, but it is generally not well integrated with whites. One scholar, Robert Lake, among many who have noticed the trend, explains that "blacks are moving to those suburban communities where blacks already live and from which whites are moving away." Some of this resegregation has been due to choice, but most blacks have become isolated due to a different trend. As soon as black people begin to buy in large numbers, the white people usually move, and property values often decline. Many suburbs that appear to be integrated, usually in what are termed "spillover" areas adjacent to majority black ghettos, are only temporarily integrated and soon resegregate as whites flee and more black residents buy homes.[1]

If every suburban community had achieved the racial integration of Columbia or Reston, America would be a quite different, if still imperfectly integrated, nation. Black residents of these new towns, unlike their counterparts in most cities and many suburbs, have access to a high quality educational system, excellent housing, safe neighborhoods, and plentiful cultural offerings. White residents in these towns, if they choose, have the opportunity to move toward more openness to racial difference and greater understanding of black culture. An economic benefit for both blacks and whites is the creation of neighborhoods that maintain their value and status even after racial integration. By their very existence, Reston and Columbia called into question prevailing ideas about the necessity of suburban racial exclusivity.

Reston's Black Focus: Low-Key, High-Quality Integration

A visitor to Reston is still immediately impressed by the level of integration of the community. Schools, shopping centers, and residential areas are filled with a mix of both black and white residents as well as new immigrants from around the world. Reston has pioneered a quiet form of integration that stresses individual black achievement as much as black/white integration.

Simon made it clear to the nation that Reston would be an "open" community, but he hoped that the community would evolve slowly into a racially integrated town. In a 1966 interview, he explained that "there has been no effort on our part to influence the percentage of Negroes that live in Reston. At the moment we have three Negro families out of, let's say, 150 families. To put it another way, we're not engineering this thing. It's going to happen naturally. Reston is going to be effectively but not politically a city, and we're going to have living in Reston all kinds of people that live in a city—low income whites and high income whites and Negroes."[2] Simon was building his community in northern Virginia, an area notoriously hostile to integration, so one detects in his voice a note of caution that is belied by his other activities on behalf of integration. According to sociologist Peggy Wireman, Simon found himself in a quandary when trying to market the community: "Local realtors refused to market homes in Reston on an integrated basis. Simon was forced to obtain money from New York banks and market directly himself."[3]

The development companies that followed maintained integrationist policies but had the benefit of momentum. Black professionals came to Reston because of national publicity and word-of-mouth. Gulf Reston had to be pressured to promote black home purchases in the community; however, they eventually used pictures of black and white residents in publicity materials during the 1970s. Despite the company's lack of enthusiasm, the growth in black population continued. Publicity materials for Reston created by Mobil Land in the 1990s continued to feature glossy images of prosperous black and white families socializing, of black families enjoying life in Reston, and of black professionals working with whites.[4] In the mid-1970s, Reston's population was 11 percent black, as compared with 5 percent in the county as a whole.[5] By 1980, Reston's population was 14 percent black, and the racial mixture has remained stable since then.[6]

A sense of the heady early days of integration in Reston is reflected in *Ebony* magazine of 1966. The magazine published an article that included extensive pictures of the few prosperous black families living in Reston. For instance, readers met the Williams family, inhabitants of a Lake Anne town house, who shared a patio with white neighbors. Other black families were pictured around town and involving themselves with whites in cluster politics. The article visually demonstrated that black residents of Reston found themselves full participants in the cultural, political, and daily life of the community. "Liberalism is way of life in Reston," explained the article's authors. Integration did not frighten people because "people who move to Reston are not running away from anything. They are hunting for an ideal community where their children can mature under the best circumstances. . . . They accept anyone who is trying to achieve the same goals in a congenial atmosphere." The article even claimed that the town was more than "another integrated suburb. Its residents hesitate to call it integrated at all." Taylor Williams, a black resident, explained that "you don't identify in racial terms here. You're just an individual. You're either a gentleman or a lady and that's it. . . . You feel a part, like you're in a democracy or something." The frustration many blacks felt in American society at this time is reflected well in this man's statement. His observation illustrates how dream-like Reston felt to some, the transformation from the old style of racial politics seemed so complete.[7]

Local papers also featured the pro-integrationist attitudes at Reston. A 1971 *Washington Post* article described an incident in Hunters Woods that portrayed the continuing spirit: "Col. Mitchell, himself black, told of an attempt by a fellow Hunters Woods resident to circulate a petition barring Jews and blacks. The man got such a hot reception that he moved out." Another black resident, Marion Secundy, noted that "the blacks here are at a very high education level and are very comfortable here with minor exceptions. But as the town grows our job will get harder: to preserve our identity as blacks and yet to join in the community." She also added that "we wanted to help make this idea a reality. There's no Western frontier anymore, so we saw this as a chance to pioneer."[8]

Carlos Campbell, a longtime black resident of Reston and author of a 1978 study entitled *New Towns: Another Way to Live,* gave his readers a revealing portrait of black life in Reston. He described black residents as ambitious and mainstream: "I find that many middle-class blacks are more 'middle class' than middle-class whites. I expect that they are where whites were about 20 years ago with respect to those values that lead to the single-family detached homes, the wall-to-wall carpeting, the showcase living rooms, the custom-made drapes (professionally hung, of course), the station wagon, the riding lessons, the kids in private schools and the membership in the country club." He quoted one black professional who explained that "blacks in Reston are bourgeois. . . . There is a brother down the street and his lawn is the best on the block." Campbell recounted that in the early years, when there were few black residents, all-black parties were common; however, as the black population grew, most parties "have given way to those that are well integrated with whites." There remained a Sunday morning basketball game of black professionals, but no one seemed sensitive about or annoyed by either black-only events or growing integration. Campbell believed that race relations were good, and that "Reston is a rare instance where the racial mix is close to the national average and one that allows blacks to enjoy some real visibility in a predominantly white environment."[9]

The newspapers of Reston have promoted this visibility by creating numerous features on the black residents of Reston over the last thirty years. This attention has helped relieve white fear of blacks by accentuating the successful members of the black community. Reston attracted a talented group of black residents, including professors, government officials, teachers, business people, and even a sizable number of professional athletes. The articles feature their achievements, and while some admit that they came to Reston because it was an open community, few of the black residents interviewed seem particularly obsessed with integration as a day-to-day concern. Black residents, like their white counterparts, stress the schools, nature, and community feeling.[10] Most of the black residents featured have been at least middle class, but the newspapers did run occasional features on lower-income black residents.[11] Still, middle-class blacks, like middle-class whites, predominated in Reston civic affairs; they had the time, education, and resources to be full participants in community activity. Some critics fault the black middle-class for separating from poor blacks, but black middle-class residents have played an instrumental role in advancing the town's goals of social justice and integration through participation in local organizations.

One of the most important civic organizations in Reston, dominated by Reston's black middle class, is Reston Black Focus. This organization emerged to complement and fulfill the promise of integration in Reston. The idea and practice of integration occasionally needed nudging. Many black residents also felt the need for identity-oriented events. Black Focus was "established in 1969 by black families concerned that black people participate as citizens of Reston. . . . Reston Black Focus supports the Reston concept—a diverse racially integrated community where people can comfortably and meaningfully live, work, socialize and raise families."[12]

A 1969 letter from a member of the Black Focus described a meeting of its members with Glenn Saunders of Gulf Reston that attempted to force the hiring of black real estate salesmen. At that time, Saunders had argued that no qualified blacks had sought jobs in Reston and that the sales staff was too large in any case. Several weeks after the meeting, Edward Sharp, a member of Black Focus, found a new advertisement Gulf Reston had placed looking for a salesman, with no mention of "all qualified applicants" as part of the ad. Black Focus scolded the company: "If Gulf Reston is really planning an open, diverse community they must actively recruit qualified blacks for residential sales."[13] According to Wolf Von Eckardt in 1971, Black Focus of Reston continued to pressure the "developer to make greater efforts to open the town to black people, to show black faces in the promotion pictures, and to hire black salesmen."[14] In 1971, the company hired its first black for a management position, Bill Johnston, who worked in the human resources department where he counseled and trained the company's many employees. The organization also featured more black models in publications.[15]

Since 1969, Black Focus has spearheaded a wide variety of activities, including lobbying for affirmative action in Reston, pressure for establishing an at-large seat on the Fairfax County School Board, and holding of "training seminars on black history for Northern Virginia elementary school teachers and administrators." The organization also countered "instances of subtle racism" during the 1970s; for instance, they criticized white organizers for staging a "slave auction" as a fund-raiser. Black Focus raised money for other organizations including the United Negro College Fund and Africare. According to an article appearing in 1982, "Black Focus amassed considerable clout in its heyday."[16]

With the help of the RCA, Black Focus developed a successful sister-city program with Nyeri, Kenya.[17] William Robertson, a black resident of Reston who had spent time in Kenya while working for the Peace Corps, initiated the program in the early 1980s. Programs included art exchange, pen pals, and even training for Kenyan teachers in special education at a summer camp program."[18]

The Reston Black Focus Festival, which became the Reston Black Arts Festival, provided a yearly public display of Reston's social diversity. The Reston Times of 1969 featured pictures of black residents, the plaza fountain remade as a human figure, and a well-dressed black couple "groovin.'" In 1972, the Washington Post praised the festival as part of Reston's commitment to being "as inclusive as possible and to reflect the rich diversity of our population and culture." That the festival received press from outside Reston is significant. The Washington Post publicized the festival, describing the variety of performances by black groups including the D.C. Repertory Dance Company, the Black American Theater Company, and a variety of drummers and singers.[19] According to a 1996 article, the festival took place at Lake Anne village from 1969 until the mid-1980s, when it moved to Hunters Woods village center. Included in the events at different times have been informal athletic events; music, theater, and dance performances; African craft sales; political and religious speeches; and picnicking. In 1996, the festival, still featuring "the works of local and international acclaimed artisans," returned to Lake Anne and, as usual, attracted nearly 10,000 people to the festivities.[20]

In addition to Black Focus activities, black residents created branches of black fraternities and sororities in Reston, a branch of the National Council of Negro Women, and Jack and Jill (a black social organization "founded in 1947 to provide constructive educational, cultural, civic, recreational and social programs for African American children").[21] Black residents have formed their own church, the Martin Luther King Jr. Christian Church, in order to give their children a stronger sense of black identity. A number of black residents have also been active in primarily white community organizations including the RCA, the Reston Association, and the Reston Community Center. Margaret Boyd, an elementary school teacher in Reston, served for many years on the RCA board, and Ivan Cole served as president of RCA.[22]

In a lengthy interview in 1998, Cole offered an upbeat portrait of race relations in Reston, saying that no one seems particularly troubled about growing black institutions or the high degree of integration. He reported that while teens did tend to cluster by race, his daughter had interracial friendships and had had difficulty coming to terms with the racist attitudes outside of Reston. Cole participates in an all-black church (and socializes informally with black friends) because he believes children and adults need an occasional majority-black experience. Finally, he said he is of the opinion that the community is moving away from an "infantile" view of diversity that stresses a pretty picture—a mixture of races in restaurants, and so on—to a more sophisticated integration based upon a diversified job base and mass transit. Cole's postracial view of diversity only makes sense in a community where integration of the community is working and progress had been made. As the Reston experience demonstrates, an excellent way to get to postracial thinking is not to ignore the problem of race but to make significant progress within a community so that both black and white residents feel comfortable enough to begin thinking postracially.[23]

Many of Reston's white, middle-class residents continue to support integration and have appreciated living in an integrated community. They have also noticed changes in the community over time, including greater ethnic diversity and the development of newer areas of Reston that are less integrated.[24] Many residents report that Reston is divided between the Lake Anne, South Lakes, and Hunters Woods villages and the new North Point village, which is more uniformly white. A visual census of the area seems to bear this out, but no figures on particular areas are available. Older areas of Reston, however, seem to be more diverse and also seem to be attracting a greater variety of residents. Larger amounts of lower-priced housing available in these villages is primarily responsible for this greater diversity, as is the tradition of openness. During the last decade, Reston has had an influx of ethnic groups, including large numbers of Hispanics, mostly from Nicaragua and El Salvador, who have located in the Lake Anne and Hunters Woods areas. (In 1998, Reston as whole was 11 percent black, 5 percent Asian, and 5 percent Hispanic.)[25] Asian residents are moving to Reston in large numbers, attracted not only by its reputation for schools and employment, but also by its reputation for tolerance. These new groups have added to the complexity of race relations in Reston. In the long run, they will probably demand a wider role in community life and will further transform the black/white dichotomy.

There have been occasional problems in Reston with race relations, but the overall picture of integration is strikingly positive. Reston proved that racial integration in suburbia could work. Black residents have their own organizations, have taken a leadership role in the community, and are respected for their achievements. There does not appear to be disappointment about the lack of complete color-blindness in Reston; rather, there are expressions of satisfaction that a compromise can be reached between identity and integration. Reston, an island in racist northern Virginia, has become an important and positive model for American suburbia.

Columbia's Black Mommies and Daddies: The Search for a Color-Blind Suburbia

The Columbia experience began with integration of a most remarkable and impressive variety. Black and white residents, dedicated to the ideals of the civil-rights movement and inspired by Rouse's charismatic leadership, attempted to create a finely grained integration that would extend down to the level of friendships and casual socializing. Columbians sought to create a color-blind community. These idealistic residents seemed to be succeeding in the early years, and integration of neighborhoods still exists, but the community has become more self-critical about efforts to extinguish racial divisions.

As at Reston, the community centers, village centers, and neighborhoods are still occupied by both races, but black residents have expressed an increasingly firm belief that racial division not only still persists but also should persist. In particular, independent black organizations, churches, and clubs have emerged over the last two decades, much as at Reston. In addition, there has always been a division between the middle-class and lower-income black residents of Columbia. As at Reston, upper-class blacks have integrated more easily with whites, whose lifestyle they share.[26] Teenagers have also been more racially sensitive than children or adults, influenced as they are by popular culture and their peers.

The growing complexity of race relations could be seen as decline and has been viewed as such by many observers, but in other respects it represents a maturation of race relations that may be more sustainable than the color-blind idealism of the early years. Nor has this increasing discussion dissuaded blacks or whites from living in Columbia, as the percentage of black residents has remained consistent, at approximately 20 percent of the total population. Basic integration, tolerance, and respect, rather than color blindness, seem to be Columbia's greatest successes, not insignificant in today's racial environment.

Rouse let it be known from the beginning that Columbia would be an integrated community. According to Hamilton, "at the time of the announcement of the new town in October, 1963, Rouse was asked by a newsman if the community was to be integrated. He replied that he didn't see how anyone in this day and age could plan a community of this size that wasn't integrated." Of course, this was not actually true, as plenty of suburban developments, including Irvine, made no provisions for racial integration. Rouse, however, wanted to make integration seem a normal part of community building, and this statement brilliantly reversed conventional thinking. Rouse also predicted "that the new town would be about 15 per cent Negro, somewhat higher than the 11.3 per cent proportion in Howard County in 1963. He also suggested that in the next decade the economic and educational level of the Negro population was going to go up fast."[27] Indeed, Rouse was right about increasing black income, and his estimates proved conservative about the proportion of black residents in Columbia.

Columbia led the way in helping Howard County rethink its racist patterns. Hamilton described some of the challenges at hand:

> At speaking engagements in Howard County, this policy of integration was stated, when the speaker was asked about it, but the question was rarely asked—in white meetings. The matter came up, tho, with emphasis, at a Negro church meeting at which James Rouse spoke. Said one member of the audience—"If I had all the money Rockefeller has, I couldn't buy a house in Howard County," and other members of the audience went on to describe the elaborate methods by which realtors in the county kept Negroes from buying into white developments. . . . It was obvious that the people in the county maintained a system of segregation, in housing, and in public accommodation . . . and that the county was still in the process of desegregating its schools.[28]

Surprisingly enough, this racist, segregated county transformed itself into an integrationist county in just a few years.

Many observers and the development team feared that the new community would face hostility from the residents of the county, but the opposite actually happened:

> HRD's policy of open occupancy was clear and stated. Yet there was no backlash, and little overt comment. Indeed, when it came to trying to get the Patent Office for the new town (with its appreciable percentage of Negro employees), HRD had had the enthusiastic support and assistance of the County Commissioners. . . . Desegregation efforts in housing and public accommodation apparently had needed more leadership and HRD had, by its policy, supplied it.[29]

Integration worked well in Columbia and Reston, *as part of a well-conceived plan for community and economic development.* In most suburban communities, integration arises as a legal strategy that arouses opposition from whites who see little to be gained by the inclusion of black residents in their community. Often the consequences of these adversarial struggles are neighborhood decline or protracted legal battles rather than economic benefit for both whites and blacks.

The company affirmed this integrationist policy through the use of "visual language" in the publicity for the new town. While almost never openly stating the policy in printed or other materials, the company mixed images of blacks and whites in guidebooks, the exhibit building, and similar venues. Rouse recalled as well that "we had black hostesses and white hostesses in the exhibit building." Mal Sherman—an early HRD official responsible for land sales and marketing, Baltimore developer, and friend of James Rouse—remembered that "Rouse insisted on showing a slide presentation to potential buyers and builders in 1967, in which people of all races were seen sharing a swimming pool." Even today, such a photograph might well spell the end of a development in a more conventionally racist community. In Columbia, however, the use of mixed-race images has continued in publications created by the Rouse Company and the CA.[30]

A combination of this kind of publicity and word of mouth brought blacks to Columbia in large numbers. By 1974, Columbia already had an 18 percent black population, a high figure for a predominantly middle-class white suburb, and that proportion has remained constant.[31] In addition, these black residents have been deliberately spread throughout the community. Rouse himself specified that real-estate agents should not group black families together in neighborhoods.

Some builders in Columbia and some real-estate agents had trouble coming to terms with Rouse's policy in the early years. To make sure that the open-housing policy was enforced and racial steering discouraged, in the late 1960s, HRD sent "shoppers" of different races to test the builders and realtors. Sherman remembered that one of the builders was not obeying the policy: "We sent black and white shoppers out separately. We found that one of the builders and his sales agent were steering black buyers to one section of the lots by telling them that they would be happy in a cul-de-sac because other blacks had bought in the cul-de-sac." Whites were then steered away from this area. According to Sherman, Rouse was "visibly shaken by the news" and formed a local task force of Columbia residents. The residents, with Rouse, decided that the builder would have to leave the community. Such a strong action sent a warning to builders.

Racial balancing demanded some occasional radical measures. For instance, with the backing of Rouse and the residential board, Sherman bought out a black buyer in a row-house development because too many black residents had already purchased there. HRD also worked to make sure that subsidized housing was integrated, and the company convinced Interfaith to broaden their search for low-income tenants. An original advertisement in a Baltimore newspaper had brought all black responses. Subsequent appeals to local businesses and industries in the Columbia area balanced the applications.

Integration, then, was not simply a matter of stating of policy and featuring blacks in photographs. HRD had to monitor and occasionally socially engineer the community in order to achieve the integration desired. Fortunately, most builders and realtors accepted the policy. For instance, Jim Ryan, founder of Ryland Homes, is well known for his adherence to integration and affordable housing, and has built approximately half of all homes in Columbia. Ryan, incidentally, began his business in Columbia and is now one of the largest homebuilders in America, proving that building integrated housing need not be philanthropic. Sherman explained that early and successful Columbia builders such as Ryan "understood this policy [of racial integration], and they accepted it."[32]

Rouse himself was not opposed to blacks living together; instead he opposed forcing people to live together, as had happened in urban areas. In 1992 he explained, in response to growing racial separatism in Columbia, that "we won't have a truly open community until blacks have their own housing together if they want it." It may well be the case that the color-blind idealism of many early residents exceeded Rouse's own.[33] Columbia, however, has yet to develop any separate black residential areas. In 1987, indeed, one resident boasted that "there is no 'black area' of Columbia. There is no 'Jewish area.' There is no 'poor area.'" He noted that everything was instead "a mixture of some sort." Certain areas, particularly the earlier villages such as Wilde Lake and Harper's Choice, are more ethnically diverse than newer villages, but they are by no means black neighborhoods.[34]

Blacks moved to Columbia for a variety of reasons and from a variety of backgrounds. Columbia attracted a large and growing middle-class black population, now reputedly the third richest black community in the country. According to 1990 census figures, for instance, 2,400 black households in Columbia had incomes over $50,000 per year, and of those families, about half had yearly incomes over $75,000 per year. A middle-class black couple in the 1970s described how on a visit to their new home with their realtor, a white neighbor came over and "handed them glasses of lemonade." In addition, "for the first few months, it seemed [this couple] did nothing but attend parties in the neighborhood." Some of their friends from their former black neighborhood in northwest Baltimore moved to Columbia in part because of their friends' positive experience. Bill and Pinnie Ross, affluent leaders in the black community, "moved to Columbia from Catonsville in 1968, because they wanted to see 'what opportunities would exist in an open community.'"[35]

Columbia also attracted a number of local black celebrities. Six Bullets basketball players lived in Columbia during the 1970s, including then-coach K. C. Jones, who noted that he was attracted to the recreational and educational facilities for his children. Another member of the team noted that it was a "nice place to live . . . and the integration thing, there have been no hassles thus far. They have lived up to what they said."[36] A number of prominent black television personalities also lived in Columbia.[37] One white resident explained that "the most affluent families here tend to be black. They have the biggest, most expensive homes, the fanciest cars and they tend to be the friendliest people."[38]

Not all those who came to Columbia were professionals or even middle-class. Others, such as the Collins family, had a more unorthodox introduction: "Theresa and her sister Lamour [Collins] were taking a sociology course . . . at the Community College of Baltimore. The instructor, a white woman . . . took her entire class to the Exhibit building in Columbia as part of a study of new towns." The Collins sisters decided to move to the city after their visit and were satisfied with their life in Columbia, although the family maintained close ties to its former black neighborhood in Baltimore. The visual language of the center could attract blacks as well as inform whites of what they would have to expect as residents.[39]

Once ensconced in Columbia, blacks and whites seemed to be getting along rather well. Visitors in the early years noticed this striking, detailed mixture of blacks and whites. Jeanne O'Neill in *American Home* gave her readers a vivid picture of the state of racial affairs in Columbia in 1970:

> Every street, apartment and neighborhood is integrated. Peeking into a dancing class, you see pink legs and black legs pointing left and right together. Waiting outside class for her baby sister is 10 year old Sue O'Donnell. "Columbia is beautiful!" breathes Sue. Smilingly, her mother agrees. "And," she adds, "integration is working." Her girls play with black children, eat and sleep at their houses (and vice versa) without a second thought. Black and white grown-ups, too, mingle easily and naturally in Columbia.[40]

Teenagers, however, as O'Neill pointed out, were not having an easy time. She described a basketball game where "all the white students [from Columbia] sat on the home side—all the black students [from Columbia] sat with the visitors." In the *New York Times Magazine* in 1971, Jack Rosenthal described his experience in Columbia: "Another kind of openness dawns on you as you drive on. Quickly you recognize that there are black daddies washing cars, black mommies grilling hamburgers, black kids on trikes." Rosenthal described a suburban world with people acting completely as expected but looking entirely different. The article also described Mary Lee Smith, a member of the first family to buy a home in Columbia and a "former Memphis debutante" who described herself as "Southern oriented." She had found the "black professionals and middle-class in Columbia 'to be just like the rest of us.'" Rosenthal also described interracial socializing: "In the Friday night crowd at the Hobbit's Glen Gold Club bar, a gray haired woman gracefully ignores a drunk. Next to them, a big affable black man, a college librarian, swaps stories with a young white couple, she in granny glasses and he in bells. The music swells. So does the crowd, black and white. Jack Daniels double on the rocks." Rosenthal, however, also found black teens who "hoot obscenities at a white housewife" and explained that a teen center had become "all black turf." Although children and adults integrated more easily than teenagers, the level of integration remained striking.[41] Still, identity remained important. Neil Sandberg found that Columbia in the late 1970s had "discussion groups on black identity, black theater groups, the teaching of Black Muslim philosophy,

FIGURE 10 Interracial reunion at Old Buggy Court, 1977. Residents of one of Columbia's first neighborhoods recall past pleasures. (*Columbia Flier*, 1977)

and social interactions that involve black people to the exclusion of others."[42]

Columbia publications contributed to racial integration by featuring numerous photographs of black residents, running stories on black and interracial couples, and offering frank discussion of race relations. Readers of a special edition of the *Columbia Flier* in 1977 celebrating Columbia's tenth anniversary, for instance, found an article entitled "On the Street Where I Lived," by Ginnie Manuel. Manuel described her integrated cul-de-sac, Old Buggy Court, the views and careers of its various members, and the early years of their life in Columbia (figure 10). Manuel portrayed a time in the early 1970s when a group of families had an extensive social life that crossed racial boundaries. Perhaps most striking is a reunion photo of the couples from the original group of pioneers. The photo of these residents, taken in a neat, suburban living room, shows whites and blacks intimately seated and comfortably sharing the space. The anniversary issue also included a number of profiles of interesting and influential black families and individuals in Columbia.[43]

The *Columbia Flier* has never ceased to feature black residents and interracial issues. The *Flier* used Rouse's memorial service in 1996 to laud the community's racial attitudes. The authors of the article on the service featured residents Mike Crable and Greg Philips, who "stood jiggling their baby girls . . . away from the crowd listening to the speeches. The two men, who became friends at Wilde Lake High School, said they may never have come together, since they are of different races, except in Columbia. 'I was born in Brooklyn,' Philips said, 'Whites and blacks didn't mix. Mr. Rouse was a great role model for us. He was a great leveler.'"[44] In the 1980s and 1990s, *Calendar* magazine, which later became *Columbia Magazine,* featured pictures of blacks, as did *Newcomers Guides* during this period. Residents would see black residents modeling the latest fashions, sharing schoolrooms, and enjoying the great outdoors at Columbia. Anyone interested in moving to Columbia would know that integration was not hidden or temporary, but part of the new-town culture.[45]

Over the last three decades, Columbia has offered its residents programs that have helped the cause of integration. In the late 1970s, Harper's Choice was the site of a program entitled "Survival of Black and White in the Next America," which featured a series of seminars and performances by respected members of the Columbia black arts establishment and was designed to raise awareness of race issues.[46] A number of smaller organizations also operated in the 1970s and 1980s to promote better treatment of black students in the school system and to raise black awareness in general. In the 1980s and 1990s, the Columbia Forum promoted improved racial interaction. An event organized by the forum celebrating black history in Howard County was described in a newsletter. The event reflects that, in 1985, integration remained the norm in Columbia:

> The crowd of 500 who attended last month's Forum event was typical for Columbia—there were community leaders and citizens, corporate executives and school teachers, a general cross-section of bright, active, and involved residents of Howard County. Twenty years ago it would have been noteworthy that the people included blacks and whites together—sharing tables, food, ideas, jokes and rest rooms. In February of 1985, however, the racial mix was unimportant; the common link among the people was an interest in the evening's theme, "Toward a Just Society: A History of Race Relations in Howard County."[47]

The forum also sponsored a workshop entitled "Black/White Styles Discussed." Nearly three hundred residents attended the workshop led by Thomas Kochman, a professor of communications at the University of Illinois, in the hope of learning how blacks and whites could improve communication.[48]

Leadership in Columbia has consistently stood behind the integrationist ideals of the community. Rouse's vision of a more diverse community received its first challenge when George Wallace came to Columbia to speak in 1968 (figure 11). Although he stood by Wallace's right to speak in Columbia, Rouse participated in a heartfelt meeting of community residents. At that meeting he explained, in a prayer, that "we are being strengthened by these trying, testing days this week. We are discovering that we are up to it; that we have the character, the competence, the will to bring faith to the next America. . . . We thank you God, for our awareness of our strength, our unity and our love, that George Wallace generates among us tonight" and "reaffirm the spirit and ideals upon which this community is based."[49] At the same community meeting, Charles Russell, an African American member of the Wilde Lake board, gave his opinion of what made Columbia special: "Columbia is the place where the American dream is struggling to be born. It is a place where I can feel that I belong; where I can walk with dignity and confidence; where I know that I will be judged on my ability and not on the color of my skin or some other idiosyncrasy. I was glad when I came here that nobody tried to make me feel overly welcome. This is the point so many people miss. All we want is to be treated plainly, to be treated just as anybody else."[50] Rouse remained a strong believer in integration until his death. Reporters constantly tried to see if he was becoming frustrated by the occasional racial incidents in Columbia, but his faith remained firm.

Attesting to the long-term success of integration is that most middle-class black and some white teenagers of Columbia featured in local stories in the 1980s and 1990s have had difficulty adjusting to the contrast between the relative racial harmony of Columbia and the often virulent racism of American society outside the community. Black students who attended predominantly black colleges sometimes found themselves seen as different or strange for lacking a strong black identity, dating interracially, and having white friends; some white students at predominantly white universities found themselves chastised for not being intolerant, dating interracially, and having black friends. A black college student from Columbia, Francesca Black, stated that "Columbia is a melting pot full of a wide variety of people who get along with one another. But at the same time, it's

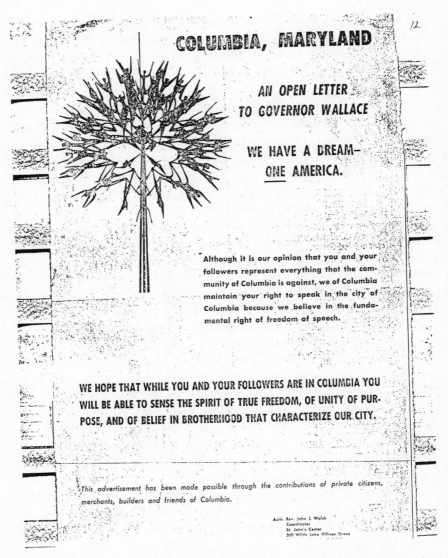

COLUMBIA, MARYLAND

AN OPEN LETTER TO GOVERNOR WALLACE

WE HAVE A DREAM—
ONE AMERICA.

Although it is our opinion that you and your followers represent everything that the community of Columbia is against, we of Columbia maintain your right to speak in the city of Columbia because we believe in the fundamental right of freedom of speech.

WE HOPE THAT WHILE YOU AND YOUR FOLLOWERS ARE IN COLUMBIA YOU WILL BE ABLE TO SENSE THE SPIRIT OF TRUE FREEDOM, OF UNITY OF PURPOSE, AND OF BELIEF IN BROTHERHOOD THAT CHARACTERIZE OUR CITY.

This advertisement has been made possible through the contributions of private citizens, merchants, builders and friends of Columbia.

Auth: Rev. John J. Walsh
Coordinator
St. John's Center
300 Wilde Lake Village Green

FIGURE 11 Statement published by local residents in support of integration. (*Columbia Flier*, 1968)

like a Utopia and not always very realistic." A local psychologist explained that "many of these children, both black and white, have had parents who participated or were part of the civil rights era in the 60s. They are unaware—because of growing up in Columbia—of the most oppressive forms of racism. Upon exiting the community, they encounter more aggressive and assertive types of racism. . . . For many this becomes a real problem." Many black teenagers go through "a phase of more intense identification with the Afro-American experience. And that may include a need to withdraw from predominantly white culture for a period of time." Other teenagers have preserved their more liberal and open-minded racial attitudes, managing "to walk that tightrope" between white and black worlds. One could fault Columbia for being unrealistic, but it is the outside world that has failed these teenagers.[51]

Another indication of the success of integration at Columbia is the attractiveness of the community to interracial couples. In 1973, 3 percent of Columbia's population lived in interracial families, "20 times the national average." According to a recent article in the *Columbia Magazine*, "many of the city's interracial families say they've found a place where they feel comfortable raising their children and going about their lives." One man in an interracial relationship explained, "It's just so nice to walk in the mall, for instance, and see other interracial families. There's a sense of belonging." One white mother reported that she was glad her children were growing up in Columbia because the community did not "identify them as outcasts." She explained, "I think their self-image is going to be so positive and that's going to help them overcome any problems they face when they leave." Her black husband, however, responded, "I'm worried more about them being snobs than about the world accepting them with open arms. And I'm not sure the world won't accept them better than we might expect."[52] Laura Nesbitt, a white woman in an interracial marriage, described how she felt about Columbia in 1985: "In Columbia our children know more interracial couples and have a wider range of friends than they would if we lived someplace else. I don't think they are naive or unaware, but I don't think they are color conscious. They see people as people."[53]

Many whites found living in an integrated community as liberating as did black residents. In 1977, Manuel Lazerov, a white real-estate developer and Columbia resident, explained, "People here tend to look less at race and religion and social background. It's a society built more on talent than pedigree. . . . I get a tremendous satisfaction from seeing all kinds of kids—white, black, yellow, orange—running down the street together, laughing and playing. Our children will probably grow up stronger because of it."[54] The young children, particularly, had positive attitudes about race. Tom Scott, a nine year old who gave his pictorial view of what he considered best about Columbia, included a drawing of black, white, and Asian "friends of many colors."[55]

There have been dissenting voices. Occasional racial incidents have occurred, mostly coming from residents outside the community. These have included attacks on black teenagers and racist leaflets left on lawns, but events like these are extremely rare. Black teenagers hanging around have frightened many Columbians. Their mere presence in a village center has sometimes been enough to scare off patrons. Some black residents have also criticized Columbia's racial idealism. June Caldwell, a black psychologist, described in 1971 how the community enforced white middle-class hegemony: "The little kids, they're very much together. But as they become adolescent, the barriers go up. . . . On balance this is a very good environment for Chip [her son]. But this community simply can't give him an awareness of being black. It demands—subtly—that I be middle-class white."[56] Caldwell saw that the teenagers seemed to have more problems getting along and believed that blacks suffered a loss of expressiveness in Columbia.

Many low-income blacks objected to being separated from middle-class blacks. One of the low-income black residents interviewed by Sandberg in the 1970s explained, "We call 'em [middle-class blacks] black bourgeoisie; they're sort of separate. They're livin' in the white man's town now, not joinin' any black nothin'." A teenager from the project explained, "In Columbia, you're considered poor if you live in this kind of housing. It's like there's a lower class group and higher class group. I've never really tried to associate with the higher class blacks because they've never tried to associate with me."[57] Jean Warrick Toomer, a black leader interviewed in 1975, offered a more compelling critique of Columbia. After six years, she found "the same white power world in which blacks are not a significant part of the 'system' just as I had always experienced in that other America I knew before moving to Columbia." As evidence of this, Toomer pointed out that in the areas of government, the Rouse Company, health services, business, and the CA, blacks had made few inroads. She did, however, note that progress had been made in black leadership in public education, religion, and local village boards. Toomer was right that whites dominated the local structure, but then again, whites outnumbered blacks four to one even in Columbia.[58]

Efraim Ben-Zadok found, as Toomer had, that blacks did not occupy a proportional number of political positions in the new town, although they were represented. Ironically, part of this low number was related to black reticence. Although whites enthusiastically supported black candidates for village positions, blacks reluctantly ran for office. Many felt that whites were not interested in the needs of blacks; others did not feel secure seeking office because of historical conditioning; and still others had developed all-black groups that provided an outlet for leadership. Ben-Zadok found that while blacks participated in CA facilities and local sport leagues, they were not involved to a great extent in village activities and tended to travel to Washington or Baltimore for many cultural activities. On the whole, however, he noted that Columbians remained positive about racial integration and that they were more negative about class integration. The residents he interviewed even believed that racial integration improved the community's reputation.[59]

Since the 1970s, significant progress has been made in many areas singled out as problematic. Black residents now occupy prominent positions. For example, C. Vernon Gray, a Columbia resident, was the first black person elected to the Howard County Council (in 1982) and the first black person in Howard County history to become chairman of the council in 1984. In 1997, he was elected the vice president of NACO, the National Association of Counties, a lobbying group for 3,000 county governments and is believed to be in line to become president of the association in the future.[60] Maggie Brown, another longtime black resident, has been an activist in Columbia and is now a high-ranking executive in the CA. From 1982 to 1988, she supervised customer service with the CA and then served briefly in the county government. In 1993, she was appointed to head the community services division of CA, which oversees a multimillion dollar budget and activities including "Columbia's lakefront summer festival, its many summer camps, ColumBus, its 25 community buildings, its before- and after-school day care programs, Oakland [Manor], the teen center, the arts center, CA's sister city program, its scholarship program" and related activities. Brown was selected in 2001 as president of CA, making her one of the most powerful people in Columbia.[61]

Over the last two decades, institutions associated with black life have developed in Columbia, including branches of Jack and Jill and the NAACP, branches of the National Association of Negro Business and Professional Women's Club and the National Council of Negro Women, black fraternities and sororities, and a variety of black churches. Long Reach Church of God, for instance, was established in 1983 and is both a congregation and a religious school. The fraternal organization, Alpha Phi Alpha, holds social and educational events both in Columbia and in the surrounding community. Members conduct tutoring at local low-income projects, offer scholarships to historically black Morgan State University, and sponsor related events to raise black awareness. A reporter in 1992 also found that "nightclubs have opened that tend to draw one group or the other, and churches are less integrated. Black high school graduates are increasingly enrolling in black colleges and universities. . . . While blacks and whites are still seen together in shopping malls, restaurants and movie theaters, one nightspot, the Silver Shadows, now is attended primarily by blacks, while a second 'black club' is under renovation. 'I love whites as much as blacks, but blacks feel more comfortable' in their own nightclub, says a black patron."[62]

Complementing these activities has been the growth of two museums in Columbia. In 1980, Columbia resident Doris Ligon founded the African Art Museum of Maryland, which operated at a variety of locations in Columbia before settling into the Oakland Manor building in 1989. The museum maintains a collection of art, photographs, and textiles from a variety of African traditions; mounts regular art exhibitions and a yearly jazzfest; organizes a yearly trip to Africa; sponsors a literary society; and offers children's events. Ligon explained in an interview that she does not believe that African-Americans need to "become part of African culture, but should understand, or gain a deeper appreciation, of art that has for so long been misunderstood." The CA, which owns and runs Oakland Manor, and the Columbia Foundation have provided valuable resources and support to the museum, as have a number of dedicated volunteers. Ligon believes that the museum's location in Columbia is related to Rouse's dream, and she has developed an interracial following both inside Columbia and in the region.[63]

The Howard County Center of African American Culture, founded in 1987, details the history of black life in Howard County. Exhibits in the museum display objects of everyday use from the old Howard County African American community and offers exhibits to schools and senior centers.[64] The founder of the museum, Wylene Bunch, began "setting up displays on African American history in schools, churches and community centers. When she and her family moved to Columbia in the early 1980s, Wylene decided there was need for a permanent exhibit." The center's collection, now housed on the grounds of Oakland Manor, includes "African-American memorabilia and artwork, a children's room, a military heroes display, a music collection, turn-of-the-century artifacts, a salute to Howard Countians, a library with over 3,000 books, and more. One section of the museum is designed to evoke images of an old Howard County home, with representation of a dining room, a bedroom, a kitchen, and a back porch."[65]

Even with all this racial progress, and perhaps because of it, journalists have been quick to jump on any racial tension. The Howard Sun, for instance, in 1992 ran a prominent article that highlighted the dissatisfaction of many black residents, particularly after a white-supremacist group left racist materials on some lawns.[66] Increases in the proportion of black students in some elementary schools located in older villages have also become a subject for debate in Columbia and Howard County over the past decade. Efforts by the Howard County school system to reduce racial concentration, however, seemed to be having the desired effect by the fall of 2000. Most Columbians, although aware of these flaws, continue to feel that race relations are good. A 1997 *Columbia Flier* survey of residents found that Columbia residents, both black and white, thought that race relations continued to be positive: 8 percent believed relations were excellent, 53 percent good, 28 percent fair, and only 10 percent poor.[67] Part of the shift to more negative coverage is related to the fact that in the early years Columbia was probably the most successfully integrated community in the nation, whereas in recent years many residents feel that although blacks and whites still live near each other, they have developed their own social and cultural circles. They believe Columbia has not lived up to its promise of complete and thorough integration. Negative reporting also reflects the decline of journalism and the American discussion of race into a scorecard of racial relations. Most recently articles have appeared in national magazines that laud Columbia's progress in race relations. Reporters are again realizing that although Columbia may not be perfect, it is less imperfect than many other communities.[68]

Columbia pioneered a new kind of American community. Although not as color-blind as originally hoped, it has developed a deserved reputation for tolerance and racial equality—two very important accomplishments. It serves as a healthy community for interracial families, black families, white families, and growing numbers of Asians and Hispanics drawn in large part by the community's tolerance of diversity (5 percent Asian and 2 percent Hispanic in 1998).[69] During the last two decades, black residents have taken a leadership role in civic life and added cultural institutions to the community. Columbia, like Reston, has pioneered an integrated society that, so far, can adjust to growing numbers of nonwhite residents rather than running from them.[70]

Irvine: Little Asia

In Irvine, no effort has been made to attract black residents. Although the Irvine Company inserted black faces into public relations during the 1960s as a result of a NAACP suit, no effort on a par with Reston or Columbia was made to attract black residents. The Irvine Company claimed in 1977 that "the Plan deals basically with the use of land. And therefore cannot determine racial balance. However, the Irvine Company does have a policy of non-discrimination and is trying to provide an opportunity for a community which is open to all persons, regardless of race, creed or color."[71] Recent sales materials do feature photographs of Hispanic and Asian people, but they feature few black faces. Although, as the developers' policies in Reston and Columbia have made clear, racial integration can be promoted without damaging profits, because the company did not make racial integration part of the early development process, it was unlikely that it would happen. Company officials believed that they had less responsibility for building an integrated community than the other new towns because blacks constituted a lower proportion of the population in Los Angeles than in the Baltimore-Washington corridor.[72]

What Irvine does have is growing numbers of Asian residents. In 1988, whereas blacks accounted for 1.5 percent of the population of Irvine, Asians accounted for 7.8 percent. Whites remained 87.8 per cent of the population.[73] By 1998, the Asian population had doubled to 18 percent, while blacks remained about 1.8 percent and Hispanics 6 percent.[74] The University of California-Irvine is also a predominantly Asian campus. Irvine residents stress international diversity, "a perfect multi-cultural environment," rather than racial diversity. Residents are quite proud of living in what they consider to be a very diverse community with growing numbers of residents from Asia and the rest of the world. After all, nearly fifty-eight languages are spoken in the schools, and the Asian population is skyrocketing. The Asian residents, with their family orientation, appreciate the educational opportunities and other provisions for family life in Irvine.[75]

The residents seem to have much less enthusiasm for black residents, as is indicated by the lack of interest on both the residents' and developers' parts. In the records there is no evidence of any attempt by either group to increase the presence of blacks in their community. The university has been the site of affirmative action programs and black-identity events, but these have not become community events.[76] One recent commentator noted that residents were mostly "white, middle-class, church-going, and working at white-collar jobs."[77] The residents could have insisted on greater racial integration but did not. The status quo seems to have been fine with the residents of Irvine.

❖

The developers and residents of Columbia and Reston have succeeded in creating communities that are more integrated than most other suburbs. Although integration is not as comprehensive as some originally hoped, heightened tolerance and racial equality have been achieved. Black residents have equal access to the high quality of life in each of these communities. White and black residents are able to shed some of their racism. Maintenance of integration over time will remain a challenge, but the new-town experience has already undermined conventional wisdom on suburban development.

Most members of the American middle-class remain committed to maintaining suburban racial homogeneity in the mistaken belief that homogeneity is the only way to preserve the value of their neighborhoods. Both suburban developers and residents share a belief in the superiority of racial exclusivism. With the few exceptions of integrated suburbs such as Oak Park, Illinois, and Shaker Heights, Ohio—communities where strong marketing programs seek to balance white and black purchase—most locales face difficulties when black citizens buy homes. Many suburbs unwillingly integrate because of fair housing laws developed since the 1960s, and then begin to resegregate as whites flee. As with many belief systems, the ideology of racial and class homogeneity as determinants for neighborhood stability becomes a self-fulfilling prophecy. Such wrong-headed beliefs lead to white flight. Residents are unaware that they are making a choice about the future of their community rather than obeying some iron law of neighborhood decline.

10

Trapped in Suburbia:
Feminism and Teenage Angst

Being a white, middle-class resident of conventional suburban subdivisions did not guarantee happiness. Critics argued that existing inhabitants of suburbia faced a different set of obstacles. Women seemed trapped in a deadening circle of chauffeuring, socializing, house cleaning, and child raising. Teenagers also seemed ill-suited to suburbia. With their high energy and participation in the growing counterculture, they appeared to many observers the most neglected group within suburban society.

Many social critics, as well as new-town developers and residents, believed that these groups needed special attention. As in other areas of social reform, the goal was to improve opportunities for community involvement and leadership. The new-town reformers also hoped to extend cooperation across seemingly fixed categories in order to make a happier and more satisfying community. The results have been more complex than the original planning predicted. Women made great progress in all of the new towns. A political and social landscape of strong women leaders and professionals called into question male dominance and conventional suburban ideas—even those of developers and planners—about women's sphere. Adolescents did not fare as well in this new landscape. Progress was made in providing activities for some teenagers, but the isolation of teenagers did not disappear in the new towns.

Women in the New Towns:
Careers, Leadership, Feminism, and Families

Suburban women of the 1950s and 1960s responded differently to the new suburbs. Many found the lifestyle of suburbia congenial, developed long-term friendships, and volunteered extensively. These women happily inhabited communities filled during most of the week by women and children and seemed undisturbed by male domination of the public and business realms. Critics acknowledged that suburban women seemed to be in control within the suburbs, although they might lack power in the public world beyond the borders: "Women wear the pants not only literally, around the house and in the super market, but figuratively as well. Suburban men have abdicated their traditional role as head of the household."[1] These women had a round of activities, including clubs and kaffee-klatsches, to keep them busy.

Another group of women found less to recommend in their new lives. They lived distant from cultural stimulation and discovered few challenges for their many talents. These women disliked chauffeuring their children and rounds of neighboring and gardening clubs. Betty Friedan believed that women had been incorrectly led to believe that fulfillment would only come through "sexual passivity, male domination, and nurturing maternal love." This mistaken belief had led the great majority of educated women to give up a public role, even at the local community level, for domestic duties. Housewifery then expanded in importance for these women, even with laborsaving devices, to fill all the hours of a day. Friedan believed that the sole focus on the domestic role had a damaging effect on women, as indicated, for instance, in the high rates of mental illness among suburban housewives. Most women, moreover, could not find jobs, educational, or cultural opportunities in suburbia even if they had wanted them. A very few women, Friedan herself acknowledged, refused to be bounded by the suburban role set for them and found careers, public roles, and educational opportunities. Most women, however, were not so lucky.[2]

The new towns attracted both women content in their suburban role and those seeking a more active role in public affairs. Although the development of the new towns coincided with the return of women to the workforce and public life, the social ferment, educational profile, and spatial organization of new towns advanced women's activity outside the home. Many married women with children benefited from having elementary schools, child-care centers, and recreational facilities in close proximity. These convenient facilities reduced the demand for constant chauffeuring and stay-at-home mothering. Women found other activities—volunteer and professional—that sharpened their political and business skills. In addition, the structure of the community associations in the new towns proved a boon to female leadership. Cutting their political teeth at the local village level, women moved up into county and state politics. Some of these women found a supportive environment for a challenge to traditional gender roles as they became caught up in the women's movement of the 1970s.

The current trend in women's history has been to question "the stereotype of postwar women as quiescent, docile and domestic," the stereotype embodied in *The Feminine Mystique*. A group of younger scholars have found that women participated widely in the workplace and public life during the period that antedates the women's movement. Friedan, in fact, acknowledged that some women remained active outside of the home, but these women remained the exceptions. The evidence from the new towns supports both the findings of these revisionists and also sustains some of the truth of the "feminine mystique." The revisionists have underestimated the constraints of suburban life and the catalyzing effect of the women's movement. Many women, for instance, welcomed the new freedom of new towns and became involved in the feminist movement, the workplace, and politics. Others, however, arrived with a strong political consciousness and experience in the workplace. For them, the women's movement meant less, but they still benefited from having a community that made child rearing less onerous and expectations of women's working more commonplace. And, of course, many women declined to either take jobs or participate in the women's movement. This short study of women in new towns contributes to the deepening of historians' view of women's experience after World War II by adding more local dimension.[3]

Reston's Leading Women

In Reston, feminism and women's activity blossomed. The physical design of the community had the desired effect of liberating mothers from the isolation of traditional suburbs. The developer and his staff realized that women faced special constraints in suburbia. A report published by the Reston Foundation, which Simon established to promote cultural and social activity, noted in 1967, "when we speak of a Reston Children's Center, we are not simply talking about day care for youngsters. We are talking about freeing young American women from 24-hour child rearing so that they may further their education, follow a career or otherwise enrich their lives."[4] One Reston mother commented, "I'm a working mother and when

I'm away my children have everything available here. They walk to the community center and shop for me, or get their hair cut, or take music lessons. . . . A mother doesn't have to put a chauffeur's cap on and take her children everywhere."[5]

Simon placed a woman in a high-profile position in Reston by hiring Jane Wilhelm as community relations director in 1964. She recalled in a recent interview that not only did she spy on Columbia in order to borrow some of their innovations but she decided which "facilities we should have or not have, such as playgrounds, nursery schools, day care centers, and I was supposed to facilitate the coming of churches, schools, and decide where they should be and help them get in." Wilhelm also helped establish Reston's first elderly housing complex, in which she herself is now a resident. Very early in Reston's history, under Wilhelm's direction, the community organized child-care centers, one of the earliest being Lake Anne Nursery Kindergarten. Since then, the number of child care centers has expanded; at last count there were approximately sixteen, and they are operated by a variety of different organizations, including nonprofits such as Reston Interfaith, religious groups, private organizations, and Montessori. Fairfax County also offers child care, including before- and after-school programs.[6]

Reston's attractiveness to women was reflected in a study by the Reston Association in the mid-1970s. The study found that the "number of families headed by just the female parent has increased from 139 to 960 in the last five years, and they now make up 16.5 percent of 5,815 families in the town." The director of the study noted that "single head of household families believe they will be more readily accepted in Reston and that the many facilities and activities available there will help occupy their children's time." Forty percent of those families headed by women were at the poverty level and had moved to the many new subsidized housing units. Certainly some of the rising numbers of single-headed families resulted from divorce within the town, too. Reston residents have told me that it was common for divorcing couples to find separate accommodations within the community.[7]

Many Reston women wanted nothing to do with feminism, but many others became involved in the women's movement. A women's center "grew out of Reston participation in the women's movement of the early '70s." The center offered referral services and workshops. The referral service gave information on child care, senior-citizen service programs, abortion and counseling information. Members also organized workshops, forums, and consciousness-raising groups. The workshops were "designed to answer women's questions about themselves. For example, they recently sponsored two workshops on the woman's reproductive system. Past workshops have covered such subjects as women's legal rights, divorce and separation, and sexism in education." The group also lobbied for women's-rights legislation on Capitol Hill. Not surprisingly, "most active members . . . [were] white, middle-class homemakers in their late twenties or early thirties, usually with children."[8] During the early 1970s, there also was a "Reston Women's Lib" group, and Diane Gore hosted and produced a feminist program for the local cable channel, entitled "Women and the Issues," that dealt "with a wide variety of issues relating to women and therefore to men and children in the Reston area." No one seems to remember when these institutions and programs ceased operating, but they probably dissolved some time during the late 1970s as the women's movement lost strength.[9]

Reston women have been particularly active in guiding the community's political and social growth. It is remarkable to consider the many institutions that have been run or influenced by women in Reston. The resident women, not just the developer's staff, played an important role in establishing the early institutions of the community. The Reston Directory, both a telephone book and a guide to local activities, was founded by Carol Lindberg and Janet Hays. Over the years the directory has grown to many hundreds of pages and is currently published by Nancy Larson, another longtime community activist. GRACE, the Greater Reston Art Center (discussed in the next chapter) also benefited from female leadership, as did Reston Interfaith during Connie Pettinger's tenure, which lasted from 1982 to 1997. Pettinger built the organization into a well-funded social-service organization for the community. The Reston Association, the main form of local governance, has had a number of female leaders, including Susan Jones and Lindberg.

Martha Pennino, "Mother Fairfax," represented Reston (and surrounding areas) at the county level from 1968 to 1991. Although not a resident of Reston, she certainly benefited from the liberal, feminist ethos of the community. Pennino worked with Restonians to develop a number of institutions: the homeless shelter, low-income housing at Stonegate and Cedar Ridge, the regional library, Reston hospital, the town center, and South Lakes High School. She considered "Reston her second home and spent a considerable amount of time working out of her office on Bowman Town Drive." She began her career on the county board in 1968 and, according to a recent article, "was one of the few politicians during the late 1960s who still believed in and fought to maintain Robert Simon's dream. . . . Pennino once said, 'It was Bob Simon's symphony, but I got to play it.'" Indeed, Pennino is in large measure responsible for preserving the new-town vision. She worked closely with members of the RCA; in particular, she collaborated with members of the Planning and Zoning Committee to make sure the developers held to both the spirit and law of the new-town vision.[10]

RCA has also had a number of female presidents, including Joanne Brownsward, Larson, and Janet Howell. Howell is a longtime community activist who has worked her way up to significant power and prestige. After her arrival in Reston in 1974, she served for many years as president of local PTAs. She also served on the Reston Interfaith board and directed Interfaith's Laurel Learning Center, providing day care for low-income families. Her political career in Reston began at the RCA. During the 1980s, she served for three years as president of the association and by all accounts was a dynamic leader. She worked for three years as an aide to Reston state delegate Ken Plum. In large measure because of this leadership experience, she was able to attain higher office, and unseated a popular Republican in a close race for the Virginia state senate in 1992. Howell recently became the first woman in Virginia history to hold a seat on the influential Finance Committee.[11]

Another woman in a position of importance in the community is Priscilla Ames, a member of one of Reston's pioneer families. Since the 1970s, she has struggled to remind residents of new-town ideals and to build new institutions for the community. Ames, with Embry Rucker, her companion, helped run the Common Ground Foundation, which created many of Reston's social institutions. Affordable housing remains a serious concern for her, and she is involved with efforts to increase affordable housing opportunities in Reston.

Reston, then, answered many different needs for women: traditional housewives enjoyed the convenience of less driving; single parents found a nurturing environment; and activist women found a supportive setting for feminism, political careers, and social service. The original planning did not stress women's liberation, but an unintentional outcome of the planning was the creation of an environment particularly conducive to it.

Taking Charge in Columbia

The Columbia work group and planners made provisions for women in their planning, but they viewed most adult women as mothers who would be primarily interested in culture and education, not a career. The community they created, however, as at Reston, turned out to be well designed for working women, political women, and feminists. Furthermore, the sophistication of the new-town planning effort attracted an educated group of middle-class women who took matters into their own hands.

Some of the first women to arrive in Columbia seemed happy simply to have less driving every day. Marian Shrode, originally a housewife in Annapolis, explained in 1968 that "the day we decided to move to Columbia I had driven 43 miles around Annapolis doing errands." By moving to Columbia, she noted, "We gave up trees and a house on the water, but now the kids walk everywhere."[12] Another early resident illustrated the benefits of the new town: "I came to Columbia to get back to people, and I feel I've been able to do that. In Annapolis, we had a lovely home, but I seemed to spend the whole day chauffeuring the children. Columbia has changed my whole way of life. I'm doing things I never thought I'd be doing before. I think that may be true for a lot of people." Indeed, many women found that they had much more time to develop their personal interests and careers.[13]

Charlotte Temple, a new-town developer in Rochester, New York, published a report on Columbia (ca. 1973) that provides insight into why these communities worked well for many women. She had a number of criticisms for the developer, however, particularly "the assumption that the woman will be at home with children, that children are 'her job.'" She pointed out that neighborhood centers had failed to provide "communities of interest" that would have created a support system for women. Nonetheless, she found the women's movement to be strong in Columbia: "The very openness of the new town to new ideas and institutions, coupled with affluence and high educational levels, seems to promote this questioning process." She believed that "an additional force here is the existence of a large number of divorced men and women who are attempting to create new life styles." Temple found that many women already worked in Columbia: "Thirty eight percent of the women with children under five years of age work." Temple also found about a dozen child-care centers in operation in the mid-1970s. Although not perfect, the community seemed to be working well for women whose ambitions carried them beyond the home.[14]

Women residents of Columbia took it upon themselves to develop better day-care services, and they were aided by the CA. A report from 1971, entitled "A Model for the Nation: Child Care and Learning at Columbia," detailed the numerous innovations. The report noted that new-town zoning allowed for more flexibility when it came to creating child-care options in residential neighborhoods. In addition, many neighborhood centers contained day- or child-care buildings. By 1971, Columbia had seven cooperative preschools in operation, administered and initiated by parents of enrolled children but run by professional staff (with help from parents). By the early 1970s, the CA also operated two children's centers that provided nursery school and day care, had created an Early Childhood Education Board, offered a path-breaking hourly child-care program (with hourly rates), and supplied extensive recreational after-school programs for older children. Interfaith Day Care opened in 1970 to serve lower-income residents at Roslyn Rise Day Care Center. A Montessori program operated in the early years, and a large number of private day-care options have expanded over the years. In 1999, there were nine cooperative nursery schools, eight private nursery schools, two religious nursery schools, five Montessori schools, and approximately fifteen private day-care centers. The CA runs before- and after-school programs at approximately twenty schools and still operates two extended kindergarten care programs at neighborhood centers.[15]

A number of women took the opportunities offered by Columbia to return to a career, begin a new one, or become part of the growing women's movement. Scotty Loje, for instance, put off her law-school plans in the early 1970s for a few years while raising her children but "devoted most of her free time to the Committee Against Sexual Stereotyping, a group which lobbied to eliminate sex discrimination in education. Calling herself 'a moderate feminist,' she [said], 'I confined myself to a specific area of the women's movement where I felt I could make some changes.'"[16]

As at Reston, many women wanted more than careers; they sought to restructure relationships and society as part of the women's liberation movement. Temple described two other organizations "deeply involved in the growing pains of women here." One was the Family Life Center, which offered "family life education such as parent effectiveness training, family and marriage counseling, and educational workshops." The Women's Center sponsored "special-interest study groups which focus[ed] on issues of special relevance to women. There are groups for women over 35, for separated or divorced women, and for couples." Louise Eberhardt, the head of the center, felt that the "Center would not have been there if Columbia had not been a new town." The Women's Center, for instance, found space in one of the Interfaith centers, received funding from the Columbia Foundation, and benefited from the new town's openness "to new ideas."[17] One visiting reporter, in 1972, found a "young, blue-jeaned woman sitting in a feminist circle on the floor of the Interfaith Center, exploring her feelings with a women's [therapy] group." [18] Another reporter in the 1970s noted that the Women's Center "with its discussions and training sessions attracts the younger, turned-on set."[19]

Many women evidently found new ideas at the Women's Center. Columbia resident Karen Wexler in 1971 described how although everything seemed fine in her life (new baby, successful husband), "she thought she would go 'bonkers' at home." She explained that "when she moved to Columbia, she found people who felt the same way at the Women's Center. And in the consciousness-raising group, she found people to share her unhappiness and her anger 'at the role I was expected to play.'"[20] Mary Jefery, another Columbia resident, had moved from Massachusetts where she had been a full-time housewife. At first, in Columbia, she had felt alone, but that changed when "she started going to the Women's Center, took a number of women's courses at Howard Community College, and joined a consciousness-raising group." She decided to go back into teaching, and she and her husband began sharing housework and child rearing. The women's movement helped many women transform their lives. The Family Life Center continues to be an important Columbia institution, but the Women's Center, like the one in Reston, no longer exists.[21]

The *Columbia Flier* also helped make feminism and women's careers part of Columbia's culture. Not only did the magazine feature writing and editing by women, but it published articles that explored women's issues (figure 12). The *Flier*'s tenth-anniversary-edition magazine in 1977 featured women in an article entitled "Working Women: Out of the Rut and Rising to Unique Opportunities." Ruth Glick, the author, introduced Marian Shrode, the publisher of the Columbia Directory, a guide to the community. Shrode explained, "I probably never would have worked if it hadn't been for Columbia. This is my second marriage. And during the four years before we moved to Columbia, I was the housewife. . . . Now my house is a wreck, and I don't cook anymore." She believed that the openness of the community had encouraged her to take a leading role in business. Glick also introduced readers to Mickey Dunham, a representative for HRD. Glick discussed how "as a working mother, with a consuming job, Dunham feels that the convenience of the new town was a substantial help in allowing her to take on the responsibilities of a full time career." Her son was able to walk to school, participate in extracurricular activities, and go to the library. He also used the bus system as an adolescent. Judy Foster, an X-ray technician and working mother of three, explained, "in Columbia, it seems almost expected that women will do something interesting. In fact,

FIGURE 12 Humorous inversion of a traditional scene in the feminist world of Columbia. ("The People of Columbia," *Columbia Flier*, 1977)

there seems to be a competition here—not about who can bake the best cakes but who has the best job."[22]

From the very beginning, too, Columbia women became involved in local politics. Helen Ruther initiated a League of Women Voters chapter in Columbia in 1968, just one year after the opening of the community.[23] An article in the *Columbia Flier's* tenth anniversary edition entitled "Hatch Act Baby: The Emergence of Women as a Political Force," by Kay Wisniweski, explained some of the reasons for women's successful activism. The new-town concept had attracted a "disproportionate number of highly educated, idealistic women endowed with the self-confidence peculiar to their generation and class." Columbia had another special condition that encouraged women's leadership: many women had husbands who were covered by the federal Hatch Act, which prevented them from participating in partisan politics.

Wisniweski explained that village boards acted as springboards to wider power, because "it doesn't take much in the way of money or courage to get elected to one. . . . Women who might have quailed at the thought of running for state or county office can get their feet wet in the shallow lagoons of Columbia's village government." Village boards, which seemed to many men to be dead-end organizations because of developer control, offered a stepping stone to greater power: "After a couple of terms as village board chairman or Columbia Council representative, women like Ginny Thomas and Ruth Keeton found themselves local celebrities with an embryonic campaign organization composed for the most part of other women who shared their passion for consumer protection or fair housing or some other grassroots cause." The Democratic party, too, was female dominated in Columbia, and "affirmative action at CDC [the Columbia Democratic Committee] consisted of beating the bushes for token males." Wisniweski described the new kind of "political boss" to be found in Columbia: "We have the thirtyish housewife running a door-to-door canvass operation with a baby in a backpack or a toddler clinging to one blue-jeaned leg, a strong new branch on Mr. Rouse's People Tree." Lani Clark of Columbia, a mother of two, for instance, "worked in succession with the McGovern campaign, PTA, the Women's Center, the county's Democratic Central Committee and now Womanscope, a career guidance service of which she is now director." Women have been and remain a strong force in Columbia and Howard County politics.[24]

In 1974, Columbia residents elected Keeton and Thomas to the county council, an organizational body not previously known for female participation. Thomas and Keeton each served terms as chair of the council, and Thomas went on to become a Maryland state delegate. Elizabeth Bobo, although not a resident, represented Columbia and was aided by the support for female leadership. Bobo served on the county council in the 1970s and 1980s and eventually became the first female county executive in Maryland.[25] Jacqueline Dewey developed community services at the CA for twenty years, supervising a budget that grew to over $4 million by the time she retired. Maggie Brown, another leader of Columbia, replaced Dewey and became the new president of the association in 2001. Brown took the reins of what has become one of the largest homeowner associations in America with an annual budget of $44 million and eight hundred employees. Women have also served in large numbers on the Columbia Council, which now oversees the CA.

Ruth Keeton's political career reflects the new kind of female leadership at Columbia. Known for her gentle but persistent lobbying, she was never afraid to take on what might have been considered unpopular stands. Keeton spent her life engaged in social action of one kind or another, including work with the American Friends Service Committee and the Congress of Racial Equality. When she and her family moved to Columbia, she was first elected to the CA board, then to the Howard County council. She served four terms on the council and was a leader in social and environmental issues, in which she always had a strong interest. During her fourth term, she succumbed to Alzheimer's disease and passed away in 1997. Keeton probably would have succeeded anywhere, but her ability to gain political power resulted from Columbia's liberal politics, the open nature of the political system, and the feminist attitudes of the community that supported women's bid for political power.[26]

Columbia's planners created a suburban environment that proved supportive of women's efforts to work, to engage in feminist activities, and to become politically active. Women chose their degree of involvement in homemaking, work, politics, and feminism, and the new town offered suburban women a number of viable choices.

Active Women in a Traditional Irvine

Irvine's women, like their counterparts in the other new towns, have taken a leadership role in the community, as the design of the town proved congenial to women's working and political activity. As in the other new towns, children were provided with extensive recreational facilities within walking distance; schools were conveniently located; and a child-care network has developed over the last three decades.

Recently, *Working Mother* magazine "rated the City of Irvine as one of the top five cities nationwide for its provision and maintenance of child care and pre-school services." More than thirty preschools are currently operated by a variety of organizations. The City of Irvine, beginning in the 1980s, hired a full-time child-care coordinator and in 1987 adopted "the state's most comprehensive municipal child care ordinance," with the goal of providing "quality child care for all residents who need it." The city operates a "child development center . . . [and] the 11,000 square-foot facility is one of California's few city-operated child care centers available to municipal employees as well as the community at large." The Irvine Child Care project, coordinated with local nonprofits, provides child care in modular units at eighteen elementary schools. The city also operates child-care and after-school programs and summer day camps at local community centers, as well as a "kid phone" that offers thousands of children every year a "reassuring adult voice." A Child Care Coordination Office promotes the creation of new child-care opportunities, distributes information, and offers technical assistance to new child-care providers. Some residents complained in the early days about the lack of services, but the residents have more than compensated for any early deficiencies.[27]

The number of working women in Irvine demonstrated that women found it possible to combine work and child rearing there. In 1979, one survey found that "sixty-five percent of the county's women are working, which is sixteen percent above the national average."[28] Many of the residents of the ranch, after all, needed the extra income to afford the high cost of housing and living. There is no evidence of extensive feminist activity beyond the university, but the high degree of female participation in the economy and in local government reflects both the type of women attracted to Irvine and the relative ease of parenting in new towns, where schools, day care, and recreational facilities were conveniently located.

Women have played a leadership role during much of the city's history. Gabrielle Pryor represented a type of female leadership similar to that found in other new towns. She began her political career in her local homeowner's association as editor of the *Village Park Community Association Newsletter*.[29] In the first elections in Irvine, she became one of the first five city councilors (out of field of thirty). In 1974, she was elected mayor. An article in *New Worlds*, titled "The Mayor Is a Hometown Girl," explained that even though Pryor's job as mayor was full-time, "the 34-year-old mayor is a housewife by profession and choice." Pryor proved a dedicated mayor. She led the fight for more moderate cost housing, and also worked on improving emergency and teen services. She saw a special and limited role for women in politics: "Women know what the community needs are, and they adopt the fulfillment of those needs as a goal. Most of the women I know in local government are that type of politician, they don't really hold ambitions for higher office." Pryor herself had mixed feelings about the women's movement. Although she was a member of the National Women's Political Caucus, she had little interest in consciousness raising: "I can think of nothing more counterproductive than sitting around in a circle and griping about your circumstances. For heaven's sake, if you're not happy with what's happening . . . go out and change [it]. . . . If I can encourage other women to do their own thing the way I've done mine, I'll do it, but I'm not going to encourage women to tear men apart because it makes them feel superior."[30]

The City of Irvine has had a large number of female city councilors, including Mary Gaido, Paula Werner, Barbara Wiener, Christina Shea, and Sally Anne Sheridan. Sheridan, a political conservative, defeated the better funded and more liberal incumbent, Larry Agran, to become mayor in 1990. Whereas Reston and Columbia have fostered largely liberal female politicians, Irvine's women leaders include many more politically conservative women, in part reflecting the conservatism of the community. One of those is Shea, the current mayor of Irvine.

Shea is a fascinating political figure whose rapid political rise reflects the openness of Irvine to women's political ambition. A longtime resident and single parent of two children, Shea is a self-described businesswoman who has served on the board of directors of the American Cancer Society, as president of the Irvine Child Care Project, and as a fund-raiser for Human Options, dedicated to helping abused women and children. Shea also distinguished herself in her opposition to the proposed conversion of El Toro military base into a civilian airport.

Her affiliations with nonprofits might make one expect her to be liberal, but since her election to the Irvine city council in 1992, Shea has been unerringly conservative in her stances. For example, as a council member in 1995, she voted against the Santa Alicia low-cost housing project in Westpark.[31] Still, in 1996, she received a surprising and important endorsement from Agran, who shares her strong opposition to the El Toro airport plan. As mayor, Shea has expressed her opinion that the city council needs to do more to guide policy: "I will not rubber stamp suggestions by staff, particularly with regard to the Irvine Company." She acknowledged that Irvine residents supported female leadership: "In 1992, I won [a City Council seat] by a landslide . . . so I knew I was popular and women were doing well. From the standpoint of a female in office, I think that certainly says something about the electorate."[32]

Irvine experienced less organized feminist activity than did Reston or Columbia, but many women engaged in professional development and political organizing. The openness of the political system, the growth of local child-care options, and the support in the general population for female leadership have made Irvine an exceptional community.

In the new towns, the physical and institutional environment helped liberate suburban women from the most onerous aspects of full-time housework and child rearing. Complementing this physical arrangement has been the development of a social environment of educated, middle-class activist women, women-oriented institutions, and a more open political system. These conditions in tandem aided women's participation in community life and propelled them to the leading edge of the women's movement and local suburban politics. Much of the same activity could be found in other suburbs and cities at the time, but the scale, ambition, and success of women in the new towns over the decades remains striking.

Teenagers in the New Towns: Coercion, Kindness, and Defiance

> Got to find a way to keep the young ones moral after school. . . .
>
> DR. HAROLD HILL, *The Music Man*

The adolescent represented a challenge for the new town. In the standard suburb, according to the critics, the adolescent was the outcast, poorly suited to the suburb's emphasis on conformity and the nuclear family. In a *New Republic* article, Wolf Von Eckardt sketched a familiar portrait of teenage delinquency, this one set in suburban Montgomery County, Maryland, where "kids from good homes with all the 'privilege' our society can offer, smash windows, throw home-made bombs into libraries, race about in stolen cars and crash parties."[33] Even Herbert Gans, in his respected and moderate study of Levittown, found adolescents cut out of suburban society, lacking extensive extracurricular activities, possessing few public places for socializing, and bereft of domestic privacy.[34] Many suburban residents genuinely feared that the growing numbers of adolescent baby boomers would create chaos in suburbia. When trouble started, the police used coercion and control of teenage behavior as the most common recourse, especially as the 1960s and 1970s counterculture grew.

The new-town reformers, on the other hand, believed that they could transform the life of the adolescent. Developers and residents did not endorse the teenage subculture, but they believed that, instead of trying to simply coerce youngsters, they could divert their energy into patterns adults considered more socially acceptable. Youths would be converted with kindness as much as authority. The new towns sponsored teen centers and initiated special programs, many of which remain in place. Paul Goodman's *Growing Up Absurd: Problems of Youth in the Organized System* (1956) seems to have had some indirect influence on new towns. Goodman proposed that the solution to teenage rebellion was to reshape corporate, governmental, and educational systems, not repress the rebellious adolescent.

Indeed, many teenagers expressed satisfaction with their environment and the activities available. The new towns have high rates of college attendance, and many teens have returned as adults to live in the community. Some teenagers, however, still chafed against the restriction of life in new towns, especially during the 1960s and early 1970s. Teenagers were not always interested in the wholesome activities designed for them and remained under the sway of the counterculture and teen culture. Many wanted merely to hang around in public spaces, use drugs, and "make out." Some parents found ways to control teenage behavior; some teens found ways to get out of town, create parties in parentless houses, or gather clandestinely in the woods.[35]

The 1960s brand of counterculture has all but disappeared, but teenagers remain some of the most visible members of these communities. Teenagers are the only community members who wish to spend leisure time out of doors in public spaces, simply hanging around. Teenagers often speak their minds to journalists and offer unconventional or negative analyses of their communities. New-town residents, especially adults with hectic job and family responsibilities, have trouble coming to terms with any idle and critical people in their community. Teenagers are an annoying reminder to adults that the busy lifestyle they have chosen is not the only choice and perhaps not the best choice, when their children seem so defiant. Teenagers can be seen as living embodiments of aggression, overt sexuality, and free-spiritedness, qualities eschewed by the respectable middle-class culture of the new towns. Their very presence in community spaces is a form of street theater, an effective visual criticism of the achievement-oriented life of the new towns and suburbia in general.

Reston's Enterprising Lads and Lasses

Reston, the first of these new towns, sought to make adolescents more comfortable and content. Teenagers would have every resource imaginable: from recreational facilities to special gathering spots. The planning and construction of the first part of Reston, however, preceded the counterculture. Youth rebellion led to greater drug use among adolescents and a discontent with "square" towns such as Reston. Many residents complained about these "hippies," but after the 1960s-style counterculture passed, so too did much of the overt problem. Drug use continued; teens still congregated at village centers; and gangs occasionally operated in the community, but the adolescent "problem" faded from view.

The developer featured a Rathskeller club in the *Reston Letter* as a promotional feature for potential residents: "Located in the Lake Anne Center, the Rathskeller is a spot specially reserved for young people in the ninth grade and up. . . . It is currently decorated wall-to-wall with teenage objets d'art; street signs, every conceivable model of the four-on-the-floor variety, pop art. . . . These enterprising young lads and lasses are currently engaged in various fund-raising activities—records, future dances." In time, the planning also incorporated extensive recreational facilities, parks and woods, and an excellent educational system with numerous extracurricular offerings that proved satisfying to many teenage residents.[36]

Many teenagers gathered at the Rathskeller, but life in Reston had certain limitations. In 1969, an important article on teenage life, penned by sixteen-year-old Sarah Larson, appeared in the *Reston Times*. Larson, an active and successful young woman, began her article on an optimistic note: "Reston at a glance might seem to be mainly a town of outstanding architecture. A second or third look, however, reveals a community of varying interests from politics to art shows, a community that supports over 300 meetings a month. And, of front-running town contributors, the Reston teens must be included." Teenagers acted as the babysitters of the town, and "so, it is upon the teenagers that the adult social life of Reston depends." Also, teenagers participated in "school oriented programs such as debate, sports, the student council" and they were, of course, important to the "financial health of the merchants in town." Parents and teens had also started meeting in a group entitled Community Action, or "Let's-all-get-together-and-hash-it-out." At these meetings, "those who attend come perhaps to find out what teenagers can do to further the Reston dream and what adults can do to help teenagers continue their program. They are finding out that while discussion is lively, there are not many nitty-gritty disputes. In fact, it's a pretty amiable organization."[37]

Out of four hundred high-school-age kids in Reston, Larson counted seventy-five who had joined the Rathskeller. The article explained why a designated space was so necessary in Reston:

> High school students in Reston find that they are not particularly welcome to gather in unorganized groups in the parking lots of the plaza. The Reston Rent-a-Cop is forced to break up groups of people that meet around the lake. Teens are not welcome to sit in the drug store to talk because they slow up business. Property guards keep people off the vacant lots in Reston. Homeowners are not particularly pleased when teens who don't live on the block use the recreational courts. Life is different for teens in Reston merely because the community doesn't have any street corners.

Larson's description gives a sense of both the satisfactions and challenges of living in a new town. Reston teenagers had plenty to do, but nowhere to go or simply "be." The village center had developed a reputation during this period as a hippie hang-out, an unintentional consequence of being one of the finest public spaces in northern Virginia, and the community responded by trying, unsuccessfully, to force teens out of the area.[38]

Larson described problems that have never been resolved. In the early 1970s, conditions seemed to be worsening. In 1970, the Common Ground (formerly the Rathskeller) and the lunch counter at the drug store reduced their hours: "Cutting the hours of the two favorite teenage hang-outs on the Plaza was done to relieve what some saw as intolerable pressures. Pressures of the young and their new life styles upon the old life styles was part of it, perhaps a major part. Some of the young committed vandalism?" The editors reminded residents that "daddy lurching off the Booze Bus" made it difficult to criticize teenager "grass" usage. (The Booze Bus was the name given to the commuter bus to Washington chartered by Reston residents that at one time featured heavy drinking.) The editorial encouraged communication between the generations, not "new and bigger community centers, flossier teenage gathering places, more elaborate youth programs." This communication, as well as "flossier" gathering places,

FIGURE 13 Plucky teenagers in the Lake Anne village center. (*Reston Times,* 25 March 1971)

failed to materialize, but the teenagers did not disappear from Lake Anne plaza or Reston in general (figure 13).[39]

During this time, the community received one of its first teenage surprises. According to a lawyer who had his offices in Lake Anne village, "by about 1970 this was the New York Stock Exchange of drugs in the Washington area. The traffic must have been every bit of 10,000 dollars a day. I could look out my window and see dealing on the plaza." He defended many Reston teenagers when a crackdown began that ended in the arrest of thirty-five individuals, primarily teenagers, in 1972. Many middle- and upper-middle-class residents were surprised that such activity took place in Reston, particularly when it involved their own children. In addition, a shocking drug-related murder occurred in 1972. Gwen Ames— daughter of ArDee Ames, an assistant secretary of HUD—was found strangled about 2 A.M. on June 4, on her way home from a dance. Apparently Gwen Ames had a heroin habit and was "just emerging from deep involvement in the drug world." To make matters worse, another Reston teenager had died in 1971 of an overdose. Many observers both within and outside the community predicted grave problems for Reston, but these remain the most disastrous of Reston events. Lake Anne and Hunters Woods drug activity declined, and while there still have been occasional crackdowns on teenagers involved in drug use and shoplifting, few more serious problems have surfaced.[40]

The teenage problems calmed with the end of the 1960s counterculture. Drug use went underground, and attention focused on low-income teenagers and drug dealing in projects in Reston. As at Columbia, the presence of teenagers, particularly minority teenagers, in village centers tended to scare off patrons and create a perception of crime even if actual crime remained very low. In recent years, a few teenagers, some even from affluent families, have become involved in gang activity. As always, a small number of teenagers has been involved in these activities. After all, if larger numbers had been involved, the community would have had much more than a few incidents of violence.[41]

Reston adults have not abandoned their commitment to diverting teenage energy into more socially acceptable channels. The Reston Association not only maintains a number of athletic facilities but for many years also has sponsored a number of teen events during the summer. The association sponsors parties, summer camps, and outdoor weekend trips for teenagers. Community pools remain popular gathering places for teenagers. Teenagers also attend parties at the Pit Teen Centers in Reston town center and at Forest Edge Elementary on weekend nights. Many teenagers gather at the town center to ice skate, watch movies, and simply "hang-out" into the late hours. Others travel to Washington or Georgetown for entertainment. Meanwhile, the schools of Reston still offer numerous extracurricular activities; many teenagers hold jobs in the community; and approximately 93 percent of Reston's students go on to college.[42]

A popular new book that has attracted national attention, *A Tribe Apart* (1998), promises "A Journey into the Heart of American Adolescence." The author, Patricia Hersch, a former contributing editor to

Psychology Today and a Reston resident, followed a group of Reston teenagers over the course of a few years and documented, through observation and interview, their every action. Hersch understands that Reston, as a new town, is very different from most communities, but she sees the teenage experience there as representative of the adolescent experience nationally. Her primary argument is that adults in Reston, and nationally, have abandoned their adolescents to a teen culture that is often destructive.

The stories in the book are harrowing, including those about teenage sex, partying, drug use, and graffiti pranks. Many Reston teenagers leave school and congregate in empty homes to use drugs and alcohol, and they engage in sexual activity. With some parents tolerant of such behavior, the teenagers, even those from strict homes, can be drawn easily into this permissive lifestyle. Hersch also gives vivid descriptions of the "hip-hop" subculture, which integrates upper-income whites and low-income blacks. Offering insecure teenagers a countercultural style, the hip-hop scene, which emphasizes aggression, violence, and anti-intellectualism, is an unsettling force in the local community. At the high school, too, there remains a racial divide between the gifted and talented program (with more whites) and the rest of the school (with more blacks).

Hersch is particularly skilled at making adolescent and community problems seem tragic, although she herself admits that "few kids are in Real Trouble" and most go on to college or other adventures. Even her largely critical observations bring into focus certain aspects of the new town vision. It is true that many parents seem to have little time for the adolescents, but the community as a whole offers a great deal more than many suburbs in terms of activities and experiences, particularly of the kind that Gans thought were missing in Levittown. Many adolescents find jobs in the community, and many seem to enjoy them; having shopping centers convenient and within residential areas facilitates working by teenagers. The adolescents have also enjoyed the pathways of the community, both for nature and recreation, and the seclusion they provide for all manner of activity. While they are often shooed from the town center, teenagers do gather there in large numbers to skate, enjoy the public space, and go to the movies. The community pools also serve as gathering places for adolescents, and special events are held for them. Although in declining numbers, according to Hersch, many adolescents participate in extracurricular offerings at the high school, including sports, band, newspaper, and student government. Reston may not be a teenage utopia, and many teens, particularly those from divorced homes, find themselves without strong guidance or support, but the new town provides wholesome alternatives to rebellious teenage behavior.[43]

New-town residents only partially succeeded in finding a middle path between the coercion of more traditional communities and the lawless counterculture with which many teenagers identified. Adults had to resort to coercion to keep the well-ordered communal image they wanted in village centers and the town center. In the long run, the decline of the 1960s counterculture probably helped dispel the perception of a teen crisis more effectively than the wholesome activities provided by the community.

"Products of a New Eden," Life in the Columbia "Bubble"

> It is perplexing to me to see twenty-five young people on a warm sunny day on the wall of the village center just sitting, not even talking to one another. They can hear people swimming, listen to people singing, see tennis courts across the street and yet not be inclined to do any of these things.
>
> COLUMBIA RESIDENT

A teenager in Columbia sticks out like a sore thumb. Reston is more thickly wooded than Columbia, so teens are less visible, but Columbia teens can be seen on afternoons wandering around the edges of village centers, disappearing onto paths, and just hanging around village centers and apartment complexes. In most communities they would excite little comment, but in Columbia, as in Reston, they represent unfinished business. Adults have made more extensive efforts in Columbia than Reston to divert teenage energy into socially acceptable activities, but they cannot and apparently will never endorse the wilder aspects of American teenage life that are more closely connected to mainstream popular culture.[44]

Teenagers of Columbia, particularly middle-class ones, began their lives as the privileged, indulged children of Columbia. Those who had lived there for a time spent years perhaps in the open-classroom system of the elementary schools of Columbia, where "teachers are viewed more as resource persons than disciplinarians." In these classes, teachers encouraged students to be creative and self-directed, and classes changed not with a harsh bell but "a soft pinging sound."[45] Even though Columbia has slowly moved away from the open-classroom model, the town's children remain the recipients of an impressive educational and recreational system that

stresses individual development, free thinking, and personal satisfaction.[46]
The CA complements school activities with a system of open spaces, outdoor recreational programs and pools, summer camps, athletic leagues,
and indoor recreational programs including dance and the arts. Through
participation in these activities, children have been encouraged to be expressive, creative, and even a little rebellious.

When these children became teenagers, however, their parents and
the administrators of the community found that their expressive children
had exceeded their own conception of freedom. The rise of the 1960s
counterculture, the drug scene, and the simple persistence of teenage energy spelled trouble in the peaceful greens of Columbia's town center and
village centers. During work-group meetings in 1964, Gans foresaw difficulties with teenagers and recommended that they "should be provided
with their own centers for sociability, their own projects, their own responsibilities with a minimum of adult supervision."[47] One of the final reports
of the work group encouraged the creation of a series of teen hangouts.
Teen centers would be located in the neighborhood centers, where a store
would provide focus for teen activity in the evening. The report hoped that
"rather than prohibiting this activity, the more sensible thing would be to
recognize it and provide adequate facilities for its use by adolescents." The
report also recommended a separate room for the teens adjacent to an outdoor eating terrace.[48] In the village centers, the work group called for teen
centers as part of the high school; the school cafeteria would be transformed in the evenings into a coffee house.

The planners, responding to these ideas, created a series of teen centers in village centers during the 1960s and 1970s. The early planners of
Columbia realized that the growing number of adolescents needed attention. One early official at HRD, James Wannemacher, explained that teens
"were beginning to become disenfranchised. They didn't much like the
adult world and few adults wanted them hanging around." The early planners decided to build special centers for the teenagers at Wilde Lake,
Harper's Choice, Oakland Mills, and a special teen center known as the Orange Propeller (discussed below). The first teen center, in Wilde Lake, was
designed about 1968 by Morton Hoppenfeld to reflect the "unstructured"
lifestyle of teenagers. The space, connected to the community center, was
"open and free-flowing." But "both the space and the concept were
doomed from the beginning. To begin with, teen facilities must be chaper-
oned at all times. Otherwise, even the gods shudder." The early management at CA could not find sufficient number of chaperones, and the Wilde

Lake Teen Center was closed within a year. Wannemacher gives a telling description of his experience chaperoning a teen event:

> Things went poorly from the outset. It was supposed to be an informal dance and social affair. A few couples actually did dance (to records) but most seemed to drift in and out of the space looking for friends or someplace else to drive to. We weren't quite sure what to do, if anything, so we kept out of the way. As the evening wore on, small groups of boys began to show up. Some were loud and rowdy. . . . Apparently some of the kids were raising a little hell out in the parking lot. The police seemed to feel our Center was causing the congregation of youngsters and actually suggested we close down a little early. I felt kind of helpless at the time.[49]

The Orange Propeller, another teen center, became enormously popular—so popular that adults feared it would be destroyed by its own success. Columbia's leadership decided that they would restrict access to the center to Columbia residents, a move that alienated many youths. Rouse explained why outsiders had to be banned: "Here we are out in the Baltimore-Washington corridor, with 400,000 or 500,000 people between the two beltways, and very few valid meeting places for people of any kind, and we (in Columbia) create beautiful meeting places. These beautiful meeting places attract people, and they attract young people. The fact that we attract them in abnormal quantities is an expression of the vacuum, of the void, that exists." Columbia teens, of course, disliked the restrictive policy that went counter to the spontaneity of that generation. Gael Hilson, a local teenager, used new-town rhetoric to criticize the policy: "A new city should be really open just like any other city. There shouldn't be so many rules. You shouldn't have to have a card to use the pool or to notify people four days in advance if you want to bring some friends from outside to the teen center." Other teen centers suffered from a more serious problem: turf battles between whites and blacks. While such confrontations were rarely violent, teen centers became associated with one racial group or another. Separatism eventually resulted in low turnouts, and most centers had ceased to operate by the mid-1970s.[50]

The lakeshore area developed its own teen problem. In 1971, Jack Rosenthal of the *New York Times Magazine* described the situation: "During the last two years, difficulties growing out of the youth problem have mounted steadily. Young people from Columbia and the county gathered nightly on the broad lawns overlooking Lake Kittamaqundi. . . . Drug traffic grew heavy. Adults leaving the expensive restaurant protested that young people were heckling obscenely, even fornicating alfresco. And then came rock concerts in the pavilion, drawing thousands. . . . With the crowds came scuffles and finally, in August, an assault on guards." The CA developed a summer concert series that neutralized the teen situation by bringing a greater diversity of residents to the lakeshore. Teenagers continued to congregate there, but the summer festival had the desired effect of neutralizing the teenage subculture.

By 1972, the teen situation had not noticeably improved. If anything, it had worsened. According to Jean Moon, "there isn't even one 'picture show' in Columbia, nor are there bowling alleys or pool halls. The Jack-in-the-Box fast food restaurant is the only facility that approximates a teenage 'hamburger hangout,' as they used to be called. The village teen centers have been touched by racial strife and are notoriously underattended, predominantly attracting younger teens."[51] Moon discussed the situation with director of community services for the CA, Harvey Brookin, who admitted a problem existed: "Cultural and background differences are rarely taken into account. This, he notes, can be disconcerting, for example, to those who come from the city to Columbia and find things they took for granted missing. He cites late night basketball playing by city teens as a case in point. Columbia has no lighted basketball courts, while it has plenty of youngsters who would take advantage of such an amenity."[52]

The leadership of Columbia did not remain inflexible. They saw that the relatively unstructured teen centers had failed and began designing activity-oriented programs to replace them. The goal remained the same, to divert energy from socially unacceptable behavior, but the methods had changed. In the 1980s, the CA began designing activity-oriented teen centers to replace the unstructured ones. By the mid-1980s, a teen activity center in the Barn in Oakland Mills village center served over 1,000 teenagers a year, "with activities ranging from woodworking to job counseling." Teens could join discussion groups designed to help them cope with life, participate in arts and crafts activities, view films, and attend seminars. Apparently the center enjoyed some success. A teenage participant explained that "[the staff] are great people. Everybody there cares about you and there's a lot going on. It's an okay place."[53] High praise from a teenager. Even in the negative article discussed above, Moon enumerated a variety of programs available to Columbia teenagers. Many village centers offered rooms for gathering and pool playing; other villages offered courses and sports; and a popular dance continued to be held weekly at Wilde Lake during the 1970s.[54] The *Columbia Flier* itself offered a "teen" page during the 1970s and 1980s.[55] Columbia residents sponsored an impressive soccer league, and schools offered sports and extracurricular activities.

The association still offers many activities, including homework clubs and three teen centers that are open for three hours a day and offer a series of activities. A weekly open-mike night during the summer by Lake Kittamaqundi is a popular teenage venue. Low-income teenagers can earn membership to the association's fee based recreational facilities, and other teens use these facilities—which include skating, horseback riding, swimming, and tennis—on a regular basis. Teens can take classes at the Columbia Arts Center, participate in midnight basketball at Howard Community College in the summer months (an innovation directly linked to earlier complaints of its absence), join a variety of sporting clubs, or call a teen line.

The community made strides in developing more successful programs, but the problems did not disappear. Teens continued to lounge in public spaces; perceptions of a teen problem are hard to dispel. Harper's Choice village-center manager Wendy Tzuker explained that the misperception that crime was high in the village center (when it was, in fact, quite low—the center and village had some of the lowest crime rates in Howard County) came from the fact that "teenagers have 'hung out' at the village center for 20 to 25 years." Teenagers remain the most conspicuous members of the community because they spend leisure time out of doors, simply hanging around.[56]

Diagnoses of teenage life in Columbia, complete with sensational details, appeared during the 1970s and 1980s. A resident, Roger Karsk, wrote a book entitled *Teenagers in the Next America,* which detailed teen life in 1973–74 by asking a group of teens to keep journals of daily activities. Readers of the review of his book in the *Flier* would hear about heavy drug use (including alcohol), truancy, racial conflict, sexual promiscuity, and a lack of "hang-out" space in Columbia. The reviewer believed that because the community lacked information about teens, the book would prove "valuable" to Columbia parents—regardless of whether these diaries were truly representative.[57]

Karsk viewed Columbia as only partially successful in improving life for suburban teens. Juvenile delinquency and crime, for instance, were comparable to those in other suburban communities. He noted ominously that "in Columbia, as in other communities it was not possible to keep [teenagers] isolated in separate teen centers or other such programs." Most teenagers never used the teen centers and instead gathered in homes for socializing and parties. The teen centers, as described earlier, had become the turf of low-income blacks, who discouraged other users from congregating there. These low-income teenagers, he explained, had a greater need for lounge space than their middle-class peers, who had recreational spaces in their homes.[58]

Karsk understood why race relations between black and white teenagers seemed so difficult. Adults had chosen to live in Columbia for its integrated characteristics and chose the places and situations in which they would integrate themselves, but teenagers did not have this liberty. Not only were many teenagers caught up in the identity movements of the 1960s and 1970s, but teens, unlike their parents, "dealt with the realities of association every day by attending the same high schools." Teenagers lived in a much more radically integrated world, and although there was integration among teenagers, conflicts occurred more frequently and turned to violence more easily. Many black teenagers, too, came from lower-income backgrounds and found themselves cut off from the affluent world around them. Low-income teenagers "underwent their first exposure to affluence [in Columbia]. . . . The teens wanted their share but knew no way to obtain it." Some teenagers thus turned to pressuring other teenagers for money, other aggressive acts, or to outright crime.[59]

For all its failings, Karsk found much to praise in Columbia. It compared well with Levittown. Gans had found that teenagers disliked life in the child- and family-centered world of Levittown and tended to become bored and isolated. The situation was different in Columbia: "Teens in our study did not call Columbia 'Endsville' as had the adolescents in Levittown from which Gans drew many of his ideas. The degree of mobility, excellent recreational facilities and job opportunities have generated a more positive attitude. The majority enjoyed the economic benefits of upper-middle class families such as a room of their own, use of the second car, and spending money." Karsk praised the community for putting "quantities of energy into developing both innovative and traditional programs that dovetailed into a variety of physical amenities in Columbia. These included neighborhood swim teams, soccer . . . and the variety of programs offered at the village centers." Columbia was no teenage utopia, but it was an improvement over standard suburbia, much as the reformers had hoped.[60]

Karsk was only one of many people to present critical portraits of teenage life in Columbia, and his account was more balanced than many. For instance, a 1989 article on teenage life in Columbia pointed to problems. The reporter for the *Flier* found large groups of teenagers hanging around the convenience stores in the neighborhoods of Hawthorne and

Running Brook, "the hot spots in town." From twenty-five to one hundred teenagers could be found at the stores on a summer night, where they "cruise the parking lot, stroll from car to car, and buy snacks." They stole from the stores, bought and sold drugs, and harassed the store employees. In addition, each store collected a specific racial clientele. One had a largely black group of loiterers, while the other store attracted a more mixed crowd. Teenagers also described their other activities: "They go to Bennigans [restaurant], the movies, Pizza Hut, Merriweather concerts in the summer. And there are weekly 'under 21' evenings at Maxwell's and P.T. Flaggs—Baltimore nightclubs—when no alcohol is served. And, of course, there are parties. Often, kids meet at the stores to find out just where the parties are." One young man said that they gathered at convenience stores because "it's Columbia, it's boring." This judgment is apparently "in" among some teenagers.[61]

How representative are these accounts of teenage life in Columbia? One must remember, as most observers have not, that the most visible and unhappy teenagers are not necessarily representative. Adults and visitors have taken an interest in these teens because, after all, they make the best copy. Thousands found lives of sufficient interest and variation, but they only occasionally made the papers. Some reporters have taken a more balanced approach. A reporter for the *Washingtonian* in 1971, for instance, found that "the kids aren't bored and restless. . . . They have every imaginable kind of facility, from an elaborate teen club to swimming pools and rock concerts. A pretty fifteen year old blond named Kathy McNealy summed up the attitudes of the kids I talked with. 'It's got a spell over you,' she said, 'When I came here . . . I changed completely. I mean we're all together here. There's plenty to do and the air smells good here.'"[62] Such attitudes were also reflected almost twenty years later. The *Washingtonian* of 1988 offered its readers a revealing paragraph on the subject of Columbia: "An honors student at the University of Maryland is writing a paper on his hometown as Utopia. He talks of growing up amid lakes and trees, of walking to school and sports, of feeling that his environment embraced him. He is writing about Columbia, MD." Columbia may be well liked by many teenagers.[63]

Teenagers have given their community some of the more insightful social critiques, having more distance from the community's experimentation. In 1977, Kevin Young, a black teenager, explained why he thought little of the village concept: "I mean, people that stay in the village don't stay together. . . . They're just in the village to lie there. It's not that they want to live there to meet the people, they're just there." He had moved to

Columbia from Evanston, Illinois, when he was ten, and he believed that "the only way to have a real neighborhood . . . is to never leave where you were born." In Columbia, he noted, "people don't stay as long here. Back in Evanston, we were the first family to move out. . . . We had relatives right around the corner." Even Young conceded, however, that Columbia was an easier place in which to participate in recreational activities, and he liked the fact that he was not dependent on his parents to drive him to facilities. Finally, despite tension between races, he observed, "I have plenty of white and black friends, probably more white than black."[64] In 1987, Kristin Bacon, a teenage resident of Columbia, admitted, "I remember the first time I saw a bum at The Mall. I was shocked. You have the feeling growing up here that they will always be in Baltimore or Washington. I always assumed they weren't allowed in Columbia. It's like a glass bubble."[65] Teenagers, then, appreciated the special nature of their environment but could see that the new-town culture concealed persistent problems.

Of the three new towns, Columbia has invested the most resources and creativity in redirecting teenage energy without the use of coercion. Residents have studied their teenagers, created numerous teen centers, and adjusted activities. As at Reston, however, no amount of redirection satisfied all teenagers. The teenage culture and the counterculture proved too spontaneous to contain within the wholesome cultural activity of the new town.

Irvine's Minority of Kids

> Some have compared Irvine to the class nerd—smarter than everybody else and dressed by its mother.
>
> TOM BERG, *Orange County Register*

In Irvine, the young people ripened in a world of indulgence with access to exceptional recreational facilities provided by both the city and the particular village in which they lived. They attended some of the best schools in the country, including alternative options, and had the opportunity to learn in attractive, comfortable, contemporary settings.

Inevitably, however, problems arose. A detailed feature in 1974 on teen life offered a bleak portrait. Mike Stockstill, city editor of the *Irvine World News*, examined the social habits of teenagers at a local village shopping center and on greenbelts. According to Stockstill, teenagers had abundant recreational activities to choose from, including swimming, community centers, and sports, but few gathering spots. One teenager explained, "You can't even walk around the fields. I did that and the Irvine Company cops busted me for trespassing. . . . And the cops around here will stop you for just walking home." On greenbelts where they often gathered, they would be "rousted" by police, and cars were frequently stopped and searched. Stockstill found, as well, that teenagers he met believed that use of marijuana should be legalized. One teenager, however, stopped him before the evening was over and drew him aside. The teenager explained, "I don't want you to get the idea that the majority of kids in Irvine are like this. Not everyone is blowing pot or hanging out here at night. Lots of people are at home, or studying or at work, or doing something, this is just a minority of kids."[66]

In most cases, neglect seemed to be the primary cause of delinquency. A 1979 *New Worlds* article entitled "More Than Enough Isn't Everything" chronicled some of the problems by introducing a number of troubled residents. One of these was an adolescent named "Brian, the fourteen-year-old son of a salesman and a bookkeeper who between them earn $35,000 a year. Instead of going to school, Brian spends afternoons with friends, smoking pot and bathing his mind in the colors of the television screen." According to this article, these teens had not adjusted to life in paradise: "The most common forms of delinquency in [Irvine] are . . . vandalism in schools and parks, and truancy. Away from school, teenage boys hang out, sitting on cars and drinking alcohol in the shopping center parking lots."[67]

Teens in 1989 could still be heard complaining that "they feel unwelcome in this community full of parks and sports fields but without a downtown area or after-dark recreation." A contemporary observer confirmed adolescent frustration. Discussing the community's reputation for high rates of teenage drug and alcohol abuse, he gave a glimpse into teen life there: "The main communal goals for adults—cleanliness, safety, and rising property values—do not exhaust the ambitions of a still-free people, which in this community can only mean teenagers. The kids complain that the strict paternalism of the Irvine Company's design has left them with nothing more to do at night than to drive around in their cars and hang out at the local fast-food places." He also noted that teens tended to go to nearby Newport or Laguna to "wreak havoc."[68]

Irvine political leader Sally Sheridan admitted in 1989 that many residents disliked teenagers, but she explained that "teens all complain that there's no place to go and nothing to do. They always do that. That's justification for their parents to buy them a car so they can go somewhere else and say there's nothing to do. There are tons of things for teens to do here."

She listed "school sports and activities, music and dance lesson, charity clubs and jobs." Sheridan noted that a teen center had been constructed in Heritage Park, and "teen-agers helped design and run center programs," which had been successful. According to the article, however, "older teens didn't like mixing with younger teens," and so younger teens and children ended up as the primary patrons.[69]

Over the last decades, the city has developed a number of programs for teenagers. In the early years of cityhood, the city government operated a bus to take kids to the beach.[70] During the 1980s and 1990s a wider variety of services developed. A teen-activities hot line gives teenagers information about concerts, sporting events, volunteer opportunities, local activities, and classes in the area. A middle-school program offers after-school programs, classes, and special events. A teen camp run by the city provides trips during school breaks to local sites, the beach, the mall, and similar venues. A youth employment service run by the city helps teens find jobs. Irvine operates a youth action team that includes student representatives from each of Irvine's four high schools. These students represent their peers to various community groups and coordinate a variety of services for teenagers. Classes for teens run by the city include study stills, baby-sitting courses, "French for teens," and even movie-making. The Irvine Fine Arts Center, run by the city, sponsors activities specifically for teens, including the option to register for art classes.[71]

An installation at the Irvine Fine Arts Center explored life in Irvine from a teenage perspective in 1994. Entitled "Irvana: A Different Perspective," the exhibit brought together the vision of twenty youths who "snapped pictures of their environment, focusing on places where they felt either comfortable or unwelcome." The teens provided text and recorded commentary that they integrated. The exhibit included a phone where visitors could "eavesdrop on frank conversations about sex education at school, censorship and uptight adults. For every picture of a lived-in untidy bedroom or favorite hangout there were shots taken outside of gated communities or pools off-limits to teens."[72]

Irvine residents were shocked in 1992 when gang violence erupted in the community. A shoot-out took place in the Stonecreek Plaza between gang members, and two bystanders were wounded. This event sent city officials into a special session of both the city council and the school board, and a special task force was created to look into problems. Most teenagers seemed nonplussed by the whole affair and thought that not only was the attention unwarranted but that Irvine was long overdue for an event of this nature.[73]

As at Columbia and Reston, teenagers made choices about their activities. Many and probably most teenagers participated in the structured activities of the community, while others favored secluded spots or traveled to other communities to engage in more unstructured activity. In all likelihood, there will forever remain a divide between the values of certain rebellious teenagers, well-adjusted teenagers who participate in both teenage and regular activities, and their even more conventional, middle-class parents. These communities are notable precisely because they tried to bridge this gap rather than pushing the issue out of sight.

The creation of "teenagers" in the last fifty years has presented numerous opportunities and problems. Adults have exempted teenagers from labor without offering a satisfying alternative. The new-town attempt to neutralize teenage identity through a mixture of redirection and mild coercion has been only partly successful. Many teenagers found these communities congenial, but others objected not just to the lack of public space in the community but to the mainstream values of their parents. No number of teen centers and activities overcame these differences in values. Teenagers during the 1960s and 1970s, and even some today, question the busy, achievement-oriented society around them—especially if it has left them without significant adult guidance. They questioned this lifestyle not only in the local press but in their own forms of street theater, where they did exactly what their parents forbade: used drugs, engaged in open sexual activity, lounged around, stole, and seemed vaguely menacing. New towns deserve credit for adapting and expanding choices for teenagers in suburbia, even though many teenagers will have nothing to do with these activities.

❖

It is easy to fault the developers and the middle-class residents of these new towns for what they did not achieve—more subsidized housing, a truly colorblind society, or uniformly happy adolescents—but it is more important to highlight their successes. These communities demonstrated that social and racial mixture, even if expressed in unexpected ways, could be a unifying force for a suburban community, not an impetus to community abandonment. They also showed that suburban communities could be made better for some women and adolescents.

In these social reform efforts the new towns embodied the suburban social critique. Their translation of ideas into flesh and bone disarmed those who believed that suburban criticism was strictly a dreamy utopian vision. It was one thing to argue for social change and quite another to live the critique. The rewards for being part of this extraordinary transformation of ideas into social reality were great: a sense of satisfaction that came with feeling that one was doing the right thing, a less tense racial environment, journalists treating you as though you were a star, new political and career possibilities, visitors amusingly shocked by the alternative landscape, and a sense of camaraderie. There were costs, too. Acting as poster children for a cause began to tire some people in the new towns, particularly adolescents. Others became so perfectionistic and critical that they proved unable to see the good in what they were doing. This was the price of ambition. Social reform at the new towns was not all for the best, but it certainly was unconventional and exciting.

11

Suburban Chautauquas: Patronage in the New Towns

So you see there is no chance to loaf or kill time, no pretext for evading work; no taverns, or alehouses, or brothels; no chances for corruption; no hiding places, no spots for secret meetings. Because they live in the full view of all, they are bound to be either working at their usual trades, or enjoying their leisure in a respectable way.

SIR THOMAS MORE, *Utopia*

The hope was to produce a community among people, a release of creativity by people who felt a sense of support from one another . . . that it would be a freer society and that there would be the development of a much greater sense of tolerance, more openness, more trust, more freedom, more creativity.

JAMES ROUSE, in *Columbia Flier*

For thousands of years, visionaries have dreamed of creating a society dominated by creativity and expressiveness. The developers and the planners of new towns, inspired by this ancient vision, designed institutions and public spaces for uplifting, community-wide cultural expression. Like the fictional inhabitants of More's Utopia, the residents of new towns found themselves with plentiful and respectable cultural opportunities. Wealthy developers such as Rouse and Simon, as well as many new-town residents, believed that Americans should recommit themselves to creativity and made every effort to expand opportunities for cultural participation.

By democratizing cultural activity, new-town developers and residents sought to reinvigorate a middle-class tradition of cultural participation that had been stronger in the nineteenth century. In Chautauqua, New York, a cultural retreat, attendees participated in the arts and applauded concerts, lectures, and symposia by eminent individuals. But the rapidly expanding twentieth century middle class had less interest in such cultural activities and more interest in mass spectatorial pursuits, including movies, television, professional sports, and radio. The middle-class suburbs seemed particularly emblematic of this new passivity. Suburbanites consumed films, TV programs, and art reproductions irrespective of quality and produced little original of their own.[1] Not only had mass culture achieved great power in suburbs, but suburbs lacked cultural institutions such as universities, museums, symphonies, and artists' colonies that might mediate against passivity. The new-town reformers, in order to be seen as part of a solution to criticism, had to demonstrate that in cultural affairs they could reverse the conventional image of suburban boorishness and passivity.[2]

Cultural Sponsorship in the New Towns

The developers of new towns initially provided cultural activities—including concerts, community centers, art exhibitions, and public art displays—to attract cultured residents and distinguish their communities from standard subdivisions. As the new towns grew, however, some of the developers retreated from cultural underwriting. Developer-sponsored cultural events and special community and cultural centers from the early years attracted arts-oriented residents, but it has been the residents who, over forty years, have created a network of cultural activities and organizations including concerts, festivals, theaters, art courses and exhibitions, galleries, and continuing education. New towns in particular placed a premium on wide participation in the arts and culture; professionals performed, but what mattered most was that a relatively broad group of residents felt free to be creative.

Reston's State of Grace

In exchange for space, scale, liberty and individuality, the new "laird of the manor" [in Reston] acquires a new set of standards/assets, if you please. Vast public grounds, parks, gardens (without care), lakes, entertainment, and "packaged" culture in the form of imported theater and arts, a Total Community . . . a kibbutz for the American capitalist.

VLADIMIR KAGAN, *Interiors Magazine*

Vladimir Kagan derided the ambitions of Reston's developer because cultural life was to be "imported" rather than generated by residents. Because of Simon's untimely departure from the community, however, just the opposite has happened. Reston has not developed cultural activities to the extent envisioned by its founder, but residents have created the important cultural institutions and activities in the new town.

Simon began with a bold program of cultural patronage that in all likelihood would have expanded had he remained the developer. An accomplished pianist and the one-time owner of Carnegie Hall, he valued cultural activity. Simon laid particular emphasis on stimulating the creativity of residents rather than promoting cultural consumption: "Our function is to stimulate participation. This is not a spectator business I'm talking about, it's a participation business, based on the belief that there is more reward from doing than watching someone else do. To put it less facilely, you get more fun out of getting the fun yourself than out of watching the other guy have his fun."[3]

This emphasis on participatory culture reduced the need for movie theaters, large stadiums, and even bars—institutions that have either failed or only slowly developed. In the first year he claimed, "My experience at Reston has shown that facilities do lead to participation. The fact of Reston's community hall, art gallery and multi-purpose educational and religious facilities has been responsible for the high degree of participation by the residents in cultural, educational, and recreation activities."[4] The original plan called for community centers in each village to include "gymnasiums, concert and exhibition halls, craft and photographic rooms." Unfortunately, although Simon created Lake Anne Hall and a gallery space, he was unable to carry out this part of the project, and later developers were not interested.[5]

Simon sponsored a number of performances in the early years in order to attract cultured residents. By bringing professional artists to Reston he helped establish a high level of cultural expectation. A one day "Salute to the Arts" on December 4, 1965 (the dedication day of Lake Anne village), featured the poet Stephen Spender and included performances by the Mclean Ballet, the Washington Brass Quintet, the Potomac English Handbell Ringers, the Lywen String Quartet, Frederic Franklin of the

National Ballet, and even a demonstration of pottery making by a famous Austrian potter. After only one year, Simon proudly listed all the activities that had occurred in the community:

> We have had lectures there, motion pictures, Stephen Spender did his poetry reading there, we've had a string quartet play there. . . . Next to the community center is a rathskeller for young people and on the other side is a space which will be occupied by a branch of the county library this spring. We have an art gallery and studio. The gallery is largely for exhibitions, the studio is set up for ceramics and painting classes. Dance is a very big thing with us here. We have ballet classes going on here now. And we're going to have folk dancing.[6]

The shops that first opened in Lake Anne village center also reflected the community's cultural sophistication. A shop named Gudrun, for instance, offered Scandinavian home furnishings, which at that time represented the cutting edge in home decorating. Dyer Brothers in Lake Anne specialized in art supplies, custom framing, and restoration.[7]

Reston residents interviewed in the 1960s appreciated the community's cultural opportunities. They reported that in Reston "'the cultural aspects are limitless.' . . . 'It has many conveniences not found in most subdivisions: cultural activities, the community center, the outdoors.' . . . 'I didn't realize there would be so many cultural things for us to do.'" One resident boasted that Reston "has all the advantages of a large city without being one."[8] An editorial in the 1970 Reston Times opined that "one of the amazing things about Reston is that there is forever the opportunity to enrich one's life. This is what separates Reston—and indeed, the major cities—from the sterile suburbs; there is a natural dynamism which rarely exists outside a truly urban area."[9]

The Reston Foundation, which was essentially Simon himself, provided much of the seed money for the early cultural activity of the town.[10] The foundation provided support until Gulf Reston lost interest in the late 1960s. In a Washington Post article of 1972, Gulf officials maintained that "despite the town's growth and evolution, the Simon concept is still very much alive." In the same article, Simon countered that he believed that cultural growth had in fact slowed because the developer "is putting the entire burden of creating (cultural, educational and recreational) programs on the people, instead of serving as a catalyst." Jack Guinee of Gulf Reston, however, maintained that "programs that required the active interest of the

developer when the town was small have simply become self-generating."
Mobil, Gulf Reston's successor, had a better reputation for cultural patronage, but none of the later developers placed a strong emphasis on cultural
development.[11] Lake Anne, designed as much as a community and cultural
center as shopping center, included provisions for community activities,
a gallery, and public art. Hunters Woods, Tall Oaks, South Lakes, and
North Point are relatively well designed, mixed-use shopping centers and
nothing more.

Even after Simon's dismissal, the arts continued to flourish. Residents
had to abandon the high-profile performers; however, they did not abandon Simon's cultural agenda. Design, or in this case the cessation of planning, did not end resident interest in cultural affairs. One of the most
successful resident-developed organizations has been GRACE. The organization began when two resident couples took over operation of the Heron
House gallery space in 1970. The new gallery "was an instant smash,"
shows changed every three weeks, and after a few successful years, residents
involved with the gallery formed GRACE to combine the gallery operation
with a flexible, community-oriented art program.[12] GRACE still operates a
gallery space in the town center that features local artists and shows and
continues to sponsor community art classes, a summer art camp for children, and an art-in-the-schools program. The art-in-the-schools project,
with the help of three hundred volunteers, provides five hours of art instruction for approximately 12,000 students in Fairfax County each
month.[13]

GRACE initiated a successful craft/art show. The Northern Virginia
Fine Arts Festival is held in town center each summer for one weekend.
The festival, founded in 1991, has developed a regional reputation and attracts artists from around the nation. In 1997, the 71,000 individuals who
attended the fair enjoyed juried arts and crafts displays and music performances. Particularly notable was a children's art area that included participatory art activities for children including printmaking, hat making,
weaving, *gyotaku* (Japanese fish painting), and pottery making. As in the
early days, participation in cultural activity, not just spectatorship or consumption, informs the new-town cultural efforts.[14]

Reston supports a number of other organizations that provide opportunities for art instruction and exhibitions. An umbrella organization,
the Arts Alliance of Reston, promotes the different organizations, including GRACE, the League of Reston Artists and Photographic Society, and
the Reston Art Gallery and Studio in Lake Anne. Artists also show their
work at their own residences (during open studio opportunities), at the

U.S. Geological Survey building, and in local restaurants. The Reston Community Center also offers residents access to a number of craft studios.[15]

Performing arts have always been popular in Reston and received a boost with the construction of the Reston Community Center in 1975. The community center offers rehearsal space and a professional theater and a schedule of nationally known performers in dance, music, and theater and a foreign-film series.[16] Its theater also hosts a number of local amateur music and drama groups. Since the first years of the town, the Reston Community Players have staged theatrical productions. The Players are serious amateurs who stage four productions each year, conduct a play-reading series, a stage-combat troupe, theater workshops, and according to their own publicity at least, offer "a level of professionalism rarely aspired to in amateur theater."[17]

Musical societies performing in Reston include a string ensemble, a baroque ensemble, a group specializing in Renaissance and early American music, a classical choral chamber, a contemporary music ensemble, and the Reston Chorale. The Chorale, an accomplished amateur group, takes on challenging compositions and originated in Reston's early years.[18] As the organizer of an arts-oriented festival in Reston noted, "it seems odd that we're in the suburbs and have such high-quality groups." Given the deliberate efforts of Reston's founders and residents, that outcome is not odd at all.[19]

Public-access cable Channel 8, one of "the first public access cable television channels in the nation," has added to the cultural life of the community. Simon disliked the look of television antennas and saw cable as a potential substitute. He also viewed the local channel as a "community newsletter." The early broadcasts included "singers, dancers, would-be comedians," and by 1990 there were fifteen different series featuring live broadcasts of community events, popular art programs, county government shows, religious programs, folk music, and more. The station has even received three ACE awards, cable TV's highest honor.[20]

Culture in Reston has not achieved its early promise. At the same time, the community offers both professional and serious amateur cultural activity. Residents attracted by the early vision have achieved a remarkable level of cultural ferment, even in the face of significant regional competition and the general loss of support by the developer. When the designs the developers promised failed to materialize, resident initiative took up the slack. In this case, then, the lack of planning and provision did not limit local activities valued by many residents. The complex interaction of planning and resident behavior has thus been reproduced in cultural patronage.

Columbia's Cultural Democracy

The endless series of garden apartments, split-levels, and parks of Columbia do not connote cultural ferment. Look closer, however, and the signs of cultural activity appear. On kiosks in village centers are announcements of numerous events. Community centers feature exhibits and spaces for performances and dance classes of all types; a cultural center operates in one village center; and a thriving community college houses a professional theater company. During the summer, residents attend free performances by the lakefront, popular concerts at the Merriweather Post Pavilion, and now the growing Columbia Festival of the Arts. Columbia has developed as an extraordinary suburb—a true suburban Chautauqua. Unlike Reston, the original developer in Columbia has continued to be a generous patron, and the citizens have added their own institutions and efforts. The early planning, in fact, helped set the tone of the community. Design affected culture by providing spaces for activities and attracting the culturally ambitious. Like Reston, the accent was placed as much on direct cultural participation as on spectatorship.

The work group sought to shift residents' interests away from mass culture and spectatorial leisure activities by offering more attractive substitutes. They hoped to use culture as a means to break down social divisions (which meant at least a nod to popular culture, as represented, for instance, in the Tivoli complex). The description of the Tivoli entertainment district reveals the interrelationship of cultural and social goals at Columbia, and the way in which the work group hoped to use culture as a social tool:

> Since Tivoli is by definition a place to have fun, it is also by definition a permissive place and under the guise of having or seeking fun, experiences could be tried and behaviors and attitudes learned which are at variance with the workaday style of the individual. In particular, by mixing in with games the arts . . . those people who usually would not expose themselves to these "highbrow" activities for fear of neighbor or family disapproval, might feel freer to so here. . . . In the same way, those who believe they are required by station in life to look down on some activities might feel free to try them here. Such

cultural exchange should contribute to the consolidation of Columbia.[21]

Hamilton recorded that "perhaps the boldest idea put forward in these early stages was from HRD Consultant Wayne Thompson, City Manager of Oakland, California. Thompson proposed that leisure activities in the new community be focused on a 'Center for Cultural Achievement' which would accent the *doing* of cultural activities, and not the performing or spectating."[22]

Not all the members of the work group supported participatory culture, but Rouse stood up for it. According to Hamilton, discussions during the work-group sessions provoked a response from Rouse, who defended his desire to provide leisure options: "After a great deal of talk about getting people to participate in adult education and recreation programs, a certain anchorite reaction set in. Some consultants and individuals within the organization began muttering about 'What if I don't want to participate in all those pottery classes?' . . . Rouse went on to suggest that the freedom of choice is now highly restricted in communities of suburban sprawl, and that because options for satisfying leisure activity were not available, individual loneliness was becoming more and more prevalent." He made sure that the plans for cultural participation, an essential part of suburban reform, reached fruition.[23]

The Tivoli failed to materialize, as did the Center for Cultural Achievement, but the thinking that inspired these institutions did not disappear. The direction of the work group's thinking had a more general impact: Columbia became a model of decentralized participatory culture. This is evident in the abundance of community/cultural centers, a community college, a foundation to underwrite cultural activity, and a homeowner's association committed to cultural development. A mixture of institutional and design innovations energized the cultural scene.

One of the first cultural institutions to be constructed was the Merriweather Post Pavilion in the town center. The work group had recommended creating "a bowl cut into a hillside, overlooking a lovely natural scene" for artistic performances, including instrumental music, opera, ballet, and theater. No mention was made of popular music concerts, the form that eventually predominated at the amphitheater. Hamilton remembered that "the first thing we got in was the Merriweather Post Pavilion, and we had the National Symphony Orchestra, and we had this and we had that. And they (the people who lived in Howard County before Columbia) were in seventh heaven. It's dull exurbanite life. So we put George Balanchine in

CULTURAL PATRONAGE ◆ 249

the middle of Howard County, for the love of Pete."[24] The National Symphony even temporarily established its summer home at the Pavilion. Branches of cultural institutions, such as the Corcoran School of Art and the Peabody Institute (a music conservatory) also established branches in Columbia in the early years.[25] Even though these branches proved temporary, and most left within a few years, they were impressive attractions for a town with a population of just a few thousand.[26]

Another indication of Columbia's efforts to provide culture was the formation of the Columbia campus of Antioch College, which was written up in the *Washington Post* in 1971 as a vibrant, alternative college: "Antioch . . . is exploding with creative energy. Students and teachers alike wear beards, long hair, raffish clothing and attitudes. The venerable walls are covered with signs, notices, drawings, and remarks. It has precisely the vitality . . . that makes a city a city."[27] Antioch also had the distinction of having America's only inflatable campus—structures usually employed for indoor tennis centers—created in 1972 in some of Columbia's open fields. The Antioch program, weighted heavily toward student-run and initiated activities, defied easy definition: a combination of hands-on cooperative projects in areas as diverse as art and administrative services, as well as a busy schedule of radical politics. By the late 1970s, Antioch began scaling back its Columbia activities, mostly because of problems with the school's ambitious expansion plans.[28] Indeed, culture in general, had difficulty taking root in Columbia. According to Len Lazarick, looking back in the *Columbia Flier* of 1977, "the population was not big enough to support many of its great expectations." He noted that "cultural institutions floundered. Lack of support caused the symphony to depart. The rock concerts which replaced it caused too much trouble. The Pavilion was often bare."[29]

Columbia was the site of so many different experiments in culture that it was easy to overlook the successes. Lazarick acknowledged that three other higher education institutions—Howard Community College, Loyola College, and Johns Hopkins University—offered a fine selection of undergraduate and graduate options. After many years of growth, Howard Community College today offers both day and evening courses at its town center campus. It has developed a two-year program in the liberal arts, premed, and computer science and serves 15,000 students yearly. These educational institutions all offer a variety of noncredit personal enrichment courses as well.[30]

Although the high-profile cultural institutions made slow headway, decentralized cultural participation became Columbia's forte, as the work group had planned. The village centers in particular nurtured creativity.

Morton Hoppenfeld explained that "early work group discussions moved away from the concept of a single agglomeration of bricks and mortar that might serve as a 'cultural center,' and looked instead towards the possibility that the arts, in a variety of forms, might permeate the life of the community. . . . This has led us to put emphasis on the development of arts and crafts programs in the villages and the construction of a multi-purpose community center in each village which will serve the needs of teenagers and adults in a variety of programs ranging all the way from physical fitness to pottery making and amateur theatricals." Provision of these facilities played a significant role in furthering cultural life by providing space and support for the budding cultural scene.[31]

In 1971, Albert Mayer of the *Village Voice* praised the town's cultural effervescence: "In music (symphonic and rock), in theater, on the central ambitious spectator level, the earnest experimental level, and the 'homemade' intimate level, a lively situation—somewhat on the plane of big city central sophistication, and of its neighborhoods' local productive ferment."[32] In the village centers, numerous cultural activities were available, including coffee houses, community festivals, galleries, "a visual arts center, several theater groups, a few dance companies . . . and several film groups." Many of these institutions continue to prosper in Columbia to this day.[33]

The Columbia Film Society formed in 1968 when "four Columbia housewives [realized] they missed having a convenient, local cinema." After deciding to show films themselves, they then made a trip to Slayton House (Wilde Lake's community center) and "gained access to movie catalogues." The fare they provided was, and still is, atypical for suburbia. The series opened in 1969 with *Yojimbo,* and featured international, cutting-edge films. It continues to offer high quality cinema available only at urban arthouse cinemas. Nine films are offered each year to growing audiences. Early on the cinema was moved from Slayton House to Bryant Woods Elementary, "where more space was available";[34] the film series now attracts approximately four hundred people at each showing, held at Howard Community College.

Dance proved particularly popular in Columbia, and the community centers supported a number of talented, first-rate instructors. Anne Allen, a dynamic dance teacher, began with classes in one community center and quickly expanded her offerings. She created first the Columbia Multi-Media Theatre and "as dancers developed, the Columbia Dance Theater was founded, and a vital interest in the art of dance as an integral part of community life began to blossom." Because of Allen's efforts, "every village community center has a large room with a wood floor," and later came barres and mirrors. In 1983, the *Newcomers Guide* noted that "sixteen different dance teachers offer classes at the village centers and in local private studios and master classes are also scheduled frequently."[35]

A reporter in 1977 recorded the "Happenings Noted on a Kiosk in Wilde Lake Village" for the readers of the *Washington Star:* "A childbirth workshop . . . a psychodrama group meeting. An evening of one-act plays. A marriage seminar. An Apricot Brandy concert. A 'Freer men' group meeting. A family dance class."[36] An outside observer from Baltimore in 1979 noticed that Columbians kept very busy: "Everything . . . is open at night in Columbia. That's when much of the business is done. All the stores in the Mall are open until 9:30 and many shops in the village centers stay open until 10." He admitted that he had "never encountered so much tedious, stay-busy, nighttime activity: government board and committee meetings; village open space and architectural committee meetings; art, dancing, drama and karate classes; men's divorce reform group meetings, innumerable workshops." What he found, in fact, was a thriving participatory culture, much as the work group had predicted.[37]

The 1980s witnessed significant improvements to the performance and cultural scene. This resulted from the maturation of existing institutions and the creation of new ones. One of the growing institutions nurtured from within Columbia was HoCoPoLitSo, the Howard County Poetry and Literary Society. In 1983, the *Newcomers Guide* noted that "five years ago, just the idea of a poetry reading in Columbia seemed farfetched. Today, there are public readings and discussions, a supporting organization known as the Howard County Poetry and Literature Society and scheduled weekend workshops that feature guest artists and local talent." The society had been in operation since 1974 but received more attention in the 1980s, as it started to attract famous authors. Since the 1970s, the society has featured writers like Isaac Bashevis Singer, Saul Bellow, Edward Albee, and Grace Paley, and many less well-known but respected writers. The emphasis is as much on participation as performance, and the society has worked to bring both adults and high school students into contact with poets and writers.[38]

Beginning in the 1980s, the Howard County Arts Council, growing entirely out of Columbia resident efforts, took a leadership role in developing the county's limited arts scene. Fearful of alienating more conservative county residents, Brenda Bell, the founder of the council and a Columbia resident, used a post-office box in neighboring Ellicot City to disguise the Columbia origins of the organization. The council creates artist-in-residence and related cultural programs in the Howard County schools.

252 ◆ CHAPTER ELEVEN

On a yearly basis, more than 8,000 students participate in these programs. The council also provides grants to county arts organizations, primarily Columbia institutions. The council operates the Howard County Center for the Arts in Ellicott City, which boasts a $1 million annual budget. The center, located in an old elementary school, contains artists' studios, performance spaces, and large gallery spaces. Professional artists on a year-round basis teach classes for all ages in art, dance, and theater; the galleries mount nearly eighteen shows a year; and the theater space features ballet, modern dance, experimental theater, concerts, and recitals.[39]

The Columbia Festival of the Arts, like the arts council, reflects a blend of participatory culture with high standards. With help from the Columbia Foundation, the Howard County Arts Council, and the CA, Columbia residents have sponsored an arts festival each summer since 1989. While the feeling has been informal, with an attempt to have residents "directly engage the artists," the schedule of professional and local performers has been impressive. In 1994, for instance, the festival included performances by Bill T. Jones, Taj Mahal, Garrison Keillor, a documentary theater piece on "Images of Emancipation," and the Baltimore Symphony.[40] Attendance had reached 30,000 by 1997 and more than three hundred volunteers gave their time each year. The 1998 festival included more than sixty performances, three hundred artists, and fifty workshops. The festival is the source of much pride for the community.[41]

The Columbia Foundation has nurtured cultural development. The foundation's support for the Columbia Festival of the Arts, for instance, has been significant. Beginning in 1988, the foundation provided "seed funding to help pay for the coordinator's salaries, promotional materials for fundraising, and expert consultants so they can build on the experience of other comparable festivals."[42] The following years brought ever larger grants to the festival and to a variety of other Columbia arts organizations.[43]

The CA has facilitated cultural development much more actively than its Reston counterpart. Since the early 1970s, the association's Lakefront Festival during the summer has brought movies, musicians, and a variety of other live entertainment to the lakefront seven nights a week from June through August. Originally designed to neutralize the overwhelming teenage presence at the lakefront, the festival quickly became popular in its own right and still includes a wide range of live performances.[44] An article in 1986 noted that in the summer of 1985, "a total audience of over 15,000 gathered on the shores on Lake Kittamaqundi to hear everything from blue-grass to big band, and to see everyone from Miss Piggy and Kermit to Romeo and Juliet."[45]

The association also helps organize the Columbia Festival of the Arts, donating staff hours and logistical support to the event. The Visual Arts Center in Long Reach, which changed hands among a number of institutions, including Antioch, the Columbia Cultural Institute, and Towson State University, is now run by the association. High-quality hand-made crafts are on display, a gallery mounts regular shows, and professional-level participatory craft and art programs are offered.[46]

Central to the association's cultural role are the many community centers that provide space for cultural activities. In 1975, for instance, the four community centers offered "744 different courses, enrolling over 7,600 people" in every imaginable kind of course.[47] By 1983, the *Newcomers Guide* of 1983–84 explained that "in older areas of the city, the village center community buildings have become a focus of community life. They are the place to go for meetings, dance, art or exercise classes or to see a community theater group perform."[48] Eight community centers are now managed by local village boards. The CA renovated Oakland Manor, a "179-year-old Federal style beauty" in the geographic center of Columbia. Home to community events, gatherings, and special-interest groups, including the new African Art Museum of Maryland, the manor has featured music performances, teas, and school programs. During the 1990s, the Howard County Arts Council, with the CA, led the creation of the Jim Rouse Performing Arts Center, a professional theater and dance studio designed for both community and school use, at Wilde Lake High School.[49]

The planners and residents proved unsuccessful in weaning a majority of residents from mass-cultural pursuits, but Columbia nevertheless features an impressive array of cultural events and organizations. Good planning, generous patronage, and extensive citizen action wove creativity into the fabric of the community. Columbia is a contemporary suburban Chautauqua, chock full of uplifting and serious cultural activity for both participation and consumption.

Irvine: Town and Gown

> Things like residential development and business and such are only part of Irvine as a place. It takes culture to give a city a real community identity.
>
> LOUISE SCOTT AND FRANK O'DONNEL, *New Worlds*

William Pereira's early plans for the Irvine Ranch envisioned a university town filled with artisans, intellectuals, and performers. Although the Irvine

Company abandoned elements of Pereira's plan, the university does offer Irvine residents some cultural sophistication. Residents have created additional cultural opportunities through city government sponsorship. Like Reston and Columbia, however, the signs of cultural life are not immediately recognizable, and the high cost of living in Irvine, as well as its increasingly conservative reputation, have given Irvine a worse cultural reputation than it deserves.[50]

In the 1960s and 1970s, the Irvine Company fostered cultural development. Most importantly, of course, it donated the 1,000 acres that became UCI, now one of America's leading educational institutions. The company also sponsored outdoor summer concerts and art shows, ice shows, boat shows, and craft shows at Fashion Island in Newport Beach to promote the mall and the community growing around it. As in Reston and Columbia, big name performers were imported.[51] Individuals associated with the company have donated money and land to the Orange County Museum of Art in Newport Beach, which features contemporary art from California and the world. The museum offers arts-related lectures, a wide range of art classes, an art camp for children, and it sponsors courses in conjunction with the UCI extension. The company, however, left the majority of cultural sponsorship to the ranch residents and the university.

The City of Irvine has sponsored its own cultural activities. A 1980 description of a busy Sunday in Irvine gave a sense of Irvine's ambitions: "Irvine residents settle into chairs in a city park building to view a dance concert; or maybe it's a brass band, or a visiting mime. A couple of neighborhoods away, UCI's Symphony Orchestra is tuning up. . . . A continent or two away, the Irvine Master Chorale is off on a tour of Europe."[52] Not only did Irvine offer fine arts performances, and for many years transported residents to cultural activities in nearby cities, but city residents organized amateur music, theater, and arts groups.

The city sponsored a cultural-affairs division during the 1980s that worked to augment participation in the arts. Their activities included public art projects, performing-art sponsorship (free programs around the city), awards to businesses and individuals who supported the arts, partnerships to increase art education in the schools, grants to arts organizations, promotion of intercultural participation in the arts, and running of the fine arts center. Irvine has maintained an active sister-city program with both Tsukuba, Japan (a planned city), and Hermosillo, an agricultural town in Mexico: "Trips, student exchanges, and cultural programs are used to share ideas in the arts, education, law, business and industry, urban planning and medicine."[53]

Community centers run by the city in different neighborhoods also offer courses and activities for residents. These centers, like those in Columbia, sponsor a remarkable number of child- and teen-oriented programs, including camps, foreign-language programs, performing-arts opportunities, dance, and crafts. For adults, the city sponsors numerous affordable enrichment courses in computers, dance, writing, sports, and martial arts. Many of these same courses are offered in continuing education programs in the area, but their availability at affordable prices in convenient community settings adds to the richness and accessibility of cultural participation in the community.

Since 1980 residents and others have enjoyed exhibitions, classes and workshops for adults and children, festivals, lectures, open studio spaces, and performances at the 18,000-square-foot city-sponsored Irvine Fine Arts Center. The Arts Center has been complimented for mounting "well-thought-out shows" over the years and has been lauded as a gallery that "does the most with the least." The center also runs a variety of off-site display areas. One is a Floating Storefront Studio at the University Center shopping area. At this site, artists work in studio space provided by the Irvine Company.[54]

The city government and UCI have created a world-class theater on the campus. The two organizations sponsored the $17 million Irvine Barclay Theater as a venue for both professional and university events. The 750-seat theater regularly sells out. The program is, as the director of the theater notes, eclectic, because "Orange County has become a place of extraordinary diversity with people whose tastes and interests are as far ranging as any other place in this country." The schedule for 1998–99 included African dancers, sitar music, Tibetan singers, Cuban jazz, blues, magic, klezmer, drama (including Eric Bogosian), classical concerts (including Yo-Yo Ma and the Emerson String Quartet), and contemporary dance (including Mark Morris and Momix). In addition, university arts organizations offer plays, concerts, and dances. The outreach program of the theater compliments these activities with performances of plays and workshops for schools. Few suburban communities boast such a high-quality performance program.[55]

The university attracted culturally sophisticated residents and events. One longtime resident remembered, in 1965 "the evening after I moved in, I went over to the new university and sat on bleachers in a gymnasium and watched Martha Graham dance. And I said to myself, like Brigham Young,

'This is the place.'"[56] The campus features world-class art facilities with nationally known programs in dance, drama, music, and studio art. Approximately 18,000 students now attend the university and are served by a 1,400 member faculty. The continuing education program of the school offers 1,800 courses, seminars, and workshops on the campus and around Orange County. Irvine hosts other colleges as well. Irvine Valley College (now Saddleback Community College) offers 8,000 students each year a chance for affordable community college education in a broad range of fields from art to chemistry. Concordia College also offers numerous theater and music performances. The UCI campus, nonetheless, is Irvine's principal cultural center.

The City of Irvine does not have the intimate college-town feel associated with older university towns, yet residents have taken advantage of the campus. A survey in 1975 found that 30 percent of residents visited the campus monthly, and 57 percent visited a few times a year.[57] One resident explained recently, "Our piece of Paradise is near the University of California, Irvine. A short walk to University Extension courses offered at night or on weekends stimulates our intellectual interest. The artistic displays, the variety of lectures, and the plays and musical performances fuel our cultural interests."[58] Louis Fridhandler, the community activist and a longtime resident, explained in an interview that not only did he take advantage of university cultural offerings but many other members of the community did as well.[59]

On the other hand, a rift separates many of the cutting-edge, liberal artists and university students and the more conservative members of the Irvine community. In a 1998 interview, the former president of UCI, Jack Peltason, described the relationship of the university to the community. The university offers world-class cultural events, but Orange County and Irvine residents, most of whom are newcomers, do not see their local community as having a defining role in where they spend time. Irvine residents are most interested in schools, recreational activities, low crime, more affordable housing, and convenient access to work. Peltason also believes that the building of the University Hill faculty-staff housing complex has separated faculty from the community. More than four hundred faculty live in the complex and need to venture out into the community very seldom. In addition, most of these faculty members, like those throughout America, are more interested in publishing books and creating art for their academic peers and distant audiences than participating in local civic, cultural, or social activity. UCI is a great research university, after all, not an incubator of social or cultural movements.

University students of the 1960s and 1970s took more interest in Irvine affairs, but contemporary students focus on academics or socializing. Most students choose to live on campus or in one of the surrounding communities rather than in the city. Many can be found in the more student-friendly communities of Newport Beach, Lido Island and Peninsula, Laguna Beach, and Costa Mesa. These communities offer the café, pizza, bar, and beach lifestyle students seek, rather than the family-centered lifestyle of Irvine.[60]

Irvine, through a combination of city and university efforts, has achieved a comparable level of cultural participation to Columbia and Reston. The university town envisioned by Pereira has not yet emerged, but the commitment of residents to cultural pursuits has grown over the decades. Planning played a role in creating facilities for cultural expression, but in the case of the university, for instance, only partially succeeded in extending that cultural life to the community in general. Only when the city became involved in cultural patronage did the community as a whole begin to develop more impressive cultural affairs.

If not immediately apparent to visitors, and often of little interest to many residents, the cultural scene as it developed in these new towns did answer at least part of the intellectual critique of suburban life. The cultural life of the new towns never replaced the mass cultural offerings of the wider society, but the programs presented an option for those who wanted more distance from conventional leisure pursuits. In new towns, creative residents found a sufficient number of like-minded people who supported, attended, and participated in cultural affairs. During the early years, construction of community and cultural centers and imported events set a promising tone and attracted arts-oriented residents. When patronage faltered or ambition increased, the residents developed new facilities and local organizations to foster cultural activity. Many suburbs may be catching up with the new towns in cultural affairs, but few have achieved the same scale and ambition. Nor did they achieve such cultural ferment forty years ago when the arts were an even lower priority in most American communities. The new towns successfully demonstrated that suburbia could, with the right conditions and a great deal of effort, provide a conducive environment for artistic expression and consumption.

Public Art in the New Towns

The finest suburbs of the last century developed a "sculptural" landscape of trees, homes, and streets. Many suburbs included monuments to war heroes or swallowed up older monuments as they expanded. Modern mass suburbs, however, had few public art projects or monuments to help establish a sense of history or place. Most developers, trying their best to keep costs at a minimum, ignored the possibility of public art. Suburban residents, generally distrustful of the arts, were wary of commissioning public art projects. Cities remained the location of most public art in America, for better and worse.

By the 1950s and 1960s, urban public art took two principal forms. Cities had added hundreds of monuments over centuries, including realistic sculptures of former civic and national leaders and famous artists or writers and allegorical sculptures designed to celebrate themes like patriotism and justice. Many of these pieces had been carefully positioned in parks or in civic centers to accent both the sculptures and their urban spaces. During the 1950s and 1960s many corporations decided to fill empty plazas adjoining their buildings with large public sculptures by well-known artists to boost corporate identity, to raise the status of buildings they had created, and to give interest to what were often seen as windy, uncomfortable spaces. The government commissioned public art for the open spaces surrounding its buildings; the Kennedy and Johnson administrations' vision of art and artists as fundamental to a democratic society contributed to this process. There remains serious doubt about the relative artistic merit of many of these projects, but cities remained the beneficiaries of such efforts.[61]

The new-town developers set out to change this pattern, but they did not simply mimic contemporary, urban public art; instead, they sought to connect to an older, nineteenth-century sculptural tradition. Like nineteenth-century public art, the public art in new towns was designed either as an integrated part of new spaces or to boost community identity through symbolism. At Reston and Irvine, developers linked early public-art projects to architecture and planning. The patrons of Columbia's public art, on the other hand, hoped to use these pieces to communicate and affirm community values.

The developers initiated public-art programs, and residents have commissioned their own pieces, but the programs have not been maintained at the level initially envisioned. The primary role of public art in these places, to help distinguish the new towns from other subdivisions, faded after the communities' reputations were well established. Concerns about cost and changes in management also contributed to the drying up of these projects. Large sculptures still appeared but usually not as part of the comprehensive vision initiated in the early years.

Public Space and Public Art in Reston

Reston's public art is located principally in Lake Anne and the new town center. At these two locations, public art is integrated with the architecture and planning of the community, consciously adding a touch of urbanity to the surroundings. The sculptures created in the early years set a high standard for the other new towns, but the program fell victim to the later development companies' turn toward more conservative designs. Only in recent years has a surprising public-art renaissance occurred in the new town center.

Simon wanted Lake Anne to have sculptures integrated into the plaza and pathways of the community. The sculptures, by James Rossant (also a designer of the Village), and Gonzalo Fonseca, a New York painter and sculptor originally from Uruguay, were fashioned of cast concrete and wood. Fonseca spent a year in Reston "designing, carving, and building alongside of architect and planner, contractor and craftsman, free to consult, absorb, and follow his own predilections." He created sculptures in the Village Plaza, one between the high-rise and garden apartments and one underneath the pedestrian underpass on the walkway from the Goodman cluster to the village center.[62] The sculpture in the underpass resembled a miniature boat and was accompanied by other concrete relief work. Sculptures by Fonseca along the plaza included a wooden climbing sculpture and a sculpture that incorporated the flattened shape of a boat. These sculptures introduced a playfulness to the town and reinforced the nautical theme sought by the developer.[63]

Rossant's fountain at Lake Anne village center (figure 14) echoed the village center's "hemi-cycle" design and was "composed of simple pyramids, cones, and cubes with water spraying from the tops and splashing down on them. It is most unique in that it has no definitive sides or edges. There is only a shallow depression in the brick paving to retain most of the water but it doesn't keep the younger set from getting into and really enjoying the fountain."[64] Rossant also designed a pyramid sculpture that included a play space within and a tower overlooking the lake. The lightness of these designs helped break down the formal character of the overall planning and helped shape unconventional spaces.

FIGURE 14 Fountain designed by James Rossant accented the unconventional designs around it. (1999)

The Reston Foundation described how these sculptures and play areas contributed to the cultural mission of the new town: "There is abstract play sculpture both in concrete and wood that is functional and beautiful. A concrete underpass was enhanced with a variety of sculptural forms, coordinated with dramatic lighting effects and the use of street furniture. . . . People, especially children, took great delight in watching these artists at work, and enjoyed sharing the creative experience itself. To the visitor as well as the resident, a latent curiosity was aroused in the public use of art." This foundation affirmed Simon's belief that art should become an "integral part of the public environment," so that America would develop more beautiful public spaces that compared with "so many of the public places of the great cities of Europe."[65]

Reston is one of the few communities in America in which sculpture was intimately designed with the buildings and landscape, rather than placed as an afterthought. These rather bold, concrete sculptures are sensitively matched to their modern surroundings and enliven the spaces. Placed in another context, they might not work as well. New village centers by later development companies entirely lacked any public art.

A revealing controversy erupted in 1988 over a proposed mammoth public sculpture by a respected Soviet artist, Zurab Tzereteli, who became inspired by Reston's design and spirit during a visit. He designed a thirty-foot sculpture, entitled *Breaking Through the Wall of Misunderstanding*, that he wished to donate to the community. The sculpture, as the title implied, featured a large figure breaking through a wall, in a "Soviet proletarian" style, and was to be sculpted in bronze and granite. The potential donation resulted in numerous meetings, articles, and arguments over whether the piece constituted propaganda, its relative aesthetic merits, and its suitability.

The sculpture received support from many local community leaders, including Martha Pennino, who thought that it represented an attempt by Restonians to be "better world citizens." Others wrote angry letters and editorials arguing that the donation was a cynical attempt to promote a simplistic view of Russian and American differences, sugarcoating the repressive nature of the Soviet regime. Some residents argued simply that the proposed sculpture was "vulgar and pretentious." Objections like these forced those who supported the donation to ask the artist at his studio to either change the design or create an entirely different piece. The artist, however, when confronted with objections, proposed an even larger sculpture. One of the Reston residents who visited the artist at his studio in the Soviet Union, on close examination of the original model, was surprised to find that "the stones of the wall were covered with three-dimensional images of angels, Christ and saints." This man exclaimed "my hair stood up on end. . . . I gulped and had to loosen my tie. . . . We thought we had problems with political messages. Wait until I have to explain problems with mixing church and state." The sculpture did not, after all, end up in Reston. The successful defeat of the sculpture reflects a healthy democratic spirit and the power of citizens to control the destiny of their community.[66]

A few public sculptures appeared in Reston during the 1980s and 1990s without the subtlety of placement that characterized the early years. A modern metal sculpture called *Restosauria* by John Parker, installed in Lake Newport in 1990, was selected by the director of GRACE. Unfortunately, trees have overgrown the piece, and it is now in need of repair.[67] At the Walker Nature Center, a large sundial was dedicated to the memory of Vernon Walker, Reston's pioneering environmental educator. The sundial, according to the piece's inscription, "is dedicated to Vernon J. Walker . . . for whom sundials were the symbol of man's unity with the natural environment." This is the only piece of public sculpture in Reston that refers directly to community life.

In the 1990s, the developer, then Reston Land Corporation, surprisingly reintroduced art as a shaper of public space in the town center. The

art chosen for the town center was designed to heighten the urban character of the center, much like earlier sculptures. As at Lake Anne, the developer matched the sculpture to the architecture and planning; a figurative,
neoclassical sculptural style was chosen to accent the neoclassical buildings
and Beaux-Arts planning. The *Washington Post* praised the main sculpture
at the town center, Mercury Fountain, "designed by sculptor Saint Clair
Cemin in collaboration with RTKL associates. . . . Cemin's concept of a
slightly off-balance bronze figure of Mercury atop a twisting column of
Carrara marble, itself dotted with snail-like bronze appurtenances that
spew water into a broad-brimmed bowl, is at once traditional and idiosyn-
cratic. . . . It's an odd blend that gives immediate and promises long-term
identity to the place." Indeed, the fountain helps frame the public space
and adds a dynamic element to the plaza.[68] At the entrance to the town
center are "two polychrome, gold-leaf, oversize versions of astrolabes
dubbed 'Day' and 'Night.'" The astrolabes use lighting and colored glass to
good effect and are well sited at the main entrance.[69]

Many of the sculptures of Reston are conspicuous and well integrated with their surroundings, perhaps better integrated than much modern urban public sculpture. As was hoped, they add a sophistication to
their environments and accentuate the self-conscious urbanity of the community. That the program was not maintained at its original level is a great
disappointment.

Columbia: Community Values in Public Art

Public sculpture dots Columbia's landscape. The community has a wide
range of allegorical, realistic, and abstract public sculptures designed
specifically to reflect and affirm Columbia's values. These pieces are numerous, and some are well positioned, but many are poorly integrated
with their sites. As in Reston, the ambitious public art program of the early
years has not been maintained.

When the Rouse company commissioned a series of sculptures for the
new town, the man hired "to oversee the production of Columbia's signs,
symbols, fountains and sculptures" was Pierre du Fayet, a French sculptor
living in the United States. The most memorable of the pieces, finished in
1967, and a sculpture still associated with Columbia, is the People Tree located near Lake Kittamaqundi in Columbia's town center, officially titled
The Tree of Life. The sculpture (figure 15), made of metalized glass fiber and
stained glass resin, is "a 'tree' composed of sixty six abstract human figures
reaching outward from a central core." The piece is strategically placed near

FIGURE 15 The People Tree sculpture by Pierre du Fayet remains the symbol of Columbia's innovative spirit. (1999)

the site of many of Columbia's public celebrations and has come to be associated with Columbia's experimental community ethos.[70]

The piece has served as a symbol of Columbia's spirit. Helen Ruther, a Columbia pioneer interviewed in 1991, explained that "in the early days, seeing the logo of the 'People Tree' as it is commonly called, on someone's car or clothing was an automatic signal that 'this person was from Columbia, and right away you felt a sort of kinship." A variety of products—T-shirts, coffee mugs, greeting cards—festooned with the People Tree logo are still available from the CA, which uses the image as its logo.[71]

The sculpture appeared in local publications and came to be used as a symbol for Columbia's aspirations. In a 1973 article, Jean Moon chastised fellow residents by claiming that the "the people tree is no Stature of Liberty" because of the town's failure to welcome large numbers of the poor and old.[72] One gentleman, James Bohanan, the manager of Copperstone Terrace, responded to Moon's article by drawing out the metaphor:

> The "Statue of Liberty" is one individual standing alone holding high a torch. She was a gift from another country in recognition of what this country stood for. The "People Tree"

was commissioned by a developer who said "we want to create a city that stays in scale with people—we *hope* those people can create the Next America". . . . To me the "People Tree" depicts active interaction between all kinds of people. To me the "People Tree" says the hope of "Next America" is in that interaction.[73]

The analysis evident in this paragraph is in keeping with the idealistic tone of the new-town effort in Columbia. The People Tree is one of the few pieces of modern public sculpture anywhere in America that has been invested with positive community symbolism.

Du Fayet also created a sculpture, *Family Group*, for Wilde Lake village green (figure 16). Again, this sculpture (set inside a fountain) had a community function. Robert Tennenbaum, one of the original planners, explained that the sculpture was commissioned because the designers wanted "public art to be become part of everyday life in Columbia."[74] The sculpture itself is a statement of the centrality of the family, but it is a stylized, modern vision of the family. In 1985, *Columbia Magazine* explained the sculpture's significance: "Situated in front of the Family Life Center, the three abstract figures symbolize another motivating spirit of Columbia: family love and togetherness. More than any other sculpture in Columbia, this one elicits human—read 'children'—interaction. When the fountain's off the sculpture frequently serves as an interesting jungle gym."[75]

Other pieces in the town center also reflect communal values and help to introduce visitors to the town's philosophy. *Bear with Nursing Cubs* in town center affirms the nurturing goals of the community. *Columbia Magazine* explained that the "sculpture nestles in town center, dispensing its quiet gracefulness and a message as soothing as mother's milk."[76] Unfortunately, the sculpture is hidden away near the American City building and the CA. Nearby *Hug*, by artist Jimilu Mason, in Columbia town center, was commissioned by the Rouse Company and the Enterprise Development Company (a nonprofit development company) in honor of Morton Hoppenfeld, who died in 1985. The artist's statement distributed with the press release revealed his hopes for the sculpture: "There were many clues to Mort's vision. He liked people and was a person who easily included them in his circle. I knew that he wanted Columbia to be a city where anyone would feel welcome . . . an all embracing city. I was told he envisioned this bosque overlooking the lake, as a place for lovers."[77]

More-recent sculptures are used to make speculative developments more attractive. The excitement of the early years has shifted to a greater

FIGURE 16 Pierre du Fayet's *Family Group* sculpture in Wilde Lake village center. Photo by the author.

focus on money making at both the Rouse Company and at other Columbia concerns. Columbia, for instance, has numerous realistic sculptures, most of which are sited in business parks. There, one can find statues of bears, mallard ducks, a pair of Canada geese, and two foxes. Many of these pieces are by "cowboy-turned-artist Jim Dolan," known for combining stainless steel, brass, and copper. Dolan's wildlife art was selected by Rouse and Associates (a developer of office parks run by James Rouse's nephew) because "his wildlife sculptures help preserve the natural setting; they blend with the environment and create a pleasant place for those who work there."[78] Not all the public sculpture at Columbia of more recent vintage is uninteresting. Many of these pieces are abstract, like the early work, and some are well integrated in the environment. *Completed Circle Waterfall*, a sculpture of burnished stainless steel in the Columbia mall by Jimilu Mason (1975), is a circular fountain "completed" by falling water. Rather than being merely an abstract metal sculpture, then, it becomes a fountain to which people are drawn.[79] Most recent pubic art has been placed as an afterthought and does not reflect in any way the actual values of the community.

The residents only occasionally commissioned public art projects, and when they did, they reverted to the older allegorical style. For instance, on its twentieth birthday, Oakland Mills village commissioned a commemorative sculpture. Artist Rodney Carroll, of the Maryland Art Institute, created a family group cut out of "one-inch thick aluminum for the roughly 11-foot-tall sculpture." Carroll explained that he designed the sculpture to reflect "the idea that Columbia is family oriented, and the idea of pioneering a new city." He also wanted it to give "the sense of Columbia, of everybody going to the promised land" where the "individual can make a difference."[80] The finish of the piece was also "randomly sanded . . . [to] reflect any ambient light, which, the artist feels, gives the whole sculpture a sense of change." This sculpture is prominently sited in the Oakland Mills village center and adds a bit of life to the space it inhabits.[81]

Columbia has developed a quirky mixture of allegorical, abstract, and realistic sculptures. Allegorical pieces like the People Tree proved important in defining the Columbia mission and sense of community. Unfortunately, the program of public art has not kept pace with the growth of the community. By turning to "plop art" instead of art designed for the community, corporations undermined the legitimacy of the public art ideal established in the 1960s. The early pieces remain striking and, reflecting their importance, have been well preserved by the community over the decades.

Irvine's Public Art Tradition

The Irvine Company made public art an integral part of the Newport Center complex. Later developments by the company have also placed an emphasis on public-art projects at strategic locations, although in less profusion than during the early years. The Irvine Company, unlike the developers of Columbia or Reston (and with little resistance from residents), has also removed quite a number of the older sculptures during renovations—a sense of new-town historical importance does not hold sway in Irvine. The city government has added new public art projects, many of which compare favorably to earlier ones.

In 1972, William Mason, then president of the company, wrote, "public expressions of art are an important part of any activity center. Much of what makes Rome or Paris great cities is the availability of art to the public." The most impressive of the early public art projects centered on Newport Center. There, the Irvine Company hired two artists to "bring art to the places people naturally congregate." Tom Van Sant, an artist who had four commissions at Newport Center, selected native animals to be rendered in life-size groups in relief on the walls of Irvine Company headquarters and used an original sculpting method that was integrated with

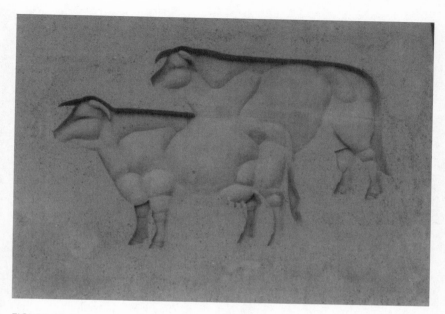

FIGURE 17 Unconventional portraits of animals, by artist Tom Van Sant, on the Irvine Company headquarters in Newport Center highlighted the developer's interest in public art. (1999)

building construction: "Once molds for the reliefs were carved, they were placed as liners in the forms for concrete. The images were thus created at the same time the contractor poured the structural walls of the building, making them an integral part of the architecture." The result is an impressive series of deep relief sculptures visible to even the most casual observer (figure 17). Another artist, Aristides Demetrius, created a sculpture for Fashion Island consisting of three figures that appear to be free-falling. It is reminiscent of Columbia's People Tree, although never invested with so much communal symbolism. These two projects were not the only commissions, but they can still be seen. Other early projects, including a set of large bells, have been replaced during renovations. New sculptures and fountains have taken their places.[82]

The Irvine Business Center also contains a notable series of sculptures of more recent vintage. Most notable are the abstract, colorful metal sculptures by prominent artist George Sugarman. The Sugarman pieces are well integrated with their site: they are set in a landscaped area that features fountains and a small artificial body of water. Many other fountains and sculptures also dot Irvine's business parks and landscape. The fountains, particularly favored by Donald Bren, reflect the community's affluence. Water, after all, is so precious in California that to have it bubbling and evaporating in such quantities is as much a reflection of power as taste.[83]

The City of Irvine has, during the last two decades, expanded the number of public-art sites in the city. During the 1980s, it sponsored the creation of a number of projects under its Art in Public Places program, which was designed to create "a sense of place by bringing outdoor art to the community." Among the many projects, particularly notable is a sculpture by artist Mark Lere at the entrance to Heritage Park regional library. Commissioned in 1985, the piece includes three elements: a spiraling marble time line embedded in the ground, a marble chair, and a twelve-foot "headless figure made of 200 stacked pieces of anodized aluminum." According to an article about the piece, the artist believed that the three elements, representing "the three basic positions of the human body (sitting, standing and lying down), share a unifying theme of 'accumulation.' The figure represents man and his accumulation of experiences. The time line represents the accumulation of culture, and the rock chair, he said, is a symbol of nature and the stacking of time." The piece is well sited at the entrance to the library, and Lere worked with the community to determine events to be placed on the time line. The sculpture's ability to communicate its message as described by the artist, on the other hand, is less clear; the subtle symbolism is probably lost on most observers.[84]

A number of other sculptures grace Irvine's landscape and were placed in strategic public locations as part of the city's public art program. Among the most notable is a sculpture by artist Ross Powers. The piece, composed of metal triangles spiraling toward the ceiling in the University Park library, compliments the building's attractive wood beams. That the city has installed this piece, among many others, reflects the fact that the interest in public art had not faded. Most of these sculptures are placed in locations where residents will see them in the course of everyday activities.

❖

Public art has played a role in distinguishing the new towns from conventional suburbs. In Reston, the best public art is well conceived for its location and adds a touch of urbanity. In Columbia, the finest public-art projects, like the People Tree, are designed to reflect community values. In Irvine, the company and the city have attempted at times to make public art a part of the planned fabric. That new towns had any public sculpture at all distinguished them from most suburbs; that they had some pieces that were inspiring, attracted public notice, and worked well in their locations was notable. The new-town experience with public art indicates that such objects could help define a suburban community, both in terms of design (a unique sense of place) and in the affirmation of social ideals. The rapid dissolution of the many programs, with only temporary reinstatements, also reflects the difficulty of maintaining a coherent cultural program in such a dynamic environment.

Emerald Cities: Environmentalism in New Towns

Protected by a carefully designed street pattern which minimizes traffic and which provides pedestrian underpasses beneath even moderately busy streets, these boys and girls are free to explore their new city. There are streams to ford, woods to explore, bike paths to ride, formal playgrounds with swings and slides and completely unplanned fields and meadows in which to romp.

COLUMBIA PUBLIC RELATIONS

America's first planned suburb, Llewellyn Park, New Jersey, preserved much of the natural landscape within its borders. Suburbs that followed replaced natural areas with a highly cultivated landscape incorporating lawns, hedges, and trees. Manicured nature served as a delightful setting for homes, and few residents or developers saved or valued wild open spaces around them. The new towns have manicured lawns and playing fields, but they also have natural spaces in abundance. These areas are remarkably pristine, and are appreciated by many residents who live next to nature preserves and by still others who use the pathways that weave through them. Developers initiated environmental conservation, but residents took upon themselves the preservation and expansion of environmental corridors.

The open spaces of new towns are cultural resources. The pleasure that Americans, particularly the middle class, take in nature is a growing cultural phenomenon. Nature appreciation by city dwellers has its roots in nineteenth-century environmental efforts that led to the creation of city and national parks and national forests. Americans preserved and created these early parks as much for their cultural importance—a reminder of American greatness, the belief in the ability of nature to inspire citizens and artists, and as a release from the pressures of urban living—as for their natural resources. The middle class of America, while in large part responsible for environmental destruction, has also provided much of the leadership in environmental preservation and education. The 1960s and 1970s witnessed a new vitality in environmental efforts, spurred by the publication of Rachel Carson's *Silent Spring,* the growing counterculture, and the increasing popularity of tourism that brought more Americans into contact with nature. The burgeoning environmental ethic had an effect on new towns, and new towns attracted many people who valued the natural environment as a cultural resource.[85]

This environmental ethic was designed to spread beyond the creation of natural areas. In all the towns, the planners may have provided highways, shopping malls, cul-de-sacs, and parking lots, but they also tried to make shopping areas and schools within walking or biking distance on grade-separated walkways. At Columbia, planners envisioned a shuttle bus moving rapidly through town on its very own road. Even when this system proved too expensive and was abandoned, the local community association kept an internal bus system running through decades of low ridership. Idealistic Reston residents developed their own internal transit system and commuter bus service that proved popular for many years. The Irvine city government created a remarkable system of bike paths that stretch across the city. These innovations, however, have had a negligible effect on use of the automobile. In 1976, Burby and Weiss found that although bus use was higher among new-town residents than those living in conventional subdivisions, "community residents overwhelmingly use their cars to travel to work, and to convenience stores, supermarkets, and shopping centers." The only appreciable change in habits came in the children's use of pathways for walking to school.[86] The dominance of the car has only increased with time. As in other parts of new-town life, design and services did not invariably revolutionize behavior.

Reston's Environmental Pioneers

Mature forest blanketed many of the thousands of acres Simon purchased. Reston still boasts forests, streams, lakes, fields, and wetlands throughout 1,100 acres of open space. Joseph Stowers, a longtime Reston activist, and other members of the RCA, fought to expand and connect the pathways system in Reston: a system that now includes fifty-five miles of paths, including ninety-five bridges. The Reston Association has made space available for garden plots on open land, too, an innovation not part of the original plans. Alternative environmental management techniques are also employed by the association: carp are used to control aquatic weeds and wasps to attack gypsy moth eggs; nature's own processes are employed to help restore stream beds; and native plant species are encouraged.[87]

The community, with help from the developer, has attempted to understand and appreciate the natural landscape preserved around them. Reston during the 1960s developed an innovative environmental education program. Vernon Walker, hired by Simon to run a nature center, had been trained as a science educator and came to Reston from New York, where he had developed a relationship with L. B. Sharp, a pioneer in outdoor education. Walker convinced Simon "that the best environmental teacher was the outdoors itself." The open space philosophy at Reston was described by Walker in 1969: "What is the character of the open space [in Reston]? . . . We have learned to avoid building permanent structures on floodplains. There is hope! The land is used for walkways . . . bridle paths, tot lots, and other recreation."[88] Walker helped create environmental management committees in the two existing villages to look after their respective open spaces and was pictured in a newspaper article talking to kindergarten children about the "need for trees as dwellings for animals," leading other children on an interpretive walk, and showing still others how erosion changed their environment.[89] Walker ran the center for many years, but died in 1982 at the age of fifty.[90]

The community created the aforementioned Walker Nature Center in 1987. Seventy acres of trees, trails, streams and wildlife have been "dedicated to Vernon Walker's vision of Reston's open space as an all-season educational experience." The center includes trails, a picnic pavilion, wildflower garden, a meditation area, outdoor displays, and a demonstration meadow. In 1989, the Reston Environmental Education Foundation was formed to promote a broader range of programs, and with the support of the Reston Association, now offers on a yearly basis "200 programs and reaches 7,000 participants." Nature education activities include preschool and school programs, summer camps, teen programs, teacher workshops, service projects, family programs, lectures, and much more.[91]

The community makes full use of the different environmental corridors available. Occasional crimes have occurred on the secluded pathways, but good weather finds numerous Restonians out walking and enjoying the attractive natural surroundings. Outside the natural areas, the traffic of Reston has worsened as residents and visitors fight for space on roads and in parking lots. The internal bus system has not kept pace with community growth and barely manages to serve the different commercial centers it links. Residents decline to use the walkway system as a daily commuting or shopping route, on either foot or bike, and drive to their nearby village centers and schools. Reston's land preservation system is lovely and a great treasure, but it is no defense against the growth of environmental problems around it.

Columbia's Abundant Nature

HRD has preserved approximately one third of the land area of Columbia as open space. Rouse remembered in 1977 that after the purchase of the land "we said in the first communication we ever sent to the people of the county that we believed it was possible to build an urban community that could respect the land and preserve the stream valleys and the flood plains, while providing a human habitat." Rouse not only valued nature for itself, but he was a great believer in the positive effect of nature on the human heart: "How do you measure the value of seeing a muskrat swim across the lake? A whistling swan? You don't have to measure it to know that extraordinary things happen to the human soul and human heart and human mind when there is this natural association with nature." Rouse's belief in the effect of environment on character was unshakable.[92]

Some of Columbia's open spaces are manicured, while others are thickly wooded stream valleys and woods. The beauty and the clarity of the streams and the thick foliage that still blankets the community are remarkable. The natural areas do much, especially in summer, to compensate for architectural blandness. Not only did the Rouse Company preserve thousands of trees, but it planted hundreds of thousands more, many of which are now nearing maturity. The CA maintains the open spaces—3,600 acres of open space, with 5,000 acres planned when complete—and pathways with the help of the county. The association also uses minimal amounts of pesticides and fertilizers and mows smaller areas than originally planned.[93] A full-time ecologist is responsible for the open-space areas and conducts regular environmental education programs for local groups. The association stocks the lakes with fish and monitors water quality to ensure "that open spaces are habitable for birds and other wildlife."[94]

Preservation of the environment has remained a priority of the association and residents during the last decades. A 1984 planning report prepared by the Columbia Forum reflects the many efforts of residents and developer:

> In terms of respect for the land, Columbia has set a high standard for other large scale developments. More than one

third of Columbia's land is permanent open space; there is more wildlife and more trees than existed in the area prior to development. Most of the watercourses have been protected and add considerably to the beauty of the area. Through the Columbia Association and through other state and local organizations, including large numbers of volunteers, the open space, trees, and wildlife have been protected and made accessible to an appreciative population.[95]

The Waterfowl and Habitat Advisory Committee, a resident organization, looks out for the open spaces in Columbia and makes sure the animals that live there are protected. The committee also organizes regular clean-ups at local lakes; members work to keep waste out of the open-space system. Local schools, scout groups, and environmental groups conduct their own programs. Although Columbia does not have the same level of environmental education as Reston, that will change in coming years, in large part because resident efforts have led to the creation of the Middle Patuxent Wildlife Area.

Residents lobbied hard for the creation of the wildlife area, one of the largest parcels of open space left in Howard County. Dr. Aelred Geis with other citizens led the effort to preserve 1,000 acres in Columbia's last village, River Hill. The parcel contains forests, meadows, wetlands, and a river, as well as abundant wildlife. The area has been well studied over the last thirty years, and eight reports by professionals and citizens have focused on its potential as open space. Originally, the valley was to be flooded and turned into a lakefront community, but Geis convinced Rouse that the land should be preserved because of its environmental richness. On a visit to the area in 1967, Rouse, "dressed in a suit . . . [lay down] on his stomach in a ditch to watch the [mating flight of the woodcock] and was so enchanted by the bird's towering flight that he declared the area off limits to the bulldozers." The establishment of the refuge did not occur until after Rouse's death, but the parcel will be preserved in its natural state, and plans call for trails and a nature center that will educate the community about the many habitats present there.[96]

Columbia developed the wild natural areas envisioned in the original plans. Natural spaces preserved on such a large scale, along with the high degree of environmental activism, made this community very different from the suburbs it sought to replace. The reliance on the automobile and worsening traffic outside the preserved areas, however, threatens the community's quality of life. Columbia may have convenient schools, shopping, and recreation areas linked by pathways, but this has not necessarily led to a decrease in automobile use. There is no viable transit alternative, the internal bus system barely functions, and air pollution and noise from automobiles is noticeable even from many of the preserved natural areas. Like Reston, the planning has failed to diminish the American love affair with the automobile.

An Irvine Paradise

Irvine residents played a leading role in making natural space part of their community. The company preserved open space for greenbelts and turned what was a dusty ranch into a lush environment, but it had not developed environmental preservation programs on the scale of either Columbia and Reston. Over time, however, the community and the company have come to an understanding. Slow-growth and environmental movements, with the often reluctant cooperation of the Irvine Company, have led a successful effort to preserve 30,000 acres of wilderness of the original 90,000 acres of the ranch. This radical change from the initial plans brings the environmental planning of Irvine into line with those of the other new towns—perhaps even exceeding them.

The Irvine Company created a number of attractive greenbelts running through residential areas beginning in the 1960s. These are narrow greenbelts in comparison to their Columbia and Reston counterparts, but they offer attractive views for residents and space for tot lots, walking, running, and rollerblading. Because they run through residential areas and because many houses have sight lines, the greenbelts are also more easily monitored by residents than the wooded paths of Reston and Columbia. The numerous plantings and grass of the greenbelts added luxuriant growth to an area that was essentially semiarid and have demanded extensive water use. In the late 1970s the Irvine Ranch Water District initiated a "'total water management program' under which all sewage effluent is recycled for use as irrigation water in greenbelts and croplands."[97]

Residents introduced a grand environmental vision for the city that has enjoyed tremendous success. Community members had started expanding the preservation of open land in the early 1970s by approving a bond issue to create parks and bike paths. The bike-path system, consisting of well-marked trails along roads and grade-separated pathways, covers the entire city. By 1988, the city had created more than 1,000 acres of park space and 900 acres of preserved open space. The city also opened a nature-education program out of a center in Turtle Rock Park.[98] In 1989 the city adopted a plan to preserve 9,500 undeveloped acres within and around Irvine while shifting development to other areas of the city. The Irvine Company, surrounding municipalities, and the city agreed to an extraordinary plan in which the city and surrounding municipalities gained extensive open space without paying for it, and the company gave up development in certain areas in exchange for higher-density residential and industrial expansion in others. The plan, now expanded to preserve 30,000 acres of the former ranch, includes major acreage in the northern foothills, and even "3.2 miles of beautiful Pacific Ocean shoreline" in Crystal Cove State Park. Much of the preserved land lies in an open space reserve split between the southern and northern sections of the ranch and is managed by both the Nature Conservancy and the state and local government. This management includes restoration of indigenous plant and animal species, long-term plans, and a schedule of hikes and tours of the properties. It remains to be seen how some areas will be reached, who will manage them, and what the exact nature of open space will be.[99]

Other areas, such as Newport Back Bay, Crystal Cove State Park, Peters Canyon Regional Park, and Wilderness Park, are already part of the reserve system. Crystal Cove, for instance, is open to the public and contains a stunning beach, high cliffs, fields, and foothills. The reserves are an important resource for the communities that surround them because not only do they provide a respite and cultural edification, but they offer a reminder of the arid, rugged landscape that has been replaced by the manicured development on the Irvine Ranch. Without these preserves, the landscape's earlier identity would have been completely lost.

Irvine has nature preserves and also traffic problems as serious, and perhaps worse, than the other new towns. There is no internal bus system, as there is in Reston and Columbia, and Orange County buses are infrequent in the community. The convenient schools, shopping, and community facilities are primarily attended by people arriving in cars. The bike-path system is extensive, but it is rare that people can be seen actually using it. Cars rule the road in Irvine. As at the other new towns, the environmental ethic has not transformed the daily lives of individuals in any appreciable manner.

❖

In all these communities, nature is part of the cultural life of residents. They appreciate both the cultivated and wild areas of their communities, and many have sought to expand and improve upon them. Developers and

residents have added to the suburban landscape an element usually reserved for distant parks and forests: a sense of wildness, free from the or-
dered system of gardening usually found in suburbia. These natural spaces
add a great deal to the sense of well-being and help protect natural ecosys-
tems from development. The new towns are notable for integrating homes
and other developments in a well-wooded and verdant landscape. Few
suburban communities have achieved a similar level of environmental
preservation.

These natural areas are important achievements, and rare in themselves, but there remain threats to environmental quality. In order to make
new towns marketable to suburbanites, the planners provided automobile
oriented amenities—malls, ample parkways, parking lots, and highway
connections—that undermined the popularity of walkway systems, mass
transit, and pedestrian oriented mixed-use village centers they also designed. New Urbanist critics such as Peter Calthorpe and Andres Duany
have criticized new-town planners for conceding too much to the automobile and designing communities that did not take pedestrians into account.
Calthorpe, for instance, has designed his communities around transit stops
and mixed-use town centers in the hope of diminishing the American auto
addiction. New-town planners, however, also made substantial provisions
for an auto-free lifestyle. Residents, unfortunately, have not augmented the
original vision to the same degree that they have in other aspects of community life. A minority of concerned citizens has tried to build on the
work of the early planners by supporting pathway creation, mass transit,
and mixed-use developments, but even they have failed to make an appreciable difference in driving habits. New Urbanists will likely face similar issues as their communities grow from small towns to large suburbs. It is
unlikely that even their physical redesign of suburbia will, in the long term,
appreciably change suburban habits.

Conclusion

The new-town reformers set out on a daring voyage of cultural and social redefinition. By the 1960s suburbanization had been cast as a fixed process, impervious to criticism and reform. The inexorable spread of cookie-cutter subdivisions dominated the academic and popular perception of suburban potential. New-town reformers, however, expanded the frontiers of suburban life by promoting innovations few critics or average Americans imagined possible.

Critics had portrayed the subdivisions of the 1950s and 1960s as uniformly ugly and poorly planned for community life. New-town developers, architects, and residents brought comprehensive planning back into contemporary suburbia. They fused older suburban community builder traditions with modernist styles and their own original ideas. Unique master plans, unconventional architecture, village and town centers, and landscape design gave definition to their suburban landscapes.

Problems inevitably developed over forty years, and plans have been adjusted. Modernist architectural design and quirky recreational themes at Reston, for instance, had to be scaled back in order to restore financial equilibrium. The environmental determinism that influenced the planning at Reston and Columbia village centers has also been largely abandoned. Although design has been occasionally successful in getting people out of their cars and into public spaces—Reston's town center, for instance—most of the communities have had to adjust design in order to fit suburban habits. In addition, it remains unclear if these new towns have actually slowed sprawl in their respective regions. Their large-scale, innovative office and retail developments have done more to promote sprawl than planners predicted.

Even after all these changes and compromises, the new town physical landscape remains distinct from most suburbs and has contributed to residents' sense of identity. Although conventional suburban housing styles in the new towns sometimes blurred the line between these communities and the suburban subdivisions they were supposed to replace, there are noticeable results of planning, such as convenient mixed-use shopping areas, an uncluttered landscape, unconventional housing styles, town centers with civic and commercial functions, nature preservation, and strong local institutions. Visitors can also find forty years of different planning and architectural styles. This layering and juxtaposition has proved to be one of the most welcome aspects of the new-town experience. By introducing variety, time has proved to be one of the best designers.

Civic apathy and anomie had been considered to be a byproduct of suburbanization by many critics. Reformers demonstrated that suburban communities could sustain activism over many decades. The process began with education on new-town ideals provided by the developers and planners. Corporate public relations successfully made the connections between the new town and the suburban critique. Many residents took the company public relations seriously, perhaps more seriously than some development officials may have expected or desired.

Residents built on company materials by making the new town concept a community ideal in their own local publications. Civic organizations translated ideas into substantive action as residents tried to preserve the new-town vision. Residents learned to use whatever resources they could muster to defend master plans and hold developers to their promises. They created their own public relations and exhibits, organized meetings, critiqued plans and made their own, goaded politicians, and created special services such as mass transit, affordable housing, and child care. Those activists who stayed the course over the decades kept their ideals intact but also learned to choose their battles carefully and compromise when necessary.

Buttressing traditional political activity was a new kind of civic culture unexpected in suburbia. "Pioneers" reminded new residents of the original vision and established many powerful organizations. Community gatherings celebrated the new towns' unconventional lifestyle and added a little levity to their serious attitude. Celebrations also provided times for recommitment to the new towns' ideals and bolstered community identification. Devoted developers often became public figures and helped popularize concepts. Many could be found living in the communities they had envisioned and participating in daily life and community organizations.

This mixture of hardheaded political activity with a personable civic culture attracted residents and guided the communities' growth over time.

Subdivisions of the 1950s and 1960s had become notorious among critics for their social exclusivity. Reformers showed that the conventional social characteristics of suburbia were contingent on beliefs. A mix of housing types and prices brought a wide range of new residents. Open housing and marketing, and even occasional social engineering, mixed black residents into the community in Reston and Columbia.

New social institutions founded by residents nurtured this potentially explosive mixture through the ups and downs of this difficult process. New-town journalists and political leaders could be counted on to support social integration while other residents helped create low-cost housing opportunities and new social-service organizations. Many black residents created organizations to safeguard and promote black life. Social mixture attracted national attention as visitors, journalists, and intellectuals realized that suburbanites were undertaking a new approach to community life. Social integration has proved successful for forty years yet remains the most fragile of the reforms. Increasing affluence, self-segregation, loss of federal subsidies, and continuing problems in low-income complexes may erode the new towns' reputation for social equality.

Minorities and the poor had been locked out of suburbia, but many critics also believed that middle-class white women and adolescents faced a troubling future there. In new towns, however, women benefited from and helped to create resources such as child care, pathways, and recreational facilities that removed some of the most burdensome aspects of motherhood. The women's movement, liberating many women from the domestic sphere, found a home in the liberal atmosphere of the new towns. Women's activity extended beyond consciousness raising and women's-rights activities to careers and politics. Leadership in local political organizations initiated women into the local power structure and helped launch the careers of many women politicians and administrators.

Attempts to improve life for adolescents met with less success. Residents underestimated the strength of a growing counterculture and teenage subculture. The attempted redirection of teenager activity to more wholesome pursuits yielded only partial results. Teenagers' interest in what many considered to be unconventional use of pubic space and deviant behavior, and conflict between some black and white teenagers forced into integrated environments, challenged the patience of many reformers. Over time a variety of activities directed at teenagers have been well utilized, but there remains dissatisfaction on both sides. Generational divisions did not disappear at the new towns.

No less important than these social reforms was the expansion of cultural boundaries at new towns. While conventional subdivisions made few provisions for cultural activity, new towns pushed cultural patronage on a number of fronts. Sponsored performances, citizen participation in the arts, public art programs, and nature preservation attracted many residents and enhanced the quality of life of many others. The story has not been without its wrinkles. Some of the original sponsored art programs failed to establish themselves. Comprehensive public art programs showed early promise but faltered. Nature conservation succeeded even better than the original plans but has proved unequal to the challenges of regional environmental decline related to automobiles. In most respects, however, cultural patronage flourished and helped distinguish the new-town scene from conventional suburbs of the time.

There have been many successes, but the movement was a failure when judged in relation to its stated goal of positively affecting the patterns of regional suburban development. In their own regions, the new towns may have inadvertently contributed to sprawl by creating innovative office and retail areas that attracted more people not only to the towns but to new subdivisions designed to capitalize on their resources. Construction of highways either through or adjacent to these communities has also made new towns regional centers or "edge cities" that only partially fulfill their goals of being balanced communities. The opportunity to live, work, and shop in the same community remains, but it is only one option, and an increasingly expensive one, for the people in their respective regions. Because nearby new towns failed to materialize, overflow from the existing towns and suburban growth generally have left these communities planned islands.

On a national level, although many developers around the country integrated new-town innovations, their adoption of these concepts proved superficial. Suburban developers who did borrow the new-town concepts built much smaller communities, known as "planned unit developments," that proved profitable and fit the tastes of most suburbanites. The well-publicized financial problems of Reston in particular scared many potential developers from undertaking such large, complicated, and expensive projects. Residents in planned unit developments would find a regulated environment, more amenities, and a homeowner's association, but not the wider reform spirit of the new towns. The concept of the good life promoted by the new towns—socially diverse, architecturally innovative, comprehensively planned, and culturally effervescent—was not shared by most developers or potential buyers.

A brief but expensive federal commitment to new town planning in the 1970s, under what was known as the Title VII program, did not help spread the new-town gospel. Congress, under pressure from liberals, intellectuals, and designers, offered long-term financial support for large, innovative, socially progressive new towns. Sixteen projects across the country, most modeled on the three studied here, received funding. The developers of these projects, even with $500,000,000 of total federal support, proved unable to build, market, and sell their communities, and most declared bankruptcy within the decade. The recession of the early 1970s stalled growth in many towns, the government was slow to provide promised grants for facilities, and many developers lacked experience and sufficient outside financing.[1]

Financial problems, however, were just part of the problem. Federal supporters seemed only to talk to each other. They rarely speculated on their actual relationship to the suburban public, or when they did, naively believed that suburbanites were just as excited as they were by the new-town concept. As this book has shown, however, extensive ideological baggage accompanied new-town development. Developers at the federal new towns—like those at Reston, Columbia, and Irvine—mixed suburban elements with modernist architecture and planning, higher density housing, social integration, and cultural experimentation. This mixture pleased intellectuals, designers, and liberals but frightened off many potential buyers. Marketing experts who studied these expensive federal disasters noted the negative effect of this alternative vision on potential residents, but developers and new-town supporters downplayed the unpopularity of their vision when explaining their failure. The special qualities that had kept Reston, Columbia, and Irvine growing—good timing, excellent press, talented financial leadership with deep pockets, and sufficient numbers of activist residents—was in short supply at federal new towns.

The new towns, both private and federally sponsored, may have failed to change suburban development nationally, but Columbia, Reston, and Irvine achieved spectacular results in redefining suburbia. These communities expanded the concept of suburbia by demonstrating that almost all of the conventional wisdom about it was wrong. Reformers showed in three dimensions that suburbanization had no inevitable outcomes on community life, as Gans himself had argued in *The Levittowners*. The principles of the new towns, including comprehensive planning, civic idealism, social mixture, and cultural participation, thrived in their suburban context. The reformers demonstrated that even though it was unlikely that developers and suburbanites would adopt their innovations, this indifference had not rendered reform an impossibility.

Millions of people learned about this experiment in redefinition, particularly in the first two decades, through the national media and visits to the new towns. The visitor centers, tours, television reports, and numerous articles and books on new-town life made the experiment known nationally and catalyzed discussion about the suburban future. Columbia, Reston, and Irvine slowly faded from popular view in the 1970s and 1980s, but the process of redefinition did not end there. Later developments in community life, as described in this book, have been just as important in redefining suburban limits.

Because of the reformers' long-term commitment to ambitious reforms, the new-town experience should be part of current suburban debates. The much discussed New Urbanist movement—at Celebration, Florida; Kentlands, Maryland; Laguna West, California; and many other projects—shares the new-town interest in suburban criticism and reform. This architectural and planning movement, led by Peter Calthorpe, Elizabeth Plater-Zyberk, and Andres Duany, has generated considerable excitement by introducing design innovations that are intended to improve on both new towns and conventional suburban subdivisions.[2]

New Urbanists deride the 1960s new towns for their superblock style of planning, separation of uses, high-speed parkways, cul-de-sacs, and conventional suburban styling. Breakthroughs pioneered by New Urbanists include pedestrian-oriented planning, the reintroduction of the street grid, and adoption of older styles of architecture. The New Urbanists, including many residents, have placed their faith in environmental determinism. They believe that they can restore healthy community life through planning and architecture that mimics older neighborhoods and main streets. Porches, old fashioned blocks and alleys, mixed-use developments, main streets, and village squares are provided in order to restore an idealized public life of the past. Designers consciously ignore the effects of automobiles, occupational and geographic mobility, high-technology, multiculturalism, and class differences on modern communities— something that Rouse and Simon could have been rightly accused of doing almost forty years ago.

These New Urbanists should look more closely at the new-town experience. The environmental determinism that guided much of the new-town movement in the early years had less effect than developers hoped and after forty years has largely dissolved as a guiding principle. Planners did attempt to make their communities pedestrian friendly and neigh-borly, and they also created mixed-use developments (similar to those pro-moted by New Urbanists), but their designs rarely yielded the intended benefits. The failure of "village centers" to act as town greens and pathways or minibus systems to become daily transportation networks has steered new-town designers and residents from putting too much emphasis on planning as a means to community intimacy. New-town residents ac-knowledge that design has made a difference in their local insitutions, community feeling, and sense of distinctiveness, but most reformers have learned that involvement in civic activism, social reform, and cultural ac-tivities have built the strongest community bonds. Even though these ac-tivities rarely create visible tableaux of community so enamored by New Urbanists, they have been more significant in building a lively public life.

The alternative values and aspirations of both residents and develop-ers further distinguish the 1960s new-town movement from New Urban-ism. Andrew Ross's insightful portrait of Celebration, Florida, *The Celebration Chronicals*, documents his year-long experience of living in an apartment in the community's town center. The residents he describes are primarily concerned with issues relating to construction quality, property values, education, and family life, not unlike most of the residents of Co-lumbia, Reston, and Irvine. The resident leadership of Celebration, how-ever, unlike that of the towns in this study, has focused exclusively on these traditional suburban issues. Ambitious programs relating to social or racial integration, mass transit, feminism, teenagers, or cultural affairs have not emerged and have not even been much discussed. Nor has the developer shown much interest in these issues. The Celebration experience, so far, re-flects the thinning of social and cultural idealism and imagination since the 1960s. The 1960s new towns, although elitist in their own way, provide a needed contrast to the even more upper-class reform spirit of New Urbanism.

The new towns and New Urbanism, even with their differences in philosophy and timing, share a mission. It is not just population and em-ployment that have shifted to suburbia; reform ideals are taking root in fits and starts. Historians and social scientists have only slowly awakened to the growing complexity of suburbia. They have, over the last decades, sketched a taxonomy of suburbia that includes working class, elite, and in-dustrial suburbs. After a century of experiments, some of them successful and all of them interesting, a new classification should be added to this list. Some older suburban communities, the new towns, and New Urban-ism have created a "reform suburb" tradition. Columbia, Reston, Irvine,

Celebration, and Kentlands share a lineage with older towns like Forest Hills, New York; Radburn, New Jersey; and Greenbelt, Maryland. These communities should not be considered in the lineage of utopianism, because they did not propose to revolutionize society and usher in an age of perfection. Pioneers of these communities have instead sought incremental improvements within the existing framework of American society.

The developers and residents of these communities have nurtured landscapes that are similar to the mainstream yet strategically different. They mixed the comforting arrangements of suburbia with alternatives to various urban and suburban problems. Some innovations have become nationally popular; master planning, homeowner associations, nature preserves, and even public art programs have been adapted for use in more conventional suburban developments. Other reforms, like social experimentation and unconventional architecture, have had much less national influence.

These reform suburbs have primarily become flashpoints for discussions about the future of community life in America. Although many critics have dismissed them for being too conventional, their recognizably suburban character has actually given them more cultural power. By being similar to conventional suburbia, their strategic changes in areas such as design, society, politics, and culture have had more impact. The alternative landscapes they have pioneered have served as effective foils to mainstream suburban society in newspapers, television, magazines, and books such as this. If they had been more dreamy, they could have been more easily dismissed. That the reforms of these places proved possible, rather than merely utopian dreams, has made them a surpisingly strong force in American culture and society.

Notes

INTRODUCTION

1. The 1950s and 1960s witnessed the creation of many communities calling them-selves new towns. These included the California new towns of Mission Viejo, Foster City, Valencia, Westlake Village, and Laguna Niguel. Others around the country included Park Forest and Elk Grove Village, Illinois; Lake Havasu, Arizona; Sharpstown, Texas; Forest Park, Ohio; and North Palm Beach, Florida. These communities shared many features with the towns studied here, yet were not as innovative or comprehensively developed as Reston, Columbia, and Irvine. Nor did they attract a similar cadre of reformers who expanded and maintained the reform ideals over time.

   Early confirmation of the special status of Columbia, Reston, and Irvine can be found in Raymond Burby and Shirley Weiss's famous 1976 study of new towns, *New Communities, U.S.A.* When ranking fourteen new towns (those mentioned above plus the three in this study) on the adherence to new town ideals, Columbia, Reston, and Irvine occupied the first, second, and third positions respectively. The indicators, equally weighted, included "(1) architectural controls; (2) bus service; (3) commercial facilities grouped in centers; (4) communications media; (5) ease of access to facilities; (6) environmental protection; (7) housing choice; (8) landscaping of public and common areas; (9) master plan; (10) open space preservation; (11) pedestrian-vehicular mix; (12) self-government; (13) self-sufficiency; (14) income mix; (15) racial mix; (16) underground utilities; (17) unified development by a single entrepreneur; (18) preservation or creation of water bodies; [and] (19) variety of land uses." The superiority of these towns in these areas has only been expanded over time by actions of the developers and the residents. See Burby and Weiss, *New Communities U.S.A.*, 97.

CHAPTER 1

1. Overviews of suburban development include Kenneth Jackson, *Crabgrass Frontier: The Suburbanization of the United States;* John Stilgoe, *Borderland: Origins of the American Suburb, 1820–1939;* and Robert Fishman, *Bourgeois Utopias: The Rise and Fall of Suburbia.*

   Books that consider the process of suburban development include Sam Bass

Warner Jr., *Streetcar Suburbs: The Process of Growth in Boston (1870–1900)*; Henry Binford, *The First Suburbs: Residential Communities on the Boston Periphery, 1815–1860*; Ann Durkin Keating, *Building Chicago: Suburban Developers and the Creation of a Divided Metropolis*; and Marc Weiss, *The Rise of the Community Builders: The American Real Estate Industry and Urban Land Planning.*

A number of case histories have enriched our view of suburban life: Zane Miller, *Suburb: Neighborhood and Community in Forest Park, Ohio, 1935–1976*; Michael H. Ebner, *Creating Chicago's North Shore: A Suburban History*; William S. Worley, *J. C. Nichols and the Shaping of Kansas City: Innovation in Planned Residential Communities*; David R. Contosta, *Suburb in the City: Chestnut Hill, Philadelphia, 1850–1990.*

2. Early critics included Sinclair Lewis, *Babbitt*; Lewis Mumford, *The Culture of Cities*; Frederick A. Allen, "Suburban Nightmare," *The Independent*, 13 June 1925, 670–71; Edward Yeomens, "The Suburban Deluxe," *Atlantic Monthly*, January 1920.

The 1950s and 1960s critics included Lewis Mumford, *The City in History*; Richard and Katherine Gordon, *The Split-Level Trap*; John Keats, *The Crack in the Picture Window*; and Peter Blake, *God's Own Junkyard: The Planned Deterioration of America's Landscape.* Some books had a wider goal than suburban criticism but nevertheless provided ammunition critics. See John Seeley, Alexander Sim, and Elizabeth Loosely, *Crestwood Heights*; William Whyte, *The Organization Man*; David Reisman, *The Lonely Crowd*; and Betty Friedan, *The Feminine Mystique.*

3. Keats, *The Crack in the Picture Window*, xiv.

4. Blake, *God's Own Junkyard*, 21.

5. Keats, *The Crack in the Picture Window*, xvi.

6. Whyte, *The Organization Man*, 344. Park Forest eventually did become an integrated community, long after Whyte's visit, and remains one of the few successfully integrated communities in America.

7. Richard H. Pells, *The Liberal Mind in a Conservative Age*, 197.

8. Andrew M. Greely, *The Church and the Suburbs*, 149.

9. A number of intellectuals offered corrections to the suburban critique. See Herbert Gans, *The Levittowners*; Scott Donaldson, *The Suburban Myth*; Robert C. Wood, *Suburbia: Its People and Their Politics*; Bennett Berger, *Working Class Suburbs*; and William Dobriner, *Class in Suburbia.*

10. James Rouse, "Cities That Work for Man—Victory Ahead," 1967, 2–3.

11. Janelee Keidel, "4 Our Men of Columbia," *The People of Columbia: A Commemorative Magazine [Columbia Flier]*, 16 June 1977, 39–40.

12. "What Is a New Town? One Answer Is Reston," *Fortune*, December 1964.

13. Robert Simon, "Statement . . . before the National Advisory Commission on Rural Poverty," ca. 1966, 11.

14. "May Move," *Reston Times*, 3 November 1967.

15. "The Festival," *Reston Times*, 21 May 1970, 6.

16. Irvine Company, "Irvine Villages: Welcome Home: Your Guide to a New Environment," April 1977, 1–38.

17. Pereira quoted in Frank McGee, "Affection for This Hunk of Earth," *New Worlds,* December 1970, 3–32.

18. Beverly Bush Smith, "The New Pioneers: Some Recollections," *New Worlds,* June 1976, 39–42.

19. Ada Louise Huxtable, "First Light of New Town Era Is on Horizon," *New York Times,* 17 February 1964.

20. Whyte, *The Last Landscape,* 257. See also these articles, among others, that treat the new town as antidote to suburban sprawl: Wolfgang Langewiesche, "The Suburbs Are Changing," *Reader's Digest,* November 1969, 157–64; Edmund Faltermayer, "We Can Cope with the Coming Suburban Explosion," *Fortune,* September 1996, 147; "A City Made to Human Measure," *Life,* 8 January 1971, 76; and "The City in the Country," *Washington Star,* 22 November 1964.

CHAPTER 2

1. Pauline Donatuti, interview by Amanda Harrison, Reston Oral History Project, 21 December 1994.

2. Benjamin Ruhe, "City Builder," *Washington Star,* 8 May 1966.

3. *Reston Letter,* 3 December 1963.

4. See Daniel Schaffer, *Garden Cities for America: The Radburn Experience,* and Clarence Stein, *Toward New Towns For America.*

5. In *Building a New Town: Finland's New Garden City,* Heikki von Hertzen shows the integration of modernist buildings with natural elements and describes social and cultural planning (the city was built by a group of social and trade organizations). See also Pierre Merlin, *New Towns: Regional Planning and Development,* and Ann Louise Strong, *Planned Urban Environments: Sweden, Finland, Israel, the Netherlands, France.*

6. William Conklin, "Planning Approaches to New Towns: Focus on Reston Virginia," *Building Research,* January/February 1966, 18–20.

7. Simon quoted in Philip Goyert, "Reston, Virginia: An Architectural History."

8. Edward Carpenter, "Brave New Town," *Industrial Design,* March 1964.

9. Goyert, "Reston, Virginia," 9–76, and Gulf Reston, *Brief History of Reston, Virginia,* 12.

10. Conklin, "Planning Approaches to New Towns," 18–20.

11. Tim Dietz, "Reston Founder Tours Town Center," *Reston Times,* 24 October 1990, A13.

12. Marcia Fram, "Architect Discourse on Plaza's Rationale," *Reston Times,* 1 June 1972, 6.

13. "Golf Course Island Opening," *Reston Letter,* 21 May 1966, 9.

14. Ellen Lupton and J. Abbott Miller, "A Time Line of Graphic Design," in Milton Friedman, et al., *Graphic Design in America: A Visual Language History,* 60–61.

15. Robert Philips, "Reston," *The Washingtonian,* February 1966.

16. Carpenter, "Brave New Town."

17. *Reston Letter,* 3 December 1963.

18. Fram, "Architect Discourses on Plaza's Rationale," 6. See also Gulf Oil Corporation, "Reston: A City in a Park," *The Orange Disc,* April 1968; Goyert, "Reston, Virginia," 9–76; Bob Bunnell, "Gulf-RCA Relationship Improved," *Reston Times,* 28 February 1980, A1.

19. Goyert, "Reston, Virginia," 9–76.

20. U.S. Department of Housing and Urban Development, Division of Policy Studies, *An Evaluation of the Federal New Communities Program,* 1984, 4.5; David Hughes and Ruth Larsen, "Reston: 15 Years after Simon," *Reston Times,* 2 September 1982.

21. Michael Kernan, "The Green Dream—II," *Washington Post,* 15 February 1971. See also Ken Ringle, "Reston at 7 Years: New Town Loses Its Innocence," *Washington Post,* 16 July 1972.

22. Ruhe, "City Builder." See also "The New Town and Major Spaces," *Progressive Architecture,* June 1965, 192, and Simon, "Original Center Promise Should Be Kept," *Reston Times,* 27 October 1993, A5.

23. Thomas Grubishich, "Plan Ahead: Father of Reston Town Center Leaves for Baltimore," *Connection,* 6 November 1991, 23.

24. Grubishich, "Town Center's Style Strikes Familiar Notes," *Connection,* 3 April 1991, TC4.

25. Jay Sherman, "Reston Unveils Town Center," *Fairfax Journal,* 24 October 1990, 1.

26. Nicholas Lanyi, "Santa Gets Big Reception," *Connection,* 1 December 1993, 4.

27. Sherman, "Reston Unveils Town Center," 1. See also Benjamin Forgey, "Quicksilver and Mercury: A Gleaming Pavilion of Glass and Steel Joins Reston's Fountain Square Statue," *Washington Post,* 31 July 1993, D1; Simon, "Original Center Promise Should Be Kept," A5; C. D. Tony Hylton III, "Is Town Center a Town Center or Not?" *Reston Times,* 4 June 1986, A8; Grubishich, "At Last, Town Center," *Connection,* 26 February 1986, 3; Ben Franklin, "Downtown Look for a New Town," *New York Times,* 21 December 1986, sec. 8, p. 1; Fran Rensbarger, "A Downtown for the Planned Community of Reston," *New York Times,* 11 December 1990.

28. Reston Association Web site, "About Reston." Available at <http://www.reston.org/> (22 April 2000).

29. Barbara Gyles, "RCA Wants Preservation of Plaza Community Space," *Reston Times,* 16 October 1980, A8. See also Grubishich, "A Bit of 'Downtown' on the Plaza," *Connection,* 15 June 1983, 2; Tara Coonin, "Lake Anne: Food to Die for, Atmosphere to Live By," *Connection,* 18 June 1997.

30. "HW Village Center Designs Complete," *Reston Times,* 12 February 1970, 3; Hughes, "Hunters Woods Enters 2nd Decade," *Reston Times,* 25 November 1982; Eugenia Gratto, "A Tale of Reston's Changing Village Centers," *Connection,* 19 July 1995, 8. On crime, see Dina Anders, "Hunters Woods Center Crime Rate In-

creases," *Reston Times*, 3 June 1982, A1; David Lerman, "Shopping Center Crime Low," *Connection*, 2 April 1986, 6.

31. D. Quyhn Nguyen, "Upgrading of Hunters Woods Gets Underway," *Reston Times*, 2 July 1997, A1, and also Jonah Keri, "Village Centers at Turning Point," *Reston Times*, 10 September 1997.

32. Amelia Gray, interview by Peter Hotz, Reston Oral History Project, 2 January 1995.

33. Gratto, "A Tale of Reston's Changing Village Centers," 8.

CHAPTER 3

Epigraphs from "Rouse on Problems and Wifely Help," *Life*, 24 January 1967, and Wallace Hamilton, "Interim Memo: Social Structure," Howard Research and Development, Columbia Archive Collection, 1 July 1964.

1. Urban renewal had a mixed record of success. See James Q. Wilson, ed., *Urban Renewal: The Record and the Controversy*; Peter Hall, *Cities of Tomorrow: An Intellectual History of Urban Planning and Design in the Twentieth Century*; and Mel Scott, *American City Planning since 1890*.

 A number of books helped turn citizens and many planners against urban renewal and modernist design. See Jane Jacobs, *The Death and Life of Great American Cities*; Herbert Gans, *The Urban Villagers: Group and Class in the Life of Italian-Americans*; and Robert Goodman, *After the Planners*.

2. Rouse, "Great Cities for a Great Society," 8 April 1965, 16.

3. Ibid., 16.

4. Ibid., 1.

5. The Rouse Company, primarily a mortgage banking and real-estate development company, is publicly owned. "Real estate development of The Rouse Company includes new communities, office buildings, and regional shopping centers." Reprinted from a publication of the Columbia Forum '82, 15. Business reporters welcomed the new-town experiment because it promised to be a profitable, nongovernmental solution to urban problems. See "New Towns: Businessman's Answer to Bleeding Heart Types," *American Industrial Properties Report*, November/December 1970, 8; see also "Master Builder with a New Concept," *Business Week*, 20 August 1966.

6. Rouse, "Cities That Work for Man," 18 October 1967, 6.

7. Morton Hoppenfeld, quoted in Gurney Breckenfeld, *Columbia and the New Cities*, 251.

8. Rouse, "Columbia—New City—New Hope," *Columbia Flier*, 16 December 1970; see also Willmon White, "He's Building a New City," *Together Magazine*, December 1968.

9. Hoppenfeld, "The Columbia Process: The Potential for New Towns," 1970, 75–80.

10. Ibid., 69–94.

11. Rouse, "It Can Happen Here: A Paper on Metropolitan Growth," 23 September 1963, 6.

12. "The Village of Cross Keys," CRD public relations materials, ca. 1961; Missy Zane, "James Rouse Looks to the Future," *Columbia Times*, 18 June 1977, 3A.
13. Margaret Guroff, "The Dream vs. the Reality," *Columbia Magazine*, summer 1992, 73. See also Donald N. Michael, "The Role and Technique of Community Planning," memo to CRD, Columbia Archives, April 1964, 9–10.
14. J. W. Anderson, "A New City for Maryland," *Harper's*, November 1964.
15. Robert Tennenbaum, *Creating a New City: Columbia, Maryland*, 33.
16. Tennenbaum, "Planning Determinants for Columbia," *Urban Land*, April 1965.
17. Hamilton, "The Physical Plan," HRD, 17 September 1964.
18. Ibid.
19. Hoppenfeld, "The Columbia Process," 1970, 81–88.
20. Breckenfeld, *Columbia and the New Cities*, 259.
21. Tennenbaum, *Creating a New City*, 57, 65.
22. *Columbia: A New City*, Rouse Company, 1966.
23. Edward Gunts, "Gehry's First Big Commissions Were from the Rouse Co.," *Baltimore Sun*, 19 October 1997, 2E.
24. Peter Hanrahan, "In the Beginning: The Good Capitalists Have a Certain Visionary Madness: An Interview with Wallace Hamilton," *Columbia Flier*, 19 June 1975.
25. Breckenfeld, *Columbia and the New Cities*, 257–82.
26. *Columbia: A New City*.
27. Nancy Baggett, "Columbia Milestones," *People of Columbia*.
28. "Columbia: Planned City with a Planned Approach to Signing," *Signs of the Times*, March 1972, 31–37.
29. Hanrahan, "In the Beginning."
30. Pamphlet, Columbia Foundation Inc., 1979; letter from Rouse to Leister Graffis, Bendix Corp., 17 July 1970; Columbia Foundation Annual Reports, 1984, 1988, 1989, 1990, 1993, 1996, and 1998. See also "Statement of Purpose of The Columbia Foundation," ca. 1972, Columbia Archives.
31. United States Department of Housing and Urban Development, *An Evaluation of the Federal New Communities Program*, 4.5. See also the Web site <www.therousecompany.com/operation/commdevel/Columbia-md/Colcommunity.html> for current statistics on Columbia.
32. See Tom Girvin, "Mrs. Z's: A Restaurant, Coffeehouse, Social Club and Living Room—Anyway, It's Different," *Columbia Flier*, 11 April 1974; Kernan, "The Green Dream—I," *Washington Post*, ca. 15 February 1971; and Albert Mayer, "A Visit to Columbia, MD: Dreamy Living in the New City," *Village Voice*, 22 July 1971, 64.
33. Dan Morse, "Traditional Town Centers in Trouble," *Baltimore Sun*, 14 July 1996; "30 Years and Counting: Survey Finds Columbians Are Happy with Their Hometown," *Columbia Flier*, 19 June 1997.
34. Deborah McCarty, "State of Columbia," *Washington Post*, 20 January 2000, 3.
35. Ibid.

36. Chuck Petrowski, "Loitering Bill Proposed," *Columbia Flier*, 25 July 1971.

37. Lisa Leff, "Columbia, 20 Years Young: New Town Still Coming of Age," *Washington Post*, 5 July 1987.

38. Natalie Spingarn, "Columbians," *Washington Star*, 30 July 1972.

39. Geoffrey Himes, "Hanging Out on Friday Night," *Columbia Flier*, 7 October 1976.

40. Extensive literature has emerged on public space in America. See Margaret Crawford, "The World in a Shopping Mall," in *Variations on a Theme Park: The New American City and the End of Public Space*, ed. Michael Sorkin; Lizabeth Cohen, "From Town Center to Shopping Center: The Reconfiguration of Community Marketplaces in Postwar America," *American Historical Review*, October 1996; Mike Davis, *City of Quartz: Excavating the Future in Los Angeles*; Sharon Zukin, *The Cultures of Cities*; and Russell Jacoby, *The Last Intellectuals: American Culture in the Age of Academe.*

41. Morse, "Mall Tries to Attract New Anchors," *Baltimore Sun*, 15 July 1996.

42. Adam Sachs, "Residents Debate New Businesses," *Baltimore Sun*, 7 May 1995. See also Morse, "Traditional Town Centers in Trouble."

CHAPTER 4

Epigraph from Raymond Watson, interview by the author, 18 November 1998.

1. A series of Irvine Company presidents, including William Mason, Raymond Watson, and Peter Kremer, led the transformation of the Irvine Company into a major development corporation. See Martin Brower, "A Time for People: How an Old Company Moved into a New Era," *New Worlds*, June 1976, 59–74; Coast Media News Group, "Irvine: the Birth of a City," 9 December 1981; and Judy Liebeck, *Irvine: A History of Innovation and Growth.*

2. Watson, "The University of California's and Irvine Company's Historic Agreement," 1998.

3. Brower, "A Time for People," 60.

4. Martin Schiesl, "Designing the Model Community: The Irvine Company and Suburban Development, 1950–1988," in Rob Kling, Spencer Olin, and Mark Poster, *Postsuburban California: The Transformation of Orange County since World War II*, 59–60.

5. William C. Pereira and Associates, "A Preliminary Report for a University-Community Development in Orange County," prepared for the Irvine Company, 1959, 21.

6. Amy Wilson, "Irvine at 25: Did the Dream Succeed," *Orange County Register*, 29 September 1996, A1.

7. Ibid.

8. Kevin Lynch, *The Image of the City*; Watson, interview by the author, 18 November 1998.

9. Nathaniel M. Griffin, *Irvine: The Genesis of a New Community*, 53.

10. Brower, "Architectural Achievements Are Important in Development," *Irvine World News*, 1 May 1975, 6.

11. Wes Nowa, "Community Landscaping Gives Irvine Villages Aesthetic Themes," *New Worlds,* 17 April 1975, 6; Watson, interview by the author, 18 November 1998.
12. "An Introduction to the City of Irvine," City of Irvine, ca. 1990, 16.
13. Many of the shopping areas located in Irvine villages have never been viewed as village centers. Heritage Plaza, Crossroads Center, and Tustin Market Place are attractive but are notable for their convenience more than anything else. See also *Irvine Sign Manual,* Irvine Company, ca. 1975, for details on new sign controls.
14. Brower, "A Time for People."
15. Thomas J. Ashley, "Planning a New City: Irvine, California," ca. 1964; Brower, "A Time for People." See also Liebeck, *Irvine: A History,* 91.
16. "City of Irvine Announced," *Irvine World News,* April 1970, 2; Jan Hunsinger, "Woodbridge: From Plans to People: An Historical Beginning," *New Worlds,* February 1977, 41–85.
17. Liebeck, *Irvine: A History,* 92.
18. Hunsinger, "Lakeside Living at Woodbridge," *New Worlds,* June 1977, 66–70; Brower, "A Time for People"; "Woodbridge Lottery Draws Thousands," *Irvine World News,* 24 June 1976, 1.
19. "If It's Nasturtiums, This Must Be Big Canyon," *New Worlds,* October 1975, 13–16; Marshall Brewer, "The Gestation of a Planned City," 57; Watson, "The Irvine Company Report: A Discussion on Park Standards," *Irvine World News,* 7 June 1974, 6; Kitty Morgan, "Billionaire Puts Personal Stamp on Design," *Orange County Register,* 2 July 1990.
20. Watson, interview by the author, 18 November 1998.
21. Linda Herington, "From Hub to Home," in *Irvine: I Call It Home: A Collection of Essays and Poetry,* 53.
22. Morgan, "Billionaire Puts Personal Stamp on Design." Descriptions also from Fashion Island Web site: <www.irvine.co.com/html/shop/nb/fshi/fshi/html>.
23. Jennifer Lowe, "A Mall Finds an Image," *Orange County Register,* 10 September 1992, C1.
24. Christopher Warren, "Legend of Alhambra Transported to Spectrum Center," *Irvine World News,* 9 July 1998, B14–15.
25. Mark Gottdiener, *The Theming of America: Dreams, Visions, and Commercial Spaces,* 115.
26. New-town residents rated the planning of their communities highly in the study undertaken by Burby and Weiss: "Three fourths of the new community respondents, versus just over half of the conventional community respondents, rated the planning of their communities as better than that of the communities from which they had moved. Planning was rated highest in those new communities and conventional communities characterized by landscaping of public and common areas, preservation of environmental corridors, existence of architectural controls, and the grouping of all commercial facilities in centers. Planning was also rated better in communities that provided walking paths, a greater degree of

pedestrian vehicular separation, and greater accessibility of community facilities and services" (Burby and Weiss, *New Communities U.S.A.*, 21).

27. Some planning historians have praised the new town. See Scott, *American City Planning since 1890;* Robert Fishman, *Bourgeois Utopias,* and "The American Garden City: Still Relevant?" in *The Garden City: Past, Present and Future,* ed. Stephen Ward.

   Most other historians have been less generous. See Ervin Galanty, *New Towns: Antiquity to the Present;* Eduardo Lozano, *Community Design and the Culture of Cities;* Carol Corden, *New Towns in Britain and America;* and Robert Whelan, "New Towns: An Idea Whose Time Has Passed," *Journal of Urban History* 10, no. 2 (February 1984), 195–209.

CHAPTER 5

Epigraph from Dave Rose, "Planning: It's More than Making Road Maps," *New Worlds,* May 1971, 44.

1. Friedman et al., *Graphic Design in America,* 53, 78. See also Robert Haddow, *Pavilions of Plenty: Exhibiting American Culture Abroad in the 1950s;* Robert Rydell, in *All the World's a Fair;* Michael L. Smith, "Making Time: Representations of Technology at the 1964 World's Fair," in *The Power of Culture: Critical Essays in American History,* ed. Richard Wightman Fox and T. J. Jackson Lears, 223–44.
2. Edward Carpenter, "Brave New Town"; "What Is a New Town?"
3. "What Is a New Town?"; "Program Notes," *Reston Letter,* December 1965; Goyert, "Reston, Virginia," 9–76.
4. Tom Grubishich and Peter McCandless, *Reston: The First Twenty Years.*
5. "Von Eckardt Sees Urban Crisis," *Reston Times,* 15 April 1966, 7.
6. Ibid.; "Living at Reston," *Reston Letter,* 1966.
7. Robert Dawson, "Wasserman Leaving for Florida Post," *Reston Times,* 29 June 1972, 6, 12.
8. Kathleen Vitale, "Architect Eyes Changes in Waterview Cluster," *Reston Times,* 23 June 1977; Grubishich, "Plaza Designers Leave Hopeful," *Connection,* 26 September 1984, 4.
9. "Reston's National Publicity," *Reston Letter,* December 1965, 4; Anne and Robert Simon, *Reston Letter,* 21 May 1966.
10. *Restonian,* Gulf Reston, 1974.
11. "Reston," *Mobil Land Communities,* ca. 1996.
12. Hamilton, "Interim Memo: The Presentation of the Plan," 30 November 1964.
13. Ibid.; Tennenbaum, *Creating a New City,* 81.
14. "Absence of an Evaluation and Feedback Component Task Force on Neighborhood and Village Planning," 1972, quoted in "Columbia Voyage: Discovering Columbia's Tomorrows," 14 October 1989.
15. "Welcome to Columbia," *Columbia,* spring 1968.
16. "Exhibition Center Crosses 1,000,000 Mark," *Columbia Flier,* 24 November 1971.

17. Len Lazarick, "New Images in Columbia Show," *Columbia Flier,* 15 December 1977.

18. C. William Michaels, "Does Columbia Still Have the 'Element of Quest' That It Began With?" *Howard Sun,* 17 May 1981. See also Lazarick, "Exhibit Center Gets a Facelift," *Columbia Flier,* 24 January 1979.

19. *Columbia: A New City; Welcome to Columbia: A Visitor's Guide,* Rouse Company, ca. 1968.

20. Donald Michael, "Recommendations for the Social Planning of Columbia: Physical Facilities and Social Organization," July 1964; *Columbia Magazine,* spring 1967, 16.

21. *Columbia Magazine,* spring 1967.

22. Hoppenfeld, "Intra Office Memorandum: General Objectives for Community Development," 4 November 1963.

23. "The Next America at Columbia, Maryland," *Columbia Magazine,* spring 1967.

24. Jeanne Lamb O'Neill, "Columbia, Gem of America's 'New Towns,'" *American Home,* May 1970.

25. Willmon White, "He's Building a New City."

26. Tennenbaum, *Creating a New City,* treats planning, sales, interracial issues, and educational and institutional development.

27. Zane, "James Rouse Looks to the Future," 3A; Judith Tripp, "Holliday Poster for Holiday Giving," *Columbia Forum Newsletter,* December 1989; Frank O'Neill, "Next America's Brave New Worlds," *Atlanta Magazine,* ca. May 1969, 55; Charles Price, "House of the Chief Planner of Columbia," *Baltimore Sun Magazine,* 13 October 1968; Lelba LaCholter, "Michael Spear: 'Columbia Has a Great Opportunity Ahead of It,'" *Times,* 22 June 1977.

28. Jean Moon, "Work Group Returns: Views of Columbia Planners," *Columbia Flier,* 23 June 1977.

29. Hunsinger, "Woodbridge: From Plans to People," 41–85.

30. Irvine Company, "Irvine Villages," April 1977, 1–38.

31. Don Moe, "House Prices, Traffic Problems Could Threaten Home's Value," *Irvine World News,* 13 September 1979, 6. See also Donald Cameron, "The Dream: How Is It Faring?" *Irvine World News,* 6 September 1973, 6; Lansing Eberling, "Corporate Profits: Where Most of Them Go," *Irvine World News,* 28 June 1973, 6; Watson, "The Irvine Company Report: Some Questions Asked and Answered," *Irvine World News,* 20 September 1973, 6; Mason, "Understanding Opportunities and Limits," *Irvine World News,* 5 July 1973, 6.

32. Michael Manahan, "Some Concepts for a New City," *Irvine World News,* 21 June 1973, 6.

33. David Swan, "Research: Finding Out What People Want," *Irvine World News,* 25 October 1973, 6.

34. Philip Bettencourt, "Neighborly Ads: Why They're Different," *Irvine World News,* 7 February 1974, 6–13. See also Michael J. Roach, "Irvine Company Report,"

Irvine World News, 13 December 1973, 6; Richard Reese, "A View of the Village Concept," *Irvine World News*, 12 July 1973, 6.

35. Frank McGee, "The Way It Was: The Land and Its History," *New Worlds*, June 1976, 16–21, and "Do We Have to Take It Like It Is," *New Worlds*, ca. 1970–71, 5–11. See also Nan Flink, "Images," *New Worlds*, June 1975, 13–16.

36. Jerome Collins, "Just Building Isn't Enough," *New Worlds*, June/July 1974, 54–62.

37. Ashley, "Growth: Is Saying No Enough?" *New Worlds*, midsummer 1972, 67–86.

CHAPTER 6

1. Donaldson, *The Suburban Myth*, 16, 156.

2. Burby and Weiss, *New Communities U.S.A*, 20.

3. See, for example, "Group Marks Anniversary," *Reston Times*, 20 September 1979, C5; Bunnell, "Gulf Reston Followed Master Plan," *Reston Times*, 21 February 1980; and Bunnell, "Gulf-R.C.A. Relationship Improved," *Reston Times*, 28 February 1980, A1.

4. Vernon George, "New Towners and Urban Dilemma," *Reston Times*, 2 August 1968.

5. Nan Netherton, "Early Reston: A Budding Community Draws Worldwide Attention," *Reston Times*, 27 September 1989, A3. See also Martha Pennino, "After 25 Years, What Makes Reston Special," *Reston Times*, 14 May 1989, A7; Grubishich, "Reston's Beginning: A 20th Anniversary," *Connection*, 14 July 1982, 15.

6. Gratto, "The Dream at 30," *Connection*, 12 April 1995.

7. Zeke Orlinsky, "A Letter from the Publisher," *Columbia Flier*, 17 June 1971; Charles Flowers, "On Assignment in Columbia," *Baltimore Sun*, 15 July 1979. See also Lazarick, "Rouse Sees New Life for Center Cities," *Columbia Flier*, 30 November 1978, or Lazarick, "New Towns Meeting Out of Focus," *Columbia Flier*, 2 November 1978; and Lazarick, "New Town in the Old Country: Columbia's Sister City," *Columbia Flier*, 13 July 1978, 51. See also "Living and Sharing the 200-Acre Dream," *Columbia Flier*, 3 February 1977, and Ellen Theologus, "Nude Art Controversy: Pastor Objects to Paintings," *Columbia Flier*, 15 July 1976.

8. Burby and Weiss, *New Communities U.S.A.*, 7–11.

9. Moon, "Rouse Dream Gets Setback," *Columbia Flier*, 29 August 1974. See also Moon, "An Extraordinary Success Story," *Columbia Flier*, 3 September 1972; Lazarick, "New Town in the Old Country: Columbia's Sister City," *Columbia Flier*, 13 July 1978, 51; Moon, "No More Village Centers?" *Columbia Flier*, 5 December 1974; and Moon, "The People Tree Isn't the Statue of Liberty," *Columbia Flier*, 20 June 1973.

10. This phrase was used to describe the paper by Watson, interview by the author, 18 November 1998.

11. According to political scientist Evan McKenzie, by 1992 there were 150,000 associations governing 32,000,000 Americans, and the numbers are growing. As will become clear, new towns possess community associations for the management of covenants and recreational facilities, but these associations are either more

comprehensive in their approach to local community needs or supplemented by numerous nonprofits and, in Irvine, an incorporated city government. See Evan McKenzie, *Privatopia: Homeowner Associations and the Rise of Residential Private Government.*

12. Larry Pryor, "Community Newsletters: A Survey of Grass Roots Journalism," *New Worlds,* midsummer 1972, 61–65; Baggett, "Columbia: Did the Planning Pay Off?" *Columbia Flier,* 19 June 1975, 14–17.

13. Simon, "Statement . . . before the National Advisory Commission on Rural Poverty," 1966, 2–5.

14. Grubishich amd McCandless, *Reston: The First Twenty Years.*

15. Ibid. See also Lee Lanz-Stewart, "An Historical Perspective of the Planning, Development and Provision of Leisure Services in a Planned Community: Reston, Virginia."

16. John Frece, "Reston Explores Center Options," *Reston Times,* 28 February 1974, 1–8.

17. Marlene Veach, "The Ultimate Trip," *Restonian* 5, no. 3 (1989), 34–35.

18. "Study Group Proposal for the Formation of a Reston Community Association," ca. 1967, 2.

19. Donald D. Fusaro, "Signs of an Open Community," *Reston Times,* 23 October 1969, 6.

20. "The 1974 Candidates for the R.C.A. Board," *Reston Times,* 14 February 1974, A8, A11; See also Fred Flaxman, "On Changes," *Reston Times,* 3 November 1967; "The 1972 Candidates for the R.C.A. Board," *Reston Times,* 17 February 1972, 1.

21. Bunnell, "Gulf Reston Followed Master Plan."

22. John Dockery, "Tactical Considerations for 'New Town' Citizens Groups: An Urban Guerrilla Warfare Manual", presented as part of a panel discussion on "Toward Improved New Community Governance," 1972.

23. Ibid.

24. Ibid.

25. "Reston Community Association Comments on Gulf Reston Planning," *Reston Times,* 19 August, 1971, 18; Lanyi, "R.C.A.'s Man of Principles Retires," *Connection,* 8 December 1993, 4; Joseph Stowers and George Toop, *Reston on Foot: A Prioritized Plan for Completing the Sidewalk and Trail System,* RCA, RHOA, and Reston Transportation Committee, July 1993, 2–4; Veach, "Boosting Cooperation in Transportation: Pioneer Activist Karl Ingrebritsen," *Restonian* 5, no. 3 (1989), 30–31.

26. Carolyn Marino, "R.C.A. Endorses Town Charter for Reston," *Reston Times,* 21 December 1978, A3; Barbara Gyles, "R.C.A. Backs Town Status," *Reston Times,* 5 June 1980; Pat Bauer, "Reston Goes to Richmond with Its Identity Crisis," *Washington Post,* 30 January 1980, C1, C5.

27. Gyles, "R.C.A. Issues Report on Town Status: Residents Question Costs," *Reston Times,* 29 May 1980, A1–A12. See also RCA meeting minutes, 5 December 1974; "R.C.A. Backs Service District Concept Idea," *Reston Times,* 16 March 1972, 1–8.

28. Susan Ferrechio, "Reston Land Modifying Spectrum," *Reston Times*, 16 February 1994, A2; "Spectrum Designers Alter Plans," *Reston Times*, 2 March 1994, A11; Lanyi, "Spectrum Nearing Citizen Approval," *Connection*, 9 March 1994, 3; Ferrechio, "Spectrum Unveils Town Center Link," *Reston Times*, 9 March 1994, 1; Ferrechio, "Spectrum Shopping Center Garners Support," *Reston Times*, 16 March 1994, A16; Lanyi, "Spectrum Developers Accept R.C.A. Conditions," *Connection*, 6 April 1994, 3; Ferrechio, "Factions Clash over Spectrum: R.C.A. Board Rejects Approval," *Reston Times*, 4 May 1994, A1; Lanyi, "R.C.A. Is Easing Up on Spectrum: Simon Refuses to Bend," *Connection*, 8 June 1994, 3; Ferrechio, "Spectrum Wins Local Support," *Reston Times*, 13 July 1994, A1; Ferrechio, "It's Official: Spectrum Retail Center Ok'd," *Reston Times*, 20 July 1994, A1.
29. Robert Myers, "The Reverend Embry Rucker of Reston: The Last Word in Ministering to the Needs of a Community," *Washington Post*, 3 June 1976; Grubishich, "Embry Rucker Dies at 79," *Connection*, 3 August 1994, 3; Ferrechio, "Reston's Spiritual Guide Dies," *Reston Times*, 3 August 1994; Vitale, "Master Builder Embry Rucker Retires as Episcopal Rector," *Reston Times*, 20 May 1976, A5; "Reston: Where Dreams Live: Community Resources," Mobil Land Corporation, March 1996.
30. Interfaith Action newsletters, 1983–1991, in the collection of the Fairfax County Library; David Lerman, "Comeback at Interfaith," *Connection*, 14 January 1987, 35.
31. "Historic District," proposal ca. 1983; Charles Fishman and Molly Moore, "Fairfax Board Gives Reston Center a Place in History," *Washington Post*, 14 February 1984, B3; Bruce Kriviskey, "Saving the Suburban Sixties: Historic Preservation in Fairfax County, Virginia," *Fairfax Chronicles*, Heritage Resources Branch of the Office of Comprehensive Planning, Fairfax County, 1995, 4–5; Gratto, "Residents, Merchants Gladly Suffer for Renovation," *Connection*, 6 December 1995, 6. See also Grubishich, "Plaza Should Be Named a Historic District," *Connection*, 4 January 1984, 5; Hughes, "A Shrine to Planned Development," *Reston Times*, 3 February 1983, 1.
32. Jane Shufer, "GMU to Store Reston Archives," *Connection*, 29 October 1986, 14; Gina Voss, "Remembering Reston," *Reston Times*, 18 February 1995, A2; Coonin, "New Trust to Open Museum," *Connection*, 12 February 1997, 5.
33. Hanrahan, "In the Beginning."
34. Hamilton, "Interim Memo: Government," 28 July 1964.
35. Hamilton, "Interim Memo: Communications and Transportation," 10 August 1964.
36. Ellen Hoffman, "Columbians Seek a Voice," *Washington Post*, 4 December 1969.
37. "End of the Year Report," *Crown Prints*, 18 July 1996.
38. "Statement of Delroy Cornick, Chairman Technical Advisory Committee, The Columbia Council before the Maryland Commission on Intergovernmental Cooperation, 6 December 1977," 1–7.
39. Steve Kelly, "Mr. Charm," *Columbia Magazine*, May 1989, 35–39. See also Jean

Moon, "The Illusion of Democracy," *Columbia Flier*, 9 May 1974; Peggy Wireman, "Meanings of Community in Modern America: Some Implications from New Towns" (Ph.D. diss., American University, 1976), 274; Janis Johnson, "Columbia: When a New Town Grows Up," *Washington Post*, 27 April 1978, 1.

40. Adam Sachs, "Rebel Works from Within," *Howard Sun*, 3 October ca. 1994.

41. Chuck Rees, "Of Council," *Crown Prints*, 7 July 1994; Sachs, "Rebel Works from Within."

42. Steve Kelly, "Rabbi with a Cause," *Columbia Flier*, 27 April 1995, 49.

43. "30 Years and Counting: Survey Finds Columbians Are Happy with Their Hometown," *Columbia Flier*, 19 June 1997.

44. Rouse, "Columbia System Works, Rouse Says," and Rabbi Martin Siegel, "Siegel Seeks Cooperation," *Howard Sun*, 22 January 1995, 6B; Sachs, "Incorporation Group Faces Skepticism, Other Hurdles," *Baltimore Sun*, 4 April 1995, 1, 14B; "30 Years and Counting"; Kevin Thomas, "Columbia: A (Rouse) Company Town?" *Howard Sun*, 14 June 1992; Sachs, "Yoga-Loving 'Visionary' Is Behind Drive to Incorporate Columbia," *Baltimore Sun*, 16 October 1994; and "An Agenda for Columbia," Columbia Forum, 1992, 33.

45. "30 Years and Counting"; Doug Miller, "It Ain't Broke, Just a Little Bent," *Columbia Flier*, 11 June 1992; Erik Nelson, "Columbia Faces a Governance Crossroads," *Howard Sun*, 14 June 1992; Moon, "How Much Control?" *Columbia Flier*, 28 August 1975; and Jean Peterson, "Columbia: A Company Town," *Columbia Flier*, 28 July 1977.

46. Paul Newman, "Rabbi Can't Tell Me Columbia Is Lacking a Soul," *Columbia Flier*, 19 May 1995.

47. Tennenbaum, "Don't Incorporate," *Howard Sun*, 6 November 1994.

48. "An Update on What Has Happened since Last June's Forum," Columbia Forum Meeting Guide, 1983, 9.

49. "Designing the Last Village: Changes in the New Town Ordinance," Columbia Forum Meeting Guide, 1983, 30; Steve Kelly, "The End Is Near," *Columbia Magazine*, 1989, 27; and "Video History of Columbia's Last Village: Planning a Village for the 1990s," The Columbia Forum Meeting Guide, 1983, 33.

50. Susan Hall, "To Build a Better City," *Columbia Magazine*, October 1987, 24; Tripp, *Columbia Forum Newsletter*, September 1984.

51. Tripp, "April Forum Event Inspires Ideas and Action for 'People Places,'" *Columbia Forum Newsletter*, June 1986. Fleming also spoke in Reston in 1985 on the subject of public art and community development, "Recipe for Public Art," *Connection*, 15 July 1985, 37.

52. John Gregory Brown, "Columbia Voyage Needs Sailors," *Columbia Flier*, 1988.

53. Ibid., 9.

54. "Columbia Forum—A Commitment to the Realization of Columbia's Potential," brochure, 1988; *Our Town—Columbia*, video produced by the Columbia Forum, in the Collection of the Columbia Archives, 1987.

55. Nancy Robinson, "Ruth Digs into Organizing the City Archives," *Columbia Flier*, 29 March 1984.

56. Mary Lorsung and Ruth Anne Becker, "Background on Establishment of Columbia Archives," 12 July 1983, Collection of the Columbia Archives.

57. Christine Devaney, "Orlinsky Needs a Few Old T-Shirts," *Columbia Flier*, 16 June 1983.

58. David Towner, "Since You Asked," *Columbia Magazine*, May 1987, 16. See also Ivan Penn, "Columbia Archives Provides Window on Community's Past," *Baltimore Sun*, 4 January 1995, and Erin Texeira, "10-Day Festival of Arts to Open," *Columbia Flier*, 19 June 1997.

59. Hunsinger, "What Woodbridge Is . . . ," *New Worlds*, February/March 1976, 53–66.

60. Cynthia Simone, "Irvine: A New Town Comes of Age," *Orange County Magazine*, March 1983, 50–64.

61. Brewer, "The Gestation of a Planned City: Irvine, California, from 1958–1971," 101–4. See also Louise Scott and Frank O'Donnel, "Irvine: Ten Years into a Fifty Year Plan, There's Already a Lot Going On," *New Worlds*, April 1980, 11–36.

62. Brewer, "The Gestation of a Planned City," 45–50.

63. "Learning from Experience," *Irvine World News*, 24 April 1980, 4; Gabrielle Pryor, "A General Plan," *Irvine World News*, 18 January 1973, 4; Schiesl, "Designing the Model Community," 55–91; "Irvine Bucks State Trends, Approves Park, Bike Bonds," *Irvine World News*, 6 June 1974, 1. See also Brewer, "The Gestation of a Planned City," 99; "An Introduction to the City of Irvine," City of Irvine Document, Irvine Public Library, Ready Reference Drawer, ca. 1990; and Lynn Smith, "Urban Design," *Irvine World News*, 6 May 1976.

64. Susan Kelleher, "Irvine Council's 'Liberal' View Stirs Controversy," *Orange County Register*, 25 September 1989, A1.

65. "Council Okays Irvine Blueprint," *Irvine World News*, 22 September 1977, 1, 19; Kelleher, "Irvine Council's 'Liberal' View," A1.

66. Penelope Crittenden, "Beyond the 3 R's," *New Worlds*, September 1973, 50–52; Michael Copeland, "A Tale of Two Cities: Irvine's Story: It's a Long Way to Recovery," *Orange County Register*, 16 March 1995, 4.

67. "For Families Program," pamphlet, City of Irvine Community Services and Family Services, 1998.

68. Simone, "Irvine: A New Town Comes of Age," 50–64.

69. Kelleher, "Irvine Council's 'Liberal' View," A1.

70. Melissa Weiner, "Consultants Give Officials Ideas for an Irvine Downtown," *Orange County Register*, 26 January 1989, 10; "Irvine Oks 137-Acre Development, Plans Calls for 'Urban Village' within Business Complex," *Orange County Register*, 19 August 1989, A1.

71. Kelleher, "Irvine Council's 'Liberal' View," A1; Cheryl Downey, "Irvine Plans to Increase Investment in Open Space: One-Third of Land in City to Be Saved under New Proposal," *Orange County Register*, 25 January 1988, B1; Kelleher, "Sheridan Triumph a Shocker in Irvine," *Orange County Register*, 6 June 1990, 1.

See also Jack Evans, "Irvine Drops Village Plan," *Orange County Register*, 25 October 1990, 1, and Weiner, "Irvine Council Calls for Study on Turtle Rock Development," *Orange County Register*, 25 August 1988, 7.

72. "No More, No Less," *Irvine World News*, 12 April 1979, 4; Louis Fridhandler, "Editorial Rebutted," *Irvine World News*, 19 April 1979, 4; Evans, "Irvine Drops Village Plan," 1; Evans, "Speak Up? Professor Sure Does," *Orange County Register*, 8 August 1991. Interviews with Louis Fridhandler (18 May 2000) and Mark Petracca (17 November 1998) added to my understanding of Irvine Tomorrow's activities.

73. Thomas Wilk, "The Council Campaigns: Where We Stand," *Irvine World News*, 24 January 1974, 6; Pryor, "Fifth Anniversary Address to Community," *Irvine World News*, 30 December 1976, 4. See also Angelo Vassos, "Irvine's Quality of Life," *Irvine World News*, 17 April 1980, 4.

74. Mark Petracca, interview by the author, 17 November 1998, UCI.

75. McGee, "The Way It Was: The Land and Its History," 24–35.

76. Liebeck, *Irvine: A History of Innovation and Growth*, 101; Weiner, "Old Town Irvine Adds a Touch of the New," *Orange County Register*, 21 April 1988, 1.

CHAPTER 7

Epigraph from Lester David, "We Made a Fresh Start in a New City," *Family Circle*, May 1975, 59–62, 76.

1. Frederick Jackson Turner, *The Frontier in American History*, 1–156.

2. Cathie Sullivan, "'Old Comers' Return to Hometown," *Connection*, 12 December 1984, 12.

3. Editorial, *Restonian*, October 1967.

4. James F. Grady, Restonian Town Crier, *Reston Times*, 12 July 1968.

5. Thomas Huth, Restonian Town Crier, "Social Center for Reston," *Reston Times*, 24 December 1970, 6.

6. Ringle, "Reston at 7 Years."

7. Reston Town Crier, *Reston Times*, 4 June 1970, 4.

8. "A History of James Rouse," *Columbia Flier*, 11 April 1996.

9. Lazarick, "How We Got to Be Where We Are Today," *Columbia Magazine*, summer 1992, 26.

10. Ruth Seidel, in *Our Town—Columbia*.

11. Diane Brown, "The Way We Were," *Columbia Magazine*, summer 1992, 44.

12. Harriet Scarupa, "The Columbia Pioneers," *Columbia Magazine*, November 1970.

13. Ibid.

14. Pat Carto, "The Kandy-Kolored Kommunicator," *Columbia Flier*, 28 October 1970.

15. Moon, "Editor's Note," *Columbia Flier*, 16 June 1977, 7.

16. Mary Strasburg, "Out Beyond the High-Rise, A New Horizon," *Washington Post*, 25 February 1968, section G.

17. Jeanne Lamb O'Neill, "Columbia, Gem of America's 'New Towns,'" *American Home*, May 1970.

18. Margaret Guroff, "The Dream vs. the Reality," *Columbia Magazine*, summer 1992, 73–74.

19. Diane Brown, "The Way We Were," 44.

20. Adele Levine, "Columbia at 20—A Renewed Idealism," *Columbia Flier*, 22 March 1987.

21. *Irvine, I Call It Home*, 37, 39.

22. Amy Wilson, "Irvine at 25," A5.

23. Ibid.

24. Mike Stockstill, "The Mayor Is Hometown Girl," *New Worlds*, August 1974, 15–24.

25. Scott and O'Donnel, "Irvine: Ten Years into a Fifty Year Plan," 11–36.

26. For information on public celebration in America, see Mary Ryan, "The American Parade: Representations of the Nineteenth Century Social Order," in *The New Cultural History*, ed. Lynn Hunt; Susan G. Davis, *Parades and Power: Street Theatre in Nineteenth-Century Philadelphia;* and Judith Young, *Celebrations: America's Best Festivals, Jamborees, Carnivals and Parades.*

27. This kind of family-center event was pioneered in Radburn, which Simon probably knew or may have attended. The event is described in Daniel Schaffer, *Garden Cities for America: The Radburn Experience;* "Festival Marks Birthday," *Reston Times,* 17 May 1968; "Flotilla Climaxes Festival," *Reston Times,* 7 June 1968.

28. Dick Hays, "Restonians Rededicate the Town," *Reston Times,* 31 May 1968.

29. "This Is RCA . . . A Commitment to the New Town Concept," RCA, 1970, 14.

30. "The Festival," *Reston Times,* 21 May 1970, 6.

31. "RCA Spring Festival," *Reston Times,* 8 June 1972, 1; "What's Happening at the Festival," *Reston Times,* 9 June 1977, section D; "A Smashing Success," *Reston Times,* 25 May 1978, A6.

32. Kirsten Boyd, "Festival Idea Began with a Ph.D. Thesis," *Connection,* 19 May 1982; Paul Clancy, "Festival Gets Wet, but It Still Sizzles," *Connection,* 26 May 1982, 5; "Parade Has Cast of Thousands," *Connection,* 15 May 1985, 28; and John Pitcher, "Reston Festival Draws Thousands," *Reston Times,* 24 May 1989, A1.

33. Nate Geffert, interview by Kurt Pronske (ca. 1994), Reston Oral History Project.

34. Grubishich, "Facelift for Reston Festival," *Connection,* 17 October 1990, 5; Ellen King, "Reston Festival Organizers Begin Counting Down," *Connection,* 7 April 1999.

35. Lanyi, "Santa Gets Big Reception," 4.

36. "A to Z Program Guide," Reston Association, summer 1997.

37. "The Village of Cross Keys," CRD public relations materials, ca. 1961.

38. Jeanne Lamb O'Neill, "Columbia, Gem of America's 'New Towns.'"

39. Harper's Choice Community Association Community Report, 1975.

40. Theologus, "Village Festivities," *Columbia Flier,* 23 June 1977.

41. "Neighborhoods," *Newcomer's Guide,* 1983–84.

42. "These Are a Few of Our Favorite Things," *Columbia Magazine,* November 1986, 22.

43. Phyllis Greenbaum, "What Columbia Is All About," *Columbia Flier,* 23 June 1976.

44. "Schedule for Columbia Birthday Week," *Columbia Flier,* June 1970.

45. "Columbia's Birthday," *Columbia Flier,* 27 June 1973.

46. "Cardboard Boat Regatta Sets Sail," *Columbia Flier,* 11 June 1992.

47. Virginia Kirk, "They Came Back," *Columbia Magazine,* October 1985, 19.

48. Brian Sullam, "Longfellow Community Puts on Its 20th July 4th Party," *Baltimore Sun,* 5 July 1990.

49. Susan Thornton, "Strange Things That Have Happened Along the Way," *Columbia Magazine,* Summer 1992, 23.

50. Phyllis Krepner, "Reigning On: The Longfellow Parade," Columbia Archive, date and newspaper unknown.

51. Sullam, "Longfellow Community."

52. Beverly Smith, "A Feast of Festivals," *New Worlds,* June 1981, 54–55.

53. *Irvine, I Call It Home,* 37.

54. Gary Granville, "The Business of Putting Down Roots: Community Keeping," *New Worlds,* May 1973, 26–52.

55. Scott and O'Donnel, "Irvine: Ten Years into a Fifty Year Plan," 11–36.

56. "Kids, Bikes, Flags and Fireworks Spell Spectacular Woodbridge Fourth," *Irvine World News,* 12 July 1979.

57. Gail Sharrocks, "Irvine Is . . . ," *New Worlds,* July 1973, 33–37.

58. "Freshly Harvested Field Is Festival Site," *Irvine World News,* 14 August 1975, 1.

59. "Plans Underway for Festival," *Irvine World News,* 13 May 1976; see also "Through the Looking Glass," *Irvine World News,* 26 October 1978, 4.

60. "1981 Harvest Festival: A Special Celebration," *Irvine World News,* 1 October 1981, 42.

61. *Irvine: I Call It Home,* 37.

62. Carol McGill, "Harvest Fest to Celebrate 20th Year," *Orange County Register,* 28 September 1995.

63. Debra Gold Hansen and Mary P. Ryan, "Public Ceremony in a Private Culture: Orange County Celebrates the Fourth of July," in Kling, Olin, and Poster, *Postsuburban California,* 55–91, and McGill, "Irvine's Festival Weekend Kicks Off with Food . . . ," *Orange County Register,* 7 October 1995, B4.

64. Numerous historians have examined paternalistic efforts. See Stanley Buder, *Pullman: An Experiment in Industrial Order and Community Planning;* John Phillips Coolidge, *Mill and Mansion: A Study of Architecture and Society in Lowell, Massachusetts, 1820–1865;* and John S. Garner, *The Model Company Town: Urban Design through Private Enterprise in Nineteenth Century New England.*

65. Mrs. Karl Ingrebritsen, *Reston Times,* 20 October 1967.

66. Hughes and Larsen, "Reston: 15 Years after Simon."

67. "Hundreds Honor Robert E. Simon at Fall Festival," *Reston Times,* 17 November 1967.

68. Simon, "Article Inaccurate," *Reston Times,* 23 February 1978, A1.

69. Paul Clancy and Joe Stowers, "Robert E. Simon Speaks Out on Issues Facing Reston," *Reston Times,* 24 May 1979, A7.

70. Simon, "A Letter from Simon," *Connection,* 11 November 1987, 8.

71. Dietz, "Reston Founder Tours Town Center," A13.

72. Carrington Cunningham, "Robert Simon Rediscovers Reston," *Reston Times,* 30 June 1993, A1–A11.

73. Grubishich, "Reston's Newest Resident Is Founder Simon," *Connection,*" 5 May 1993, 4.

74. Gina Voss Edwards, "Simon to Run for RA Board," *Reston Times,* 31 January 1996, A1.

75. Carlton English, "Robert E. Simon: In the Present Tense," *Connection,* 26 February 1994, 20.

76. Eric Lipton, "Father of Reston Vies for Its Soul," *Washington Post,* 24 July 1994, B1, B5.

77. Ferrechio, "Reston's Spiritual Guide Dies."

78. Grubishich, "Embry Rucker Dies at 79," 3.

79. "Embry C. Rucker *Times* 1970 'Man of the Year,'" *Reston Times,* 31 December 1970, 3.

80. Grubishich, "Embry Rucker Dies at 79," 3.

81. Fran Fanshel, "Planner Planted Spiritual Garden in Many Hearts," *Columbia Flier,* 18 April 1996.

82. J. W. Anderson, "A Brand New City for Maryland," *Harpers,* November 1964.

83. Jeanne Lamb O'Neill, "Columbia, Gem of America's 'New Towns.'"

84. Moon, "Guts, Brass, Love and Hardheadedness," *Columbia Flier,* 3 September 1972, 14.

85. Rouse, "Columbia—New City—New Hope."

86. W. D. Crawford, Columbia Council Representative, Columbia Association executive committee, 2–3 (ca. 1970).

87. Wolf Von Eckardt, "A Fresh Scene in the Clean Dream," *Saturday Review,* 15 May 1971, 23.

88. Dan Beyers, "Columbia Memories," *Washington Post Magazine,* 22 November 1992.

89. Natalie Davis Spingarn, "Columbians," *Sunday Star,* 30 July 1972.

90. Tim Miller, "Columbia's First 15 Years," *Washington Post,* 27 February 1982, real estate section.

91. Moon, "Robin Hood in Columbia: Good Living, If You Can Pay," *Columbia Flier,* 2 May 1974.

92. "Child's Eye View of Columbia," *Columbia Today,* February 1970.

93. "These Are a Few of Our Favorite Things," *Columbia Magazine,* November 1986, 23.

94. James Coran, "A Visionary's 'Enthusiasm for Life,'" *Baltimore Sun,* 13 April 1996.

95. Kelly and Thornton, "A Visionary's Dream Embodied," *Columbia Flier*, 18 April 1996.
96. *Irvine, I Call It Home*, 81.
97. Beverly Bush Smith, "The New Pioneers," 39–42.
98. Louis Fridhandler, interview by the author, 18 May 2000.
99. Watson, interview by the author, 18 November 1998.
100. G. W. Fleith, "Irvine's Mason: Enthusiasm Comes Big," *New Worlds*, May 1971.
101. Collins, "Proud but Not Prideful: Bill Mason: A Life Centered on People, Not Honors," *Irvine World News*, 19 July 1973, 3.
102. Brower, "A Time for People," 59–74.
103. Ibid.
104. Teri Sforza, "The Man in the Middle," *Orange County Register*, 26 February 1996, E1; Amy Wilson, "Irvine at 25," A3.
105. Sforza, "The Man in the Middle," E1.
106. Collins, "The Architect as President: Perspective on the Irvine Company's Raymond Watson," *New Worlds*, November 1973, 43–57.
107. The Newport Beach Light, "Donald Bren Recalls 1st Race—From the Winning Yacht," *Orange County Register*, 24 April 1997, 14.
108. Carol Humphreys, "Society: Medals Are Awarded to Supporters at Fund-Raising Dinner," *Orange County Register*, 10 February 1998, E3.
109. Pat Brennan, "The Compromise Coast," *Orange County Register*, 12 August 1996, B1.
110. Andrew Horan, "Irvine Co. Puts 17,000 Acres in Natural Reserves," *Orange County Register*, 7 August 1992, A1.
111. Jane Haas, "Donald Bren, Land Baron: How Orange County Created a Billionaire," *Orange County Register*, 1 July 1990, N1.

CHAPTER 8

Epigraph from Michael Kernan, "The Green Dream—II."
1. "The Shape of Reston," *Reston Times*, 1 June 1966.
2. George, "New Towners and the Urban Dilemma," *Reston Times*, 2 August 1968.
3. Walter Knorr, "Crossings," *Restonian* 5, no. 3 (1989).
4. "Rouse on Problems and Wifely Help," *Life*, 24 January 1967.
5. Rouse, "Cities That Work for Man," 5.
6. Mark Woodhams, "James Rouse: Profile of a Believer," *Planning*, September 1979, 36.
7. Ray N. Bird, "If You Can't Afford a $25,000-Plus House, Should Columbia Be Off-Limits?" *Columbia Magazine*, April 1970, 14.
8. Paul Imre, "Drug Crisis," letter to Wilde Lake Village Board, 4 September 1970.
9. Wes Yamaka, "Low Income Housing," *Columbia Today*, April 1969, 6.
10. Irvine Company, "Irvine Villages: Welcome Home" 1–38.
11. Watt quoted in Larry Peterson, "A New Lease on Lifestyles," *New Worlds*, January 1973, 15–22; Helen Hurd, "My Home Town," in *Irvine: I Call It Home*, 32.

12. Mayer, "A Visit to Columbia," 64.

13. Warner, *The Urban Wilderness: A History of the American City,* and *Streetcar Suburbs: The Process of Growth in Boston (1870–1900);* and Jackson, *Crabgrass Frontier: The Suburbanization of the United States.*

14. Burby and Weiss, *New Communities U.S.A.,* 8–9.

15. Historians have generally overlooked class integration in new towns because even though the new towns have achieved greater social mixture than most suburbs, they have not achieved the class mixture envisioned at the outset. In *The Evolution of American Urban Society,* Howard P. Chudacoff debates the actual value of new towns: "New towns offer more orderly land use, but to date they have done little to help the poor because their housing costs and job opportunities remain outside the capabilities of low-income families," 300. In *The American Garden City and the New Towns Movement,* Carol Christensen faults the planned communities of Radburn, New Jersey; Levittown, New York; and Columbia, Maryland, for failing to address economic inequality. Columbia, in particular, "embodies postindustrial society as the work group perceived it: affluent, educated, and leisured. . . . It is for this very reason that the city is not a viable model for American urbanization," 105–25.

16. Mark Pitsch, "ZIP Codes Tell Tales of Local Lifestyles," *Connection,* 15 November 1989, 5.

17. Simon, *Reston Letter,* December 1965, 2.

18. David, "We Made a Fresh Start in a New City," 59–62, 76; see also Gyles, "Island Walk Said the Key to Reston Couple's Future," *Reston Times,* 4 June 1987, A5.

19. Dorothy Bredesen, interview by Arvind Kannan, 4 December 1994. Reston Oral History Project.

20. Huth, Restonian Town Crier, "Social Center for Reston."

21. Ruhe, "City Builder."

22. Jody Beck, "Housing Plan for Reston is Opposed," *Washington Star,* 26 September 1978, B1, B2.

23. Wireman, "Meanings of Community in Modern America: Some Implications from New Towns," 276.

24. Gyles, "Island Walk Said the Key," A5.

25. Gyles, "Tenants to Control Island Walk Complex," *Reston Times,* 31 July 1980, A1.

26. Beck, "Housing Plan for Reston Is Opposed," B1, B2; "Exploring the Housing Needs," *Reston Times,* 19 July 1979, A6.

27. Stacy Kalmus, "Crime at Stonegate Declines 54 Percent in Two Years," *Reston Times,* 20 February 1991, A1.

28. Elise Burroughs, "RCA Plans Subsidized Housing Meeting," *Reston Times,* 19 July 1979.

29. Simon, "Reston Town Center Fulfills the Dream," *Reston Times,* 28 November 1990, A8; Kalmus, "Reston's Town Center Public Housing Opens," *Reston Times,* 23 January 1991, A7.

30. Jerry Geary, interview by the author, 27 March 1997.

31. Ivan Cole, interview by the author, 14 March 1998.
32. Donald Fusaro "Signs of an Open Community," *Reston Times*, 23 October 1969, 6.
33. Bill Richards, "Life in Reston Can Be Easy—For a Price," *Washington Post*, 16 January 1975, A5.
34. Betsy Schultz, interview by Lisa Carlivati, 16 December 1994, Reston Oral History Project.
35. Kernan, "The Green Dream—II."
36. "Reston's Elderly Residents Terrorized by Young Criminals," *Washington Post*, 20 September 1979, A13. On crime, see Dina Anders, "Police Claim Reston among Safest Communities in County," *Reston Times*, 3 February 1983; Willem Scheltema, "Crime Arrests Up in Area," *Reston Times*, 5 March 1986, 1; Lerman, "Shopping Center Crime Low," 6; Jennifer Burcham, "Reston Crime Is on the Decline," *Reston Times*, 25 July 1990, A1; Gratto, "A Safe Place to Live?" *Connection*, 8 August 1995.
37. "Reston Residents Have Formed a Unified Front in Defense of the Lower Income Housing Plans," signed by a number of residents, *Reston Times*, 18 August 1967, 1.
38. Megan Rosenfeld, "Reston Becomes Richer, Blacker," *Washington Post*, ca. 1977.
39. Kirsten Boyd, "Drive Set to Beautify The Green," *Connection*, 26 June 1985, 6.
40. "What's with Affordable Housing?" *Interfaith Housing Newsletter*, spring 1985; Reston Interfaith Inc. pamphlet, 23 February 1985.
41. "This Is RCA . . . A Commitment to the New Town Concept," RCA, 1970, 13.
42. Catherine Grim, "RCA Backs Apartment Plan," *Reston Times*, 14 July 1977, A8; Kristan Metzler, "RCA Demands Affordable Housing," *Reston Times*, 29 November 1989, A4.
43. Carolyn Marino, "RCA, Pennino Disagree on South Lake Gardens," *Reston Times*, 3 May 1979, A5; Elizabeth Deschamps, "RCA Liberals Are Challenged," *Connection*, 26 August 1987, 3.
44. Steve Langdon, "County Cancels Fence Plans," *Connection*, 28 February 1990, 3.
45. Eckardt, "America Tomorrow: Creating the Great Society," *New Republic*, 7 November 1964.
46. Section epigraph from Bird, "If You Can't Afford a $25,000-Plus House," 10. Hamilton, "Interim Memo: Social Structure," 1 July 1964.
47. Ibid.
48. Michael, "Recommendations for the Social Planning of Columbia: Physical Facilities and Social Organization," July 1964, 1–2.
49. Ibid.
50. Jack Anderson and Jean Lundin, "Columbia in the 80's," ca. 1986, prepared for the Columbia Forum. There were also eleven group homes for the mentally retarded in Columbia by 1982, a significant accomplishment for an upper-income community, and more than Reston, which had only two in 1984 (Elizabeth Cosin, "Group Home Wins Support," *Connection*, 1 April 1984, 45).

51. "Release on Columbia Survey," Columbia Association, October 1981.
52. Kirk, "They Came Back," 19.
53. Orlinsky, "Do Something about It," *Columbia Flier,* 1 November 1977.
54. Leff, "Columbia, 20 Years Young."
55. "Aging: Older Villages Confront Typical Urban Troubles," *Baltimore Sun,* 19 March 1995; see also Sachs, "Harpers Choice Grapples with Future," *Baltimore Sun,* 6 April 1995.
56. Michael Olesker, "Columbia at 30, Shows Its Age," *Baltimore Sun,* 17 April 1997; Lazarick, "Where Are We Now?" *People of Columbia,* 19.
57. 1999 SAT scores for Columbia high schools can be found at <http://www.howard.k12.md.us/parent/satscores.html>.
58. Sachs, "Columbia Falls Short of Rouse's 60's Vision," *Baltimore Sun,* 10 October 1995; see statistics sources above. See also Daniel Barkin, "River Hill: Columbia's Grand Finale Unfolds," *Baltimore Sun,* 4 February 1996.
59. Lazarick, "No Promised Land, No Next America—Just Columbia," *Columbia Flier,* 16 June 1977, 12–13.
60. J. Michael Marshall, "What the Real Problem Is," *Columbia Flier,* 28 September 1978.
61. Columbia Cooperative Ministry, "Open Letter," 19 April 1967, reprinted in *Columbia Forum,* 1982, 62.
62. James Hoffman, "New Model for City Living," *Presbyterian Life,* 1 November 1971.
63. "Housing," *Newcomer's Guide,* 1983–84, prepared by the staff of the *Columbia Flier,* 29; see Sachs, "Residents Criticize Affordable Housing Project," *Baltimore Sun,* 12 July 1994.
64. Lazarick, "Housing for Everyone," *Columbia Flier,* 3 November 1979.
65. Moon, "Rouse Dream Gets Setback: Study Cited 'Mediocre Performance' of New Towns," *Columbia Flier,* 29 August 1974.
66. Dan Beyers, "Columbia Memories," *Washington Post Magazine,* 22 November 1992.
67. Tim Miller, "Columbia's First 15 Years," *Washington Post,* 27 February 1982.
68. "Aging: Older Villages Confront Typical Urban Troubles."
69. Kernan, "The Green Dream—I."
70. Efriam Ben-Zadok, "Economic and Racial Integration in a New Town."
71. Stephen Ater, "The Ghetto Mob's Violence . . . ," *Columbia Flier,* 3 December 1976, and Marshall, "And Undoing the Damage," *Columbia Flier,* 3 December 1976.
72. Michael G. Riemer, "Building a Better Community," *Columbia Flier,* 12 January 1977; see also Vincent Pisacane, "Interfaith Housing Issue Not Addressed," *Columbia Flier,* 27 January 1977.
73. Philip Davis, "Columbia: Zero to 68,000 in 20 Years," *Baltimore Sun,* 7 June 1987, A1–A4.

74. Mike and Mary Ann Gates, "Hannibal Grove Becomes 'Ghetto,'" *Columbia Flier,* 27 June 1974.
75. Margaret Taite, "Copperstone: Two Signs Humiliate Resident," *Columbia Flier,* 28 August 1975.
76. Statistics from Subsidized Units in Howard County, prepared by the Maryland Office of Planning, April 1992; Texeira, "Howard Housing Reaches the Roof," *Howard Sun,* 15 June 1997, 1B; see also Shanon Murray, "Hickory Ridge Still Battles Apartment for the Elderly," *Howard Sun,* 21 February 1996.
77. Moon, "Robin Hood in Columbia." See also Moon, "The People Tree Isn't the Statue of Liberty."
78. "Housing," *Newcomer's Guide,* 1983–84, prepared by the staff of the *Columbia Flier,* 29. Tensions have not disappeared, even over more affordable housing: see Sachs, "Residents Criticize Affordable Housing Project"; Joe Murchison, "Columbia: How Does It Compare with Its Image," *Columbia Flier,* 13 July 1985.
79. Columbia Council, 23 August 1979, resolution reprinted in the *Columbia Forum,* 1982, 63.
80. "Second Annual Columbia Forum: The Columbia Concept: Facing New Realities," newsletter published 1983; see also Michael J. Clark, "Ryland's Ex-CEO Leads Effort to Build Affordable Housing," *Baltimore Sun,* 31 March 1991.
81. Leff, "Columbia, 20 Years Young."
82. Evelyn Richardson, "Incorporation Re-Examined," *Columbia Flier,* 9 March 1995, 55.
83. Section epigraph from Amy Wilson, "Irvine at 25," A4. Collins, "The Architect as President," 43–51. See also Irvine Company, "Irvine Villages: Welcome Home" 14.
84. Sharrocks, "The Alternative Lifestyle: In Apartment Neighborhoods, There's a Lot Going On," *New Worlds,* October 1974, 46–52.
85. Eugene O'Toole, "Who Am I to Deprive a Man . . . ," *Irvine World News,* reprinted from a local newsletter, 15 February 1973.
86. "Petitioners Don't Want Apartment-Dwellers," *Irvine World News,* 6 September 1973, 1.
87. Simone, "Irvine: A New Town Comes of Age," 50–64.
88. Lynn Smith, "More Than Enough Isn't Everything," *New Worlds of Irvine,* October 1979, 94–112. Average household income and median home price comes from the Irvine City Government Web site at <www.ci.irvine.ca.us/about_irvine/demo.htm>.
89. Gary Granville, "Politics and Poetry," *New Worlds,* September 1973, 25–27.
90. Ashley, "Growth: Is Saying No Enough?" 67–86.
91. Pryor, "Fifth Anniversary Address to Community," 4.
92. Schiesl, "Designing the Model Community," 55–91.
93. Scott and O'Donnel, "Irvine: Ten Years into a Fifty Year Plan," 11–36.
94. "Irvine: A New Town Comes of Age," 50–64.
95. "Irvine at 20: Planning Ahead," Irvine Company, 1972.

96. For a gripping account of suburban evasion of social responsibility, see Larry Rosenthal, *Our Town: Race, Housing and the Soul of Suburbia.*

CHAPTER 9

Epigraph from Ramsey Flynn, "Eighteen Years Later," *Baltimore Magazine,* December 1985, 142.

1. Suburban segregation continues to be a concern of many sociologists, historians, and social-policy experts. Most studies by historians have found little progress in genuine integration. In *The Suburban Racial Dilemma: Housing and Neighborhoods,* W. Dennis Keating discusses successful affirmative-action integration policies in Shaker Heights and Cleveland Heights, as well as the more common resegregation of other suburbs. Residents and social activists in Shaker Heights, as at the new towns, have made racial integration an open goal. Affirmative action policies there include promoting white purchase in the community to maintain the racial balance. In *The New Suburbanites: Race and Housing in the Suburbs,* Robert Lake finds blacks moving into suburban areas from which whites were fleeing. Resegregation of communities followed and perpetuated a "dual housing market for blacks and whites," 240. In *Our Town: Race, Housing and the Soul of Suburbia,* David Kirp, John Dwyer, and Larry Rosenthal document the difficulties in including affordable housing directed primarily at black residents, even after decades of legal battles.

Those involved in social policy have offered similarly depressing stories. In *Urban Housing Segregation of Minorities in Western Europe and the United States,* edited by Elizabeth Huttman, the various authors pinpoint limited progress in certain suburban areas, particularly around Atlanta, Washington, D.C., and New York, but a continuation of racial segregation in most other suburban communities. Spillover from ghetto areas tends to be the most common form of black suburban expansion. *Residential Apartheid: The American Legacy,* edited by Robert Bullard, documents the persistence of high degrees of segregation in all American cities and the continuing concentration of poor black families in the inner city. J. John Palen, in *The Urban World,* describes the growth of the suburban black population, particularly in what are termed "inner ring" suburbs adjacent to black ghettos. He notes that "in such cases, black suburbanization can hardly be equated with racial integration," 174. See also Morris Milgram, in *Good Neighborhood: The Challenge of Open Housing.*

2. Ruhe, "City Builder."
3. Peggy Wireman, "Meaning of Community," 282.
4. "Mobil Land Communities: Where Dreams Live," Mobil Land Communities, ca. 1996.
5. Rosenfeld, "Reston Becomes Richer, Blacker."
6. Robert Andrews, "Reston, Virginia Went from 'New Town' of 1960s to 'Boom Town,'" *Syracuse Herald,* 17 August 1986, H6.
7. "Reston, Virginia: New Design for an Ideal City," *Ebony,* December 1966, 90–96.

8. Kernan, "The Green Dream—II."

9. Carlos Campbell, *New Towns: Another Way to Live,* 43–45.

10. See, for instance, "Citizen of the Year: Robertson, Heart for People," *Reston Times,* 3 January 1990, A1; Lanyi, "400 Pay Tribute to Reston's Tom Wilkins," *Connection,* 5 May 1993, 3

11. Metzler, "Gordon Offers Help to Stonegate's Kids," *Reston Times,* 1 November 1984, A3; Lanyi, "Stonegate Village Activist Pearline Hogan Dies at 56," *Connection,* 11 May 1994, 8.

12. Reston Black Focus, "Fact Sheet," 1989.

13. Edward Sharp, "Does Ad Seek Blacks," *Reston Times,* 4 September 1969, 6.

14. Eckardt, "A Fresh Scene in the Clean Dream," *Saturday Review,* 15 May 1971, 23.

15. Vitale, "Cameo: Bill Johnston," *Reston Times,* 26 May 1977, C1.

16. Wireman, "Meanings of Community," 283; Reston Black Focus, "Fact Sheet," 1989; Wendy Swallow, "Black Group Back in Focus," *Connection,* 16 June 1982, 5.

17. Clare Fiore, "Sister City a Reality," *Connection,* 11 January 1984.

18. Sullivan, "RCA Honors Nyeri Effort," *Connection,* 5 May 1985, 7.

19. "A Glimmer of Our Own Beauty," *Washington Post,* 2 September 1972.

20. Kim Heanue, "Black Arts Fest Returns Home," *Connection,* 7 August 1996, 7.

21. D. Quynh Nguyen, "Jack and Jill Presents Young African Americans," *Reston Times,* 4 December 1996, A3.

22. Betty Reed, "Goals Vary among Local Black Service Organizations," *Reston Times,* 21 February 1980, C1.

23. Cole, interview by the author, May 1998. In *Postethnic America,* David Hollinger proposes that Americans need to move beyond the concept of multiculturalism. For Hollinger, multiculturalism places too great an emphasis on involuntary membership in groups rather than examining the important role of voluntary affiliation in shaping identity (his postethnic view). Particularly disappointing for Hollinger is the acceptance by multiculturalists of racial or ethnic categories (originally designed by the government) as "involuntary communities of descent." Hollinger, unfortunately, puts the cart before the horse. As an intellectual, he overlooks the necessity of initial social change to a change in thinking. In communities such as Reston and Columbia, a hard-fought battle has been waged to create the sociological basis for postethnic thinking. The change in sociological reality has allowed the change in attitudes. Most American communities have not come close to achieving racial integration, so it is unrealistic to expect the majority of blacks and whites to have anything but a pessimistic attitude about race or that they will see beyond crude, multicultural categorizations.

24. Carol Williams, interview by Maya Scott, 23 May 1995; Lora Haus, interview by Jon Schumacher, 29 December 1994; Sarah Larson, interview by Ben Feldman, 1994; Betsy Schultz, interview by Lisa Carlivati, 16 December 1994; Tim Stapelton, interview by Dave Zawitz, 18 December 1994; unknown person, interview by Kenny Borelli, 19 December 1994. Reston Oral History Project.

25. *Places, Towns and Townships,* 859.

26. Alisa Samuels, "Columbia Chosen for First Forum on African Americans," *Howard Sun*, 22 March 1996.

27. Hamilton, "Interim Memo: Social Structure," 1 July 1964.

28. Ibid.

29. Ibid.

30. "Praise for a Man with 'Faith in the American Spirit,'" *Columbia Flier*, 11 April 1996.

31. Moon, "Rouse Dream Gets Setback."

32. Tennenbaum, *Creating a New City*, 118–24.

33. James Hirsch, "Columbia, Md., at 25, Sees Integration Goal Sliding From Its Grasp," *Wall Street Journal*, 27 February 1992.

34. Myron Beckstein, "The Idea Works," *Baltimore Sun*, 21 June 1987.

35. Bureau of the Census, "Occupation, Income in 1989 of Black Persons," *Figures from the Columbia, MD, CDP, of the Balitimore, MD, MSA*, 1990 Census (Washington, D.C.), 828; Ruth Glick, "Bill and Pinnie Ross," *Columbia Flier*, 16 June 1977, 66. See also Robert Keller, "Columbia Nearing Its First Birthday, Most Residents Like It There," *Baltimore Evening Sun*, 19 June 1968; Scarupa, "Columbia, This Piece of the Next America, Is a Neophyte Melting Pot," *Columbia Today*, April 1970, 24.

36. John Hammond, "Six NBA Bullets Attracted to Columbia," *Baltimore Sun*, November 1975, 12.

37. Ellen Rhudy, "On the News: T.V. Personalities, Fellow Columbians," *Calendar*, July 1983, 14–17.

38. Keidel, "4 Our Men of Columbia," *People of Columbia*, 37–43.

39. "Two Black Families: Old Roots, New Roots," *Columbia Flier*, 12 May 1977.

40. Jeanne Lamb O'Neill, "Columbia, Gem of America's 'New Towns.'"

41. Jack Rosenthal, "A Tale of One City," *New York Times Magazine*, 26 December 1971.

42. Neil Sandberg, *Stairwell 7: Family Life in the Welfare State*, 24.

43. Ginnie Manuel, "On the Street Where I Lived," *People Of Columbia*, 29–35.

44. Kelly and Thornton, "A Visionary's Dreams Embodied."

45. "Fashion As . . . ," *Calendar*, 21 September 1984.

46. Manuel, "Black and White Follow-Up," *Columbia Flier*, 16 June 1977; "Programs Examine Black Cultural Identity," *Columbia Flier*, 10 March 1977.

47. Tripp, "Forum Event Celebrates Black History," *Columbia Forum Newsletter*, March 1985.

48. "Black/White Styles Discussed," *Columbia Forum Newsletter*, December 1985; Jack Anderson and Jean Lundin, "Columbia in the 80's," ca. 1986, prepared for the Columbia Forum.

49. Dave Barkley, "'Fear Knocked; Faith Answered,'" *Columbia Times*, 1 July 1968.

50. Ibid.

51. Bryan Burkert, "Color Blindness: Columbia's Kids Wake Up from Their Dream,"

Baltimore City Paper, 11 October 1993; Susan Hall and Judith Tripp, "Columbia: My Hometown," *Columbia Magazine,* November 1986, 25.

52. John Brown, "When Black Meets White: Columbia's Interracial Families," *Columbia Magazine,* fall 1990.

53. Kirk, "They Came Back," 22.

54. Hall and Tripp, "Columbia: My Hometown," 25; Keidel, "4 Our Men of Columbia," 37–43.

55. "Kids' Views of Columbia," *Columbia Flier,* 9 June 1977.

56. Rosenthal, "A Tale of One City."

57. Sandberg, *Stairwell 7,* 11–229.

58. Moon, "Integration," *Columbia Flier,* 9 October 1975, 21.

59. Ben-Zadok, "Economic and Racial Integration in a New Town," 1–326.

60. Thom Loverro, "Gray Is First Black Elected as Chairman of Council," *Howard Sun,* 5 December 1984; Doug Miller, "Vernon Gray," *Columbia Flier,* 2 March 1989, 33; Craig Timberg, "Gray Elected Vice President of NACO," *Baltimore Sun,* 16 July 1997, section B.

61. Rogers, "Brown Takes Over for Dewey at CA," *Columbia Flier,* 1 July 1993, 7.

62. Hirsch, "Columbia, Md., at 25."

63. Doris Ligon, interview by the author, 26 March 1998; Samuels, "Columbia Chosen for First Forum on African-Americans."

64. Amy Klein, "Museum's Basics of History: Everyday Objects Shed Light on African American Lives," *Washington Post,* 28 August 1997.

65. "Biography: Wylene Bunch," *Montage Magazine,* February 1997, 4.

66. Lan Nguyen, "Time Tempers Columbia's Lofty Ideals," *Howard Sun,* 14 June 1992.

67. "30 Years and Counting"; Myriam Marquez, "Entering Its 3rd Decade, Columbia Called No Place for Racial Hate," *Baltimore Afro American,* 23 June 1987.

68. Eckardt, "A Fresh Scene in the Clean Dream," 23; James Hoffman, "New Model for City Living." One example of a positive article is Alex Marshall, "Columbia, Maryland," *Metropolis,* June 1997, 37–42.

69. *Places, Towns and Townships,* 456.

70. Texeira, "Gays Find Acceptance in Liberal Columbia," *Howard Sun,* 3 August 1997. See also Catherine Grim, "Homosexuals Resent Secrecy," *Reston Times,* 21 July 1977, A8, A15.

71. Irvine Company, "Irvine Villages: Welcome Home," 35.

72. Watson, personal correspondence with the author, 12 January 2000.

73. Downey, "Community Close-Up," *Orange County Register,* 25 March 1988, B2.

74. *Places, Towns and Townships,* 332.

75. *Irvine: I Call It Home,* 77.

76. Pryor, "Fifth Anniversary Address to Community," 4.

77. Robert Scheer, "Withering on the Irvine," *Lears,* May 1991, 55–98.

CHAPTER 10

1. Donaldson, *The Suburban Myth,* 122.
2. Friedan, *The Feminine Mystique* , 37–233.
3. The debates on the relative happiness of women in suburbia continue. See Joanne Meyerowitz, "Beyond the Feminine Mystique: A Reassessment of Postwar Mass Culture, 1946–1958," *Journal of American History,* March 1993, 1455–81; Daniel Horowitz, *Betty Friedan and the Making of the "Feminine Mystique"*; Donald Rothblatt, *The Suburban Environment and Women;* and Nancy Rubin, *The New Suburban Woman.*
4. "Social Planning and Programs," Reston Virginia Foundation for Community Programs Inc., March 1967, 103.
5. Gail Norcross, "What Buyers Think of Reston," *Urban Land* 25, no. 2 (ca. 1968).
6. Jane Wilhelm, interview by Matt Craft, 15 December 1994, Reston Oral History Project.
7. Rosenfeld, "Reston Becomes Richer, Blacker."
8. Janice Greene, "Reston's Women's Center Offers Programs, Education, Counseling," *Reston Times,* 22 April 1976, A1.
9. "The 1974 Candidates for the RCA Board," A8, A11.
10. "Pennino: 'Citizen of the Year,'" *Reston Times,* 1 January 1992.
11. Elizabeth Cosin, "RCA's Janet Howell: Civic Sparkplug," *Connection,* 20 May 1987, 45; Matthew Brown, "Howell Breaks Political Ground for Women," *Reston Times,* 15 January 1997, A6.
12. Strasburg, "Out Beyond the High-Rise."
13. Scarupa, "The Columbia Pioneers," 17.
14. Charlotte Temple, "Planning and the Married Woman with Children—A New Town Perspective," Collection of the Columbia Archives, ca. 1974.
15. "A Model for the Nation: Child Care and Learning at Columbia," Childhood Resources Inc., September 1971.
16. Manuel, "On the Street Where I Lived," 29–35.
17. Temple, "Planning and the Married Woman with Children."
18. Spingarn, "Columbians."
19. Zane, "Feminists," *Columbia Flier,* 1 February 1979, 36.
20. Ibid.
21. Glick, "Working Women: Out of the Rut and Rising to Unique Opportunities." *Columbia Flier,* 16 June 1977, 45–49.
22. Ibid.
23. Strasburg, "Out Beyond the High-Rise."
24. Kay Wisniweski, "Hatch Act Baby: The Emergence of Women as a Political Force," *Columbia Flier,* 16 June 1977, 51.
25. "With Little Fanfare, Bobo Shakes Up Howard County," *Baltimore Sun,* 13 December 1987, 1.
26. "Ruth Keeton," memorial service pamphlet from the Kittamaqundi Community, 1997.

27. "Community Guide," Irvine Company, advertisement supplement to the *Orange County Register,* 24 February 1996, 8, and "Irvine," Chamber of Commerce and City of Irvine, 1990.

28. Lynn Smith, "More Than Enough Isn't Everything."

29. Beverly Bush Smith, "The Quest for Community," 18–25.

30. Stockstill, "The Mayor Is Hometown Girl," 15–24.

31. McGill, "Housing Plan OK Stirs Opposition," *Orange County Register,* 31 December 1995.

32. The Irvine Citizen, "Interview: Shea: I Plan to Take a More Serious Approach to Government," *Orange County Register,* 14 November 1996, 1.

33. Eckardt, "America Tomorrow."

34. Herbert Gans, *The Levittowners.*

35. Glen Elder's article, "Adolescence in Historical Perspective," in *Growing Up in America: Historical Experiences,* edited by Harvey Graff, is a comprehensive review of the literature of adolescence, including summaries of important work in anthropology, sociology, psychology, and history.

36. "Rathskeller," *Reston Letter,* 21 May 1966, 8

37. Sally Larson, Restonian Town Crier, "Reston Teens," *Reston Times,* 3 January 1969.

38. Ibid.; see also Larson, interview by Ben Feldman, 1994, Reston Oral History Project.

39. "Uncommon Ground," *Reston Times,* 12 November 1970, 6.

40. Ringle, "Reston at 7 Years." See also Helen Merryman Legg, "Living in Reston," *Washingtonian,* February 1966, and Ronald White, "7 Arrested in Reston Drug Raid," *Washington Post,* 15 November 1979, C1.

41. Adam Fike, "85 Gangs Roam Fairfax," *Reston Times,* 24 September 1997, A1.

42. "A to Z Program Guide," Reston Association, summer 1997.

43. Patricia Hersch, *A Tribe Apart: A Journey into the Heart of American Adolescence,* 1–375.

44. Heading quote from "The Graduates: Products of the New Eden," *Columbia Flier,* 22 May 1975. Section epigraph from Roger Karsk, *Teenagers in the Next America,* 37.

45. Vance Packard, *A Nation of Strangers,* 323.

46. Julia Malone, "Looking at Open Space: Discipline, Order Still Prevail," *Columbia Flier,* 17 November 1977; Anne Odendahl, "The Schools Go Modern," *Columbia Today,* August 1969.

47. Hamilton, "Interim Memo: Leisure," 16 April 1964.

48. Michael, "Recommendations for the Social Planning of Columbia," July 1964.

49. Tennenbaum, *Creating a New City,* 117.

50. Scarupa, "Youth in Columbia," *Columbia Magazine,* July 1970.

51. Moon, "It's a Long, Long Time from June to September . . . ," *Columbia Flier,* 26 April 1972.

52. Moon, "New City Teens: No Place to Call Their Own," *Columbia Flier*, 6 June 1974, 8.
53. Christine Devaney, "CA Tries Again to Reach Teens," *Columbia Flier*, 11 November 1982; Stuart Low, "Grant Spurs Plans for Expansion of Teen Activity Program," *Howard Sun*, 8 February 1984, 8; Sherry Wyskida, "Howard County Youth Resource Center," *Columbia Magazine*, February 1985, 11.
54. Moon, "New City Teens," 8.
55. Kids, *Newcomers Guide*, 1983–84, 73; Janet Zinzeleta, "Teens Reaching Teens," *Howard Sun*, 20 April 1983, 1–8.
56. Jill Yesko, "Village Centers Fret over Teen Loiterers," *Columbia Flier*, 1 January 1998.
57. Geoffrey Himes, Review of *Teenagers in the Next America*, *Columbia Flier*, 10 November 1977.
58. Karsk, *Teenagers in the Next America*, 1–130, 140–41.
59. Ibid., 93–107.
60. Ibid., 131–41.
61. Hollis Pachen, "Saturday Night Live," *Columbia Magazine*, winter 1989, 38–43. See also Himes, "Hanging Out on Friday Night"; Jeanne Cummings, "Summer Means Idle Hours for Youths, Frustration for Neighbors," *Columbia Times*, 8 August 1979.
62. Philip Trupp, "Langley Park and Columbia: Looking for a Way of Life," *Washingtonian Magazine*, January 1971.
63. Leslie Milk, "Gem of a Notion," *Washingtonian*, December 1988, 225.
64. Janet King, "Columbia Teens: 'I Wish Every Place Was Like This'" *Columbia Flier*, 16 June 1977, 55–59.
65. Leff, "Columbia, 20 Years Young."
66. Subhead epigraph from Tom Berg, "Tales from the Beige Side," *Orange County Register*, 1 October 1996, E1. Stockstill, "Irvine, Teenagers and Trouble: A Perspective from the Kids," *Irvine World News*, 20 June 1974, 10.
67. Lynn Smith, "More Than Enough Isn't Everything," 94–112.
68. Scheer, "Withering on the Irvine," 55–98.
69. Downey, "Irvine Youths Find Little Joy in 'Teen Hating' Community," *Orange County Register*, 17 April 1989, 1.
70. Scott and O'Donnel, "Irvine: Ten Years into a Fifty Year Plan," 11–36.
71. Irvine Community Service, summer 1998, 30–31.
72. Mary Jo Griffith, "Homing in on Teen Angst in Irvine," *Orange County Register*, 18 May 1994, F5.
73. John Wescott, "Ganging Up on Irvine Gangs," *Orange County Register*, 24 December 1992, 1.

CHAPTER 11

1. Rouse quote in epigraph from "A History of James Rouse," *Columbia Flier*, 11 April 1996. Donaldson, *The Suburban Myth*, 74.

2. On cultural patronage in suburbia see C. G. Vasiliadis, "The Arts and the Suburbs," in *Suburbia: The American Dream and Dilemma,* ed. Philip C. Dolce.

3. Section epigraph from Vladimir Kagan, *Interiors Magazine,* September 1966, 107. Ruhe, "City Builder."

4. "Statement by Robert E. Simon, Jr," Commission on Urban Problems, 28 October 1967, 4.

5. Reston Master Plan Report, May 1962, Simon Enterprises, preface; Clancy and Stowers, "Robert E. Simon Speaks Out," A7.

6. Ruhe, "City Builder."

7. "The Shops in Washington Plaza," *Reston Letter,* December 1965.

8. Norcross, "What Buyers Think of Reston."

9. "Enriching," *Reston Times,* 6 August 1970, 6.

10. John Linsenmeyer, "Letter to Residents from the Reston Virginia Foundation," *Reston Times,* 22 November 1967.

11. Ringle, "Reston at 7 Years."

12. Reed, "Participants Recall GRACE History," *Reston Times,* 5 January 1984, C1.

13. "Visions," *Greater Reston Arts Center Newsletter,* spring 1996.

14. Gratto, "Fine Arts Festival Beats the Weather," 3; Gratto, "Fine Arts Festival Draws 67,000," *Connection,* 3 July 1996, 10; and D. Quynh Nguyen, "Artists, Art Lovers Gather for Festival," A3.

15. "Reston Arts '93 Home Tour," *Connection,* 13 October 1993, 47; "Reston, Herndon Galleries Flourish," *Connection,* 26 August 1992, 32.

16. "Reston Community Center Theater: 1997–98 Performing Arts Season," pamphlet.

17. "31 Years of Theatre Excellence," Reston Community Players, 1998.

18. Program, "30 Years of Singing," The Reston Chorale, 15 March 1998.

19. "Reston Applauds the Arts with Week Long Celebration," *Reston Times,* 15 March 1995, A3.

20. Chris Gaudet, "Reston's Cable Channel 8 Celebrates Anniversary," *Reston Times,* 26 September 1990, C1; see also Grubishich, "Reston to Begin Cable TV," *Washington Post,* 18 June 1976.

21. Michael, "Recommendations for the Social Planning of Columbia," July 1964.

22. Hamilton, "Interim Memo: Leisure," 16 April 1964.

23. Hamilton, "Interim Memo: Leisure: Adult Education and Recreation," 16 April 1964.

24. Hanrahan, "In the Beginning."

25. Hoffman, "New Model for City Living."

26. Strasburg, "Out Beyond the High-Rise."

27. Kernan, "The Green Dream—I."

28. James Dilts, "The College that Snuck into Columbia," *Baltimore Sun Magazine,* 31 May 1970, 10.

29. Lazarick, "No Promised Land," 12–13.

30. Lazarick, "Where Are We Now," 19; see also Diana Dachler, "Columbia Visual Art

Exhibition Indicates Community Artistic Health," *Columbia Flier,* 11 August 1977. A high-profile NEA meeting on the arts in new communities held in Columbia at the Columbia Center for Community Research in 1972 provides an overview of cultural activity in Columbia. See Ralph Burgard, "The Creative Community: Arts and Science Programs for New and Renewing Communities," February 1973, Columbia Archive.

31. Hoppenfeld, "The Columbia Process: The Potential for New Towns," 1970, address reprinted in "Before Columbia," 69–94.

32. Mayer, "A Visit to Columbia, MD," 64.

33. Lazarick, "Where Are We Now," 19; see also Dachler, "Columbia Visual Art Exhibition Indicates Community Artistic Health."

34. "City's Film Society has 6 Movies Left," *Columbia Today,* April 1989, 22.

35. Ginna Browne, "Anne Allen," *People of Columbia,* 95.

36. Michael Kiernan, "Columbia: Maryland's New Town Turns 10," *Washington Star,* ca. 1977.

37. Flowers, "On Assignment in Columbia."

38. Kirk, "Howard County Poetry and Literary Society," September 1985, 14–17.

39. "More about the Howard County Arts Council," pamphlet, 1998; Brenda Bell, interview by the author, 15 May 1998.

40. "Want to Know More: About Local Organization the Howard County Arts Council Supports?" Directory of the HCACA Development Grant Recipient, FY, 1998; Mike Giulano, "Festival of the Arts Offers a Celebration of Enlightenment," *Baltimore Sun,* 16 June 1994.

41. Texeira, "10-Day Festival of Arts to Open"; Sherry Joe, "Columbia Fair, Arts Festival to Merge," *Howard Sun,* 21 October 1994.

42. Columbia Foundation, Update, summer 1988.

43. Columbia Foundation, newsletters, 1979–1996

44. Rebecca Krehnbrink, "How Columbia Solved Its Youth Problem and Gained a Summer Festival," *Baltimore Magazine,* June 1974, 41.

45. "These Are a Few of Our Favorite Things," 22.

46. Lynne Salsibury, "VAC May Go It Alone," *Columbia Flier,* 9 September 1981; Gail Campbell, "Arts College in Columbia Is State's Newest, Smallest." *Baltimore Sun,* 28 November 1982; Jacqueline Burrell, "CA to Consider Running Visual Arts Center with HCC," *Columbia Flier,* 13 November 1986.

47. Helen Worth, "The Saga of the Columbia Association: Its Ups, Its Downs, Its History," *Calendar,* October 1983, 25.

48. "Neighborhoods," *Newcomers Guide,* 1983–84, 8.

49. "Historic Oakland Celebrates Its First Anniversary on October 14," *Columbia Flier,* 4 October 1990.

50. Scott and O'Donnel, "Irvine: Ten Years into a Fifty Year Plan," 14.

51. Lori Basheda, "Fashion Island: 30 Glitzy Years," *Orange County Register,* 23 January 1997, B1.

52. "Promoting Cultural Maturity," *Irvine World News,* 6 January 1977, 4.

53. "Irvine," Chamber of Commerce and City of Irvine, 1990; Scott and O'Donnel, "Irvine: Ten Years into a Fifty Year Plan," 11–36.
54. "Contemporary Beadwork Art on Exhibit at Fine Arts Center," *Irvine World News,* 9 July 1998, B4; "Irvine Community Services," summer 1998, published by the City of Irvine, 58–68.
55. Barclay calendar of events, 1997–98, 1998–99.
56. Jean Pond, "Memories of Irvine," in *Irvine: I Call It Home,* 39.
57. Stockstill, "New Town, Young University: Appraising the Relationship," *Irvine World News,* 18 December 1975, 1–9.
58. Linda Herington, "From Hub to Home," in *Irvine: I Call It Home,* 53.
59. Louis Fridhandler, interview by the author, 18 May 2000.
60. Jack Peltason, interview by the author, 18 November 1998.
61. Harriet Senie and Sally Webster, eds., *Critical Issues in Public Art: Content, Context, and Controversy;* see also Casey Nelson Blake, "An Atmosphere of Effrontery: Richard Serra, *Tilted Arc,* and the Crisis of Public Art," in *The Power of Culture: Critical Essays in American History,* ed. Fox and Lears.
62. Lake Anne Village, "Community Activities at Reston," 1965.
63. Phyllis Hattis, "Sculpture: The Rest of Reston," *Connection: The Visual Arts at Harvard,* fall 1966, 28–35.
64. Goyert, "Reston, Virginia," 9–76.
65. "Social Planning and Programs for Reston, Virginia," Reston Virginia Foundation for Community Programs Inc., March 1967, 87.
66. Grubishich, "Soviet Artist, Reston, Mold Relationship," *Connection,* 25 May 1988, 5; "More on the Sculpture," *Connection,* 15 June 1988; "A Work of Art or Artful Propaganda?" *Connection,* 8 June 1988, 35; Grubishich, "'Breaking through the Wall,'" *Connection,* 1 June 1988, 24; Elizabeth Deschamps, "Reston Split on Soviet Sculpture," *Connection,* 1 June 1988; Roberta Robbins, "The Wall Keeps Getting Taller," *Connection,* 17 August 1988, 10; Cindy Chapman, "Soviet Peace Group Is 'Front' for Communists," *Connection,* 29 June 1998, 3; and Chapman, "Reston Won't Get Soviet Statue," *Connection,* 3 August 1988, 3.
67. "Reston's Dinosaur Debut," *Reston Times,* 13 June 1990, A1.
68. Forgey, "Reston's New Urban Attitude: Town Center Brings the City to Virginia's Planned Community," *Washington Post,* 13 October 1990, D1. See also Forgey, "Quicksilver and Mercury," D1.
69. Grubishich, "Town Center's Style Strikes Familiar Notes," *Connection,* 3 April 1991, TC4.
70. Michael James, "People Tree Hoped to Rekindle Spirit of Columbia," *Howard Sun,* 8 May 1991.
71. Ibid.
72. Moon, "The People Tree Isn't the Statue of Liberty."
73. James A Bohanan, "'Next America' on the Way," *Columbia Flier,* 4 July 1973.
74. Tennenbaum, *Creating a New City,* 63.

75. Kirk, "Out Beyond the People Tree: A Look at Columbia's Public Sculpture Renaissance," *Columbia Magazine,* October 1985, 27.

76. "These Are a Few of Our Favorite Things," 22.

77. Press release, P. Mack, Columbia Association, 15 June 1987.

78. Kirk, "Out Beyond the People Tree," 29.

79. "Columbia Lakefront Walking Tour," Columbia Association, ca. 1996; Mary McCoy, "Creations Bring Character to Public Spaces," *Washington Post,* 7 May 1992; Kirk, "Out Beyond the People Tree," 28.

80. Phylis Kepner, "Plans Sculpted for a Fine 20th B'day," *Columbia Flier,* undated.

81. Michael James, "People Tree Hoped to Rekindle Spirit of Columbia," *Howard Sun,* 8 May 1991.

82. Margo Mihalic, "The Artist and the Architecture: Tom Van Sant and Newport Center," *New Worlds,* November 1972, 53–56; Watson, interview by the author, 18 November 1998.

83. See Schoichiro Higuchi, *Water as Environmental Art: Creating Amenity Space.*

84. Laura Tuchman, "Irvine Dedicates Its First Permanent Piece of Public Art in a Timely Fashion," *Orange County Register,* 20 September, 1985, Show section, 1, 3.

85. Section epigraph from "Youth in Columbia," *Columbia,* September 1968, 4. See Alfred Runte, *National Parks: The American Experience;* Leo Marx, *The Machine in the Garden: Technology and the Pastoral Ideal in America;* Philip Shabecoff, *A Fierce Green Fire: The American Environmental Movement;* Roderick Nash, *Wilderness and the American Mind;* Roy Rosenzweig and Elizabeth Blackmar, *The Park and the People;* Thomas Bender, *Toward an Urban Vision: Ideas and Institutions in Nineteenth Century America.*

86. Burby and Weiss, *New Communities U.S.A.,* 28.

87. "Reston," Reston Land Corporation, ca. 1989

88. "Selling Environment Is Difficult—Walker," *Reston Times,* 30 October 1969, 13; Simon, "Article Inaccurate," A1.

89. Lyn Daniels, "A New Equation: Community Involvement," publication unknown, ca. 1970.

90. Robin Rathburn, "Nature Center Opens in Reston," *Connection,* 21 October 1987, 6.

91. Gina Voss, "RA Has Big Plans for Nature Center," *Reston Times,* 8 March 1995, A9; "Reston Gardens and Woodlands Awards Program, 1998," pamphlet, Reston Association, 1998; "Discovering the Spirit of Place," pamphlet, Reston Association, 1998.

92. Rouse, "The Value of Wildlife as an Integral Part of the Urban Community," 18 June 1977.

93. Kay Winieweski, "Water Quality in Columbia's Lakes: A $40,000 Question," *Columbia Flier,* 2 February 1978, 50.

94. "The Columbia Association," description of structure, 1998, Columbia Archives Collection, 8–10.

95. "A Planning Process for Columbia," Columbia Forum, 1984, 4.

96. Jennifer Vick, "Environmental Area Finally Opens," *Columbia Flier,* 12 June 1997; "Middle Patuxent Environmental Area," Program Committee Report and Recommendations, 15 May 1991; "Environmental Update," *Baltimore Sun,* 25 June 1997.
97. Scott and O'Donnel, "Irvine: Ten Years into a Fifty Year Plan," 11–36.
98. "Irvine Community Services," summer 1998, published by the City of Irvine, 18.
99. "Irvine," Chamber of Commerce and the City of Irvine, 1990, A42; Downey, "Irvine Plans to Increase Investment in Open Space," B1; "Wildlands Make Irvine Ranch a Special Place," *Irvine Ranch Magazine,* Irvine Company, 1998, 16.

CONCLUSION

1. See "HUD Issues Commitment for First New Community," *HUD News,* 13 February 1970; United States Department of Housing and Urban Development, Office of New Communities Development, *Report on Riverton, A New Community Proposal,* July 1971; William J. Nicoson, "Interim Economic and Financial Report-Soul City," HUD document, 15 September 1971; HUD, Office of New Communities Development, *Report on Cedar-Riverside, A New Community Proposal,* March 1971; NCDC, The Park Forest South Interdisciplinary Team, *Report on Park Forest South: Disposition Alternative,* 16 October 1979; Timothy Vanderver, "Summary of New Community Oversight Hearings," memorandum, HUD, 29 September 1975, "NCDC: Redirection Study Working Paper," 4 April 1980; NCDC board of directors, minutes of meeting, 7 April, 1982; NCDC, "Confidential Memo, Program Highlight," 1982; "Testimony before the Subcommittee on Housing and Community Development, Committee on Banking and Currency," Jonathan Howes, AIP, Center for Urban and Regional Studies, 23 September 1975. See also Thomas Lippman, "U.S. Aided New Towns Face Crisis," *Washington Post,* 15 November 1974, A1; Lippman, "HUD Ends New Town Program," *Washington Post,* 11 January 1975, A1.
2. See Andrew Ross, *The Celebration Chronicles;* Peter Calthorpe, *The Next American Metropolis: Ecology, Community and the American Dream;* Andres Duany and Elizabeth Plater-Zyberk, *Towns and Town-Making Principles,* ed. Alex Krieger; Duany and Plater-Zyberk, "Building Neotraditional Towns," *Wilson Quarterly,* winter 1992, 3; Todd Bressi, "The Neo-Traditional Revolution," *Utne Reader,* May 1992, 101–4; Kurt Andersen, "Oldfangled New Towns," *Time,* 20 May, 1991, 52–55; Herbert Muschamp, "Architecture View: Can New Urbanism Find Room for the Old?" *New York Times,* 2 June, 1996, 27; and James Howard Kunstler, *The Geography of Nowhere.*

Bibliography

LOCAL NEWSPAPERS AND MAGAZINES

Baltimore Magazine
The Baltimore Sun
The Baltimore Sun Magazine
Columbia
The Columbia Flier
Columbia Forum Newsletter
Columbia Magazine
Connection
Fairfax Journal
Howard County Sun
Irvine Ranch Magazine
The Irvine World News
New Worlds of Irvine
Orange County Magazine
The Orange County Register
The Restonian
The Reston Letter
The Reston Times
Saturday Star
The Washingtonian
The Washington Post
The Washington Post Magazine
The Washington Star

PERIODICALS

American Builder
American Historical Review
American Home
Architectural Forum
Atlanta Magazine

Atlantic Monthly
Building Research
Business Week
Catholic Review
The Communicator
Fortune
Life
Time
Harper's
House and Home
Industrial Design
Journal of the American Institute of Planners
Journal of Homebuilding
Journal of Orange County Studies
Journal of Urban History
The New Republic
The New York Times
The New York Times Magazine
The New Yorker
Newsweek
Reader's Digest
Presbyterian Life
Progressive Architecture
Together Magazine
Urban Land
Urban World
The Village Voice

INTERVIEWS

Brenda Bell
Wylene Bunch
Ivan Cole
Louis Fridhandler
Thomas Grubisich
Pat Kennedy
Barbara Kellner
Bernie King
Calvin and Nancy Larson
Sarah Larson
Doris Ligon
Ruth Ann Siedel
Jack Peltason
Mark Petracca

Joseph Stowers
Robert Tennenbaum
Raymond Watson
Jane Wilhelm

SPEECHES, ESSAYS, AND PLANS

Ashley, Thomas. "Planning a New City: Irvine, California," Director of Development Strategy Planning for the Irvine Company, ca. 1964.

Hoppenfeld, Morton. "Intra-Office Memorandum: Working Procedures for Program Planning," November 1963.

———. "The Columbia Process: The Potential for New Towns," 1970. Reprinted in "Before Columbia," by the Columbia Forum, 1984.

The Irvine Company, "Report to the Community, 1980."

———. "Irvine Sign Manual." Undated.

———. "Planned Community District Regulations." Orangetree Park, 1979.

———. "Irvine Villages: Welcome Home: Your Guide to a New Environment." April 1977.

———. "Irvine at 20, Planning Ahead." 1992.

Michael, Donald N. "Recommendations for the Social Planning of Columbia: Physical Facilities and Social Organization." Abstracted from the deliberations of the CRD Social Planning Work Group. July 1964.

Luckman, Charles. "University of California Site Selection Study: A Report on the Search for New Campus Sites." 1959.

Rouse, James. "Cities That Work for Man—Victory Ahead." Address at the Lions International Symposium of "City of the Future," University of Puerto Rico, 18 October 1967.

———. "How to Build a Whole New City from Scratch." Address at the Forty-Sixth Annual Conference National Association of Mutual Savings Banks, 17 May 1966.

———. "Columbia—A New Town by Private Business." September 1968.

———. "The New Expectancy." Address at the annual dinner of the National Conference of Christians and Jews in Baltimore, 18 November 1969.

———. "The Value of Wildlife as an Integral Part of the Urban Community." Seminar on Wildlife in Urban Areas, Howard Community College, Columbia, Maryland, 18 June 1977.

———. "Community Research and Development, Inc." Presented at the Washington Society of Investment Analysts, 2 February 1965.

———. "Great Cities for a Great Society." Presented at the honor awards luncheon of the Chicago Chamber of Commerce and Industry and the Chicago Chapter of the AIA, 8 April 1965.

———. "It Can Happen Here: A Paper on Metropolitan Growth." Presented at the Conference on the Metropolitan Future, University of California at Berkeley, 23 September 1963.

———. "Living in a New Town." Keynote address, International New Towns Congress, 9–15 December 1977.

Pereira, William. "A Preliminary Report for a University-Community Development in Orange County." Prepared for the Irvine Company. 1959.

———. "Second Phase Report for a University-Community Development in Orange County," undated.

Simon, Robert, Jr. "Statement by Robert E. Simon Jr., President of Reston, Virginia Inc., before the National Advisory Commission on Rural Poverty," ca. 1966.

———. "Statement by Robert E. Simon Jr., before the Commission on Urban Problems," 28 October 1967.

United States Department of Housing and Urban Development, Division of Policy Studies. *An Evaluation of the Federal New Communities Program.* Washington, D.C.: 1984.

Watson, Raymond. "(Irvine) General Plan, 1970."

———. "How One Developer Lives with Government Controls." Presented at the Southwest Regional Conference, American Institute of Real Estate Appraisers, Disneyland Hotel, Anaheim, California, 17 April 1975.

———. "The University of California's and Irvine Company's Historic Agreement." Unpublished article, 1998.

NEW TOWN SECONDARY SOURCES

Alanen, Arnold, and Joseph Eden. *Main Street Ready Made: The New Deal Community of Greendale, Wisconsin.* Madison: State Historical Society of Wisconsin, 1987.

Ben-Zadok, Efraim. "Economic and Racial Integration in a New Town." Ph.D. diss., New York University, 1980.

Breckenfeld, Gurney. *Columbia and the New Cities.* New York: I. Washburn, 1971.

Brewer, Marshall Glenn. "The Gestation of a Planned City: Irvine, California, from 1958–1971." Master's thesis, Northern Arizona University, 1975.

Brooks, Richard Oliver. "Hiding Place in the Wind: The New Towns Attempt." Ph.D. diss., Brandeis University, 1973.

Burby, Raymond J., and Shirley F. Weiss. *New Communities, U.S.A.* Lexington, Mass.: Lexington Books, 1976.

Burkhart, Lynne. *The Politics of Race and Class in Columbia, Maryland: Old Values in a New Town.* New York: Praeger, 1981.

Campbell, Carlos. *New Towns: Another Way to Live.* Reston: Reston, 1976.

Corden, Carol. *New Towns in Britain and America.* Berkeley Hills, Calif.: Sage, 1977.

Creese, Walter. *The Search for Environment: The Garden City—Before and After.* Baltimore: Johns Hopkins UP, 1992.

Christensen, Carol. *The American Garden City and the New Towns Movement.* Ann Arbor: UMI, 1978.

Ewing, Reid. *Developing Successful New Communities.* Washington, D.C.: ULI, 1991.

Galantay, Ervin. *New Towns: Antiquity to the Present.* New York: Braziller, 1975.

Ghirardo, Diane. *Building New Communities: New Deal America and Fascist Italy.* Princeton: Princeton UP, 1989.

Goyert, Philip. "Reston, Virginia, An Architectural History." Master's thesis, University of Virginia, 1970.

Griffin, Nathaniel M. *Irvine: The Genesis of a New Community.* Washington, D.C.: ULI, 1974.

Grubishich, Thomas, and Peter McCandless. *Reston: The First Twenty Years.* Reston: Reston, 1985.

Gulf Reston. *Brief History of Reston, Virginia.* Reston: Gulf Reston Inc., 1970.

Hersch, Patricia. *A Tribe Apart: A Journey into the Heart of American Adolescence.* New York: Ballantine, 1998.

Hertzen, Heikki von. *Building a New Town: Finland's New Garden City.* Cambridge: MIT Press, 1971.

Huntoom, Maxwell. *PUD: A Better Way for the Suburbs.* Washington, D.C.: ULI, 1971.

International City Managers' Association. *New Towns: A New Dimension of Urbanism.* Chicago: The Association, 1966.

Irvine, I Call It Home: A Collection of Essays and Poetry Presented by the Friends of Heritage Park Regional Library. Costa Mesa, Calif.: Premier, 1992.

Karsk, Roger. *Teenagers in the Next America.* Columbia: New Community Press, 1977.

Kelly, Barbara. *Expanding the American Dream: Building and Rebuilding Levittown.* Albany: SUNY UP, 1993.

Kling, Robert, Spencer Olin, and Mark Poster. *Postsuburban California: The Transformation of Orange County since World War II.* Berkeley: U California P, 1991.

Lanz-Stewart, Lee. "An Historical Perspective of the Planning, Development and Provision of Leisure Services in a Planned Community: Reston, Virginia." Ph.D. diss., University of Maryland, 1983.

Leach, Charles Bradley. "Greenhills, Ohio: The Evolution of an American New Town." Ph.D. diss., Case Western Reserve University, 1978.

Liebeck, Judy. *Irvine: A History of Innovation and Growth.* Houston: Pioneer, 1990.

McCulloch, Samuel Clyde. *Instant University: The History of the University of California, Irvine, 1957–1993.* Irvine, Calif.: UCI Alumni Association, 1996.

McGee, Frank. *UCI: The First 25 Years.* Irvine, Calif.: Regents of the University of California, 1992.

Merlin, Pierre. *New Towns: Regional Planning and Development.* London: Methuen, 1971.

Popenoe, David. *The Suburban Environment: Sweden and the United States.* Chicago: U Chicago P, 1977.

Ross, Andrew. *The Celebration Chronicles: Life, Liberty, and the Pursuit of Property Value in Disney's New Town.* New York: Random House, 1999.

Sandberg, Neil. *Stairwell 7: Family Life in the Welfare State.* Beverly Hills: Sage, 1978.

Schaffer, Daniel. *Garden Cities for America: The Radburn Experience.* Philadelphia: Temple UP, 1982.

Stein, Clarence. *Toward New Towns for America.* New York: Reinhold, 1957.

Strong, Ann Louis. *Planned Urban Environments: Sweden, Finland, Israel, the Netherlands.* Baltimore: Johns Hopkins UP, 1971.

Tennenbaum, Robert, ed. *Creating a New City: Columbia, Maryland.* Columbia, Md.: Perry, 1996.

Thorns, David. *The Quest for Community: Social Aspects of Residential Growth.* New York: Wiley, 1976.

Wireman, Peggy. "Meanings of Community in Modern America: Some Implications from New Towns." Ph.D. diss., American University, 1976.

GENERAL SECONDARY SOURCES

Arnold, Joseph. *The New Deal in the Suburbs, 1935–1954.* Columbus: Ohio State UP, 1971.

Baldassare, Mark. *Trouble in Paradise: The Suburban Transformation of America.* New York: Columbia UP, 1986.

Baumgartner, M. P. *The Moral Order of a Suburb.* New York: Oxford UP, 1988.

Bender, Thomas. *Toward an Urban Vision: Ideas and Institutions in Ninteenth-Century America.* Baltimore: Johns Hopkins UP, 1982.

Berger, Bennett. *Working-Class Suburb: A Study of Auto Workers in Suburbia.* Berkeley: U California P, 1960.

Binford, Henry. *The First Suburbs: Residential Communities on the Boston Periphery, 1815–1860.* Chicago: U Chicago P, 1985.

Blake, Peter. *God's Own Junkyard: The Planned Deterioration of America's Landscape.* New York: Holt, 1963.

Buder, Stanley. *Pullman: An Experiment in Industrial Order and Community Planning.* New York: Oxford UP, 1967.

———. *Visionaries and Planners: The Garden City Movement and the Modern Community.* New York: Oxford UP, 1990.

Bullard, Robert D., J. Eugene Grigsby III, and Charles Lee, eds. *Residential Apartheid: The American Legacy.* Los Angeles: CAAS Publications, 1994.

Calthorpe, Peter. *The Next American Metropolis: Ecology, Community and the American Dream.* Princeton: Princeton UP, 1993.

Chudacoff, Howard P. *The Evolution of American Urban Society.* Englewood Cliffs, N.J.: Prentice Hall, 1981.

Contosta, David. *Suburb in the City: Chestnut Hill, Philadelphia, 1850–1990.* Columbus: Ohio State UP, 1992.

Coolidge, John Phillips. *Mill and Mansion: A Study of Architecture and Society in Lowell, Massachusetts, 1820–1865.* 1942. New York: Russell and Russell, 1967.

Davis, Mike. *City of Quartz: Excavating the Future in Los Angeles.* New York: Verso, 1990.

Davis, Susan. *Parades and Power: Street Theatre in Nineteenth-Century Philadelphia.* Philadelphia: Temple UP, 1986.

Dobriner, William. *Class in Suburbia.* Englewood Cliffs, N.J.: Prentice Hall, 1963.

Dolce, Philip, ed. *Suburbia: The American Dream and Dilemma.* Garden City, N.Y.: Anchor, 1976.

Donaldson, Scott. *The Suburban Myth.* New York: Columbia UP, 1969.

Duany, Andres, and Elizabeth Plater-Zyberk. *Towns and Town-Making Principles.* Ed. Alex Krieger. New York: Rizzoli, 1991.

Ebner, Michael H. *Creating Chicago's North Shore: A Suburban History.* Chicago: U Chicago P, 1988.

Findlay, Mark. *Magic Lands: Western Cityscapes and American Culture after 1940.* Berkeley: U California P, 1992.

Fishman, Robert. *Bourgeois Utopias: The Rise and Fall of Suburbia.* New York: Basic, 1987.

———. *Urban Utopias: Ebenezer Howard, Frank Lloyd Wright, Le Corbusier.* New York: Basic, 1977.

Fox, Richard Wightman, and T. J. Jackson Lears, eds. *The Power of Culture: Critical Essays in American History.* Chicago: U Chicago P, 1993.

Friedan, Betty. *The Feminine Mystique.* New York: Norton, 1963.

Friedman, Milton, et al. *Graphic Design in America: A Visual Language History.* Minneapolis: Walker Art Center, 1989.

Gans, Herbert. *The Levittowners.* New York: Pantheon, 1967.

———. *The Urban Villagers: Group and Class in the Life of Italian-Americans.* New York: Free Press, 1962.

Garner, John S. *The Model Company Town: Urban Design through Private Enterprise in Nineteenth-Century New England.* Amherst: U Massachusetts P, 1984.

Garreau, Joel. *Edge City: Life on the New Frontier.* New York: Doubleday, 1991.

Gottdiener, Mark. *The Theming of America: Dreams, Visions, and Commercial Spaces.* Boulder, Colo.: Westview, 1997.

Gillette, Howard, ed. *American Urbanism: A Historiographical Review.* New York: Greenwood, 1987.

Goodman, Paul. *Growing Up Absurd: Problems of Youth in the Organized System.* New York: Random House, 1960.

Goodman, Robert. *After the Planners.* New York: Simon and Schuster, 1971.

Gordon, Richard, Katherine Gordon, and Max Gunther. *The Split-Level Trap.* New York, 1964.

Graff, Harvey, ed. *Growing Up in America: Historical Experiences.* Detroit: Wayne State UP, 1987.

Greely, Andrew. *The Church and the Suburbs.* Glen Rock, N.J.: Deus, 1959.

Haddow, Robert. *Pavilions of Plenty: Exhibiting American Culture Abroad in the 1950s.* Washington, D.C.: Smithsonian Institution P, 1997.

Hall, Peter. *Cities of Tomorrow: An Intellectual History of Urban Planning and Design in the Twentieth Century.* Oxford: Basil Blackwell, 1988.

Harvey, David. *The Condition of Postmodernity: An Enquiry into the Origins of Cultural Change.* Oxford: Basil Blackwell, 1989.

Hayden, Delores. *Seven American Utopias.* Cambridge: MIT Press, 1976.

Higuchi, Schoichiro. *Water as Environmental Art: Creating Amenity Space.* Tokyo: Kashiwashobo, 1991.

Hine, Robert. *Community on the American Frontier: Separate But Not Alone.* Norman: Oklahoma UP, 1980.

Hollinger, David. *Postethnic America.* New York: Basic, 1995.

Hollingshead, August. *Elmtown's Youth.* New York: Wiley, 1949.

Horowitz, Daniel. *Betty Friedan and the Making of the "Feminine Mystique."* Amherst: U Massachusetts P, 1998.

Howard, Ebenezer. *To-morrow: A Peaceful Path to Real Reform.* London: Swan, 1898.

Hunt, Lynn, ed. *The New Cultural History.* Berkeley: U California P, 1989.

Huttman, Elizabeth, ed. *Urban Housing Segregation of Minorities in Western Europe and the United States.* Durham: Duke UP, 1991.

Jackson, Kenneth. *Crabgrass Frontier: The Suburbanization of the United States.* New York: Oxford UP, 1985.

Jacobs, Jane. *The Death and Life of Great American Cities.* New York, 1961.

Jacoby, Russell. *The Last Intellectuals: American Culture in the Age of Academe.* New York: Noonday, 1987.

Kanter, Rosabeth. *Commitment and Community: Communes and Utopias in Sociological Perspective.* Cambridge: Harvard UP, 1972.

Keating, Ann Durkin. *Building Chicago: Suburban Developers and the Creation of a Divided Metropolis.* Columbus: Ohio State UP, 1989.

Keating, Dennis. *The Suburban Racial Dilemma: Housing and Neighborhoods.* Philadelphia: Temple UP, 1994.

Keats, John. *The Crack in the Picture Window.* Boston: Houghton Mifflin, 1956.

Kirp, David, John Dwyer, and Larry Rosenthal. *Our Town: Race, Housing and the Soul of Suburbia.* New Brunswick, N.J.: Rutgers UP, 1997.

Kunstler, James Howard. *The Geography of Nowhere: The Rise and Decline of America's Man-Made Landscape.* New York: Simon and Schuster, 1993.

Lake, Robert. *The New Suburbanites: Race and Housing in the Suburbs.* New Brunswick, N.J.: Rutgers UP, 1981.

Langdon, Philip. *A Better Place to Live: Reshaping the American Suburb.* Amherst, Mass.: Amherst UP, 1994.

Lingeman, Richard. *Small Town America: A Narrative History, 1620–The Present.* New York: Putnam, 1980.

Lockwood, George. *The New Harmony Movement.* New York: Appleton, 1905.

Lozano, Eduardo. *Community Design and the Culture of Cities.* Cambridge: Cambridge UP, 1990.

Lynch, Kevin. *The Image of the City.* Cambridge: MIT Press, 1960.

Lynd, Helen, and Robert Lynd. *Middletown.* New York: Harcourt, Brace, 1929.

Marx, Leo. *The Machine in the Garden: Technology and the Pastoral Ideal in America.* London: Oxford UP, 1964.

Masotti, Louis, ed. *The Suburban Seventies.* Philadelphia: AAPSS, 1975.

McKenzie, Evan. *Privatopia: Homeowner Associations and the Rise of Residential Private Government.* New Haven: Yale UP, 1994.

Milgram, Morris. *Good Neighborhood: The Challenge of Open Housing.* New York: Norton, 1977.

Miller, Zane. *Suburb: Neighborhood and Community in Forest Park, Ohio, 1935–1976.* Knoxville: U Tennessee P, 1981.

More, Sir Thomas. *Utopia.* 1515. Trans. Robert Adams. New York: Norton, 1992.

Mumford, Lewis. *The City in History.* New York: Harcourt, 1961.

———. *The Culture of Cities.* New York: Harcourt, 1938.

———. *The Highway and the City.* New York: Harcourt, 1963.

———. *The Urban Prospect.* New York: Harcourt, 1968.

Nash, Roderick. *Wilderness and the American Mind.* New Haven: Yale UP, 1967.

Packard, Vance. *A Nation of Strangers.* New York: McKay, 1972.

Palen, J. John. *The Suburbs.* New York: McGraw-Hill, 1995.

———. *The Urban World.* New York: McGraw-Hill, 1975.

Places, Towns and Townships. 2nd ed. Ed. Deirdre A. Gaquin and Richard W. Dodge. Lanham, Md.: Bernan, 1998.

Pells, Richard H. *The Liberal Mind in a Conservative Age: American Intellectuals in the 1940s and 1950s.* New York: Harper & Row, 1985.

Reisman, David. *The Lonely Crowd.* New Haven: Yale UP, 1950.

Rosenzweig, Roy, and Elizabeth Blackmar. *The Park and the People.* New York: Holt, 1992.

Rothblatt, Donald. *The Suburban Environment and Women.* New York: Praeger, 1979.

Rubin, Nancy. *The New Suburban Woman.* New York: Coward, 1982.

Runte, Alfred. *National Parks: The American Experience.* Lincoln: U Nebraska P, 1997.

Rydell, Robert. *All the World's a Fair.* Chicago: U Chicago P, 1984.

Schaffer, Daniel, ed. *Two Centuries of American Planning.* Baltimore: Johns Hopkins UP, 1988.

Scott, Mel. *American City Planning since 1890.* Berkeley: U California P, 1969.

Seeley, John, Alexander Sim, and Elizabeth Loosely. *Crestwood Heights.* New York: Basic Books, 1956.

Senie, Harriet, and Sally Webster, eds. *Critical Issues in Public Art: Content, Context, and Controversy.* New York: IconEditions, 1992.

Shabecoff, Philip. *A Fierce Green Fire: The American Environmental Movement.* New York: Hill and Wang, 1993.

Sorkin, Michael, ed. *Variations on a Theme Park: The New American City and the End of Public Space.* New York: Noonday, 1992.

Spectorsky, A. C. *The Exurbanites.* New Philadelphia: Lippincott, 1955.

Stanback, Thomas. *The New Suburbanization: Challenge to the Central City.* Boulder, Colo.: Westview, 1991.

Stilgoe, John. *Borderland: Origins of the American Suburb, 1820–1939.* New Haven: Yale UP, 1988.

Sugrue, Thomas. *The Origins of the Urban Crisis: Race and Inequality in Postwar Detroit.* Princeton: Princeton UP, 1996.

Teaford, Jon. *The Twentieth-Century American City: Problem, Promise and Reality.* Baltimore: Johns Hopkins UP, 1986.

Turner, Frederick Jackson. *The Frontier in American History.* New York: Holt, 1920.

Ward, Stephen, ed. *The Garden City: Past, Present and Future.* London: Spon, 1992.

Warner, Sam Bass, Jr. *The Private City: Philadelphia in Three Periods of Its Growth.* Philadelphia: U Pennsylvania P, 1968.

———. *Streetcar Suburbs: The Process of Growth in Boston (1870–1900).* Cambridge: Harvard UP, 1962.

———. *The Urban Wilderness: A History of the American City.* New York: Harper & Row, 1972.

Weiss, Marc. *The Rise of the Community Builders: The American Real Estate Industry and Urban Land Planning.* New York: Columbia UP, 1987.

Whyte, William. *The Last Landscape.* Garden City, N.Y.: Doubleday, 1968.

———. *The Organization Man.* Garden City, N.Y.: Doubleday, 1956.

Wilson, James Q., ed. *Urban Renewal: The Record and the Controversy.* Cambridge: MIT Press, 1966.

Wilson, William. *The City Beautiful Movement.* Baltimore: Johns Hopkins UP, 1989.

Wood, Robert C. *Suburbia: Its People and Their Politics.* Boston: Houghton Mifflin, 1958.

Worley, William S. *J. C. Nichols and the Shaping of Kansas City: Innovation in Planned Residential Communities.* Columbia: Missouri UP, 1990.

Young, Judith. *Celebrations: America's Best Festivals, Jamborees, Carnivals and Parades.* Santa Barbara: Capra, 1986.

Zukin, Sharon. *The Cultures of Cities.* Cambridge, Mass.: Blackwell, 1995.

Index

Adolescents, 222–40
African Art Museum of Maryland, 204, 253
Agran, Larry, 3, 112–13, 221
Ames, Priscilla, 213
Antioch College (Columbia, Md.), 249, 253

Bain, Henry, 37, 39, 81
Bren, Donald, 3, 61, 83, 148–49, 268
Brown, Maggie, 203, 219

California-Irvine, University of, 53–54, 57, 110, 149, 182, 206, 254–56
Calthorpe, Peter, 276, 282
Cedar Ridge, 161–64, 166, 212
Celebration, Florida, 282–83
Cole, Ivan, 97, 139, 163, 190
Columbia, Maryland: adolescents, 229–36; cultural affairs, 247–53; early residents, 121–26; environmental preservation, 272–74; parades and festivals, 131–33; paternalism, 140–45; planning, 33–52; politics, 99–109; public art, 262–66; race relations, 191–205; social experimentation, 167–78; women and feminism, 213–19
Columbia Archive, 108, 109, 115
Columbia Arts Center, 233, 253
Columbia Association, 38, 46, 48, 50, 78, 100–104, 114, 142, 178, 193, 202–4, 214–15, 232, 252–53, 272
Columbia Council, 38, 46, 100–104, 114, 177–78
Columbia Exhibit Center, 77–79
Columbia Festival of the Arts, 247, 252
Columbia Film Society, 250
Columbia Forum, 91, 105–9, 177, 198, 272
Columbia Foundation, 47, 81, 204, 252

Columbia Women's Center, 215, 218
Conklin, William, 20–22, 75
Country Club District, Kansas, 19
Cultural affairs, 242–57

Ditch, Scott, 77
Dockery, John, 94–95
Duany, Andres, 276, 283

Enterprise Foundation, 81, 264
Environmentalism, 269–76

Fayet, Pierre du, 262–65
Feminism, 209–22
Finley, William, 40, 81
Fonseca, Gonzalo, 259
Foote, Nelson, 37, 81
Fridhandler, Louis, 113, 146, 256
Friedan, Betty, 11, 209

Gans, Herbert, 37, 39, 124, 168–69, 222, 230, 234, 281
Gehry, Frank, 43
Greater Reston Arts Center (GRACE), 74, 212, 245, 261
Gulf Reston, 26, 73, 75, 92, 93, 161, 186, 188, 244

Hamilton, Wallace, 40, 41, 81, 100, 168, 192, 248
Harvest Festival, 134–35
Hersch, Patricia, 227–28
Hoppenfeld, Morton, 2, 37, 40–41, 45, 80–81, 230, 250, 264
Howard, Ebenezer, 19
Howard Community College, 216, 233, 249–50

Urban Life and Urban Landscape Series

ZANE L. MILLER, GENERAL EDITOR

The Series examines the history of urban life and the development of the urban landscape through works that place social, economic, and political issues in the intellectual and cultural context of their times.

Designing Modern America: The Regional Planning Association and Its Members
   Edward K. Spann

Hopedale: From Commune to Company Town, 1840–1920
   Edward K. Spann

Visions of Eden: Environmentalism, Urban Planning, and City Building in St. Petersburg, Florida, 1900–1995
   R. Bruce Stephenson

Welcome to Heights High: The Crippling Politics of Restructuring America's Public Schools
   Diana Tittle

Washing "The Great Unwashed": Public Baths in Urban America, 1840–1920
   Marilyn Thornton Williams